WALLOWING IN SEX

CONSOLE-ING PASSIONS
TELEVISION AND CULTURAL POWER
EDITED BY LYNN SPIGEL

WALLOWING

IN SEX

The New Sexual Culture
— of 1970s —
American Television

ELANA LEVINE

Duke University Press
Durham and London
2007

© 2007 Duke University Press

All rights reserved

Printed in the United States of America on acid-free paper ∞

Designed by Heather Hensley

Typeset in Minion by Tseng Information Systems, Inc.

Library of Congress Cataloging-in-Publication Data appear on the

last printed page of this book.

—CONTENTS—

—ACKNOWLEDGMENTS—

Writing the acknowledgments for a project such as this book is an overwhelming endeavor, yet it is also a pleasure for it allows me to recognize the many influences that have contributed to its creation. The project began during my graduate studies at the University of Wisconsin, Madison. I am indebted to the University Dissertator Fellowship, Vilas Travel Grant, and McCarty Dissertation Scholarship I received there, all of which supported my initial research. I am also grateful for the travel grant provided by the American Heritage Center (AHC) at the University of Wyoming, an invaluable archive. The work of the archivists and librarians at the American Heritage Center, the Library of Congress, the Cornell University Human Sexuality Collection, the Wisconsin State Historical Society (WSHS), the University of Wisconsin libraries, and the Madison and Milwaukee Public Libraries has been instrumental to this book's existence. Their efforts to preserve and catalog myriad materials pertaining to 1970s television made this project possible. Certain individuals also provided important materials. I thank Barbara Corday for sharing her memories and insights; Steven Tropiano for supplying me with a complete copy of *Alexander: The Other Side of Dawn*; R. Franklin Brown for granting me permission to reproduce the work of his father, the cartoonist Bo Brown; and Stacy for helping me find tapes of *General Hospital* from the late 1970s.

Although my material debts are major, my intellectual debts are even more significant. At the University of Wisconsin, Madison, Julie D'Acci, Michele Hilmes, Michael Curtin, and John Fiske were models of scholarly passion and rigor. Their guidance shows itself throughout this work. Just as vital were the insights and challenges posed by my graduate school colleagues. Jason Mittell was instrumental to the project's beginnings, Kelly Cole offered just the advice I needed for the book's completion, and Ron Becker was my unflagging sounding board from start to finish. Any clarity or insight this book offers is a product of his influence. At the University of Wisconsin, Milwaukee, David Pritchard, David Allen, and Jeff Smith have all provided consistent encouragement. Barbara Ley, Paul Brewer, and Melody Hoffman offered excellent suggestions in the final stages of my writing. Milo Miller was a tremendous help with the illustrations.

I also thank the editorial and production staff of Duke University Press, whose expertise and professionalism have done much to strengthen this project. My editor, Ken Wissoker, provided steady encouragement and advice and Anitra Grisales answered my many questions with patience and kindness. The suggestions of the press's three anonymous readers were crucial to this project's transition from dissertation to book.

I owe more personal thanks to the friends and family who have supported me over the course of this project, many of whom I have already mentioned. My parents, Dodie Levine and the late Elliott B. Levine, always championed my efforts, and my father in particular did much to mold a future television scholar through the models of his intellectual curiosity and his willingness to take television seriously. My sister, Alyssa Osterman, and lifelong friend Andi Simon played 1970s TV with me during many a childhood afternoon. Marla Davishoff both suggested to me the subject of chapter 6 and provided encouragement throughout. Ruby and Al Newman, Kurt Newman and Michelle Detorie, and Amy Newman have enthusiastically awaited this book's arrival for as long as I've known them. Leo Elliott Levine Newman has helped put this book's gestation and birth into perspective via his own arrival and vitality. My largest and most personal debt is to Michael Z. Newman, a stellar writer and astute scholar whose faith and commitment to my work and to me have made the biggest difference of all.

INTRODUCTION

A new sexualized popular culture pervaded American life in the 1970s, and it seemed that everyone wanted to be part of it. Watching a porn film at the local theater, flipping through a sex advice manual in line at the grocery store, dancing the hustle at a glittery discotheque — all were markers of sexual sophistication. But participating in the racy new culture did not require seeing *The Devil in Miss Jones* or visiting Studio 54. If those symbols of the sexy society were inaccessible to you, you could also join in by what you wore. Silky short-shorts, feathered hair, and tight-fitting bell-bottom jeans helped, as did slogan t-shirts with iron-on transfers, the most popular of which were sexually provocative. From the vague ("Tonight's the Night") to the raunchy ("The Word of the Day Is Legs — Spread the Word"),[1] these shirts winked salaciously at the world, heralding their wearers' embrace of a new kind of sexual expression. The shirts' double entendres were meant to be bold sexual statements, yet the slyly suggestive nature of the wordplay, as well as the placement of these sexual signifiers on commercially marketed t-shirts, also made them decidedly mainstream.

American popular culture of the 1970s was rife with just this sort of commodified sexual expression. Indeed, during the 1970s sex was for sale and millions of Americans were buying. Some were buying sexually explicit representations and experiences. *Deep Throat* (1972), the highest earning hard-core porn film to date, made $25 million through its exhibition in seventy-three U.S. cities. The vividly illustrated advice manual *The Joy of Sex* (1972) sold 3.8 million copies in its first two years of publication. And Plato's Retreat, formerly a Manhattan gay bathhouse, became a haven for heterosexual experimentation, with over six thousand men and women participating monthly in 1977.[2] Less explicit cultural products and experiences had an even wider reach. Disco music and its association with the flashing lights, repetitive beats, and hedonistic impulses of the urban discotheque was at the forefront of this innuendo-driven culture. The skin-baring costumes and macho personae of The Village People helped break the all-male group into the Top 40 with such numbers as "Y.M.C.A" (1978) and "In the Navy" (1979), pop songs that only thinly disguised their status as gay sexual anthems. The dance hit "More, More, More" hinted at orgasmic pleasures, not only by asking the provocative question, "How do you like it?" but also by publicizing the singer Andrea True's day job as a porn actress. Across the pop culture landscape of the 1970s, from t-shirts bought at the local mall to The Village People blaring out of a pre-teen girl's bedroom, from sex manuals "tossed into the grocery shopping bag with the asparagus"[3] to celebrities lining up to see the latest hard-core porn film, sexualized popular culture became a taken-for-granted element of everyday life.

Nowhere were these new forms of sexual expression more prominently, or more surprisingly, felt than in commercial network television. Despite its history as a "family" medium, in the 1970s American television was, as one anonymous TV industry executive confessed, "wallowing in sex."[4] Television of the 1970s contained innumerable references to the new sexual culture: passengers disco dancing in *The Love Boat*'s Acapulco Lounge; a young girl walking by a Hollywood Boulevard marquee advertising *Deep Throat* in *Dawn: Portrait of a Teenage Runaway*; a frustrated housewife checking out *Orgasm and You* from her local library in *Mary Hartman, Mary Hartman*. But 1970s television also contributed to the new sexual culture, doing as much as any cultural form to bring an acceptance of sexual change to the American mainstream. Television entertainment invited viewers to participate in a world in which "Would you like to come back to my cabin for a nightcap?" was an unambiguous sexual proposition, in which bralessness was an essential component of female sexual attractiveness, in which words such as "rape" and "VD" and "impotence" were part of a common vocabulary. Television of the 1970s made the new sexual culture the new American culture, and it made American culture more openly sexual than it had ever been before.

The new sexual culture of 1970s television left a legacy for the way American culture would discuss, depict, and define sex for years to come. Not only did it help shape the sexual attitudes and experiences of the generation that came of age during this era, it also helped determine how the sexual revolution would make its mark on mainstream American culture and the citizens who participated in it. Television of the 1970s made America's chief mass medium more open to sexual situations and themes, although it helped institute the parameters of TV's sexual openness, as well. Because of the steps taken by 1970s television, in the 1980s the networks could air made-for-TV movies such as *Something about Amelia* (about father-daughter incest, ABC, 9 January 1984) and *An Early Frost* (about a gay man with AIDS, NBC, 11 November 1985). In the 1990s, the sitcom protagonist Ellen Morgan could come out as a lesbian ("The Puppy Episode," *Ellen*, ABC, 30 April 1997) and *Sex and the City*'s girlfriends could celebrate a vibrator called the Rabbit ("The Turtle and the Hare," HBO, 2 August 1998). In the 2000s, *The Oprah Winfrey Show* (syndicated, 16 April 2004) could explore the phenomenon of heterosexual black men on the "down low" (that is, sleeping with other men unbeknownst to their female partners). At the same time, in keeping with the limits of television's take on sex in the 1970s, Russell's and Peter's *thirtysomething* "morning-after" scene brought an onslaught of protests ("Strangers," ABC, 7 November 1989), the brief nudity introduced in the first season of *NYPD Blue* (ABC, 1993–2005) was considered scandalous, and the Janet Jackson "wardrobe malfunction" that exposed her breast during the half-time show of the 2004 Super Bowl (CBS, 1 February 2004) incited a flurry of indecency crackdowns by the federal government. The new sexual culture of 1970s television did not *cause* these future developments, but in preceding them it helped to make them possible, and perhaps even probable. In so doing, the new sexual culture of 1970s television affected not only the future of American television but also the futures of those viewers for whom television would remain a key cultural reference point.

As a child growing up in the suburban Midwest, I was one of the many Americans introduced to the sexually revolutionized world through 1970s TV. Because I was a kid, and because I was inordinately invested in TV, television's representation of the new sexual culture in the 1970s may have had a particularly significant impact on me. But both casual conversations and historical research have shown me that my experience was hardly unique. I know of many women and some men who pretended to be Lynda Carter's powerful and sexy Wonder Woman in their 1970s childhoods. I've been told of the burning question raised for one boy by the legendary "chick-magnet," the Fonz: What do you do with twins on a date? I've heard of countless girls and women who valiantly tried, and most often failed, to achieve the hairstyle of the sex symbol Farrah Fawcett-Majors. I've found out how disturbed, excited, and confused many soap fans felt when Luke raped Laura or Roger raped Holly. I've learned how drawn some viewers were to the stories of teenage runaways, hitchhikers, and stalking victims in TV movies. And I've read of certain people's disgust with *Soap*'s gay, cross-dressing son, impotent husband, and adulterous mother. Television's representation of the new sexual culture shaped Americans' experiences with that culture and elicited strong responses in the process.

The New Sexual Culture of 1970s Television

This book tells the story of television's role in the new sexual culture of the 1970s. It asserts that television was the most significant cultural form for the dissemination and acceptance of the monumental changes in sexual identities, practices, mores, and beliefs that developed in the wake of the sexual revolution. Entertainment television of the 1970s told Americans about the impact of the women's liberation movement, the influence of the gay rights movement, and the outcomes of the sexual revolution through stories and characters, images and sounds, words and silences. It left out as much as it left in, and it was vilified as much as it was admired. Before the birth of Fox and the growth of cable, the three broadcast networks reached up to 90 percent of the viewing audience. As a result, television's take on the sexual revolution was more widely consumed than any other. The power of television's tales of individuals facing sexual change in ways innocent and jaded, irreverent and somber, tolerant and bigoted affected what America's new, post–sexual revolution culture could become.

As central as it was to America's new sexual culture, 1970s television stayed far away from the sexual explicitness of pornographic films or sex advice books. Television's version of the new sexual culture was all about sexual *suggestiveness*, teasingly offering hints of sex. It did not show explicit sex acts or nudity and it did not use graphic language. A medium funded by advertisers and regulated by the government's Federal Communications Commission, broadcast network television of the 1970s necessarily addressed the sexual revolution in ways that could be considered acceptable to advertisers fearful of controversy, to politicians fearful of public backlash, and to viewers fearful of radical challenges to their way of life. Thus television's sexual revolution was in many respects a more restrained version of the changes taking place in the world around it.

By treating the sexual revolution in this way, television's new sexual culture was particularly compatible with the advertiser-supported, capitalist system in which the medium is based. As numerous scholars have shown, American network television's commercial foundation shapes the content of its programming, sometimes by implanting blatant endorsements of consumer capitalism in television texts and sometimes with more subtle ideological messages. The new sexual culture of 1970s TV was more like the latter. Television's emphasis on idiosyncratic characters grappling with sexual change could make it seem as if the sexual revolution was not about challenging the heterosexual nuclear family, patriarchy, or the capitalist system, but only about the choices of certain individuals. American television rarely offers systemic critiques and typically endorses dominant ideologies of social identity — gender, sexuality, class, and race. In keeping with such leanings, television's construction of sex and the new sexual culture during the 1970s supported the dominance of heterosexuality over other sexual orientations and the subordination of women as objects of male sexual desire. Thus, television's sexual revolution shied away from the fully revolutionary. Instead, it made the new more familiar and the potentially radical safe.

This book explores the relatively safe tendencies of television's sexual culture in the 1970s and its endorsement of sexual and gender hierarchies, but it also reveals the complicated nature of television's relationship to the changing American culture. In the 1970s, television actively participated in the sexual revolution even as it appeared to reinforce the status quo. Certainly, television's handling of the new sexual culture necessarily went along with many of the accepted norms and values of American culture; after all, even though television's sexual culture was "new" in many respects in the 1970s, it could not have achieved the popularity it did without presenting sex in a way that seemed natural and inevitable for much of the TV audience. At the same time, however, to achieve popularity with an audience experiencing changes in sexual mores, practices, and identities in their day-to-day lives, television also necessarily accommodated and incorporated some of the emergent challenges to dominant norms and values. Television of the 1970s excelled in bringing together aspects of the "new" sexuality—premarital sex, out gays and lesbians, women with sexual desires—and such long-standing, seemingly natural ideologies as heterosexual monogamy and fundamental sexual difference. The negotiation between these two perspectives both sustained the dominant culture and acknowledged oppositional elements within it. While this may ultimately have worked to keep that dominant culture intact, it also opened the door to small, incremental instances of social change. American television of the 1970s accomplished this cultural work so effectively that it managed to construct a new, post–sexual revolution common sense, a new way of understanding and accepting the sexually altered society that would not likely have come to pass without its involvement.[5]

To explore American television's negotiation of this new sexual culture, I question exactly *how* and *why* 1970s television constructed sex the way it did. Television's cultural impact is the product of a chain of events: the multitude of choices made by television's creators, which result in a complex combination of images, sounds, and meanings in television content, which are then interpreted, discussed, and sometimes challenged by viewers. For example, the ways that the hit ABC series *The Love Boat* represented sex were shaped by ABC's desire to draw a broad audience to the commercials aired during the show, as well as by American culture's dominant ideas about sexuality and heterosexual monogamy. However, the stories this series told, and the way it told them, were also products of the program's structure (of three nonoverlapping plots, at least one of which was comedic), of the experiences of its producers (the executive producer Aaron Spelling deemed what was and was not the right kind of TV sexiness), of responses to content regulations (such as the family viewing policy of the National Association of Broadcasters [NAB]), of interactions with viewers (such as that of one father who wrote that he was embarrassed to watch the show with his daughters), and of myriad other forces that molded *The Love Boat*'s tales. Thus, while the economic pressures of the advertiser-supported television marketplace serve as an essential frame, this book is more invested in the question of how specific networks, producers, writers, actors, and regulators—as well as the resulting texts—constructed television's new sexual culture, why such choices were made, and what impact they had on the vision of sexual change the medium offered.

In addition, television's take on the sexual revolution was far from uni-vocal; television told a multitude of *different* stories about sex in the 1970s. It was this diversity of representation that gave the medium much of its power. Clearly, most television programming avoided the more radical facets of the sexual revolution, the facets that most often signify the sexual revolution in the historical record. Characters on daytime soap operas were not visit-ing bathhouses and participating in orgies, sitcoms were not set in lesbian separatist communities, and made-for-TV movies did not feature swingers' parties. Yet 1970s television still managed to represent sex and the new sexual culture in diverse ways and even to address some of the issues at the core of the sexual revolution. Take the matter of women's sexuality. The women's libera-tion and anti-rape movements, the popularization of sex advice literature, and the widespread adoption of the birth-control pill had made women's sexuality a subject of public discussion. Questions of women's sexual satisfaction, of re-productive rights, of sexual violence were all up for debate. While television did not typically take on the "myth of the vaginal orgasm"[6] or the politics of abortion (with some important exceptions, for example, "Maude's Dilemma," *Maude*, 14 and 21 November 1972), it made women's sexuality a ubiquitous theme and offered a range of variations on it. On prime-time action adventure shows such as *Charlie's Angels*, the female detective protagonists used their sex appeal to get information, disarm suspects, and gain access to such "under-world" settings as porn film sets and Playboy-style nightclubs. On the daytime soap opera *Guiding Light*, Roger Thorpe raped his wife, Holly, who then faced a criminal justice system that treated rape victims abusively and charges of marital rape incredulously. On the hit sitcom *Three's Company*, the middle-aged Helen Roper constantly griped about her husband Stanley's lackluster sexual performance, lobbing sarcastic insults at him and bemoaning her dis-satisfaction in bed. And in commercials for the vaginal deodorant spray FDS, a woman confided to the camera that FDS made her feel "grown up" and "more feminine" before she excitedly whispered, "He's home," and turned to meet the man that FDS had helped her attract. Across the television schedule, at all times of day and night and in all kinds of genres, women's sexuality was displayed, defended, and discussed. Not only was it the subject of numerous TV narratives, but women's sexuality was also addressed differently and made to mean differently in each of these representations. This was a limited diversity, to be sure, but one that spoke to many of the TV audience's hopes, fears, and uncertainties about the changes brought by the sexual revolution.

The Sexual Revolution in America

Just what was this sexual revolution in which television participated during the 1970s? How much of America's sexual mores, beliefs, identities, and practices did it really change? And what exactly was television's part in those transformations? Although the 1960s and 1970s are most often identified as the period of sexual revolution in American history, changes to American sexual culture actually came more gradually over the course of the twentieth century. At the end of the nineteenth century and the beginning of the twentieth, shifts in gender roles, economics, technology, and work and leisure patterns began to turn American sexual behavior and beliefs away from the strictures of Victorian morality and toward the greater sexual "freedom" we associate with the sexual revolution. The achievement of women's suffrage and women's concomitantly increased role in the public sphere did much to change relations between the sexes, but so did the post-war prosperity of the 1920s, the invention of the automobile, and the move to an industrialized labor force. With wages to spend, time to spare, and urban amusements such as the cinema to patronize, young men and women began to find the money, the time, and the space to develop sexual relationships beyond the boundaries of home and family.[7] Of course, many social boundaries, many conventions of propriety continued to restrict sexual behavior during the coming decades. For example, New York's flourishing gay male world of the early twentieth century became much less visible and less tolerated by mainstream America between the 1930s and the 1960s.[8] Similarly, despite women's greater public presence in the 1920s and again during World War II, repeated backlashes against equality between the sexes often reinforced traditional gender roles

8

and restricted women's sexual freedom.[9] Racial inequalities also persisted, such that men of color — African Americans, Native Americans, Asian Americans — continued to be depicted as white women's rapists in Hollywood films and continued to be suspected, and often persecuted, for such crimes in real-world experience.[10] Clearly, the path of sexual change in American history has not been one of steadily increasing progress; it has not been a move from repression to liberation but rather an ongoing series of struggles to define what sex means and to preserve or disrupt social hierarchies on the basis of those meanings.[11]

In part, the back and forth nature of sexual change before the 1960s is what has earned the 1960s and 1970s the label of "sexual revolution," for beginning in the 1960s, a convergence of social movements, scientific developments, and legal liberalizations led to a rather markedly different sexual climate. The women's liberation movement directly addressed, and spurred changes in, issues of women's sexual pleasure, lesbianism, and reproductive rights. The gay rights movement demanded visibility and voice for nonheterosexuals and challenged straight America's conception of gender roles, sexual identity, and promiscuity at the same time. The civil rights movement achieved a degree of racial equality theretofore unseen in American history and began to dent long-standing stereotypes surrounding black sexuality. The youth, anti-war, and hippie movements actively rejected the older generation's values and choices, including those of monogamy and the heterosexual nuclear family. As these social movements converged, so too were scientific advancements changing the possibilities for contraception and legal developments changing the parameters for the kinds of sexual culture that could be permissibly distributed, printed, and screened.[12] The sexual revolution was experienced on much "smaller," more private, more individual levels as well, from college students living in co-ed dorms for the first time[13] to married couples delaying pregnancy and childbirth. The rising numbers of teens engaging in sexual intercourse, the increasing frequency of divorce, the growing legions of out gay men and lesbians, and the open discussion of sexually transmitted diseases all affected Americans' everyday lives.

These changes were products of and contributors to a new meaning for sexuality, one that developed across the twentieth century and that turned the significance of sex away from reproduction and the family and toward individual gratification and fulfillment.[14] There is no consensus on whether this shift was ultimately good or bad for American culture. It was a clear mark of progress for those social groups, women and nonheterosexuals especially, for whom the previously presumed link between sexuality and reproduction could be constraining and oppressive.[15] But it also made sex fair game for the marketplace. Historically, entry into consumer capitalism is too broad and deep a phenomenon to be easily deemed of benefit or harm; however, it does shape the way one may experience and understand the commodity at hand. In the case of the commercialization of sex, the individuating drive of the sexual revolution encouraged a popular understanding of sex as something that could be sought out and acquired, not as something inherent, intangible, and fundamental to human interaction.[16] This distinction may have limited popular conceptions of sexuality to the kinds of thoughts, feelings, practices, and identities that are readily adaptable to market logics, excluding other ways of living and knowing.

But the commodification of sex can also be seen as a democratization, in that most members of a consumer culture have at least some access to the marketplace, and the influence of the market can keep sex from being solely controlled and regulated by religious, governmental, or scientific forces. Certainly, those forces have continued to shape American sexual culture, regardless of the sexual revolution and the commercialization of sex. However, the dissemination of the new sexual culture via the marketplace has lessened the more exclusive holds those forces have traditionally had over sexuality. The shift in influence from the traditional arbiters of sexuality to the marketplace may be the legacy of the sexual revolution most heavily indebted to television, for better or worse, and the one through which the other aspects of the new sexual culture have achieved their widest reach. Through 1970s commercial network television, most Americans were exposed to different aspects of the sexual revolution so regularly, with so much variety, and to such an extent that this new, market-friendly sexual culture became a part of the common sense of American everyday life.

Television and Sex in the 1970s

The new sexual culture of 1970s television developed *after* many of the social, political, and cultural shifts associated with the sexual revolution were already underway. The liberalization of obscenity laws, for example, began in the late

1950s and was complete by the 1973 *Miller vs. California* Supreme Court case. Because of its conservative tendencies and its mass-targeted mission, however, television was not a full participant in these changes until the 1970s. Certainly, the "Big Three" broadcast networks began to deal overtly with sexual themes as of the late 1960s, and one can interpret even earlier TV as being a response to changing sexual mores (for example, *Peyton Place, Honey West, 77 Sunset Strip*).[17] But television's whole-hearted engagement with the new sexual culture was a phenomenon of the 1970s. Still, I mean my use of "the 1970s" to be flexible; in fact, television's construction of the new sexual culture began around 1968, when comedy-variety shows full of sex jokes debuted (for example, *Rowan and Martin's Laugh-In*), and ended around 1981, when *Charlie's Angels* was canceled, the sex symbol Suzanne Somers left *Three's Company*, and Grant Tinker took over the presidency of NBC from Fred Silverman, the network executive most strongly associated with television's turn to sex.

The rest of this book traverses this period, exploring the different modes of sexual representation that television offered across these years. The focus is on entertainment programming, since this is the space within which most sex-themed representation occurred, as well as being the most widely viewed of television's offerings. But my analysis goes beyond television's "texts" to include the TV industry's motivations for depicting sex and the new sexual culture as it did, as well as the TV audience's responses to this material. I also examine the relationships between television programming and some of the specific debates of the sexual revolution — over the morality of "X-rated" culture, young people's sexual experimentation, women's changing roles, homosexuality, promiscuity, and sexual violence.[18] Tracing the circuit that television's new sexual culture followed through processes of production and reception, through the programming itself, and through the social debates in which that programming intervened offers a useful means of understanding not only what appeared on television but also how and why it took the shape it did.

Although the book does not proceed chronologically, the modes of sexual representation that I describe do build upon one another. Chapter 1 takes a wide view of sex and television in the 1970s, focusing on the rivalry of the Big Three broadcast networks, ABC, NBC, and CBS. This chapter offers an introduction to the TV of the period, surveying the many different kinds of sex-themed programming and the structure of network competition that both generated and supported it. These economic pressures and possibilities provided a crucial framework for television's depiction of the changing times. In the 1970s, the networks used sex-themed programming as a means of attracting viewers and distinguishing themselves from one another. Their competitive strategizing shaped television's new sexual culture in ways specific to the network system's drive for ratings and advertiser dollars.

Providing this overview of network competition and the resultant outpouring of sex-themed material in 1970s television allows me to focus on much more specific TV industry practices and the representations they produced in the subsequent chapters. In fact, chapters 2 through 6 delve in depth into chapter 1's broad history of sex and 1970s television by focusing on exactly how and why television constructed sex and the new sexual culture in the range of ways it did. Each of these chapters centers on a particular program genre or theme, beginning with television's "safest," most reserved means of constructing the new sexual culture (indeed, the first mode is so "safe" that it refuses to allow sexual elements to appear on TV at all!) and building up to the discourse of sex that I see as the most potentially open to the challenges of the sexual revolution.

Chapter 2 examines some of the representations of sex that did *not* appear on television and thus tells the story of some of television's most glaring efforts to repress, even censor, the new sexual culture in the 1970s. I focus on three different instances in which the new sexual culture was barred from TV: the uproar over the rumored broadcast of X-rated feature films, the controversy over bra ads featuring live, lingerie-clad models, and the struggle over condom commercials. By studying intra-industrial regulatory debates, as well as government and public challenges, I examine these three areas of sexual taboo and the fights that ensued over their potential appearance on TV. As much as these fights reveal the television industry's censorious tendencies, these battles were not only about keeping certain material off the air. Indeed, they were as much about determining which representations of sex *would* appear on TV as they were about outright censorship.

Chapter 3 turns to one of television's most paranoid responses to the new sexual culture, one that understood sex and the sexual revolution as a grave danger to youth. This construction of sex as danger appeared in two primary sites. One was the regulatory uproar over the impact of TV sex and violence on young people, which played out most dramatically in the case of the National Association of Broadcasters' family viewing policy. But the notion of sex as danger was also omnipresent in one particular form of programming: the made-for-TV movie. Television movies often represented the fears expressed in regulatory discourse while instigating much regulatory angst about their own effects on young viewers. These movies combined the titillation of under-age young people (usually girls) becoming involved in prostitution, rape, or other sexual horrors with hard-hitting morality lessons about the dangers of sexual freedom. To mine this cautionary representation of the new sexual culture, I explore the production and reception of these movies, including the ways they were promoted and the parts they played in regulatory squabbles between the government and the TV industry. Together with analyses of the films themselves, I offer a picture of one TV representation that expressed many of the anxieties raised by the sexual revolution.

In chapter 4, I turn to yet another of the controversial programming trends of the 1970s—the preponderance of female sex symbols across the TV schedule and most notably in action-adventure series with women leads. Focusing on popular programs such as *Charlie's Angels* and *Wonder Woman*, this chapter analyzes television's tendency to symbolize sex and the new sexual culture through the bodies of conventionally attractive young women. By associating the new sexual openness with women and identifying those women as sex symbols, television made the changing gender roles endorsed by the women's liberation movement seem less disruptive and less revolutionary. Although making these female characters (and the actors who portrayed them) into sex objects seemed to many to be in direct opposition to the changes enabled by feminism, some of the era's female stars managed to symbolize not only sexual attractiveness but also the negotiation between the new feminism and the old femininity. The TV sex symbols became a locus for American culture's debate over what it meant to be a woman, what it meant to be a man, and what the difference was between the two in a period of rapid change. The Angels, Wonder Woman, and the many other TV sex symbols who followed in their path represented an aspect of the new sexual culture that sustained many longtime inequities but that managed to make Americans confront and, to some extent, accept the changing sex and gender roles fought for during the sexual revolution.

Chapter 5 explores television's construction of sex as a source of innuendo-driven humor by examining comedy-variety shows (for example, *The Sonny and Cher Comedy Hour, Laugh-In*), sitcoms (for example, *Happy Days, Soap, Three's Company*), and game shows (for example, *Match Game, Three's a Crowd*). Television's comedic treatment of sex was the perfect fit for the medium's tendency toward hints and winks over bolder, bawdier representations. Through humor, television could speak to many aspects of the new sexual culture, including the increasing visibility of gays and lesbians and the growing acceptance of premarital, nonmonogamous or "promiscuous" sex. As much as the suggestiveness of this humor allowed for references to potentially taboo topics, it also contributed to television's ability to sidestep the more radical aspects of the sexual revolution. Being able to avoid saying or showing anything explicitly sexual kept television's innuendo-driven comedy from fully committing to depictions of the post–sexual revolution society. The bulwarks of heterosexuality, monogamy, and traditional values thereby could be upheld. Yet several aspects of television's sexual humor, namely the unconventional choices of narrative, style, performance, and distribution in which some of TV's creators engaged, allowed the comedy to suggest the acceptability and normalcy of some rather challenging ideas, including the value of women's independence and sexual satisfaction and the pleasures of non-straight, or queer, perspectives. In this respect, the representation of the new sexual culture through innuendo-driven humor at times offered viewers a site where they could safely and enjoyably grapple with some of the more disruptive aspects of the sexual revolution.

The most ambiguous of 1970s television's representations of sex and the new sexual culture appeared in daytime television and its depiction of sex as a complex mixture of pleasure and pain. Chapter 6 investigates the abundance of rape plots across daytime soap operas of the 1970s, and especially between 1978 and 1981, when there were at least nineteen such story lines. Unlike the danger associated with sex in prime-time made-for-TV movies, the soap opera rape plots represented sexual violence in a range of ways, sometimes ignoring the anti-rape movement's challenges to American culture's understanding of rape, but more often taking into account those challenges and interweaving them with the intense emotion and character drama of the soap form. In daytime's version of the new sexual culture, the meaning of rape was up for debate, much as it was in American culture at large in the 1970s. This was a time when the line between conceiving of rape as an act of sexual passion and conceiving of it as a hostile act of violence became blurred. The many soap opera rape plots delved into these debates, and while some sought to educate viewers about the "true" meaning of rape as a crime of violence, others, such as the most popular — and most infamous — of these stories, that of *General Hospital*'s Luke and Laura, remained disturbingly ambiguous, enacting the confusion many women and men felt about the meaning of rape at a time of supposed sexual freedom. While this representation of sex and the new sexual culture as a complex mixture of pleasure and pain went nowhere near the most radical feminist stances on rape, daytime's multitude of rape plots did give voice to the feminist anti-rape perspective and, even more significantly, to the confusion, fear, and excitement so many people felt in the wake of the sexual revolution.

I conclude the story of television's embrace of the new sexual culture by considering its legacy, both for the television that has come after it and for American culture more generally. How has 1970s television influenced the handling of sex on TV since the early 1980s, especially given the turn away from the "network era" dominated by the Big Three toward a more diffusely distributed "post-network" era and its fragmented audiences? In addition, I consider the ways in which 1970s TV continues to shape mainstream under-standings of sex and the sexual revolution. What traces of the sex-themed television of the 1970s persist in contemporary culture, and what can those traces reveal about the long-term impact of this earlier era?

Television's handling of sex in the 1970s presented a negotiation between long-standing values, mores, and norms and the challenges to them posed by the sexual revolution. The participants in these negotiations — the broad-cast networks; television producers, writers, and performers; government and intra-industrial regulators; advertisers; organized audience groups and indi-vidual viewers; along with the television programming itself — determined how the sexual revolution would pervade the American mainstream. Through this confluence of forces, America's new sexual culture would take root, blooming into a common-sense understanding of sex in the post–sexual revo-lution world. Television of the 1970s shaped the way that American culture would think and talk about sex for years to come.

KIDDIE PORN VERSUS ADULT PORN

INTER-NETWORK COMPETITION

As the sun rises each day in the awesome world of the three
networks, their generals send forth the stars to do battle for
the ratings that rule the realm. The battle is fierce, but the
treasures are precious. . . . Today the battle is physical—
and furious.—VOICEOVER OPENING TO THE 1976 *BATTLE OF
THE NETWORK STARS* (ABC)

Between 1976 and 1984, U.S. television viewers were treated to a bian-
nual athletic competition between the prime-time stars of the Big Three
broadcast networks—ABC, NBC, and CBS. *The Battle of the Network Stars* ran
on ABC and was hosted by the network's overzealous sports commentator,
Howard Cosell. Cosell employed his trademark verbiage to narrate the series
of competitive events that made up the *Battle*—the swimming relay, the kayak
race, the obstacle course, the baseball dunk, the climactic tug-of-war. All of
the participants were subject to Cosell's appraisals, often centered on their
bodies or at least their physical prowess. Sex-tinged descriptions of the women
—Belinda Montgomery of *The Man from Atlantis* (NBC, 1977–78) was "a lis-
some lass with a limber body" while Joyce DeWitt of *Three's Company* (ABC,
1977–84) was "a diminutive bundle of instant sexuality"—somewhat outnum-

bered Cosell's evaluations of the men's physiques, but even the male actors were subject to Cosell's appreciative eye. He exclaimed about NBC captain Robert Conrad, "Look at Conrad! That body so finely proportioned!" Alongside Cosell's narration were other sexually suggestive elements. Buxom cheerleaders shot from low camera angles encouraged the teams; male and female contestants sported the short shorts and tight swimwear popular in the day while the women often competed braless (a fact emphasized in slow-motion replays of them in athletic motion). Brief profiles of competitors often focused on their physical attractiveness and included such footage as sex symbols Suzanne Somers and Lynda Carter exercising in full make-up and striking attractive poses. Even the antics surrounding a "just for fun" round of Simon Says (a 1970s craze) placed such stars as Cathy Lee Crosby of *That's Incredible* (ABC, 1980–84) and Larry Wilcox of *CHiPs* (NBC, 1977–83) in an intimate embrace.

Battle of the Network Stars was a genuine athletic competition. The stars could win up to $20,000 each, so they took it very seriously. At the same time, however, Cosell's hyperbolic commentary, the adolescent sexual suggestiveness, and the mock-serious tenor of the introductory segments like the one quoted above tended to undercut the competition's intensity. *Battle* exemplified the fierceness of 1970s network competition and the centrality of sexual content to that competitive climate, but it also illustrated the ultimately superficial nature of both the networks' battles with each other (if they were in such fierce ratings competition, why would ABC willingly promote the other networks' shows?) and the kind of sexual material that would make it on air. *Battle of the Network Stars* was emblematic of a distinctive moment in network television history and in the history of television's new sexual culture.

Throughout the 1970s, the Big Three faced virtually no competition. No competition, that is, except from each other. In the network era, ABC, NBC, and CBS were the main options for TV entertainment and each network focused on besting the other two. All three were contending for the same advertiser dollars, and those dollars increased in proportion to the Nielsen ratings for their programming. Network rivalry centered on drawing audiences to boost ratings and thereby raise ad rates. However, because the three networks operated so similarly, with parallel corporate structures, scheduling practices, and content, their tricks for drawing audiences came from the same bag. As a result, the networks' attempts to differentiate themselves came down to small distinctions in programming—differences in story lines, in stars, in the mix of genres and the mapping of the schedule. While such distinctions may have had little impact on the larger commercial function of American network TV, they could affect how and to what extent television represented particular social issues, not least of which was sex. Whether by imitating each other's successes or countering each other with variations on a theme, in the 1970s all three networks used sex to appeal to viewers. Inter-network rivalry produced the new sexual culture, ensuring its ubiquity, its limited diversity, and its commodified base.

The story of 1970s television competition is one of the longtime third-place ABC passing runner-up NBC and perennial champ CBS on its path to ratings victory. Essential to ABC's ascension was its sex-themed programming; in many respects, ABC led the networks in bringing the sexual revolution to TV. Yet television's new sexual culture was not the product of one network's risk-taking. It was a medium-wide phenomenon born of all three networks jockeying for ratings and constructing their versions of the sexually changed times in relation to each other. Just as important as ABC's efforts were CBS's "turn to relevance" in its social issue-oriented sitcoms and NBC's experiments with sexually suggestive humor in its comedy-variety shows. Later in the decade, NBC's attempts to "out-sex" ABC had a significant impact on the made-for-TV movies' version of the new sexual culture, just as CBS's stab at hosting some buxom beauties of its own shaped the legacy of the TV sex symbol. It was through the struggles between all three networks, not just through ABC's endeavor to rise from third place to first, that the new sexual culture of 1970s television was created.

Network Positioning in the Early 1970s

When the 1970s began, CBS held a clear lead in total household ratings and ABC was seemingly stuck in third place. CBS had substantially more shows among the top twenty of the 1969–70 season than either of its competitors, while ABC, the youngest of the three, consistently held last place despite a couple of promising seasons in the early 1960s.[1] These standings were, not surprisingly, far from satisfactory to ABC management, but the network seemed mired in its inferior position. ABC had long been the butt of jokes among industry insiders. While CBS was often deemed the "Tiffany network" (especially by its self-serving executives), ABC was said to stand for the "Almost Broadcasting Company." Its rapid turnover in series, which were quickly canceled if they failed to perform, earned the quip, "If President Nixon put the Vietnam War on ABC, it would be over in thirteen weeks." CBS's imposing Manhattan headquarters were respectfully nicknamed "Black Rock"; ABC's new, rented setting was labeled "Schlock Rock."[2]

A joke circulating in the TV industry of the late 1960s aptly illustrates not only the three networks' relative reputations, but also the prevailing industry attitudes toward sex. It went like this: The three networks were marooned on an island, deserted except for a beautiful girl with whom the networks agreed they should all have sex. ABC was the first to volunteer and proceeded "to ravish the beauty unashamedly in plain view of the other two networks." Though CBS declared he did not like being second to anyone, particularly to ABC, he told the girl, "I'll be next, but come with me to the other side of the island where we can have privacy." Then it was NBC's turn. Though anxious to have sex with the girl, NBC said, "First, I've got to call New York and see what they say."[3] The joke's sexism was surely a product of the "old boy" power bloc that ran the TV industry, although it was also a relatively common, accepted stance in the early years of the women's liberation movement. The joke is perhaps most telling as an illustration of the kind of masculine potency each network was imagined to have. ABC was the impetuous adolescent, quick to jump into bed with whatever attractive offer came by, unconcerned with how it looked to the others. CBS, in contrast, was ever the gentleman, perfectly willing to debase itself but only to do so away from judgmental gazes, thus keeping its stellar reputation intact. Finally, NBC was the regular fellow, excited by the prospect of an illicit romp but nervous about the ramifications and hesitant about forging ahead as a result. This macho one-upmanship would persist throughout the 1970s, though the balance of power between the participants would change. Still, at the beginning of the decade, ABC not only trailed in ratings but also in respectability, at least in the eyes of its fellow networks.

The same relative positioning of the Big Three also played out in the networks' standings in daytime, most notably in the ratings and reputations of their respective soap operas. Until the 1970s, ABC's daytime line-up was in even worse shape than its prime-time schedule. Its first even remotely successful foray into daytime drama was *General Hospital*, which began in 1963, and its game shows and talk shows, the other staples of daytime television, had little to no sustained presence. In contrast, CBS had dominated the soap schedule from television's earliest years, airing more serials and garnering consistently higher ratings than either of the other two networks. Much of the CBS daytime schedule was filled with soaps produced by the sponsor Procter and Gamble. This marriage of CBS and Procter and Gamble was, in fact, the foundation of the network's daytime success. From 1952 to 1972, the daytime dramas produced by Procter and Gamble—*As the World Turns* (CBS, 1956–), *The Guiding Light* (CBS, 1952–), *Another World* (NBC, 1964–99), *Search for Tomorrow* (CBS, 1951–82; NBC, 1982–86), and *The Edge of Night* (CBS, 1956–75; ABC, 1975–84)—consistently placed in the top two daytime serial ratings spots and often filled the top four, with *As the World Turns* coming in first most years.[4] With the exception of *Another World*, the Procter and Gamble empire was entirely located at CBS, keeping the sponsor-producer and the network closely aligned and keeping CBS as dominant in the soap industry as it was in prime time. Because soaps were particularly profitable for the networks in the 1970s (with their relatively low production costs, many commercial minutes, and loyal viewership of the primary household consumers—women), these struggles were at least as significant to network economics as were the prime-time ratings races. Indeed, daytime fed both CBS and NBC 75 percent of their profits in the early 1970s.[5]

Youth and Sex in the Early 1970s: The New CBS

At the beginning of the 1970s, while CBS's historic leads in daytime and prime time were as strong as ever, they were beginning to face some legitimate challenges. In the 1969–70 season, CBS's winning prime-time schedule featured a slate of rural-set and family sitcoms, old-fashioned westerns, and traditional variety shows, including *Mayberry R.F.D.* (1968–71), *Family Affair* (1966–71), *Gunsmoke* (1955–75), and *The Red Skelton Hour* (NBC, 1951–53; CBS, 1953–70; NBC, 1970–71). The number one show, however, was on NBC, and its experiments with sexual humor presaged a key way in which network competition was soon to change. *Rowan and Martin's Laugh-In* (NBC, 1968–73) held the top spot for the second season in a row. *Laugh-In* depended heavily upon double entendres for its humor. In one infamous skit, the comedian Judy Carnes appeared on screen in a skull cap, making her look bald. Clearly distressed, she declared, "I've never been bald [balled] before!" The joke thus depended upon more than Carnes's absurd appearance. It depended upon the second, bawdier meaning of her exclamation. Such humor, along with topical jokes on matters from the pope to the pill, helped make *Laugh-In* one of the few series at the turn of the decade that consistently drew young audiences, the market segment increasingly valuable to advertisers from the late 1960s onward.[6] Influenced by *Laugh-In*'s success with America's youth, all of the networks sought programs to attract those viewers. This was especially challenging for CBS, since its older-skewing shows were *not* ratings successes among the young, urban viewers of the network's five owned and operated stations.[7]

Responding to this climate, Robert Wood, the president of CBS, declared that he was setting out to change "the character of the network from more bucolic material to more fresh or updated, contemporary [fare]."[8] Assisted by Fred Silverman, his programming chief, Wood gradually revamped the entire prime-time schedule, first adding some dramatic series with young casts and social issue story lines (à la ABC's *Mod Squad*, 1968–73) in 1970–71 and then, for the 1971–72 season, phasing out the older, rural appeal series such as *Green Acres* (1965–71) and *Hee Haw* (1969–71) in favor of more social issue-oriented shows, this time in comedic form.[9]

By the start of the 1972–73 season, the network had found three sitcom anchors that spoke to the changing social worlds of the young while not alienating older viewers or the institutions that supported them. *All in the Family* (1971–83), *The Mary Tyler Moore Show* (1970–77), and *M*A*S*H* (1972–83) each dealt with social change in its own way, but all three managed to use their comedic sensibilities to make both young and old, rebels and authority figures the objects of good-natured ribbing. *All in the Family*'s Archie Bunker was absurdly bigoted, but his liberal son-in-law, Mike "Meathead" Stivic, was naively idealistic; *The Mary Tyler Moore Show*'s Mary Richards coped with the sexist shenanigans of her boss, Lou Grant, and the pompous anchor, Ted Baxter, while bumbling through her own attempt at life as a single, working woman; and *M*A*S*H*'s unwilling draftee, Corporal Max Klinger, went to ridiculous lengths to be discharged from a unit in which the hilariously humorless Major Frank Burns wielded his ineffectual authority. These series dealt overtly with social issues of the day: race relations, women's roles, the generation gap, the war in Vietnam (very thinly disguised as the Korean War in *M*A*S*H*), and the changing sexual mores. They also featured characters with more depth and relationships with more complexity than had been seen in the sitcom genre before this time (with rare exceptions). Their success resulted in numerous spin-off series that dealt with similarly explosive issues, including sexual ones.

CBS's politicized brand of sexual humor in its new sitcoms helped win the 1972–73 TV season a reputation as the year TV turned to sex.[10] Developments at the other networks also contributed to TV's reputation as increasingly permissive. For example, NBC's standards and practices editors began to allow topics and language they never had before, including rape, homosexuality, and words such as "penis," "coitus," and "orgasm." The network also allowed Johnny Carson, the *Tonight Show* (1954–) host, to deliver his nightly monologues without pre-screening.[11] Although comedic treatments of sex were common, NBC and ABC began to experiment with such material in dramatic form. For example, on ABC, *The Streets of San Francisco* (1972–77), *Marcus Welby, M.D.* (1969–76), and *Owen Marshall, Counselor at Law* (1971–74) all featured gay-themed episodes, as did NBC's *The Bold Ones* (1969–73).[12] The 1972–73 season was also the season in which ABC ran the much-discussed and much-praised *That Certain Summer* (1 November 1972), a made-for-TV movie about a gay, divorced father's attempt to "explain his lifestyle" to his fourteen-year-old son.[13] Meanwhile, on PBS, the documentary series *An American Family* (1973) featured the family's openly gay son, Lance. While CBS's immensely popular sitcoms were clearly leading the TV industry into new sex-themed territory, the other networks were beginning to consider alternate ways of representing the changing sexual landscape.

The Roots of Three-Network Parity

Before ABC could become a TV industry success story, it needed to become more equivalent financially with its competitors. Two new federal policies, both of which seemed detrimental to the networks' economic fortunes, actually helped ABC achieve this parity. The FCC's ban on cigarette advertising and the Prime Time Access Rule (PTAR) both had an immediate impact on network profits. The 1971 ad ban meant a $170 million loss for the TV industry.[14] However, as Sally Bedell explains, by cutting the minimum amount of time an advertiser could buy (from one minute to thirty seconds), CBS actually managed to attract new advertisers and earn more per advertising minute. The other networks followed CBS's innovation and all three thus weathered the cigarette ban crisis.[15] In addition, PTAR shortened network prime time by a half-hour as of the 1971–72 season, returning that time to the local affiliates. Although this meant a potentially damaging loss of sixty-three commercial minutes per week for the networks, it actually improved ad sales for the new, shortened prime time because national advertisers panicked about scarcity and eagerly paid even higher rates. Coupled with the networks' ad strategy enacted after the ban on cigarette advertising, PTAR left all three networks with an unanticipated *increase* in profits for 1971. The Prime Time Access Rule was particularly instrumental in ABC's improved fortunes. The rule meant that ABC could relieve itself of three and one-half hours of poorly sponsored, poorly rated shows each week, without the expense of replacing them.[16]

ABC also managed to acquire more affiliates and to put competitive pressure on CBS's and NBC's ad rates in the early 1970s, which allowed all three to regularly sell out their ad time.[17] Combined, these measures helped ABC-TV to make its first profit in ten years in 1972. As the ABC executive Elton Rule happily told *Business Week*, "In today's marketplace, there is no longer the possibility of one dominant network year after year in all the important time periods, as CBS once was. And there's no possibility of one network staying a poor third, as we once were."[18] Long the pathetic also-ran of network television, ABC was poised to compete fiercely in the network ratings race.

ABC's Innovations in Prime-time Sex

ABC paired its economic gains of the early 1970s with attempts to distinguish itself in terms of its programming, attempts that would help establish the network's reputation as the unconventional purveyor of a distinct kind of sexuality. For the 1969–70 season, ABC debuted a new series that would ultimately provide a rich source of programming for the networks and a new forum for television's sexual culture. ABC's *Movie of the Week* premiered on 23 September 1969 and quickly helped ABC establish a reputation as a television innovator.

NBC was the first network to air made-for-TV movies with its *Project 120* series, a collaboration with Universal Studios that had begun in 1964. The high cost of licensing theatrical releases for broadcast, along with the increasingly racy content of feature films, made custom movies an appealing prospect (and one that drew healthy ratings), so ABC followed NBC's lead in the late 1960s.[19] But ABC differentiated its *Movie of the Week* from NBC's movies for television in two ways, both of which helped establish ABC's reputation for sex-themed programming. First, ABC cut back on costs by scheduling 90-minute (instead of 120-minute) movies and by opening itself to pitches from a range of producers (instead of contracting with one Hollywood studio, as had NBC).[20] The second way in which ABC differentiated its TV movies from NBC's was in content. NBC's *World Premiere* movies tended toward the action-adventure and suspense genres.[21] ABC scheduled these sorts of films, as well, but also programmed many more comedic pieces and, eventually, more projects dealing with social issues. Many of ABC's airings from both genres dealt with sexual subjects, or at least with subjects that acknowledged a society affected by such phenomena as women's liberation, sexual promiscuity, and divorce. Among the comedy airings were *The Feminist and the Fuzz* (26 January 1971), about the pairing of a women's liberation activist and a chauvinistic policeman; *Congratulations, It's a Boy!* (21 September 1971), about a bachelor's "swinging life" being interrupted by a teenager who claims to be his son; and *Playmates* (3 October 1972), in which two divorced men secretly date each others' ex-wives. The more issue-oriented films touched on such social subjects as rape (*A Taste of Evil*, 12 October 1971), teenage pregnancy (*Mr. and Mrs. Bo Jo Jones*, 16 November 1971), and homosexuality (*That Certain Summer*). With certain exceptions (for example, the lauded *That Certain Summer*), most of ABC's efforts at sex-related social issues were not the sort of hard-hitting, well-respected, "quality" products that would soon draw attention to the made-for-TV movie form. Instead, ABC's typical fare framed sex-related social problems either light-heartedly or through more exploitative means. ABC's innovations in this form quickly became one of the network's few clear successes in the early 1970s, and one that would contribute to ABC's growing reputation as the most sex-saturated broadcaster.

Challenging CBS Daytime

ABC's experiments in new ways to draw desirable audiences while maintaining low programming costs also affected its daytime schedule. When Leonard

Goldberg inherited the leadership of the nearly nonexistent ABC Daytime in 1965, one of his initial steps was to schedule the first series created by his predecessor at ABC, Chuck Barris. *The Dating Game* (1965–73), soon followed by *The Newlywed Game* (1966–74), helped establish Barris's career as a producer of youth-targeted, sexually suggestive game shows and helped ABC Daytime establish an identity. Along with a revamped *General Hospital* and a new serial, *Dark Shadows* (1966–71), ABC Daytime began to compete with the other two networks for the first time.[22] *Dark Shadows* in particular drew a young audience, mainly teenagers, to ABC in the late afternoons. The popularity of this gothic serial among American youth further bolstered ABC's image as the young, unconventional network. And the sexual subtext of its vampire tales, alongside the sexual humor of the Barris shows, was increasingly making sexuality a cornerstone of ABC's image.

ABC's growing presence in daytime was matched by NBC's incursions into CBS's lead.[23] As of November 1971, both ABC and NBC had made gains over their 1970 ratings, while CBS had taken a 9 percent ratings drop.[24] By May 1972, *TV Guide* was declaring, "There is an extra measure of ferocity in the daytime battle this year. For the first time, the networks are locked in what amounts to a three-way dead heat for daytime ratings."[25] Though CBS and its serials were still performing quite well, by 1972 there were four more soaps on the air than in 1968, one at CBS, one at ABC, and two at NBC; the sheer increase in numbers provided more competition for CBS and for the Procter and Gamble programs it carried.

Along with these ratings incursions, innovations in the narratives and style of the other networks' serials, particularly ABC's, challenged the formulae the CBS shows had relied upon for years. The programs created by Procter and Gamble followed the soaps' conventional interests in subjects such as marriage, divorce, pregnancy, illness, and family relationships, subjects that remained little affected by the passage of years and that unfolded slowly over weeks and months. As one *As the World Turns* staff member put it, "We stayed in the 1950s while everybody else was moving into the 1970s."[26] The other soaps began to "move into the 1970s" primarily by injecting more contemporary social issues into their drama, making soaps more socially "relevant," much as producers of prime-time series were doing at the time. They also began to pick up the pace of daytime serials, shortening scene lengths and allowing stories to progress more rapidly. The serials ABC premiered in the late 1960s and early 1970s were at the forefront of this turn. The early days of *All My Children* (1970–) featured a Vietnam War protestor and, in 1972, television's first legal abortion.[27] ABC's image was in distinct contrast to that of CBS and the Procter and Gamble soaps that had long reigned there.

By the end of 1971, representatives of NBC and ABC were both claiming that CBS's serials were "wearing thin," implying that the old-fashioned kind of soap storytelling to be found on CBS was past its prime.[28] Although Procter and Gamble's *As the World Turns* and *Another World* retained the first and second spots in the daytime ratings throughout the middle years of the 1970s, their reign was clearly under threat. As Irna Phillips, the creator of most of the Procter and Gamble serials, complained, highlighting the difference between her generation of soaps and the soaps of television's new sexual culture: "The daytime serial is destroying itself, eating itself up with rape, abortion, illegitimacy, men falling in love with other men's wives."[29] Network competition in daytime drama was just as intense as it was in prime time, and just as focused around sexual content.

ABC Takes the Lead: Mid-1970s

By the 1973–74 season, NBC's and ABC's efforts to challenge CBS's ratings lead were beginning to have a greater impact. In particular, the other networks' innovations in such areas as made-for-TV movies and daytime soaps were keeping CBS from resting contentedly in first place. Instead, the network was beginning to consider ways to supplement its hit comedies with other programming that would retain its status in terms of both its ratings and its image. How could CBS continue to be the vanguard network, the classy industry stalwart willing to embrace new permutations in TV quality, when its competitors were finding new ways to draw attention to themselves? Increasingly, that attention was generated around sexual matters, and ABC in particular was becoming more and more adept at using sex as an attention-getter. As ABC took over CBS's ratings lead in the mid-1970s, its brand of TV sex, which was very different from CBS's handling of the topic in its sitcom hits, would come to dominate. Even as longtime industry standings were reversed, competition between the Big Three would dictate the terms of television's new sexual culture.

Sex in Daytime

In March 1973, facing the new developments in ABC's daytime schedule, CBS Daytime made its first bold move to compete in the soaps' edgy innovations that were driven by social issues. Still retaining its successful and foundational Procter and Gamble programs, the network debuted a new serial, *The Young and the Restless*. Unlike the majority of its soaps, *The Young and the Restless* was neither produced by Procter and Gamble nor shot in New York City. According to its creator, William J. Bell, it would "emphasize more the man-woman relationship than the life and death crisis situations used as the prime emotional force in many daytime dramas."[30] Along with its new focus on romance and sex, *The Young and the Restless* soon established a "Hollywood" look, with a young and glamorous cast and high production values, and it dealt frankly with sexual subjects, among them adultery and rape. It also drew those ever-valuable young audiences.

The Young and the Restless epitomized the mounting changes in soaps of the 1970s not only because it broke with the conventions of the typical CBS serial, but also because it featured more explicit sex scenes and sex talk than the soaps that came before it. In 1978, *TV Guide* described the five-year-old program as "the paradigm for the more recent soaps" due to its semi-nude scenes, "enough open-mouth kissing to humidify the atmosphere," and "some very plain pillow talk between the handsome men and beautiful young women."[31] *The Young and the Restless*'s boldness in these areas encouraged other shows to do the same, or at least to try. For example, on *General Hospital* network censors were rumored to have demanded wardrobe changes when the actress Judith McConnell was to go braless under a sexy dress in a seduction scene.[32] On NBC, a new soap, *How to Survive a Marriage* (1974–75), a "women's lib" serial about a thirty-two-year-old divorcée facing the worlds of work, parenting, and dating on her own, debuted with a semi-nude bedroom scene that drew substantial viewer protest.[33]

Along with the turn to more sexually explicit representations, the soaps of the middle 1970s continued the trend that had begun earlier in the decade of daytime dramas grappling with controversial issues. As one commentator explained in 1975, soap characters "live their lives in the modern '70s world and thus are involved (at least some of them some of the time) with many of the so-called 'relevant' issues: rape and abortion and child abuse and Pap tests and psychotherapy and women's liberation and drugs and sex."[34] For instance, in 1974–75, CBS's *Search for Tomorrow* planned a story about a draft dodger coming home at the end of the Vietnam War.[35] In 1977, NBC's *Days of Our Lives* played out an interracial love story, touched on a lesbian plot, and grappled with wife-beating. While soap fans were not always pleased with these changes, the networks and soap producers saw turns to sex and controversial social issues as ways to draw new, young viewers to daytime. Much as in prime time, youth, sex, and sensational social issues seemed a winning combination in the eyes of the networks.

New Experiments in Prime-time Sex

Just as daytime television was becoming more adventurous in its handling of sexual themes and controversial social issues, so too was prime-time programming across all three networks branching out in these areas. CBS's hit sitcoms continued to challenge TV taboos by using sex as one of many politically charged themes. But CBS and NBC also sought to establish youth-appeal credibility by including sexual themes in other genres of prime time. As ABC's competitors joined the rallying third-place network in scheduling more made-for-television movies, they sought to distinguish their kinds of tele-films from their competitors' while still cashing in on the success of ABC's *Movie of the Week* with advertisers. At the same time, ABC and NBC both experimented with a new way to inject sexuality into their programming—by featuring attractive young women as leads in action-adventure shows, a first for U.S. television. Thus, network competition in sex-themed made-for-TV movies and in new action-adventure series with sexy women stars further developed the networks' new sexual culture.

Once CBS began airing made-for-TV movies in 1971–72, all three networks used the form as a relatively economical way to draw valuable audiences, particularly young women.[36] ABC continued to feature many movies with sexual themes, although the network's experiments with comedies began to peter off, to be replaced by more social issue and exploitation-style dramas in a bid to compete with NBC and CBS.[37] Beginning in 1973–74, both CBS and NBC aired made-for-TV movies that offered "serious" treatment of sex-themed social issues, most notably CBS's *Cry Rape!* (27 November 1973) and NBC's *A*

Case of Rape (20 February 1974). Such films began to garner a "semblance of respectability" for TV movies, and both NBC and CBS saw these intimations of quality as a way to distinguish their products from that of ABC. ABC quickly rushed to keep up, programming its own "quality" fare, such as the epic QBVII in the spring of 1974.[38] Yet all three networks, and most distinctively ABC and NBC, more often treated their social issues sensationally (and chose sensational social issues to treat). For example, ABC's *Hustling* (22 February 1975) and *Someone I Touched* (26 February 1975) dealt with prostitution and venereal disease, respectively. On NBC, *Born Innocent* (10 September 1974) stirred up immense controversy about the impact of TV sex and violence on youth with its depiction of a teenage girl's same-sex gang rape in a juvenile detention center. Both networks would keep up these thematic trends throughout the decade, although NBC would come to specialize in this sort of sex-and-social-issue sensationalism. In the mid-1970s, however, both ABC and NBC distinguished their movies from CBS's by investing in these topics.

ABC and NBC also distinguished their programming from CBS by scheduling action-adventure series with sexy women leads in the 1974–75 season. Although women leads in sitcoms and made-for-TV movies were increasingly common by this point, dramatic series and action shows had yet to feature a woman as star. There was a strong bias against such representations throughout the industry. As Frank Barton, CBS's vice-president of program development, argued in 1973, "The audience tends to identify more with male heroes than female heroines . . . for some reason the audience doesn't identify with a woman lead say, a woman detective. It will accept a man, but not a woman."[39] Although this bias was widely accepted industry logic, the successes of sitcoms and made-for-TV movies starring women, as well as the increasingly influential women's liberation movement, led certain network executives to reconsider. As NBC's director of development, Terry Keegan, explained, "Now that the public's consciousness is up, it's not as hard to find a believable role [for a woman]."[40] Key to the networks' interest in such projects, however, was that these series leads be not only female but also sexually attractive. Female sex appeal and the potential sexual danger to which the female protagonist was exposed were the most important elements in the formula.[41]

ABC and NBC aired pilots for two action series with sexy women stars early in 1974. *Get Christie Love!* (ABC, 22 January 1974) and *Police Woman* (NBC, in "The Gamble," 26 March 1974, an episode of *Police Story*) proved promising in pilot form and were picked up by their respective networks for the 1974–75 season. Starring the established sex symbols Teresa Graves (known for her bikini-clad role on NBC's *Laugh-In*) and Angie Dickinson (of Hollywood films), both shows put their policewoman heroines in weekly jeopardy as they went undercover to capture criminals. Their undercover disguises were stereotypically feminine—in "A High Fashion Heist" (12 March 1975) Christie poses as a model and in "Market for Murder" (11 September 1974) she serves as "bait" to lure a jewel fence, while Dickinson's Pepper Anderson frequently took on the guises of hooker, waitress, and "stewardess." The fact that Graves/Christie was black was treated as incidental in the series (although the pilot was a more explicit blaxploitation film imitator). What mattered for both shows was that these adventuresome heroines were sexy and attractive, that their work depended upon that attractiveness, and that sex appeal and action could be so readily combined.

Although *Get Christie Love!* was canceled after one season, *Police Woman* ran through 1977–78. Both series helped to convince the networks that women could headline action-adventure series—at least if they could be classified as sex symbols. In the 1975–76 season, ABC aired four different pilots for such series, two of which (*Charlie's Angels*, 21 March 1976, and *The New, Original Wonder Woman*, 7 November 1975) would have successful runs beginning the next season.[42] In addition, the network was preparing to spin off the Six Million Dollar Man's girlfriend, Jaime Somers, in *The Bionic Woman* (ABC, 1976–77; NBC, 1977–78). Like CBS's *Kate McShane* (starring forty-six-year-old Anne Meara), NBC's efforts (*The Lives of Jenny Dolan*, 27 October 1975, starring forty-one-year-old Shirley Jones, and *McNaughton's Daughter*, 4 March 1976, starring thirty-six-year-old Susan Clark) did not have the crucial ingredient of ABC's pilots that did become hit series: their older stars lacked the youthful sex-symbol status of the ABC heroines, all of whom were in their twenties when their series began. Only NBC's *Police Woman* and ABC's new programs with sex-symbol leads would have any sustained presence. Once again, ABC's brand of TV sex—in this case, that of sexy young women in action-oriented roles—would serve to establish the network's new identity and vastly improve its standings in the Big Three's ratings race.

Fred Silverman Comes to ABC

With successful experiments in sex-themed TV in daytime and some prime-time movies and pilots, ABC's fortunes had improved by 1975. Yet CBS continued to dominate the prime-time ratings with its comedy line-ups while NBC stayed ahead of ABC with comedies such as *Sanford and Son* (1972–77) and *Chico and the Man* (1974–78), both of which dealt with hot-button racial and ethnic issues in the tradition of Norman Lear. However, a well-publicized shift in employer for one key network executive, Fred Silverman, would soon do much to assist ABC's imminent rise to first place. It would also help to solidify ABC's already-burgeoning reputation as the network willing to pander to young audiences with sexual appeals. In May 1975, Silverman left the programming vice-presidency at CBS for the presidency of ABC's newly organized Entertainment division. It was a lateral move, but ABC offered Silverman some particularly appealing remuneration, not all of it financial. Silverman's defection to the Tiffany network's most junior rival was seen by many as a journey from middle-brow tastefulness to mass pandering. But it was also a move that altered television's handling of sex and revised the standings of inter-network competition.

Fred Silverman had never seemed to fit in among the Ivy League-educated CBS executives (see figure 1). As an anonymous friend characterized him: "Freddie's a blue-collar worker — he actually reads scripts and watches shows — and he doesn't do things in the white-collar CBS way." In contrast, Silverman seemed perfectly suited to ABC, his "spiritual home" as *Time* magazine put it.[43] The president of ABC, Fred Pierce, wisely offered him not only more money and perks than he was getting at CBS, but also more respect. In certain senses it was ABC's boldest step yet in embracing its image as the younger, more free-wheeling, more unabashedly populist network. Silverman had long recognized these qualities in ABC. He had written his Ohio State University master's thesis on ABC's programming between 1953 and 1959, the period in which the new network achieved a status just shy of its two competitors. In the thesis, he argued for the value of program promotion, audience research, a flexible schedule, long-term contracts with prolific producers, series programming over "spectaculars," and merchandising tie-ins, all of which became prominent components of his own contributions to ABC in the 1970s.

1 Fred Silverman.
NBC/PHOTOFEST.

The thesis also contended that ABC's targeting of young families with children was its most important strategy, another principle from which he would borrow when he controlled the ABC schedule.[44]

Because Silverman's tenure at ABC coincided with regulatory attempts to protect young audiences from objectionable material, his interest in appealing to a cross-age "family" audience was fortuitously timed. Along with staving off regulatory pressure, this strategy served to counter-program CBS by offering shows with no apparent political message and no pretensions to artistry. The Silverman era at ABC centered around what the programming executive termed a comedy "structure" of kid-friendly characters and jokes, a structure meant to appeal to the mass audience's common denominator — they had all been kids at one time or another.[45] Thus, broad, simple comedy and comedy-action-fantasy hybrids became the foundations of the ABC schedule. By structuring ABC's kid-oriented comedy upon innuendo-laden sexual humor, Silverman's ABC was able to seem as up-to-date as CBS without taking too radical a stance on the changing culture and without alienating the mass, "family" audience. Given the juvenile sexual humor pervading the Silverman-era schedule, the "kid" in all of us seemed to be an especially horny adolescent.

These efforts led ABC to a consistent first place in the network ratings, unlike any time in its history. In the 1975–76 season ABC finally edged past NBC to finish second, signaling an impending change in network standings.[46] In 1976–77 that change arrived, as ABC came in first and achieved the highest season average rating in the history of television, placing seven shows among the season's top ten.[47] The network held this position for years, allowing it a degree of industry power it had never before experienced. As the first-place network, it set the ad price structure for the industry.[48] Its affiliate count also improved, as some stations switched affiliation to the new champion, usually away from now third-place NBC.[49] Yet ABC's rise was, in some senses, a victory for the entire network system. The fact that a perennially last-place network could not only achieve parity with its competitors but also outpace them testified to the robustness of the advertiser-supported television economy of the 1970s. The fact that all three networks substantially increased their earnings during the decade also indicated that inter-network competition would not determine which networks would survive and which would fail. By 1980, the total revenue for the networks was three times what it had been in 1970 — at $3 billion a year, the network system was thriving.[50]

The Rise of ABC Daytime

With such impressive gains in prime time, Silverman was also eager to improve ABC Daytime's performance. Continuing the pattern of ABC robbing CBS of its golden status, Silverman brought a CBS Daytime executive, Jackie Smith, to ABC in March 1977 and put her in charge of the rapidly rising network's daytime fare. Working with the elements already in place, Smith gave ABC Daytime the final push it needed to achieve number one status and match the network's nighttime performance, including its attractiveness to young viewers and its propensity for a distinctive brand of TV sex.

Smith's work with ABC's daytime line-up can be seen clearly in the rise of *General Hospital* from barely surviving soap in the mid-1970s to national phenomenon by the early 1980s. After Smith's arrival, *General Hospital* steadily climbed in the ratings. One of her first steps was to hire Gloria Monty as producer and Douglas Marland as head writer. In concert with trends throughout the soap industry, Monty and Marland began to steer the show away from its focus on the hospital and toward younger characters embroiled in intense romantic and sexual situations. As the 1970s progressed, *General Hospital* continued to change, not only with new characters and stories but also with an accelerated pace, newer sets, and rejuvenated lighting and directing. Between 1978 and 1979 the show moved from ninth place in the daytime soap ratings to first. By early 1980, it was a solid and unbeatable number one. In the fall of 1981, the serial had the highest concentration of both teenage and eighteen-to-thirty-four-year-old viewers in daytime, it averaged a 12.1 rating and a 41 share, and its network charged around $25,000 per thirty-second commercial spot, adding up to approximately $50 million in network earnings a year, one quarter of ABC-TV's annual profits.[51]

Meanwhile, CBS, the former daytime champion, held the dubious distinction of leading in men and women viewers over the age of fifty.[52] Procter and Gamble made an effort to revive its expiring line-up, even attempting storylines around controversial social issues, including some with sexual material. However, the company's programming guidelines prohibiting "excessive or gratuitous sex, violence, profanity, or other material that might be offensive to the average viewer" limited the degree to which its soaps would imitate the ground-breaking social issues of an *All My Children* or the fast-paced action and adventure of a *General Hospital*.[53] Despite Procter and Gamble's efforts, by the late 1970s sex, relevance, and youth had triumphed over tears, talk, and coffee; ABC Daytime had overtaken the long-dominant CBS.

Promoting "the Heat"

ABC's success in daytime was matched by the network's attempt to build its popularity in prime time, an effort that was assisted by a new degree of attention to program promotion, much of which relied upon allusions to sex. Although ABC led its competitors in the use of promotions before Fred Silverman even arrived, in the Silverman years the network came to specialize in sexually suggestive teases, what Silverman called "the heat."[54] As the ABC promo writer Larry Sullivan described the formula, "We sell the possibility of tits and ass and the possibility of violence. We present the stimuli and the response."[55] Sometimes these stimuli even implied a sexual element that was not, in fact, a major part of the episode. For example, the network promoted a *Happy Days* (1974–84) episode in which Fonzie goes temporarily blind by showing the character with his arms around two young women.

The tag line was "Fonzie can't eye the girls anymore."[56] Though this was a "serious" episode about Fonzie dealing with a disability, ABC played up the character's sexual prowess in its promotion, promising titillation and pretty girls if audiences tuned in. *The Love Boat's* (1977–86) sexual suggestiveness was also subject to this kind of promotion. ABC pressured the program's producers to increase the sex in the series, partly to find promotable "heat." Thus, the executive producer, Douglas Cramer, asked of a script he was reviewing whether the staff could "find some *hot promo* moments when things really are jazzed up?"[57] And another of the show's producers, Gordon Farr, complained when he felt that the network promotions were failing to do what ABC said they most wanted — to showcase sexy and provocative scenes.[58] ABC's promotions typified the network's successful strategy in the 1970s: using sex to sell itself to valuable young viewers.

Challenging ABC: Late 1970s

No promotional slogan more aptly expressed the changes in network power and in attitudes toward sexuality over the course of the 1970s than CBS's tag line for the 1978–79 season. "Turn us on, we'll turn you on," promised the Tiffany network.[59] Inter-network competition had led the most staid of the networks to openly hawk the new sexual culture right alongside that randy youngster, ABC. By the time ABC's first-place positioning was a solid reality, the other two networks were scrambling to imitate ABC's success by replicating some of the key elements of its formula. In scheduling their own incarnations of female sex symbols in action-oriented roles, made-for-TV movies with sexual themes, and discussions of sex in a range of comedies and dramas, CBS and NBC perpetuated the constructions of sex offered by ABC *and* sought to differentiate their versions of the new sexual culture from ABC's top-rated, but still disparaged, programming.

Criticism of ABC's sexual fare came from many sources inside and outside the television industry, but NBC's challenges were among the most widely circulated, a calculated move by the now third-place network to retain its status as the more significant broadcaster. For example, William S. Rubens, vice-president of research at NBC, spoke to the Association for Consumer Research about sex on television and slyly mentioned "one network [that appeared] to be giving viewers more cheesecake and making greater use of sexual overtones."[60] Most vocal was the NBC executive Paul Klein. He coined the terms "kid porn" and "jiggle television" to describe the ABC strategy. As Klein explained, "kid porn" described programs "that make kids squeal and close their eyes," like *Three's Company*, while "jiggle TV" applied "when you have a young, attractive television personality running at top speed wearing a limited amount of underwear."[61] Klein was fond of comparing ABC's fare to porn, thereby tapping into 1970s anxieties about the spread of pornographic culture throughout mainstream America. As he commented regarding the sex-heavy soap-opera parody *Soap* (1977–81), "[Silverman's] doing Lady Chatterley, making it look like a work of art, when what it really is, is a [1970s porn star] Marilyn Chambers."[62] He seemed particularly disdainful of the juvenile nature of ABC's sexual content—the fact that most of ABC's sex was presented comedically and was designed to inspire tittering and giggles of intrigued embarrassment from the sex-crazed adolescent in all of us. Despite these criticisms, however, both NBC and CBS took deliberate steps to mimic ABC's success, sometimes by replicating the tone of ABC's "kiddie porn" and "jiggle" fare and sometimes by staking out different representations of sex.

The Onslaught of "Jiggle" TV

One of NBC's and CBS's most overt attempts to duplicate ABC's formula was in the spread of "jiggling" female sex symbols across network schedules. The popularity of ABC's *Charlie's Angels* encouraged all three networks to program more series with similarly pulchritudinous leads or supporting players. Sexy young women in revealing outfits, often engaged in adventurous pursuits, became standard television fare. The previously slow process of bringing women into lead roles in action-oriented programming accelerated rapidly and industry executives left behind all their doubts about a woman's ability to carry a series—that is, as long as the woman qualified as a potential sex symbol.

ABC was at the forefront of the attempts to imitate the success of *Charlie's Angels*. Although the network declined to renew both *Wonder Woman* (1976–77; CBS, 1977–79) and *The Bionic Woman* for the 1977–78 season, this did not mean that it was giving up on sexy young women as a programming strategy. Between 1977 and 1982, ABC licensed multiple made-for-TV movies produced by Aaron Spelling that offered slight variations on the premise of *Charlie's Angels*, none of which they ultimately picked up as series.[63] ABC also tested *The*

TABLE 1 Made-for-TV Movies or Pilots Featuring Female Leads in Action-Adventure Roles

Title	Network	Air date
The Bait	ABC	13 March 1973
Get Christie Love!	ABC	22 January 1974
Wonder Woman	ABC	2 March 1974
Hit Lady	ABC	8 October 1974
Kate McShane	CBS	11 April 1975
The Lives of Jenny Dolan	NBC	27 October 1975
The New, Original Wonder Woman	ABC	7 November 1975
McNaughton's Daughter	NBC	4 March 1976
Charlie's Angels	ABC	21 March 1976
Brenda Starr	ABC	8 May 1976
Kiss Me, Kill Me	ABC	8 May 1976
Cover Girls	NBC	18 May 1977
The Hunted Lady	NBC	28 November 1977
Wild and Wooly	ABC	20 February 1978
Kate Bliss and the Ticker Tape Kid	ABC	26 May 1978
Flying High	CBS	28 August 1978
Flatbed Annie and Sweetiepie: Lady Truckers	CBS	10 February 1979
Willa	CBS	17 March 1979
Beach Patrol	ABC	30 April 1979
S.H.E.	CBS	23 February 1980
The Georgia Peaches	CBS	8 November 1980
The Secret War of Jackie's Girls	NBC	29 November 1980
The Oklahoma City Dolls	ABC	23 January 1981

Oklahoma City Dolls (23 January 1981), about a women's football team, and had big hits with two features of the *Movie of the Week* that showcased the Dallas Cowboys Cheerleaders (14 January 1979, 13 January 1980). In addition, the network also tried to make a go of *Sugar Time* (1977–78), a sitcom about three beautiful young aspiring rock singers, but it had little success. Even with such failures, ABC managed to secure another female sex symbol to showcase alongside the Angels: Suzanne Somers of the hit "sex-com" *Three's Company*. Somers's popularity even further convinced NBC and CBS that sexy women were crucial to the prime-time schedule.

During this period, the networks considered a number of pilots featuring women tagged for sex-symbol status, including *Jackie and Darlene* (ABC, a cop show), *Co-ed Fever* (CBS), *El Paso Pussycats* (CBS, cheerleaders), *California Girls* (NBC, lifeguards), and *The Cheerleaders* (NBC) (see table 1).[64] And both NBC and CBS actually aired a number of ultimately unsuccessful clones of Angels and Somers types. Despite Paul Klein's disparaging criticisms, NBC picked up *The Bionic Woman* after ABC decided not to renew it. NBC also aired pilots as movies of the week for several *Charlie's Angels*-like series, among them *Cover Girls* (18 May 1977) about fashion model spies, *The Hunted Lady* (28 November 1977) starring Donna Mills as an undercover policewoman on the run, and *The Secret War of Jackie's Girls* (29 November 1980), about a squadron of female World War II pilots. The now third-place network also revamped its existing World War II series, *Baa Baa Black Sheep* (1976–78, re-named *Black Sheep Squadron* in December 1977), and included a quartet of "nubile maidens" working as nurses on the military base.[65] New series with sex-symbol stars included *Quark* (1978), a parodic sitcom set in a futuristic space station that featured identical twin co-pilots Betty I and Betty II, as well as *Rollergirls*, which lasted for one month in the spring of 1978 and focused on a scantily-clad women's roller derby team.[66] Similarly, a Las Vegas showgirl series, *Legs*, left the air after a low-rated one-hour special in May 1978.

Although still securely capturing second place in the Nielsen ratings, CBS also struggled to keep up with ABC's sex-symbol successes. Wondering why his network couldn't capitalize on what seemed to be an easily exploitable phenomenon, CBS's chairman, William Paley, reportedly complained that there were no pretty girls on CBS. In addition to picking up ABC's *Wonder Woman* when the network canceled it, CBS ran two short-lived *Angels* imitators in the 1978–79 season: *Flying High*, about three "stewardesses" and *The American Girls*, about two TV magazine reporters working undercover to expose teenage prostitution and beauty pageant corruption (see figure 2). The Tiffany network also exploited the late 1970s trucking craze with two TV movies about female truckers: *Flatbed Annie and Sweetiepie: Lady Truckers* (10 February 1979) and *Willa* (17 March 1979). In 1980, CBS attempted movie-of-the-week pilots about sexy women going undercover: *S.H.E.* (23 February 1980), about a female James Bond, and *The Georgia Peaches* (8 November 1980), about young women working undercover for the U.S. government.

Although many of the attempts to clone *Charlie's Angels* on all three networks were failures, the presence of sexy young women in television programming did not fade away. Most frequently, women cast as sex symbols appeared as guest stars and as members of ensemble casts. Such depictions were present alongside *Charlie's Angels* in its debut season. Then, even sitcoms such as *Happy Days*, ABC's family-friendly hit, featured the sex symbol Roz

2 Connie Sellecca (as Lisa), Pat Klous (as Marcy), and Kathryn Witt (as Pam), the flight attendants in *Flying High*, CBS. WISCONSIN CENTER FOR FILM AND THEATER RESEARCH.

Kelly as Pinky Tuscadero in a three-part episode ("Fonzie Loves Pinky," 21 and 28 September 1976) (see figure 3). Pinky's satin shorts and high-heeled boots hugged her body, as did the camera as it tilted from her legs up when she entered a scene. The other networks soon followed suit. CBS's *WKRP in Cincinnati* (1978–82) began in September and included the voluptuous, blonde Loni Anderson as the station's secretary. Similarly, when CBS debuted *The Dukes of Hazzard* (1979–85) in January, the cast included the Duke boys' cousin, Daisy Duke, whose standard costume included a midriff-baring top and short shorts. *B.J. and the Bear* (NBC, 1979–81) added seven lady truckers to its cast, including "Stacks" and the twins Teri and Geri, in 1981. Even series such as *The Love Boat*, which regularly featured sexy women as guest stars, sought to increase the sex-symbol content for the 1979–80 season when, among other strategies, its producer, Gordon Farr, investigated the possibility of hiring models from the Playboy Modeling Agency in addition to the series' regular extras.[67] In the 1980–81 season, ABC scheduled a couple of new sitcoms that were clear attempts to discover the next Suzanne Somers (who had by this point basically been written out of *Three's Company* due to her salary demands). *It's a Living* (ABC, 1980–81; syndicated, 1985–89) starred five

3 Roz Kelly (as Pinky) and Henry Winkler (as Fonzie), "Fonzie Loves Pinky," *Happy Days*, 21 September 1976. ABC/PHOTOFEST.

waitresses in a Playboy-like restaurant-club and *Too Close for Comfort* (ABC, 1980–83; syndicated, 1984–86) showcased the star Ted Knight's two attractive daughters, especially Lydia Cornell as Sara, a ditzy, big-breasted blonde à la Somers's Chrissy Snow.

NBC's "Adult Porn"

NBC certainly undercut its own criticisms of ABC by actively pursuing "jiggle" series, but the network also sought to differentiate its brand of TV sex from Fred Silverman's network. Alongside Paul Klein's dismissal of ABC's sexual pandering was his announcement that "If ABC is doing kiddie porn, NBC will give the audience adult porn."[68] NBC set out to program its more "mature" version of the sexual revolution primarily through its burgeoning made-for-TV movie schedule. Of course, NBC had been programming sex-themed movies of the week since at least the 1974–75 season. With the exception of 1975–76, for the next few seasons, NBC forged ahead of ABC (and CBS) in scheduling sensational tele-films that dealt with the seamy side of sexuality.[69] In 1976–77, NBC aired *Dawn: Portrait of a Teenage Runaway* (27 September 1976) and its sequel, *Alexander: The Other Side of Dawn* (16 May 1977), which explored the hardships of teenage runaways turned prostitutes or hustlers. For the next couple of seasons, NBC continued the "portrait" theme, with *Sharon: Portrait of a Mistress* (31 October 1977) and *Katie: Portrait of a Centerfold* (23 October 1978). In addition, miniseries such as *Harold Robbins' 79 Park Avenue* (16–18 October 1977), chronicling the exploits of a call girl, and *Loose Change* (26–28 February 1978), foregrounding its female protagonists' sexual explorations amid 1960s radicalism, helped perpetuate the network's new identity as the place for sensational treatments of sex.[70]

Sex in Continuing Series: NBC

Eventually, NBC would also attempt continuing series that carried over some of the themes and the sexually "mature" tone of its made-for-TV movies. Such series as the prime-time soaps *Secrets of Midland Heights* (1980–81), set in a college town, and the heavily promoted *Number 96* (1980–81), about the entanglements of the residents of a Los Angeles apartment complex, had sexual titillation at their center. Such series would not last long, but NBC (and the programmer Paul Klein in particular) also worked to alter the sexual tenor of existing shows. Klein's involvement in the sensitive teen drama, *James at 15* (1977–78, titled *James at 16* as of 9 February 1978) offers a useful extended example. For the February 1978 ratings sweeps period, Klein asked the show's producers to have James lose his virginity at a local brothel, a "gift" from his uncle for his sixteenth birthday. The idea was not a completely foreign imposition on the program. Romance — and sex — were ongoing themes in the series. For instance, in the pilot episode (15 September 1977), as James and his family prepare to move from Oregon to Boston, James comes close to having sex with the girlfriend he is leaving behind. But the series creator, Dan Wakefield, thought the brothel idea was outdated, so he wrote a script in which James's trip to the brothel is a comedic disaster. He followed through with Klein's request for James to lose his virginity, however, by planning for him to have sex with a Swedish exchange student with whom he had fallen in love. Important to Wakefield's script was the fact that James and Gun, his girlfriend, truly cared for each other and that they acted "responsibly" by using birth control. Wakefield was willing to play the birth control discussion scene vaguely, with nothing more specific than the kids talking about being responsible. But NBC rejected the idea. They insisted that the teens *not* use birth control, that "If they have sex at all, it must be in a moment of spontaneous passion." They also insisted that Gun have a pregnancy scare afterward (though she would not, in fact, be pregnant) so that she and James would regret their actions.[71] NBC's preferred version aired ("The Gift," 9 February 1978) along with a follow-up episode ("Listless Fever," 23 February 1978) in which James fears he has contracted a venereal disease. But NBC's interference led Wakefield to resign from the show, which was canceled a few months later.

NBC's handling of *James at 15* suggests more than the network's desire to censor teen sex in an attempt to appease protest groups or avoid some other outside vituperation. Although that may have been partly the case, this incident also constructed NBC's version of the new sexual culture in distinct contrast to ABC's. NBC would allow characters to have sex instead of just suggestively referencing it, but it would also punish the same characters for their actions. In NBC's on-screen world, birth control could not be condoned, but teens engaging in sex could be condemned. In this way, NBC managed to be more sensational than its chief rival but also to seem morally superior. The network could exploit the plot development of teens having sex and at the same time come off as disapproving of it, as adhering to conventional morality by illustrating the dangers of premarital sex among the young. In developing the story of James's sexual experience, and especially by avoiding mention of birth control while dangling the threats of pregnancy and venereal disease, NBC managed to defy the boundaries of conventional TV content acceptability and reify the boundaries of conventional sexual morality. NBC's attempts to piggyback on ABC's success and make itself seem a distinctive voice multiplied television's representations of the sexual revolution while keeping traditional values intact.

Worlds Collide: Silverman Joins NBC

Paul Klein's efforts to differentiate NBC's TV sex from ABC's in order to beat the number one network were complicated by NBC's management, which hired Fred Silverman as network president early in 1978. With the increased money and prestige the position offered, Silverman decided to join the network. Given his long antipathy toward Silverman, Klein may very likely have been trying to prove that he could beat his nemesis at his own game by increasing the sex content of NBC's schedule in the months between Silverman's hiring and his arrival at the network. Everyone expected Silverman to bring a height-ened sexual sensibility to NBC, anyway, continuing the successful strategy he had employed at ABC. But the criticisms of his years at ABC seemed to have made some impact, since Silverman arrived at NBC in June 1978 pledging a change in his ways. In his first speech to NBC's annual convention he an-nounced, "True leadership requires responsibility—programming that does not violate general standards of taste. We must avoid material that would alienate significant elements of the audience, and we must continue stead-fastly to make the difficult and delicate judgments that draw the line between the offensive and the acceptable.[72] He sought to make NBC a "class act," with "a more intelligent approach to comedy" than he had developed at ABC.[73] Whether in an effort to revise his image (one NBC executive said of Silver-man's turn, "He doesn't want to be known as the tits and ass man. . . . He doesn't want to go down in history as the kiddie porn jiggler"),[74] whether in response to the intensified efforts of pressure groups such as the National Fed-eration for Decency, or whether in an attempt to paint counter-programming as ethics, Silverman strove to limit the number of overtly sexy shows on the NBC schedule and instead sought out more typically wholesome family fare. Though he found a few new hits this way, Silverman's efforts at NBC were ulti-mately rather inconsequential. He would leave the network in 1981, replaced by Grant Tinker, the former owner of MTM, and forever retain his reputation as the kiddie porn jiggler.

A New Network Marketplace: Early 1980s

NBC's initial efforts to "out-sex" ABC, followed by the network's turn away from sex-themed programming as a new marketing strategy, signaled the be-ginning of the end of television's turn to sex in the 1970s. Beginning with the 1979–80 season, CBS would make a late grab at the other networks' sexual cachet with its own made-for-TV movies in the exploitation vein (for example, *Portrait of a Stripper*, 2 October 1979; *Portrait of an Escort*, 8 October 1980; *The Two Lives of Carol Letner*, 14 October 1981; and *Jacqueline Susann's Valley of the Dolls 1981*, 19–20 October 1981). The former first-place network would also initiate the prime-time soap trend, debuting *Dallas* (1978–91) in the spring of 1978. Although the hit serial would help CBS to reclaim some of its former ratings glory, it did not do so by centering on sexual matters. Unlike the day-time soap innovations of the 1970s, *Dallas*'s drama stemmed from business and family conflicts more than sexual ones. CBS's other ratings hit in this period was the stalwart news magazine *60 Minutes* (1968–). Thus, in the early years of the 1980s, CBS would certainly improve upon its standing during the mid- and late 1970s, but its most popular fare was markedly different from the programming with which ABC had triumphed.

With NBC in a ratings free-fall and CBS reclaiming some of its earlier success, ABC played out the final years of its sex-centered glory at the beginning of the 1980s. *Charlie's Angels* ended with the 1980–81 season, also the season when Suzanne Somers exited *Three's Company*. Other successful series of the 1970s, including *Happy Days* and *The Love Boat*, ran into the 1980s, although they ceased to be the cultural and ratings forces they once were. ABC Daytime was more successful. *General Hospital* remained a first-place sensation throughout the early 1980s, followed closely by ABC's *All My Children* and *One Life to Live*. Unlike soap trends of the 1970s, however, *General Hospital*'s formula in the early 1980s combined romance and sex with action-adventure, including science-fiction and gangster plots. This drew a wider range of viewers to the genre but also led the soaps' turn away from social issues, including sexual ones.

Broadcast network competition would be irreversibly changed in the 1980s with the incursions of cable, home video, and new broadcast networks such as Fox. Thus the story of network competition in the 1970s illustrates not only the ways that these industrial imperatives directed sex-themed TV but also the ways that the network system functioned before the onset of the so-called post-network era. Characterizing the 1970s as a period of intense network competition in some senses belies the fact that so *little* competition actually existed in the U.S. television marketplace then, as now. As much as the Big Three fought each other for ratings dominance, the fact that *only* three programmers with remarkably similar corporate structures, economic interests, and funding practices held an oligopoly over a medium as widely viewed and as influential as television is *anti*-competitive in the most basic of ways. Yet the rivalry of the Big Three did provide the framework within which television's new sexual culture was created. As oligopolistic and ideologically limited as it was, the context of inter-network imitation and innovation made the new sexual culture what *it* was—a cautious, yet compelling version of America's sexual revolution.

NOT IN MY LIVING ROOM

TV SEX THAT WASN'T

In 1969, one Dallas television station ran a public service announcement prodding parents to keep tabs on their children's whereabouts. It asked, "Do you know where your boy is tonight?" One mother wrote the station in response and expressed a growing sentiment among certain members of the public. "I know precisely where my boy is tonight," she wrote. "He is looking at a dirty movie on your station."[1] Beginning in 1969 and continuing throughout the 1970s, the sexual content of theatrically released films airing on broadcast television became a matter of much controversy, so much so that an extended campaign waged on numerous fronts sought to bar certain kinds of feature films—those bearing the new "X" rating—from TV. As much as sexual material suffused the broadcast airwaves as never before in the 1970s, so too did efforts to ban many kinds of sexual material suffuse discussion about television. As this Dallas viewer's disapproval makes clear, audiences of many types, including parents, members of Congress, and the Federal Communications Commission, began to challenge the appropriateness of television's sexual content, managing to keep certain sexual representations off the air and thereby limiting those representations that would appear.

Big Three network competition clearly shaped the ways that television delivered the sexual revolution to the American public, but this chapter and the next consider a range of *regulatory* efforts that also helped to determine what kind of sex did and did not make it to television. In this chapter, I focus on three examples of sexual materials that were kept *off* of television in the 1970s: X-rated movies, bra ads, and condom commercials. What can an examination of the TV sex that wasn't reveal? After all, this book argues that unlike any previous time in U.S. television history the 1970s featured an abundance of sexual allusions and themes. If 1970s television was indeed "wallowing in sex" as never before, what is the point of considering the sexual topics that were kept away from television? In what ways can an exploration of the TV sex that wasn't help explain how television delivered a new sexual culture to its audiences?

Such an exploration might help us to understand the workings of censorship in TV's new sexual culture. But censorship is too heavy-handed a term to describe the complex negotiations over content in U.S. television. The processes by which material is barred from the airwaves are more aptly described as content *regulation* than as censorship.[2] This is because the forces of broadcast television content regulation are diverse, and no single entity has the authority to determine what does and does not appear on air. For one thing, the media's right to free speech under the U.S. Constitution prohibits direct government censorship of television content. Still, federal government regulation does play a part in determining what can be broadcast, a part that was up for negotiation during the 1970s. The television industry also engages in *self*-regulation of content. In the 1970s, this self-regulation took place at an industry-wide level, via the National Association of Broadcasters and its Television Code, as well as at the more immediate levels of individual network and station owners, executives, and standards and practices editors. In addition, both government and TV industry regulation are affected by the efforts of citizen groups and the many businesses that advertise their products and services on TV. Such influences were active during the 1970s, as both government and industry regulators sought to appease these diverse constituencies. As both a public resource and a commercial venue, U.S. television is positioned at a distinctive crossroads, subject to the regulatory efforts of public and private interests, and beholden to the citizenry and to the bottom line.

The instances in which sex was kept away from television in the 1970s helped define what the new sexual culture was, what television was, and how the two could — and could not — meet. In these debates, television's status as a family medium was upheld, as were certain traditional ideas about sex. In the efforts to keep X-rated films, bra ads featuring live models in lingerie, and condom commercials off the air, the mechanisms of TV content regulation reinforced older constructions of sex as inappropriate for youth, as embodied by women, and as linked to reproduction. This version of American sexual culture was hardly new, but the repressiveness of these choices can also be seen as helping to produce the new, negotiated version of the sexual culture that would emerge over the course of the 1970s.

The Threat of "X"

In 1977, the journalist Mary Lewis Coakley published a tirade against television's new sexual culture — *Rated X: The Moral Case Against TV*. In it, she railed against how far television had gone in its handling of sex (see figure 4). Among the instances she noted was a promotional spot for ABC's acclaimed drama, *Family* (1976–10), in which Nancy asked her twelve-year-old sister, Buddy, "Do you know what a homosexual is?" She also pointed out, with horror, that NBC's made-for-TV movie *Little Ladies of the Night* (16 January 1977) told a story of teenage prostitutes, their abusive pimp, and the ex-pimp turned policeman who sought to save them. She mentioned, with intense disapproval, a CBS news report on transsexualism, a rape story on *The Young and the Restless*, a pregnancy scare for a teenage character on *Welcome Back, Kotter* (ABC, 1975–79), a "dirty" riddle delivered by the host of *Match Game* (CBS, 1973–79), and a suggestive commercial for Underalls pantyhose — in other words, she took to task all of the diverse ways in which television was constructing its new sexual culture.[3] For Coakley, television's turn to sex was so shocking, so immoral, so excessive as to earn the medium the rating of "X." In borrowing the designation for those feature films from which all viewers under the age of sixteen were barred, Coakley was drawing upon the new, shorthand label for the furthest reaches to which the post–sexual revolution culture might go. Although the X rating was not instituted to be synonymous with "dirty movies," the meaning of "X" quickly morphed such that, by the 1970s, to be "Rated X" was to be so overtly and explicitly sexual as to be pornographic.[4] Calling her book *Rated X* thereby gave Coakley a powerful rhetorical weapon to use against television's new sexual culture.

Coakley's tirade against television's handling of sex in the 1970s was cer-

Reference Library

4 "Reference Library," Bo Brown, printed in *Rated X: The Moral Case Against TV* by Mary Lewis Coakley, Arlington House Publishers, 1977.

tainly an extreme case of the disapproval the medium's new sexual culture was generating. However, her use of the "Rated X" label was not as overzealous as it might seem. The X rating had come to signify all that was most explicit, and most morally suspect, about the post–sexual revolution culture and many began to worry that television would be no different from the other cultural products that had embraced the new sexual openness. Such fears centered around American television's historical role as a "family" medium. Since "X-rated" culture was, by definition, *not* appropriate for the whole family, the threat of X-rated culture—and X-rated feature films in particular—appearing on TV generated a rather intense panic around television's standards of sexual appropriateness. This panic played an important part in defining what television's new sexual culture would *not* become, and thus in determining what it would be.

The X on TV?

Just a few years after NBC debuted its *Saturday Night at the Movies* in the 1961–62 season, broadcasters began to hear rumblings of discontent about these feature films and their suitability for the home screen. In 1966, an FCC commissioner, Robert E. Lee, spoke of his concerns about the increasingly daring theatricals then being produced and warned of their imminent broadcast. In 1969, when the new X rating of the Motion Picture Association (MPAA) and the sexually explicit culture were both in full sway, Lee again spoke out. He claimed that current public and congressional disapproval of television content was largely due to the feature films produced in recent years and now airing on TV. He ominously asked, "What will happen four or five years hence when the television rights to current controversial movies become available?" and answered, "I am afraid to look."[5]

Other government officials joined Lee in his distress. At a hearing on subscription television in November 1969 at the House of Representatives, Representatives Torbert MacDonald and James Harvey both expressed concern that the proposed pay television system would show sexually explicit films, MacDonald wondering specifically about the Swedish import *I Am Curious (Yellow)*.[6] This film, as the first of the European-imported, X-rated, soft-core features to draw a large U.S. audience, often claimed the dubious distinction of being named in congressional hearings and press accounts as the harbinger of moral doom. Senator John O. Pastore of Rhode Island, who was the chair of the Senate's Communications Subcommittee and an ardent foe of sexual and violent program content, made something of a habit of questioning witnesses at subcommittee hearings about their thoughts on *I Am Curious (Yellow)*'s chances for a television airing. During the December 1969 hearings to revise the FCC's procedures for renewing station licenses, Pastore asked Anthony R. Martin-Trigona, a small-market broadcaster who presented himself as a proponent of free speech and diversity in station ownership, whether he would like to see the film on television. When Martin-Trigona said he would, Pastore warned, "Don't keep that up. I do not want to see it on television. God forbid if we ever do."[7]

The film was also the touchstone for an exchange between Pastore and Kenneth A. Cox, an FCC commissioner, that began to suggest the implications of the Supreme Court's recent liberalization of obscenity law for broadcast regulation. Cox explained that for the FCC to declare broadcast material obscene that material would have to meet the Department of Justice's criteria for obscenity because obscenity was, by legal definition, a prosecutable offense. In return, Pastore submitted his standard query about the Swedish import.

When Cox reiterated that the determination of obscenity rested with the Department of Justice, Pastore indignantly challenged, "Now, you are saying because it can be shown in theaters, the standards are the same, and it can be shown on television[?]"[8] For Pastore, this potential equation between a theatrical release and a broadcast airing was immensely disturbing, for it signified the easy access the sexual revolution may have had to the American home and the family within it. It challenged his—and many others'—conceptions of television's role and the place of sexual material within it.

The new MPAA ratings system, and the age-restricted films that came out of it, were particularly problematic for broadcasters because of the industry's historic role as purveyor of mass, family entertainment. If a film were deemed inappropriate for young theatrical audiences, it would be difficult to justify its appropriateness for the all-ages TV audience. Senator John McClellan of Arkansas worried that broadcasters would not know how to handle the new ratings system, so he surveyed the television networks, station groups, and individual station owners on their feature film acceptance policies, asking outright whether they would show X, R, or even M rated films. (The M rating was roughly equivalent to today's PG-13.) Most answered that they would not run X-rated films in any form, but that they would consider some R- and M-rated films. A smaller portion said they would consider X-rated films if they could be properly edited for television. Though each broadcaster surveyed surely had her or his own definition of what constituted an X, R, or M-rated film (given the recent institution of the ratings and the ambiguity over their meanings even within the MPAA), their near-universal refusal of the X suggests how widespread the category's scandalous reputation was, as well as how combustible a combination the X and broadcast television were. Some of the broadcasters' comments even indicated that in certain sections of the country, all feature films were now suspect, regardless of their rating. As the operator of Tulsa's KVOO explained, "It is getting to the point where we are having to keep a constant vigil on all films offered for home consumption."[9] In many broadcasters' eyes, the X-rated culture (and even its less explicit permutations, for example, R- and M-rated films) was ill-suited to television's mass audience and should thus be barred from the airwaves.

This station operator's concerns about the Tulsa market were prescient. A few years later, in February 1972, a fundamentalist newspaper published in the city, *The Christian Crusade Weekly*, ran a front-page editorial denouncing CBS's purchase of a "series of X-rated pictures" for broadcast.[10] Though CBS would later deny the acquisition of any such series, the paper was partially accurate in that the network had purchased and scheduled one X-rated film, Luchino Visconti's *The Damned* (1969), for its late-night movie slot on 28 February. *The Damned* dramatizes the decline of an industrialist family in 1930s Germany, a tale designed to comment on "the decay of a civilized nation," according to Tom Swafford, a CBS executive.[11] CBS claimed that Warner Bros. offered the film with twenty-five minutes already cut and that its standards and practices department had cut an additional eleven minutes. Between the two edits, the elements that presumably earned the film the X in the first place were removed—an incest scene, two child molestation scenes, bedroom scenes (including one with waist-up nudity), and a pre-teen's suicide.[12]

Though the network ran the movie as scheduled, a substantial number of stations across the country refused to air it. When members of the Cleveland City Council learned of the scheduling, they called an emergency vote to ban X-rated films from local airwaves. The Southern Baptist Convention and the Christian Life Commission submitted resolutions to the Senate and the FCC, respectively, protesting CBS's decision to show the film and calling for a halt to future broadcasts of X-rated movies.[13] None of these protestors thought it significant that Warner Bros. and CBS had removed the offending elements from the film. For instance, when Cleveland's WEWS-TV decided to air *The Damned* a couple of weeks later, after previewing it and finding no objectionable material, a city council member named Joseph Kowalski (who also previewed the film) insisted that even edited films had to be guarded against.[14] Senator Pastore also dismissed the editing process as irrelevant. During the testimony of John A. Schneider, the president of the CBS Broadcast Group, in a March 1972 Senate subcommittee hearing, Pastore insisted, "You say it has been sanitized. But the point is, it was characterized as X at one time. The minute you announce the title of the movie, everybody knows it was an X-rated movie whether you say so or not."[15] Such responses suggest that even the threat of association with the X was beyond television acceptability, that the sexual explicitness symbolized by the X surpassed the limits of television's new sexual culture.

The panic over the X appearing on broadcast television is perhaps best illustrated by the controversy that succeeded CBS's airing of *The Damned*.

Over the next seventeen months, CBS was deluged with nearly half a million letters protesting the network's supposed forthcoming series of X-rated films. CBS insisted that there was no such series, that the package of 247 films it had purchased from Warner Bros. included exactly one X-rated movie, *The Damned*. But the rumors persisted. The February 1972 story in the *Christian Crusade* seems to have planted the idea, but it was perpetuated and elaborated upon by numerous sources — other religious newspapers, church newsletters and bulletins, state and county legislatures, and local stations. In Gladewater, Texas, the Church of Christ's publication, *The Abundant Life*, reported the story. In Ohio, a publication of the Ohio Woman's Christian Temperance Union shared the news.[16] New York's Rockland County legislature, as well as South Carolina's state legislature, officially condemned CBS for "pandering to the baser instincts of man's nature."[17] As a result, stations in Spartanburg and Columbia, South Carolina, as well as one station in Los Angeles, ran editorials pledging not to air X-rated films.[18]

In all of these instances, the editing of *The Damned* (or other films with the potential for future airings) was irrelevant, as were CBS's denials of having purchased any other X-rated films. What mattered was the X and its potential appearance on television, even if devoid of the material that warranted the rating in the first place. The specific threat of the X-rated film on television indicates the limits placed upon television's handling of the sexual revolution. As the businessman John F. O'Neill explained in a 1973 poll about television "rawness," "If my family or I want to view some of the garbage available in current motion pictures we can go to the movie house. But I don't want it in my living room."[19] O'Neill and others who shared his views were not just railing against the possibility of sexually explicit movies on television. The opponents of the X were reacting to a range of sexual materials that seemed to be clearing the path for greater sexual freedom in broadcasting and altering the medium's longtime role as purveyor of mass, family entertainment. They were seeking to define the parameters of acceptable sexuality, the parameters of television content, and to determine the "safe" meeting point for the two.

Government Regulation of "X-rated" Broadcasting

By 1969, President Nixon, Congress, and the FCC were actively guarding against loosened obscenity laws bringing "X-rated" materials to the airwaves. Nixon appointed the conservative Dean Burch as chair of the FCC and Burch avidly pursued the matter, announcing to the Senate Communications Sub-committee that the FCC and the Department of Justice were ready to enforce obscenity laws in broadcasting as soon as they determined an appropriate case. Speaking in 1970 about the "disturbing trend" in pornographic mail, X-rated films, and other such products, Burch declared that "should a similar trend develop in broadcasting, it would be . . . a public cancer, and the time for effective and swift action to prevent any such occurrence is now."[20] Burch and the commission thought they had their test case in May 1970 when they fined WUHY-FM in Philadelphia for indecent language, but the station opted to pay the $100 fine instead of fighting the ruling in court. Over the next two years, the FCC failed to find an appropriate case. Meanwhile, the commission was increasingly pressured to do something, for the X was getting closer and closer to the American home. Just north of the U.S. border, in Toronto, Ontario, CITY-TV, a new, community-oriented UHF channel, instituted a Friday midnight movie series, *The Baby Blue Movie*, which showcased such unedited, X-rated films as *I Am Curious (Yellow)* and *Thérèse and Isabelle* (1968) to great audience response.[21] Meanwhile, KVVU-TV in Henderson, Nevada, briefly ran a Sunday late-night *Adult Theater* series featuring uncut R- and X-rated films.[22]

While the sexual explicitness of feature films seemed to be gradually encroaching upon the home screen, an audio version of that explicitness had already arrived. As early as 1970, but with spreading popularity by the end of 1972, radio stations across the country began to air local and syndicated sex talk shows. KGBS in Los Angeles experimented by putting the overnight disk jockey, Bill Ballance, on the air midday in a new call-in program titled *Feminine Forum*. Storer Broadcasting, the owner of KGBS, soon began similar versions at five of its stations and other broadcasters followed. By early in 1973, fifty to sixty stations programmed similar shows and Ballance's program was syndicated in twenty-two markets. Targeted to young women home during the day, often with young children, the programs generated calls by asking listeners to comment on a specific sex-related topic.[23] Branded as "X-rated" and "topless" radio, and with rumors circulating that ABC was hoping to convert *Feminine Forum* to a TV series, these programs attracted the attention of Senator Pastore and the Senate Communications Subcommittee, who in turn put pressure on the FCC to act on the fast-approaching X threat.[24]

In early April 1973, the FCC announced an official inquiry into sex on the airwaves, focusing especially on the "X-rated" radio shows. Here, it seemed, was a specific, appropriate case that would allow the commission to test the limits of obscenity in broadcasting, to fight off the X as it made its way into American living rooms and surpassed the government's imagined boundaries for broadcasting's new sexual culture. The inquiry announcement alone scared some broadcasters into canceling their "topless" radio shows, while direct FCC pressure led Sonderling Broadcasting's WGLD-FM in Oak Park, Illinois to eliminate "intimate subject matter" from its *Femme Forum* talk show.[25] Unlike X-rated films, with their self-selected audiences and their MPAA-induced age restrictions, broadcasting was constructed as a fundamental presence in everyday life, accessible to the masses, with or without the conscious choice to hear or see it, and this made "X-rated" radio especially threatening.

A few months later, the Supreme Court handed down its decision in *Miller v. California* and asserted the significance of local community standards in determining obscenity. This allowed the FCC to be morally, if not legally, vindicated in its efforts against "X-rated" radio. The commission further extended its authority with a 1975 declaratory order in the case of a 1973 broadcast of the comedian George Carlin's routine about the "seven words" forbidden on the airwaves. This order reformulated the concept of "indecent" language, defining it as "language that describes, in terms patently offense [*sic*] as measured by contemporary community standards for the broadcast medium, sexual or excretory activities and organs, at times of the day when there is a reasonable risk that children may be in the audience."[26] This order clarified the FCC's definitions of indecency and obscenity, broadened its powers to condemn on-air speech, and reasserted the special nature of broadcasting and its mass audience when it came to sexual material.

While the FCC's actions in response to "X-rated" radio solidified its authority to protect the mass broadcast audience from the indecent and the obscene, the commission soon recognized that that authority was ultimately quite limited. Title 18, section 1464 of the U.S. Criminal Code, the statute upon which the FCC's authority to restrict obscene, indecent, and profane material was based, had been instituted originally under the Communications Act of 1934 and thus had been designed to apply to radio communication, to sounds and language, and not necessarily to visual representations. When the commission, Congress, and others began to note a new "X-rated" threat—cable television—it became clear that the regulatory efforts in response to "topless" radio were insufficient in guarding the American home from the post–sexual revolution culture. As one FCC official recognized in 1975, "Right now, there's nothing keeping TV from showing *Deep Throat* if it left out some of the sound track."[27]

While broadcast television of the early 1970s took many more risks with sexual material than it had in the past, its representations of sexuality remained safely far from X-rated territory. The fast-growing cable television industry was another story. Cable television technology had been in use since the 1950s, when it served primarily as a relay service, delivering broadcast signals to remote locations via cable wires. By the early 1970s, however, many groups saw the potential in cable technology and cable systems began to grow.[28] In 1972, the FCC's "Third Report and Order" mandated that cable systems reserve channel space for public, government, and educational access and not interfere with the programming created for such stations. By 1973, access channels around the country were in operation, and some of them regularly included X-rated fare. Syracuse University's student-run station and a channel in Albany, Georgia, programmed hard-core pornographic films. In New York City, the access channels of Sterling-Manhattan Cable featured such programs as *Transsexuals* and *Body Movements*, in which a naked young woman examined her own body.[29] Pay cable stations were also experimenting with racy programming. A Pottsville, Pennsylvania pay channel promoted sexually sophisticated R-rated films such as *Klute* and *Sunday Bloody Sunday* (both 1971) as "adult" fare.[30]

Spurred by such programming, as well as by its recent assertions of control over "X-rated" radio, the FCC sought to extend its ability to regulate obscenity by making sure that Title 18, Section 1464 applied to visual depictions as well as aural ones. In its "Report on the Broadcast of Violent, Indecent, and Obscene Material" in February 1975, the commission asked Congress to amend Section 1464 so as to make clear that it could proceed against *video* depiction of obscene or indecent material. The commission also made a point of saying that such an amendment should apply to cable as well as to broadcast television.[31] Congress did not act on this recommendation, likely because the

5 Opening titles, *Midnight Blue*, Manhattan Cable Public Access.

National Association of Broadcasters' newly instituted family viewing policy seemed to be addressing such concerns.[32]

Meanwhile, cable television persisted in bringing "X-rated" material into the home, disregarding the limits of sexual material in broadcasting so assiduously fought for by government regulators. Pay cable networks specializing in adult films began to acquire a larger piece of the cable television market. For example, in October 1976, Buffalo's International Cable began two months of late-night X-rated films and, in April 1977, Hilo, Hawaii's Comtec cable system showed the X-rated *Emmanuelle* and gained two hundred new subscribers in the process.[33] Public access also continued to offer some of the medium's most risqué fare. The opening to Manhattan Cable Television's *Midnight Blue* featured a drawing of a naked woman straddling a missile-like phallic object in front of a rendering of the Manhattan skyline (see figure 5). This opening set the tone for the show, which featured segments on male strippers (including footage of performances), Annie Sprinkle's creative sex toys from the grocery store, and a weekly vox pop sex survey (for example, "How many times have you had sex in the last week?"), as well as commercials hawking such products as the Orgasmatron vibrator.[34]

Such explicit sexual content was not uncontested, however, suggesting that it was not broadcast television alone that needed "protection" from an X-rated version of the sexual revolution. Some pay cable channels shifted from X-rated films to "hard R" in response to parents' complaints while cable industry leaders urged system operators to avoid sexually explicit material in fear of congressional repercussions.[35] Manhattan Cable actually sought out congressional guidance over *Midnight Blue*. Uncomfortable with the program's boundary-pushing content and concerned about the FCC's actions against obscenity and indecency, Manhattan Cable suspended *Blue*. The system operator claimed it was unsure how to proceed, that the FCC, the New York State Cable Commission, and the New York City Bureau of Franchises all made it clear that an operator is not to interfere with access channel content, but that the FCC said that same operator should prohibit obscenity and indecency across its system.[36] Eventually, Manhattan Cable decided to institute its own obscenity and indecency standards for access programming, which included the requirement that access producers submit their programs to the cable system for pre-screening and allowed the system to refuse to air any programming it felt could subject it to prosecution.[37]

Assessing the X That Wasn't

Even with the encroaching presence of "X-rated" material on cable and, according to some, on radio, government, industry, and citizen regulators kept X-rated culture and X-rated feature films off of broadcast television throughout the 1970s. The furor that ensued over even the *potential* for X-rated features to appear on broadcast TV demonstrates the intensity with which many different parties—the government and some members of the public included—sought to police the boundaries of what was and was not suitable for television's new sexual culture. Even if the actual appearance of X-rated films on broadcast TV was always a far-fetched possibility, the fact that extensive discussion and debate, not to mention specific regulatory policies, surrounded that possibility suggests that the "X" was a limit beyond which television's construction of sex would not go. In what follows, I discuss two other instances of such limit-setting, not by the FCC but by the television industry's self-regulating body, the National Association of Broadcasters (NAB). While these cases deal with material less explicit than the X-rated culture, they also serve as cautionary tales, defining the sexual boundaries that television would not cross.

Bras without Breasts: The NAB TV Code
and Advertising Regulation

The scantily-clad women featured in the Maidenform Company's print advertising campaign from 1949 to 1969 told the world about their dreams: "I dreamed I went shopping in my Maidenform bra," "I dreamed I swayed the jury in my Maidenform bra," "I dreamed I stopped a train in my Maidenform bra." They stared out from the pages of women's magazines, boldly proclaiming their fantasies of appearing in public wearing a bra and little else. One of these imaginative women even fantasized about a major media appearance: "I dreamed I starred on television in my Maidenform bra." This Maidenform woman did not realize just how fanciful her dream was, for between 1959 and 1982, women wearing bras alone were not permitted to appear in television commercials, or at least in those commercials running on stations that subscribed to the National Association of Broadcasters Television Code.[38]

Covered under the television code's personal products category, "foundation garment advertising" was restricted by the industry's self-regulating organization, the NAB. The policy on foundation garment advertising held that live models could not be shown wearing bras (or other foundation garments) unless fully clothed. Thus, the product was displayed in one of the following ways: without a body wearing it (though a bra without breasts in it had, presumably, little appeal for a society that tends to fetishize this particular female body part); on a still mannequin; or through the "ectoplasm technique," where the body of the model was blacked out, leaving on-screen a suspended sliver of lingerie filled out with invisible breasts belonging to an invisible, yet remarkably shapely, woman. The poor Maidenform woman with the dreams of television stardom could have hoped for only an ectoplasmic version of herself on the nation's airwaves.

The story of the forbidden live models in bra commercials illustrates another of the ways that television regulation kept certain sexual material off-screen and, in the process, defined the limits of television's new sexual culture. Unlike the government's involvement in the controversy over X-rated films, however, the debates around bra advertising took place largely within the TV industry's self-regulatory organization, and between that organization and television's advertisers. Although the decision to keep live models wearing bras away from TV commercials certainly contributed to constructions of television as a family medium and of television sex as nonexplicit, the decision produced other ideas about sex, as well. In particular, the ban on live models wearing bras activated associations between sexual illicitness and the female body, reproducing long-standing social constructs of the woman as the locus of shameful sexual temptation.

The NAB TV Code

The National Association of Broadcasters had been formed in 1923, when radio station owners joined together to establish a common front against the music licensing organization, ASCAP, which sought royalties for radio play of recorded music. Throughout radio history, and continuing with the growth of television in the late 1940s and early 1950s, the NAB served to unite stations and networks by promoting their mutual interests. The organization also served as an intra-industrial regulatory body, eventually establishing guidelines for program and advertising content in an effort to keep governmental bodies from imposing guidelines of their own upon the broadcast media. Most program content regulation came from the networks' internal standards and practices departments, and adherence to the code was only superficially enforced.[39] However, the NAB's code also applied to the commercials running on code-subscribing stations. While the networks and stations still employed their own commercial clearance departments (which occasionally countermanded NAB policy), the NAB's advertising code seems to have had some significant industry-wide impact. In forbidding or allowing certain product *categories*, the NAB's code set a baseline for individual broadcaster decisions. The code had no comparable role for programming, thus the actions of the NAB TV Code Review Board regarding advertising tell us a fair bit about the TV industry's efforts at self-regulation.

Included in the advertising guidelines of the television code from its inception was a personal products provision, a provision that covered such areas as hemorrhoid treatments, feminine hygiene products (including menstrual products and douches), body, foot, and mouth odor products, laxatives, and toilet paper. Initially, advertising for any of these products was deemed unacceptable. A specialized subcommittee was formed to deal with personal products, and it would play a key role in the 1970s, when many of the restrictions on personal product advertising were initially challenged.

Bra Advertising on Television: The History of the NAB Ban

In the early years of the code, bra advertising was not included in the personal products provision. In fact, not only were bra commercials permitted on the air, but bra commercials featuring *live models wearing bras* were permitted.[40] Perhaps because these sorts of ads were so common in magazines of the day (Maidenform's dream campaign had been a hit for a couple of years already), the NAB TV Code Review Board did not think that television advertising featuring live models in bras was particularly risqué. However, in October 1959, the board changed its mind and decided to include "foundation garments" under its personal products provision. When introducing the new policy, the personal products subcommittee said, "Commercials for foundation garments, bras and girdles, because of the real or implied associations with sex, can create problems of offense to propriety or decency. The committee emphasizes the need for special care on the part of the advertiser in creating the commercial and great caution on the part of the broadcaster in scheduling it." The subcommittee also instructed that such commercials should avoid the use of live models (unless fully clothed), any shots or copy emphasizing "sexual allurement," appeals to teenagers, demonstrations with the human hand, and too many close-ups. In contrast, the committee urged advertisers to produce commercials with appeals to style and fashion that used mannequins or the ectoplasm technique to demonstrate "the garment rather than the body."[41]

Though this policy was full of restrictions and itemizations of what commercials should *not* do, it was not merely repressive. In its claims about propriety and decency, the policy participated in defining both sex and television's role in discussions of it. For one, "foundation garments," particularly those worn by women, were linked to sex, thereby linking the female body, especially body parts such as breasts, to sexual activity. While this association was nothing new for American culture, the personal products committee's reassertion of a commonly held assumption (that women's breasts are, by definition, sexual objects) echoed the overall logic by which such broad conclusions are made to seem inevitable and natural. The policy also helped to reproduce ideas about sex that alienated women from their own bodies. By limiting "demonstrations with the human hand," the personal products subcommittee perpetuated assumptions about the perversity of women touching their own bodies, especially in sexual ways. The policy also took part in already-circulating discourses about teenage sexuality, namely, that teenage sexuality was deviant and dangerous and thus should not be encouraged through titillating bra ads. While all of these ideas about sexuality were already well entrenched in American culture, the personal products committee's declaration implicated television in the social work of perpetuating and upholding them. The foundation garments policy, by its very existence, suggested that television played a part in maintaining social categories about acceptable and unacceptable sexuality. The policy's particular focus on women's bodies further suggested that the female body, and breasts especially, were the means through which television could assert itself in social discussions about sex and the new sexual culture.

"Ban the Bra!"

As consistent as the 1959 policy seemed with contemporaneous social mores, the country's attitude toward sex and toward women's bodies began to shift in the 1960s, as the hippie movement, the sexual revolution, and the burgeoning women's liberation movement began to question traditional ideas. In many quarters, the bra became a symbol of these changes. One of the first major events to generate extensive publicity for the women's movement was a protest at the Miss America pageant in 1968. Here, protestors crowned a sheep "Miss America," picketed the pageant with signs depicting women's bodies divided up into sections and labeled as different cuts of meat, and threw high-heeled shoes, fashion magazines, typing books, and other items into a "Freedom Trash Can." Most infamously, the women threw bras into the trash can, bras that they had been swinging overhead in rejection of their intended function. While the protestors initially planned to burn the contents of the trash can, they refrained for safety reasons. Still, the media widely reported on the "bra-burning" that purportedly went on outside the pageant, even though no bras were actually burned.[42]

Media representations of feminists as "bra-burners" became commonplace after the pageant of 1968. Even by the mid-1970s, this idea was still widely circulated. For instance, the *Family Feud* television game show (ABC, 1976–85; syndicated, 1977–83) listed "burns bra/braless" as the number one thing a woman does to show she is liberated (before, for example, paying her own way) in one of its survey questions. As the cultural historian Susan Douglas has argued about the news media, bra burning became a metaphor "that trivialized feminists and titillated the audience at the same time . . . [it] equated the women's movement with exhibitionism and narcissism, as if women who unstrapped their breasts were unleashing their sexuality in a way that was unseemly, laughable, and politically inconsequential, yet dangerous."[43] For mainstream media organizations that had little choice but to report on the increasingly vocal women's movement, focusing on the bra issue was a way to demean the movement while warning just how threatening it might become. If women's breasts were unleashed, the coverage seemed to indicate, there was no telling the depths to which society might fall.

Bra manufacturers were perhaps the most threatened of any in the face of the braless movement. As *Advertising Age* quipped, "The bra-less ones are really causing sagging sales these days."[44] In 1970, the Corset and Bra Council claimed that bra sales were increasing only 1 percent a year, unlike five years earlier, when the growth rate had been 5 percent a year.[45] In response, the industry came up with new products and new advertising plans, including an attempt to reverse the NAB's ban on live models in bra commercials.

One of the lingerie industry's first strategies was to create new styles of bras that allowed for a more "natural" look and targeted the youth market.[46] In effect, the bra industry set out to convince women to purchase bras in order to achieve "the feeling of being braless."[47] Countless ads linked the new "natural" bras to women's increasing freedom, seeming to accept feminist rhetoric about the restrictiveness of bras, then tying liberation to the purchase of a new product. Other advertisers tried a scare tactic that pointed out to women the potential dangers of bralessness. For example, Peter Pan's print ads offered this advice:

Before you take off your bra for good, take off your bra and take a good look at your body. Now, if your body is super firm, if you've got well-toned muscles and the somewhat flat shape — if what you have are the kind of breasts that are usually found only on a healthy young girl, and if you really think you look terrific, then you could go bra-less. Whatever the reason, you've got the body. All you need is the guts. But if you're like most girls, with a bustline that you think is too big or too little, or if you're okay, but your breasts and your muscles just aren't tight enough, and if you really don't think you look so hot, then you probably couldn't go bra-less.[48]

Giving countless women hours of terror in front of their mirrors, this campaign used the braless trend to reassert long-held, patriarchal norms for women's bodies.

Challenging the NAB Ban

Though the development of new products and print ad campaigns were two of the bra industry's major moves in the face of the braless trend, some manufacturers took an even bolder step and attempted to get the NAB to drop its ban on live models in bra commercials. The manufacturers saw television advertising, particularly advertising that would allow a demonstration of the bra on a live woman, as an effective means of reaching their customers. When the Canadian Broadcasting Corporation began to allow such ads in 1968, Playtex was among the first advertisers to buy time.[49] But the NAB reaffirmed the U.S. ban that same year.[50] Exquisite Form Industries then proceeded to challenge the U.S. policy and in 1969 the company produced two versions of commercials, one with a live model and one with a mannequin, for the NAB's review.[51] The NAB again voted to uphold the ban.[52] Still, the increasingly permissive climate and the persistence of bra advertisers led the NAB TV Code Review Board to send a memo to subscribers in February 1970, requesting their opinions on the use of live models in foundation garment ads. As of May 1970, 83 percent of the member stations had responded, and 66.2 percent of the responses favored retention of the policy. Given these results, the board decided once again to keep the ban intact.[53]

These repeated refusals to change an eleven-year-old policy designed to protect the medium from allegations of promoting sex were no longer as understandably in keeping with contemporary social mores as they had been when the policy was initiated in 1959. By 1970, bras and the breasts they contained had become major subjects of discussion in the news, in the workplace, in the home, and in the streets. Susan Douglas was a college freshman in 1968 when she and her roommate photographed themselves braless, wearing men's undershirts and holding up a sign that read, "Ban the bra."[54] Jan Andre, a welding engineer, lost her job at General Dynamics in Pomona, California, for organizing a No Bra Day at her workplace.[55] And Thomas R. Haskett, the writer of a letter to the *New York Times Magazine*, referred dismissively to "braless radical feminists" in response to an article about the National Organization for Women's position on television commercials.[56] Much of the television audience was familiar with the bra issue and many of them had strong feelings on the matter. In the television industry's ongoing attempt to keep television a truly mass medium, palatable to everyone and offensive to none, the stations and networks that formed the NAB refused to enter into the bra fracas. Bra manufacturers could advertise on TV, but the television industry did all it could to keep those bras from being too closely associated with breasts and their sexual connotations.

Not all members of the NAB were so willing to keep the bra-breast issue at bay. John T. Murphy, the president of AVCO Broadcasting, wrote to the NAB TV Code Review Board in 1969 arguing that the ban on live models was "archaic and makes no sense at all when you consider the bikinis on live models on such programs as *Laugh-In*, and the other entertainment programs such as Dean Martin, Mike Douglas, Johnny Carson, etc."[57] When the NAB refused Murphy's request and reaffirmed the ban, he wrote back to the board and chastised it for not changing with the times: "It is unfortunate, in my opinion, that in most cases we sit on our hands and do nothing in the interest of advancement, until we are challenged. During these trying days when our industry is under such severe criticism, why should we not advance our thinking in the areas where we are privileged to make such advancements, to further carry out our obligation to the public we serve and, in this case, it is approximately 75,000,000 women."[58] With Murphy's equation of product-hawking and public service as their rallying cry, AVCO stations in Cincinnati, Columbus, Dayton, Indianapolis, and San Antonio all agreed to air commercials featuring live models wearing lingerie, in direct defiance of the NAB TV Code.[59] Though AVCO stations aired such ads with few audience complaints, other station groups did not follow their precedent. The NAB's ban on live models wearing bras stayed in place, only to be challenged again later in the 1970s.

AVCO's challenge ultimately had little impact on the industry as a whole, but bra manufacturers continued to search for ways to appeal to potential customers without showing live women wearing bras alone. In 1972, Playtex ran a commercial featuring a model wearing a bra *over* her dress. That same year, Maidenform commercials featured life-size, cardboard women's bodies with bras painted on them. A spokesmodel's head appeared on top of the cardboard figure's neck, as she quipped, "Maidenform's Rated X bra makes you look beautiful" in a play on the television industry's recent controversy over X-rated films.[60] In the increasingly liberalized times, commercials such as these poked fun at the outdated NAB ban while still managing to associate bras with sex. In this way, the advertisers circumvented the original purpose of the ban—to eliminate associations with sex. While this may have helped the bra industry rebound from its dip in sales at the end of the 1960s and the beginning of the 1970s (by 1975, at least one manufacturer claimed to have doubled sales from 1969 figures), it kept in place the linkages between bras, breasts, and sex that the ban on live models attempted to repress but ultimately reproduced.[61]

Even with these gentle prods from the bra industry, the NAB kept the ban on live models in place throughout the life of the code. In 1976, the board rejected a request by Playtex to air commercials featuring live models.[62] However, in 1977 the NAB TV Code Review Board allowed Playtex to run two series of test commercials in major television markets, test commercials that featured live models wearing only bras. Yet again, the board was not convinced by these tests and refused to lift the ban.[63] As outdated as the ban must have seemed to many (especially in light of the increasingly risqué material in television programming), the conservative nature of the television industry and the desire to retain limits for television's new sexual culture won out. Women in bras would not appear in TV commercials until the early 1980s, when the code was suspended.[64]

Assessing the Bras without Breasts

The NAB TV Code Review Board likely kept the ban against lingerie-clad breasts in place for several specific reasons. First, the rebounded sales figures in the bra industry kept advertisers from putting very much pressure on the board. Other than Playtex's requests in 1976 and 1977, there were few attempts to have the policy changed and advertisers had settled into using print for the bulk of their campaigns. Second, the board was likely responding to its subscriber survey of 1970, in which the majority of stations wanted the ban kept in place. It was easy for the board to maintain the status quo when its constituents had voted in favor of doing so. Third, the board was likely acting preventively. Throughout the 1970s, various organized groups and individual audience members complained about the use of sex in advertising, much as complaints about sex on television in general rose during this time. For example, in 1969 a network clearance official told *Advertising Age* that his network regularly received letters critical of sex and "phallic symbolism" in ads:

"The mail indicates when some people hear sex appeal talked about, they think someone is pushing not just sex, but abnormal sex or sexual indulgence."[65] In 1971, the National Organization for Women's "10 worst ads" list included an ad for a Playtex girdle that depicted women competing with one another for the attention of men.[66] In 1975, a panel at the Chicago Advertising Club's meeting discussed the use of sex appeal in ads as demeaning and insulting, citing such controversial campaigns as Continental Airlines' "We really move our tail for you," which featured young, attractive "stewardesses."[67] The NAB might very well have seen removing the ban on live models in undergarment ads as a foolish step given this climate of criticism. Keeping the ban on live models in bra ads in place during this time may have been a final effort by the NAB to deflect some of the derision being heaped upon the industry. With television in general and advertising in particular already under scrutiny for their appeals to sex, the NAB TV Code Review Board may have hoped to defend the television industry's integrity with its refusal to change this one policy.

Whatever the ultimate reasons for the maintenance of the ban on live models in bra advertising, the NAB's decision did reproduce existing ideas about sex and women's bodies. By attempting to repress the cultural linkage between breasts and sex, the television industry helped keep in place not only that linkage but also a conception of sex that located its inappropriateness and indecency squarely upon the female body. Much like the controversy around the possibility of X-rated films coming to television, the debates around live models wearing bras demonstrate the limit-setting that accompanied the repression of certain sexual images and themes. Mainstream American culture —and broadcast television in particular—both sexualized women's bodies and denigrated women's bodies for being sexual temptations, a construction of sex that would continue in television representations that *did* appear on screen, as well.

Regulating Contraception: Condom Advertising and the NAB TV Code

Americans celebrated their first National Condom Week in February 1978, complete with a contest for the best condom-related rhyming couplet and a commemorative 236-foot condom tree.[68] Yet some young men, such as twenty-one-year-old Jack, were none too fond of the widely praised prophylactic. According to Jack, "You don't want to mention contraception because you don't want to ruin the opportunity. I know it's a kind of Russian roulette, but I've been willing to play it."[69] Though the dangers Jack so cavalierly chanced were venereal diseases and pregnancy (commenting, as he did, in the years just before the AIDS crisis hit), his attitude, particularly in the context of a growing awareness of the condom's effectiveness for contraception and disease prevention, represented a primary tension in the struggle by 1970s feminists, health-care providers, population control advocates, and condom manufacturers to make contraceptives in general and condoms in particular widely accepted and used. Though American culture was increasingly open to discussing sexuality in public, discussion of contraception, particularly condoms, remained uncomfortable territory for many and forbidden territory for television.

As with other "personal products" in the 1970s, contraceptives found their way into the commercial marketplace to degrees theretofore unseen. Chief among these forays into the world of commerce were attempts by condom manufacturers to bring advertisements for their products to television. Much like the struggles of undergarment manufacturers over bra ads, condom manufacturers found themselves confronted with the NAB's TV Code Review Board, a regulatory force they were unable to sway to their interests. As with the controversies over X-rated films and bra commercials, condom ads were a version of TV sex that never fully made it to television in the 1970s. However, in debates over the possibility of such material airing on TV we can see the ways that regulatory bodies such as the NAB and citizens' groups negotiated the terms of television's new sexual culture. In addition to setting limits for what television would not show, such debates also contributed to constructions of sex that, again, linked the act with women and that defined issues such as contraception and disease prevention as fundamentally unsuited for television's family audience.

Contraceptive Controversy in the 1970s

Contraception became a major subject for public discussion and a major site of social change in the 1960s. The birth control pill was first made available in 1960. Within a year, one million women were taking it and, by 1970, nine million were protected from pregnancy by the pill's daily hormonal doses.[70]

The pill was widely regarded as the premier factor in the sexual revolution, offering women freedom from fear of pregnancy and offering both men and women a means of contraception that separated birth control from the sex act itself. Television advertising was not much of an issue for the birth control pill. Because taking it required a doctor's prescription, the pill did not seem like a consumer good. Pharmaceutical companies concentrated their energies on selling their product to physicians, not on selling it to the individual consumer.

Still, the pill would in many ways be the impetus for the increased emphasis on the condom later in the 1970s, including efforts to get the NAB to allow condom advertising on TV. The demand for birth control methods other than the pill began in the late 1960s. Some dissatisfaction with the pill arose out of a backlash against women's liberation and the sexual revolution. For example, mainstream women's magazines began to question the effects of the pill on sexual satisfaction, charging that women were upsetting the balance of nature by altering their reproductive cycles.[71] Another aspect of the backlash was, as *Ladies' Home Journal* wondered, "What 'The Pill' Does to Husbands" (the answer: leads to "frustration, worry, fear and occasionally impotence").[72] While the changes brought about by the women's movement and the sexual revolution were no doubt disruptive to some marriages, placing the blame on the pill and, more specifically, on the woman's deviant sexual response made the contraceptive stand in for women's increased control over their own bodies and sexuality. Questioning the pill was a way to question women's changing social roles.

The other main dissatisfaction with the pill concerned its health risks. The historian Linda Gordon argues that the pill "drop-out" began in 1967, when women became unhappy with its many "harmless" side effects (such as nausea, rashes, weight gain, and bloating).[73] But women suffered more life-threatening damage from the pill, as well. In 1969, the journalist Barbara Seaman began to draw national attention to the pill's dangers and, in 1970, Senator Gaylord Nelson of Wisconsin led a Senate subcommittee investigation of the oral contraceptive. In response, 18 percent of American women on the pill stopped using it and another 23 percent gave serious thought to quitting, with a steep decline in use throughout the 1970s.[74]

With the pill no longer heralded as the miracle drug it once was, women sought out different forms of contraception. Condoms were not usually the method of choice. Because many of the men who had reached sexual maturity in the 1960s had come to assume that every woman was on the pill, sales of condoms had dropped in recent years.[75] In addition, many recognized the social difficulty of condom usage. Because condoms had long been associated with prostitution and with venereal disease (in most states in the 1950s condoms could only be sold as prophylaxis against venereal disease, not as contraceptives), because men complained of a decrease in sensation with their use, and because condoms reintegrated birth control with the act of intercourse, this contraceptive faced many obstacles to widespread acceptance.[76]

There were also legal barriers to the acceptance and use of condoms. In 1973, pharmacies were permitted to display condoms openly in forty-two states. However, of the fifty thousand pharmacies nationwide, no more than fifteen thousand displayed them for fear of losing customers who might be offended by the blatant display of a sex-related product.[77] Condoms were not widely advertised, either. In 1970, only *Playboy*, *Ebony*, and a few male-oriented pulp magazines accepted ads from the non-profit Population Services, Inc. for mail-order condoms.[78] This gradually changed as the 1970s wore on, assisted by the increasingly vocal women's movement, a rise in venereal disease, and a growing concern with population control. By 1976, over half of the nation's pharmacies in states where the display of condoms was legal were openly displaying the product (40 percent of which had put up their displays since 1974).[79] Open display was legalized nationwide in 1977, when the U.S. Supreme Court outlawed New York's restrictions on the distribution, display, and advertising of all nonprescription contraceptives, including prohibitions against sales to minors.[80] The effects of these changes on the sale and use of condoms were vast. In 1976, 58 percent of stores with open condom displays saw an average increase in sales of 37 percent.[81] Between 1973 and 1978, total U.S. condom sales increased by 50 percent.[82] Many people seemed to appreciate the new facility of condom purchasing, including women.

Bringing Condom Ads to Television

Armed with evidence of women's willingness to purchase condoms, condom manufacturers began to deliberately advertise their product to women, in particular to "liberated women," during the 1970s. And some of these manufacturers saw television as an ideal way to reach these women. Print advertising had become more accessible for condom sellers in recent years, and they hoped that television would follow.[83] The first ads in women's or general interest magazines used the controversy around the pill to promote the product.[84] As the targeting of women increased throughout the 1970s, the ads began to emphasize women's sexual liberation and the pleasure women could secure for themselves through the purchase of a particular brand of condom.

During this same period, the NAB's personal products division was loosening its restrictions on products such as sanitary napkins, tampons, and douches, a development that encouraged various contraceptive manufacturers to work for approval from the NAB, as well.[85] One of the earliest manufacturers to approach the NAB was the producer of Delfen Contraceptive Foam. Its ad agency, McCann Erikson, presented the case to the NAB in 1971, citing growing national concern about over-population and offering a storyboard for Delfen's proposed ad. Over shots of a woman and a baby, a voice-over talked about women wanting to delay having another child: "Delfen Foam gives you the time you need now. The time you want . . . to enjoy this child . . . Delfen. So feminine — so easy — so appealing to the woman-ess of you. . . ."[86] While the NAB refused the request, Delfen did air a slightly revised version of its spot in Canada. The Canadian Radio-Television Commission approved various radio and TV ads for contraceptives (foam and condoms) in 1971, but the NAB remained unmoved by the actions of its northern neighbor and continued to uphold its ban.[87]

In 1974, several condom manufacturers formed the National Association of Contraceptive Manufacturers to lobby the NAB on their behalf. These corporations joined with the Population Institute, Planned Parenthood, and representatives of the federal Department of Health, Education, and Welfare in their efforts to bring condom ads to television. The addition of these nonprofit interests to the contraceptive manufacturers' cause was surely a factor in the serious consideration the NAB began to give them. After an initial meeting with the TV Code Review Board, the association felt hopeful about its chances. It had many arguments on its side: the fact that laws against open display in some states kept people from getting information about contraceptive products; the need for alternate contraception given women's dissatisfaction with the pill; the audience's acceptance of contraceptive ads in Canada; and ongoing concerns about population growth, venereal disease, and abortion. They countered the "poor taste" question by pointing to the much poorer taste of other ads, in this case, "products . . . that talk about douching and diarrhea."[88] Despite the association's arguments, the NAB merely ordered the personal products committee to study the matter further and no changes were made in the current policy.

One condom manufacturer, Youngs Drug Products Corporation, was unwilling to wait for the NAB's decision. In 1975 Youngs sought clearance on noncode stations for its Trojan condoms commercials, the first of their kind on U.S. television. The two spots Youngs produced emphasized family planning and responsible parenthood. One featured a pair of hands fashioning a cradle as a voice-over stressed Trojans' role in helping people "safely practice responsible parenthood." The other offered images of a young couple on a beach and included a voice-over intoning that the "makers of Trojan condoms believe there is a time for children. The right time."[89] The ads aired in two markets, San Jose, California, and Canton-Cleveland, Ohio. In both cities, the ads stirred up significant controversy and were initially pulled from the air. In San Jose, the commercial first ran in the early evening, at 7:15 PM. KNTV, the ABC affiliate that ran the ad, got an "overwhelmingly unfavorable" response from the audience. The station quickly halted the ad run but made an unusual choice in further surveying the audience on its reactions. The station aired the ads as part of a feature story on the local newscast, asking viewers to write or call with their opinions. The response was large and positive; three hundred viewers contacted the station, with phone calls running twenty to one in favor of the ads and mail running five to one in favor. As a result, KNTV reinstated the spots and faced little controversy thereafter.[90] WJAN-TV in Canton-Cleveland only ran the ads during a news report announcing the campaign. When the general response was unfavorable (though the station's general manager claimed the calls were mostly from "kooks and nuts") and business, community, and religious leaders advised against airing the spots, the station decided not to schedule them.[91]

The reactions of these two communities to television commercials for condoms offer intriguing evidence of audience responses to this sort of advertising. It seems that audience reaction was affected very much by the frame within which the commercials were presented. Though differences in the two cities may partially account for the different responses to the ads when they aired in local news stories, it seems more likely that the two news stories either framed the ads differently or that KNTV's explicit request for audience feedback elicited a more positive response than WJAN-TV's less interactive reporting. When audiences in San Jose were confronted with an ad for condoms in the early evening, they were likely shocked and perhaps offended that such commercials would run during the newly instituted family viewing hour. However, when their opinions were solicited, when KNTV acknowledged the significance of the ads and the audience's response by producing a news story about them, audiences seemed willing to give the commercials a chance.

Youngs parlayed the positive outcome of the San Jose ads into a campaign airing on five noncode subscribing television stations and nine radio stations, hoping to build a body of evidence about the ads' acceptability to present to the NAB.[92] Meanwhile, some other condom manufacturers chose to stay away from TV, preferring to keep their advertising to more narrowly targeted — and less controversial — print forums.[93] Still, the NAB TV Code Review Board continued to consider the issue and, in 1976, it even conducted a poll of two hundred national organizations to get their opinion on the matter. Unsurprisingly, organizations such as Morality in Media and the National Right to Life Committee favored a continuation of the NAB's ban while groups such as Planned Parenthood, the Population Institute, and the American Public Health Association favored a change in the code.[94] This far from unanimous perspective kept the NAB from altering the code. Still, in 1978, the Code Review Board held a "fact-finding" session on the matter, featuring testimony from a range of public and religious groups (the groups' stances hadn't changed since 1976).[95] In 1981, the board was still debating the issue. This time, it conducted a survey of two thousand households and gathered relatively pro-advertising responses from such groups as the Girls Clubs of America, the Society for Adolescent Medicine, and the American Public Health Association.[96] That year, the NAB finally approved a test of condom ads, and commercials ran on 7 network affiliates, 15 independent stations, and 125 radio stations. After the test, 53 percent of station owners opposed the continuation of such ads, though they did approve of public service announcements on the subject.[97] Before the board could make a decision about the ultimate fate of condom ads, the code itself was suspended, keeping the industry's self-regulating body from ever officially permitting contraceptive advertising, the last holdout in the personal products division.

The TV Sex That Wasn't

Condom commercials came closer to actually appearing on television in the 1970s than did X-rated movies or live models wearing bras. All three instances of the TV sex that wasn't had brief moments of tangible appearance on air, but only condom ads received the serious consideration by industry regulators that might have led to their sustained presence. There are many reasons why condoms came closer than these other cases to breaking through the television acceptability barrier. One is the fact that a fairly wide range of citizen, activist, and professional groups took a favorable stance on their inclusion, something that could not be said for the more profit-driven interests that sought to lift the ban on bras. Because these groups were often motivated by public health concerns, their positions had greater credibility and influence with the NAB than did product manufacturers' arguments. In addition, because condom advertising could carry this public health message, it could more easily avoid the associations with sexual titillation and explicitness that X-rated films or the display of lingerie-clad breasts evoked. Condoms' connections to contraception and disease prevention, as well as to the male body, made them decidedly less "sexy" than either breasts or "X-rated" culture; because they had long been associated with men's "natural" sexual exploits, they did not carry the same aura of shocking newness that women's sexual autonomy or an increasingly mainstream "X-rated" culture did. Indeed, condom ads could be seen as helping to fulfill television's public service mandate rather than merely feeding into the sexual free-for-all that some saw as taking over the airwaves in the 1970s.

Whatever the reasons that condom commercials came closer to TV acceptability than these other cases, they clearly served as a test of television's limits. While X-rated films were clearly beyond those limits, and while bras with real breasts were just enough outside those limits to be kept off the air, condom commercials were a more ambiguous case. Just as the meanings of condoms were changing in a society beset by sexual revolution, so too was the possibility of condom ads appearing on TV a matter of changing opinion over the course of the 1970s. Even though these ads can be ultimately classified as among television's repressed, the fact that they were on the verge of TV acceptability demonstrates the ways that the *kind* of sex that could appear on television was up for negotiation.

Although different regulatory agents had differing degrees of influence in these three cases, regulation of all types affected the new sexual culture that television presented. While not operating strictly as censors, constituencies such as the U.S. Congress, the Federal Communications Commission, the National Association of Broadcasters, and citizen groups managed to keep certain representations of sex away from television during the 1970s. While some instances faced more intensive opposition than others and some came closer to appearing on television than others, all three of these examples illustrate the limits of television's new sexual culture. Through these cases, we can see how television's status as a family medium was continuously upheld, how TV sex was, by definition, more suggested than explicit, and how gendered conceptions of sexuality — in particular, of the woman's body as a locus of sexual titillation and shame — were reproduced. Clearly, television and its regulatory influences repressed many representations of the changing sexual landscape. At the same time, however, these repressions produced ways of thinking about sex, about television, and about the link between the two that would reverberate throughout television's construction of sex and the new sexual culture in the 1970s.

THE SEX THREAT

REGULATING AND REPRESENTING
SEXUALLY ENDANGERED YOUTH

> Hello Daddy, hello Mom
> I'm your ch ch ch ch ch cherry bomb!
> Hello world I'm your wild girl
> I'm your ch ch ch ch ch cherry bomb!
> —LYRICS FROM "CHERRY BOMB," THE RUNAWAYS, 1976

When Pam Brownell of Allen, Nebraska, and Lisa Stewart of Austin, Texas, saw the 1976 made-for-TV movie, *Dawn: Portrait of a Teenage Runaway* (NBC, 27 September 1976), they both wrote letters to the film's producers. Neither had anything to say about the movie's sobering look at teenage prostitution or about the family pressures that led the film's main characters to leave home in the first place. Neither asked for information about the movie's teenage star, Eve Plumb, or about Leigh McCloskey, the handsome young actor who played Dawn's sensitive love interest, Alexander. Instead, both Brownell and Stewart inquired about "a real rock and roll song" featured in the film.[1] The song was "Cherry Bomb" by The Runaways, an all-girl rock-punk band started in 1975. Made up of five teenage girls, the band soon gained notoriety for the trashy lingerie the members wore on-stage as they performed their songs of angry, sex-tinged rebellion.[2]

"Cherry Bomb" was featured in a key moment early in *Dawn*. After running away to Hollywood and being taken in by the kind and gentle Alexander, Dawn follows Alex when he goes to work one evening. Alex has been purposely vague with Dawn about his job as a street hustler, but Dawn's naiveté begins to break down as she trails Alex along Hollywood Boulevard and The Runaways' music plays on the soundtrack. As she passes the harsh neon lights and the throngs of seedy men and women gathered along the boulevard, she encounters various signs of the sex-saturated netherworld within which Alex lives — a woman in drag leeringly eyes her, an effeminate hippie-type talks to Alex, a window advertises Le Sex Shoppe. "Cherry Bomb's" raunchy lyrics — "I'll give ya something to live for / Have ya, grab ya til you're sore" — punctuated by the vocalists' orgasmic moans and screaming electric guitar solos, emphasize the menace of this world, particularly to vulnerable young women like Dawn. In the context of the scene, The Runaways' voices are those of the girls already corrupted by this exploitative life, threateningly representing the depths to which Dawn will soon fall.

The use of "Cherry Bomb" in *Dawn* turns The Runaways' rebellious message against itself, making it a warning about youth sexuality gone astray as opposed to an in-your-face assertion of youthful defiance. But Brownell's and Stewart's interest in the song resists the meanings imposed by the filmmakers. As Brownell wrote, "I love music and sing and play all the time. I love this song and I would like to know what the name is, where I can get it and who sings it."[3] She wanted to know more about the song and its performers in order to enjoy it further and even to perform it herself. Pam Brownell embraced The Runaways' rebellious spirit; she didn't see the song's raw energy as a foretelling of doom for America's youth.

"Cherry Bomb's" multiple meanings in relation to this sex-themed made-for-TV movie offer an apt example of a key element of television's new sexual culture in the 1970s. This construction of sex suggested that young people in particular were at risk in these sexually liberalized times, that sex and the supposed revolution around it were threats to America's youth and thus, by extension, to America's future. In this discourse, young people could be in sexual danger (that is, rape), physical danger, moral danger, or emotional danger; in any case, they were in danger of losing their youthful innocence. This chapter analyzes the discourse of sexual endangerment as circulated in two key sites: made-for-TV movies and regulatory debates over TV content.

Unlike those regulatory debates surrounding versions of sex that were *prevented* from appearing on TV, this strand of regulatory discussion focused on the sex that *did* show up on screen, and in particular on the effects of those sex-themed representations upon young people. In turn, this theme of sex as threat to youth was replicated in some of the very programming that governmental bodies and citizen groups criticized. In particular, the discourse of young people's sexual endangerment circulated in a subgenre of the sex-themed made-for-TV movie. This subgenre, of which *Dawn* was a part, exploited the very sexual dangers it warned against, placing young people—especially adolescent girls—under sexual threat in ways both titillating and cautionary.

The 1970s moral panic around young people, sex, and television grew out of long-standing panics around youth in general and around the media's effect on youth in particular. Since at least the early days of industrialization, childhood has been constructed as a time of innocence and, consequently, as a source of hope for the future.[4] As Lynn Spigel has detailed, this notion of childhood innocence is rooted in a strict demarcation between children and adults, a demarcation that depends upon keeping children from certain types of "adult" knowledge. Because the mass media have been seen as persuasive disseminators of various kinds of "adult" knowledge, media products as diverse as dime-store novels and video games have been subject to scrutiny, regulation, and censorship.[5] Television and young people's interactions with it have received such attention throughout the medium's history, hence the concerns about the effects of television's representations of sex in the 1970s.

Although the moral panic around young people and television in the 1970s was nothing new, it did take shape in ways specific to the historical moment. For example, both the TV movie representations of sexual danger and the regulatory rhetoric around television's harmful effects linked sex with violence. Although this pairing had long-standing resonance for American culture, the violence associated with sex in television representation and regulation spoke to many Americans' sense that they were living in an increasingly volatile world. Violence seemed to be suffusing American life by the early 1970s, not only through the images of death and destruction relayed from the war in Vietnam, but also through reports of racially charged rioting, increasing incidences of murder and violent crime, contentious confrontations between student war protestors and police, and assassinations of high-profile figures such as Martin Luther King Jr. In addition, the 1970s panic around young people, television, and sex was specific to its time in that it concerned itself with adolescents at least as much as, if not more than, younger children. With teenagers and young adults at the forefront of many of the changes brought by the sexual revolution, it was adolescent experimentation with sex that held the most potential for disrupting conventional morality and blurring the line between children and adults.

Finally, the 1970s panic around youth and sex is notable and historically specific because of its multi-sited appearance, circulating both in fictional television representation and in real-world debates over television regulation. The made-for-TV movies that focused on sexually endangered youth contributed to the regulatory maelstrom by intensifying the moral panic around young people and sex, but they also knowingly used that panic to draw audiences. In such movies' attempts to warn the viewing audience about the dangers young people faced, they also exploited the titillating pull of those dangers. Representations of sex as a danger to youthful innocence in television of the 1970s reinforced the rhetoric around youth, sex, and television in the regulatory realm, each exacerbating the other's alarmist vision of the new sexual culture.

Regulating Sexually Endangered Youth:
The Link between Sex and Violence

Across media history, regulators and censors have sought to protect young people from the media's influence in two main areas: violence and sex. At times, one or the other has been the more dominant concern, but often the two have been closely intertwined. For example, the nineteenth-century crusader Anthony Comstock warned against young people reading dime novels, which could lead to them acting out the novels' plots of "seduction, theft, and murder."[6] The panic in the 1950s around juvenile delinquency pointed to a range of media products, including music, film, television, and comic books, as delivery systems for messages of violence and of sex.[7] As Senator Robert C. Hendrickson announced at the 1954 Senate subcommittee hearings on the subject, of greatest concern were the "ideas that spring into the living room for the entertainment of the youth of America, which have to do with crime and with horror, sadism, and sex."[8] The assumed connection between violence and sex in such discourse, as well as in the regulatory debates of the 1970s, widened the address of these regulatory and censorship efforts, including both liberal perspectives (more typically concerned with violence) and conservative ones (more typically concerned with sex).

The Effects of Television Sex and Violence

In the 1970s panic over the impact of TV content, concerns about violence and those about sex developed somewhat independently of each other but merged by the middle of the decade in regulatory debates and in programming. Long-standing anxieties about the impact of TV violence accelerated in 1968, when three highly visible violent events seemed to peak a period of increasing violence across the United States. The April assassination of Martin Luther King Jr., the June assassination of Robert F. Kennedy, and the August confrontation between protestors and police at the Democratic Party Convention in Chicago served as catalysts for a host of social-science and legislative efforts aimed at understanding and controlling the unabated violence in U.S. society, including the violence appearing on television. To help explain these events, as well as the growing violence across America in the 1960s, Congress turned to television as a likely culprit, and forty-nine members of the House introduced resolutions calling for the FCC to study the effects of TV violence on the public and especially on America's youth.[9] These representatives saw a "distinct and growing relationship" between TV violence and real-world violence and were eager to control the former as a means of containing the latter.[10]

This governmental concern spread to the television industry, which was scrambling to avoid government intervention. Immediately following Kennedy's assassination in June 1968, the Association of National Advertisers urged its members to withdraw sponsorship from programs featuring excessive violence while network executives quickly announced their willingness to help the national commission charged with uncovering the causes of violence in American society.[11] The networks also rushed to the producers of some of their most popular action-oriented shows, requiring changes that deemphasized violence.[12] With most series in production for the fall start of the 1968–69 season, the networks were able to effect changes on many levels. CBS even agreed to pay for re-shoots of shows that were already completed.[13]

Despite these efforts, Senator Pastore used his Communications Subcommittee in March 1969 to call for a new study of the effects of TV violence. Pastore opened the subcommittee hearings on 4 March 1969 by highlighting the special importance of TV violence and its impact on youth as an object for the subcommittee's attention. He then floated his proposal: to ask the surgeon general to explore the causal relationship between television violence and real-world violence much as had recently been done for the relationship between cigarette smoking and lung cancer.[14] Pastore framed his concern over the cancerous effects of TV violence as an effort to protect the American public, a public that was embodied in "our most valuable and trusted resource, the minds and moral behavior of our young people."[15] While Surgeon General William H. Stewart made clear the necessity for careful, nuanced research on the subject, research that would take into account such factors as the way that violent content is interwoven with other material and the way that a child's age or family life affects the influence of television, the politicians who called for the research referred to bald statistics and anecdotal evidence to suggest that they already knew what the surgeon general's study would find.[16] Senator Vance Hartke wrote to Pastore that "studies show not only that teenagers watch television more than do their parents, but that almost 40 percent of these youngsters believe that what they see on television is an accurate representation of the character of American life."[17] Such rhetoric fueled the panic over television's impact on youth apart from the yet-to-come findings of the surgeon general.

The final surgeon general's report was released in January 1972. It concluded that there was sufficient causal evidence of a relationship between TV violence and real-world violence. Or so Pastore led the public to believe. The actual report was more tentative, suggesting that there was some evidence that there may be some effect on behavior for some audiences. When press accounts of the report began to discuss these qualifications, as well as the potential bias in the surgeon general's committee (the three networks had been allowed to "black ball" proposed members, thereby ensuring a more network-friendly outcome), the networks took up their own violence-effects studies to disprove the causal connection and, they hoped, forestall further government interference. Although the networks also sought to carefully regulate their violent programming, they put producers in a difficult position, asking them to design programming that would meet network and government expectations in terms of anti-violence but still meet network demands for large audience draws. This contradictory impulse was further complicated as concerns about the impact of sexual themes were increasingly paired with those regarding violence.

Sex was a repeated concern even in those content regulation efforts that were purportedly focused on the effects of TV violence upon young people. At the March 1969 TV violence hearings of the Senate's Subcommittee on Communications, Senator Pastore regularly referred to sexual content, often in ways that had little to do with the subject at hand. When the surgeon general spoke about the proposed study of TV violence and the limits that would necessarily need to be placed on its scope (for example, limiting it to television representations instead of including print), Pastore chimed in with this non sequitur: "On that point, the Supreme Court has held that *Lady Chatterley* is not pornographic. I would hate to see it portrayed on television."[18] During the course of the hearings, Pastore also found time to discuss a provocative shaving cream commercial, *I Am Curious (Yellow)*, and talk show guests in revealing clothing, all as affronts to morality and dangers to the youth audience. At times, other senators joined Pastore in raising issues of sexual content and its impact on children. For example, Senator Daniel Inouye questioned the appropriateness of an "adults only" promotion for a broadcast of the feature film *La Dolce Vita* (1960).[19] In addition, President Nixon's letter in support of the surgeon general's study referred to the effects of television sex on youth on equal terms with television violence, despite the fact that the proposed study was explicitly and exclusively focused on the latter.[20] The strongest articulation of the significance of sexual content in these purportedly anti-violence regulatory efforts came from Pastore, who remarked, "I don't think there is so much competition on the showing of violence as there is on the showing of sex," thereby suggesting that the impact of TV sex on America's youth was at least as disturbing to him, to the U.S. government, and to American life as was TV violence.[21]

Linking Sex and Violence in Made-for-TV Movies

The intensity of regulatory furor over violence and sex in television programming had multiple causes: the long-standing anxieties about America's youth, the changing climate of domestic and international violence, the new sexual mores, the political posturing of congressional figures, the efforts by the TV industry to forestall government interference, and the genuine concern by multiple parties that television might be harmful to children and adolescents. But the key link between these contextual influences and the regulatory measures that would follow was the content of television itself. Beginning in the late 1960s, broadcast network programming dealt increasingly with sexual matters, much of it tinged with violence. Participants in the regulatory debates indicted different parts of the TV schedule. Certainly, advertising and theatrically released feature films were frequent targets. But one of the networks' newer programming innovations was also beginning to receive some attention. As the 1970s proceeded, the made-for-TV movie was quickly becoming a major site for television's representation of sex and a major focus of regulatory inquiry. One movie in particular, NBC's *Born Innocent*, would feature strongly in the TV industry's main effort at self-regulation.

Although *Born Innocent*'s blend of sex and violence ignited the government's and the TV industry's regulatory fire, it was not the first made-for-TV movie to draw on this formula. The earliest TV movies, those aired in NBC's *World Premiere* series beginning in the 1960s, typically drew from mystery and suspense genres and thus relied on violence as part of their audience draw. As the critic Judith Crist wrote in 1969, "Most of the films fall into the mystery melodrama rut with each crisis attenuated to commercial break time, with violence more often than not the name of the game."[22] When ABC began its *Movie of the Week* series, Barry Diller, a network executive, argued that NBC's films had fallen into "an action-adventure mystery-suspense rut" and that ABC would be aiming for a greater variety of stories.[23] ABC's ninety-minute movies introduced sexual themes both comedic and dramatic to the form, but they certainly did not avoid the suspense and the violence that NBC's movies had relied upon. In fact, they helped to define the made-for-TV movie as television's site for the exploitative treatment of social issues.

TV movies treat social issues exploitatively when they focus on sex, violence, and the personal ramifications of an individual's involvement with said issue. This approach might be contrasted with one that explores the underlying social, political, or economic causes of a given issue. In addition, the issues that TV movies began to cover by the mid-1970s tended toward the salacious, including prostitution, white slavery, domestic violence, and rape—

issues that had sexual *and* violent elements at their core. In contrast, less dramatically realizable issues—such as poverty or wage discrimination—were rarely touched.[24] As both Laurie Schulze and Todd Gitlin have argued, the lack of the ongoing characters and situations of a weekly series demands that TV movies have easily promotable subjects that are both "believable" and "sensational."[25] The made-for-TV movie must provoke audiences' interest "by the promise of the unusual or the scandalous and immediately mark itself off as different. Yet it must be familiar at the same time, and reassure by its reference to the instantly recognizable."[26] Thus, stories of "regular" people (for example, average housewives) facing extreme circumstances (for example, rape) provided the compelling, attention-getting material the form required in its early years. *Born Innocent* was very much a product of this formula, but its particular choice of subject matter and its particular mode of representation drew a new wave of negative attention to the made-for-TV movie.

Born Innocent: Sexual Endangerment on and off the Screen

In September 1974, NBC began its season of *World Premiere* movies with *Born Innocent*, a film that would cement the connection between the made-for-TV movies' stories of sexually endangered youth and the regulatory uproar over the impact of TV sex and violence on young people. The two-hour movie aired at 8 PM EST on Tuesday, 10 September. Starring the teenage sensation Linda Blair, who had come to fame in the 1973 feature film *The Exorcist*, *Born Innocent* told the story of fourteen-year-old Chris Parker (Blair) and her descent from "innocence" to hardened hopelessness in a girls' juvenile detention center. As a critical commentary on the flawed juvenile justice system, the film was seen as "dramatically important" by its producers and by NBC; some involved with its production even believed it might win an Emmy Award.[27] Yet an outpouring of angry responses to the film, in particular to the feared impact of a graphic same-sex rape scene on young viewers, changed the movie's significance for the network and for the history of sex in 1970s television.

Although NBC had high hopes for the reception of the film as an important piece of social realism, the network was certainly aware of the potential controversy it might cause. After all, some of the advertisers who previewed the film retracted their sponsorship, fearful of being associated with such combustible material.[28] NBC offered the film to its affiliates for previewing and even aired an advisory at the movie's start, warning audiences about the "realistic and forthright manner" of its representation of the juvenile detention center and suggesting that viewers consider "whether the program should be viewed by young people or others in [their families] who might be disturbed by it."[29] However, broadcast standards had requested very few changes during the film's production process, suggesting that the network *wanted* the movie to be as sensational as it was, perhaps in hopes that the film's daring would draw critical acclaim.[30] Furthermore, some TV critics were allowed to see the film before the broadcast and publish reviews of it, which was atypical for made-for-TV movies of the period.[31] Thus, while NBC was no doubt aware of the movie's potential for controversy, the network seemed willing to allow that controversy, perhaps hoping that the film's educative function would be seen as surpassing its more exploitative one.

Promotion for *Born Innocent* also teetered between announcing its social importance and wallowing in its prurient pleasures. NBC advertised the film in the *New York Times*, both on the Sunday before it aired and on its airdate (see figure 6).[32] The Sunday ad was part of a larger NBC promotion for the start of the fall season. It highlighted Blair's name and face, but it also drew upon the film's dual roles as serious social realism and sexual titillation. The copy heralded the involvement of the creators of *The Autobiography of Miss Jane Pittman*, a CBS made-for-TV movie that had aired in 1971 to great critical acclaim. But it also teased, "She's in a woman's prison. She's fourteen. She's learning, fast, what you have to learn to survive there." In the accompanying photo, Blair's foreground image was menaced by the images of three sullen, tough-looking girls behind her, further intimating the sadistic lesbianism associated with the women's prison genre.

While the ad was not targeted to an audience of a particular age, it did suggest a parallel between the film and NBC's Monday night programming, the debut of the series *Born Free*, a story of game wardens protecting African wildlife. Because the series was based on a book and a movie popular with children, its presence alongside the ad for *Born Innocent* (not to mention the similarities in name between the two) might easily have led readers of the *Times* to assume *Born Innocent* was also family fare, an association that would be central to the controversy that followed the broadcast. In addition, the image of Elsa the lioness in the *Born Free* portion of the ad was remarkably

6 Display ad for *Born Free* and *Born Innocent*, *New York Times*, 8 September 1974, 138.

similar to that of Blair in the *Born Innocent* portion. Elsa's head and Blair's were roughly the same size and shape; both looked off-camera to the right; the V-neck of Blair's sweater was mirrored in the upside-down V-shape of Elsa's slightly open mouth. This pairing of the young Blair with a wild jungle animal (albeit one as gentle as Elsa) not only linked the two nights of programming but also imbued Elsa with Blair's innocence and Blair with Elsa's wildness. Because Blair's work in *The Exorcist* already led to associations between her and an out-of-control (possessed), violent sexuality, the doubling of Blair's image with a wild animal further enhanced the suggestion of forbidden, sex-tinged danger in *Born Innocent*.

The film itself trades in the contemporaneous panic around young people, sex, and violence, condemning parents and the juvenile justice system for failing teens, which leads to immoral and harmful behaviors. Blair's character, Chris Parker, is treated cruelly by most of the adults she encounters, with the exception of a caring teacher at the detention center. The film's outlook is so bleak that Chris does not find support or kindness in her peers, either. In fact, as much as the film wants to place blame with adults and the institutions to which they submit young people, the harshest treatment Chris receives is from the other girls at the center, most notably in the rape scene. Because of this, the film loses some of its critical edge and becomes more focused on the exploitative spectacle of girl-on-girl sexual violence, characterizing the girls as sexually deviant psychopaths.

In the rape scene around which so much controversy swirled, four of the girls attack Chris as she comes out of the shower. They hold her down as one of them rapes her with a broomstick, an apparent rite of passage at the center. The attack goes on for 95 seconds, a long stretch for such an explicitly sexual and violent scene. The rape is foreshadowed earlier in the film when the girls refer to the broom as "Johnny," taunting Chris about her pending introduction to him. In addition, there are disparaging references to lesbianism throughout, suggesting that Chris's fate is inevitable. For instance, Moco threateningly asks Chris if she has a girlfriend and if she wants to go out with her. In an early draft of the script, Moco is described as "Seventeen, borderline Lesbian—if she could exist on the outs, she might be straight, but that would be impossible for her, starting at zero. As the leading butch of her cottage, she has found a position in life—she's the man of the house, swaggering, flirting, courting, threatening."[33] Moco's problem, as identified in this script, is her lesbianism—it is what makes her act like a "man," it is what makes her violent. And it is this violent lesbianism that becomes the real scandal, the real spectacle, of both the narrative and the outraged responses to it.

Moco turns out to be one of the leaders of the gang rape; she is the one who ends it with, "OK, that's enough." Moco is not the one who inserts the broom into Chris, however. The scene's axis of action runs primarily between Denny, who holds the broom, and Chris. While the other girls flail every which way in their efforts to hold their struggling victim, Denny's gaze is always upon Chris and we see shots and reverse shots between them throughout the scene (the longest duration shots among a sequence of rapid cutting). One long shot shows Denny kneeling between Chris's splayed legs as she rapes her. Though the scene is thus shot primarily as Denny's rape of Chris, Moco is also a significant figure. At first, Denny ignores Moco's order to stop the rape and Moco angrily barks, a second time, "That's enough!" before Denny stops. Though Denny's deviant lesbianism is suggested in the zealous way she attacks Chris,

7 Chris Parker (Linda Blair) post-rape, *Born Innocent*, NBC, 10 September 1974.
NBC/PHOTOFEST.

the scene also reinforces Moco's menacing sexuality. In a brief shot, Moco looks from Denny to Chris with a leer, implying her perverse pleasure in the action before her. Her sharp order to Denny to stop the rape thus sounds almost jealous, as if she no longer wants Denny to be the one penetrating Chris. While the scene is remarkable for its disturbing violence, it is the sexual tenor of that violence that comes across as particularly disturbed. The film's representation of rape was quite different from most of the rapes appearing on television at that point—it was perpetrated by a gang, that gang was a group of girls, and their victim was another girl, an especially young, innocent-looking girl (see figure 7).

The rest of the film documents Chris's response to this trauma. The scene ends with her sobbing as she lies naked on the bathroom floor and is followed by a somber montage sequence of her lonely existence. When she tries to escape, she is placed in an isolation cell, where her torment grows. Eventually, she becomes as violent as the other girls, leading a riot wherein the girls violently attack the housemother and viciously destroy the recreation room. While the downbeat ending reinforces the film's social critique, the most enduring images are those of the violent rape scene, the sexually explicit spectacle that led to the movie's infamy.

The film drew a large audience; it was the highest rated program of the evening. It even drew some of the critical acclaim its producers and NBC sought.[34] But it also drew some serious complaints. Some irate viewers objected to the film's sexual and violent content while others were more disturbed by that content appearing so early in the evening, making a young audience all the more likely. In both cases, young people's exposure to "deviant" sexual violence, whether on-screen or in the living room, was at the heart of the protests. Reports indicate that NBC stations in New York, Washington, Chicago, and Los Angeles alone received three thousand critical calls and letters.[35] A Nashville station manager called it "filthy, disgusting, and degrading."[36] The group station owner, Charles Crutchfield, wrote to the FCC chairman, Richard Wiley, that "television survived and prospered quite well for more than a quarter century without training the cameras on the outhouse walls and graphically depicting rape-by-broomhandle."[37] Even the *New York Times* critic John J. O'Connor, who argued that the film's disturbing images were "used for sobering documentation, not sensational exploitation" took issue with the early evening scheduling and consequent availability to young audiences.[38]

The most damning reaction to the film was made public via a lawsuit against NBC and its San Francisco outlet, KRON. The plaintiff, Valeria Niemi, filed an $11 million negligence suit against the broadcasters, claiming that her nine-year-old daughter was the victim of a copycat gang-rape four days after the broadcast and that NBC and KRON instigated the attack by showing the film at such an early hour, thereby exposing the alleged perpetrators and her daughter to its corrupting content. The broadcasters argued that the suit was a violation of their First Amendment rights, but Niemi's attorney, Marvin Lewis, insisted that the film was a violation of the broadcasters' duty to shield America's youth from the sexually explicit culture. As he strategically and sarcastically told NBC News, "This [rape] scene, if shown in a movie house, would have had an X on it, and I see no reason for the media to worry merely because X movies are not allowed into our families at seven and eight in the evening when our kiddies are watching."[39] This case and the incendiary rhetoric surrounding it helped cement the film's reputation as the embodiment of the threats to America's youth from television and the new sexual culture.

While much of the controversy around *Born Innocent* centered on its representation of and effect on young people's sexual and/or violent behaviors, another stream of criticism came from gay, lesbian, and feminist activists. A range of groups, including the Gay Activist Alliance, the National Organization for Women, the New York Rape Coalition, the Gay Media Coalition of New York, Lesbian Feminist Liberation, and the National Gay Task Force, an organization that worked regularly with the networks on questions of gay representation, challenged the film.[40] These groups made their protests public after the initial broadcast and seem to have had some impact when the film was rerun on NBC and then sold into syndication. For example, Lesbian Feminist Liberation (LFL) claimed that it persuaded four different sponsors to pull their ads from *Born Innocent*'s rebroadcast in October 1975. The group's objection to the film was simply stated: "Men rape, women don't. . . . We regard the film as propaganda against lesbians."[41] The advertisers claimed that their decision was not influenced by the lesbian activists (a credible claim given the intense criticism of the film from more mainstream interests), but LFL's objections were still given voice, regardless of whether they had a direct effect.

NBC had decided to rebroadcast the film with a later start time and an edited version of the rape scene, standing by its initial claim that the movie was an important piece of social criticism.[42] But the National Gay Task Force (NGTF) argued that the edited rape scene *further* emphasized the girls' deviant lesbianism (even though it toned down some of the violence). It was only when ABC bought the film in syndication, intending to run it on its owned and operated stations, that NGTF's editing suggestions were finally adopted. Included in these suggestions was the elimination of the lesbian references throughout the film, such as the scene in which Moco tauntingly asks Chris if she wants to go out with her. The rape scene itself remained the same as it had been in NBC's rerun broadcast.[43] Presumably, with the lesbian references elsewhere in the film eliminated, the rape scene did not communicate the same meanings about the perversity of lesbian sexuality and thus were not as offensive to the gay activists.[44]

The fact that NBC and the film's producers edited the movie at all between its first broadcast and subsequent airings demonstrates how controversial the initial broadcast was. Whether by activists upset with the representation of lesbianism as deviance or by station owners, politicians, and parents upset about young people's exposure *to* lesbian deviance, the response solidified the connections between moral panics about young people, broadcast content regulation, and the sex-themed made-for-TV movie. Eventually, the reception of *Born Innocent* would serve as a powerful catalyst for the creation of the National Association of Broadcasters' family viewing policy, a key effort to regulate young people's exposure to sex and violence on TV. However, it was not the only representation of young people's sexual endangerment that inspired the policy. Despite the controversy around this film, the networks aired at least four additional sex-themed made-for-TV movies in the 1974–75 season, including three during the crucial February ratings sweeps period.[45] All four of these movies dealt with young female sexuality in some respect, all of them pointing out the sexual dangers young women face. At the same time, all four films shared *Born Innocent*'s attempt at using harsh social realism to deal with a serious issue.

Sexual Endangerment and Made-for-TV Movies: 1974–75

The first such film to air after *Born Innocent* was Linda Blair's second made-for-TV movie for NBC that season, *Sarah T. — Portrait of a Teenage Alcoholic* (11 February 1975). Clearly, this film's social issue was teen alcoholism, assisted in Sarah's case by a difficult home life (divorced parents, newly remarried mother). The movie depicts the many problems Sarah has as a result of her drinking, including neglecting a child for whom she is babysitting and getting into trouble at school. But Sarah's drinking also exposes her to sexual danger, most notably when she approaches a group of four young men outside a liquor store, asking if they will buy her some vodka. She promises, "I'll do anything you want." When one of the guys, Roger, takes her up on her offer, a shot of him laughing as he turns to Sarah is followed by a medium long shot of Sarah tentatively walking toward him before the film fades to black. Although none of the sex is nearly as explicit as *Born Innocent*'s rape scene, there is a clear implication that Sarah is engaging in dangerous sexual behaviors. In fact, her acquiescence to Roger induces her most destructive period to that point, during which she finally hits bottom and agrees to get help. Because the baby-faced Blair plays Sarah, she seems doomed to sexual destruction from the outset, her sexualized victimization in *The Exorcist* and *Born Innocent* making her a 1970s emblem of youthful innocence corrupted.

Another of the 1974–75 season's sex-themed made-for-TV movies featured a Linda Blair look-alike in the young Glynnis O'Connor. *Someone I Touched*

(ABC, 26 February 1975) was primarily the story of Sam and Laura Hyatt, a middle-aged married couple struggling with venereal disease and the allegations of adultery that accompany it. However, it is O'Connor's character, Terry Warner, who leads off the story, as she discovers that she has contracted syphilis. She is asked to share the names of all her sexual partners with the public health office — and the significantly older Sam turns out to be one of them. Although Terry is twenty years old and thus not as emblematic a figure of childhood innocence lost as Blair's characters, the film still represents her as more a victim than a perpetrator of sexual misdeeds. In fact, O'Connor looks and sounds enough like Blair to make her seem an older version of Blair's victimized heroines. Terry is ashamed of having had multiple sex partners and claims to have been in love with Tommy, the college student she fears gave her the disease. A key moment at the conclusion of the film centers on Sam telling Terry that she was not the source of his syphilis, as both of them had assumed (in fact, Laura gave it to her husband, having acquired the disease from her own extramarital affair). Although the characters spend a lot of time trying to figure out whom to blame for transmitting the disease, the film seems to point the finger at the sexual revolution — the "care-free love" teased in a *TV Guide* ad for the movie — and the problems it causes for single and married people alike (see figure 8). Once again, a made-for-TV movie represented the sexual dangers facing young people and in so doing further bolstered anxieties about America's youth and the sexual revolution.

Someone I Touched aired just a few days after ABC's other entry in the sex-themed made-for-TV movies of the 1974–75 season. *Hustling* (22 February 1975) was promoted and reviewed as a more serious and substantial take on prostitution than your typical tele-film.[46] Based on a book by Gail Sheehy, the film offered an exposé of Manhattan prostitution by telling the story of the reporter Fran Morrison's crusade to uncover the shady dealings of the pimps and "respectable" businessmen who profit while the young women in their employ suffer. The film's social conscience and awareness of the systemic roots of the prostitutes' sad lot make the movie less exploitative than many sex-themed films of the era and less invested in hyping the sexual dangers threatening America's youth. But in representing the young women victimized by the prostitution industry, *Hustling* still participated in the discourse of sexual endangerment.

THE POWERFUL
STORY OF
FOUR PEOPLE
WHOSE
CARE-FREE
LOVE
LED TO A
TERRIFYING
EPIDEMIC!

SOMEONE I
Touched
starring
Cloris Leachman
James Olson

ABC WEDNESDAY
MOVIE OF THE WEEK
8:30

Due to mature subject matter,
parental discretion is advised

8 Display ad for *Someone I Touched*,
TV Guide, 22 February 1975, A-84.

Perhaps the most remarkable example of the sex-themed made-for-TV movies that followed *Born Innocent* in the 1974–75 season, before family viewing had a real impact, was *Cage without a Key* (CBS, 14 March 1975), yet another women-in-prison tale, this one with a plot very similar to *Born Innocent*'s. Valerie Smith, a recent high school graduate, gets sent to the San Marcos School for Girls after she is unwittingly swept into a robbery-murder and unfairly convicted of a crime she didn't commit. Although the detention center has the attractive façade of a girls' finishing school, in fact it hosts the standard hostility, violence, and "deviant" lesbianism of such facilities in other made-for-TV movies. Although the hypocrisy of the penal facility's proper appearance comes under attack, the film focuses more on the injustices the girls perpetrate upon each other than upon the unjust system that detains them in the first place. In this respect, it panders to *Born Innocent*'s more exploitative tendencies and shies away from its more trenchant areas of social critique. *Cage* features a post-shower, same-sex sexual assault scene that leaves its victim shaken and distraught, and in that respect it clearly follows *Born Innocent*'s formula. Still, *Cage*'s treatment of the sexual dangers the girls at San Marcos face is a bit less invested in the stereotype of sadistic lesbianism, as it portrays two different lesbian characters, one of whom becomes a tragic heroine.

Valerie faces a lesbian threat soon after she arrives at San Marcos. As she joins a rap session led by one of the center's teacher-guards, Noreen—one of the girls now identified as a threatening lesbian—leers at her. During the session, Noreen reaches over and strokes Valerie's hair while looking at her longingly. Valerie quickly pulls away, signifying her discomfort with Noreen's advances. Later, when Valerie is returning to her room after a shower, clad only in a towel, Noreen is waiting for her. We first see that Noreen is in the room as Valerie looks in the mirror. Noreen is reflected as being behind her and we witness their initial interaction in this way. Valerie is at first annoyed and asks Noreen what she wants. Noreen's response, coupled with Valerie's towel-clad vulnerability, makes clear that this is a sexually charged scene. "You're pretty," says Noreen, "Prettiest bride they ever had in this cottage." She then moves toward Valerie, putting her hands to her face and trying to kiss her. Valerie backs away and asks Noreen to leave, but Noreen responds by pulling off Valerie's towel and pushing her onto the bed. With Valerie's bare back to the camera, we watch them struggle, Noreen pressing her body and mouth onto Valerie's. Another girl enters and grabs Noreen, saving Valerie from the sexual violence suffered by Chris Parker in *Born Innocent*, or so audiences might likely have inferred having seen or read about the earlier film's infamous scene. Valerie is left crying and shaking on her bed, arms clutched across her chest.

The girl who rescues Valerie is Tommy Washington, the other character identified as a lesbian. Tommy is the leader of one of two warring groups of girls at the center. (Noreen is a member of the other group, which is led by the evil Susie Kurosawa.) Noreen's assault of Valerie is framed by two scenes between Tommy and Valerie in which Tommy's lesbianism is made clear. In the earlier scene, Tommy tries to get Valerie and Sarah Harris, the younger girl who enters the center at the same time as Valerie, to join her "family." Valerie has already guessed that Tommy is a lesbian and is suspicious that she is trying to get to Sarah for sexual reasons. Tommy sees this and declares, "If I want a woman, I can have any woman around here I want. I mean, that is a whole other thing. But this, you and Sarah, that is about family. Don't ever get the two mixed up." Tommy's assurance that she is not out to exploit Sarah sexually is one of the first suggestions of her decency; her rescue of Valerie from Noreen is another. To convince viewers even further that Tommy is not the "bad" kind of lesbian that Noreen is, Valerie and Tommy have a heart-to-heart talk in a scene that follows the assault. Valerie asks Tommy, "How did you become . . . ?" in response to which Tommy offers a long description of her difficult background, including mention of a "friend" whom she "lived with for two years and loved who got shot down one night in a gay bar." Valerie's and Tommy's friendship grows from this point, and Valerie agrees to join Tommy in an escape attempt when her long-hoped-for release is indefinitely delayed. During the chaos of the attempted escape, Tommy saves Valerie's life but sacrifices her own in the process. The film ends with a freeze frame of Valerie's tormented face lying against Tommy's lifeless chest as a voice-over decries the pitiful funding for detained youth. Together, the image and the voice-over attempt to make a compelling statement about the injustice of the system, emphasizing the tragedy of Tommy's fate.

Although *Cage*'s representation of lesbianism is less stereotypical than *Born Innocent*'s, it still capitalizes on the trope of sadistic same-sex desire and implies that lesbianism is a product of a dysfunctional life. After all, one of Valerie's lowest points comes after Noreen's attack. In addition, even though Tommy is portrayed sympathetically, Valerie is depicted as being wholly different from her. This difference is marked as much by race as it is by sexuality. Tommy even remarks upon the cross-racial nature of their relationship, asking Valerie if she has ever had a black friend before. Although Tommy is an admirable character, the fact that the leaders of the school's two rival gangs are people of color (Susie is Asian American) makes the social problem the film purportedly exposes seem to be one that need not centrally concern white America. Throughout the film, Valerie insists that she does not belong at the school, not because it treats the girls poorly but because she is innocent. Although she *is* innocent, her repeated assertion to this effect implies that the other girls — chief among them Tommy and Susie — more legitimately belong at San Marcos. The film's central conflict is thus Valerie's individual effort to get out, not the larger problem of a system that treats disaffected youth in this way or that imprisons young people of color more readily than white youth.

The fact that *Cage* did not cause nearly the stir that *Born Innocent* did, despite its similar subject matter, is likely due to several factors. First, the outcry over *Born Innocent* had already catalyzed the efforts to regulate young people's exposure to sexual content; after all, the family viewing policy was already underway. Second, *Cage*'s representation of female youth under sexual threat was markedly less disturbing than the earlier film's. Certainly, the sexual assault scene was much less explicit. But perhaps as significant were the two films' different casting choices. While Linda Blair's age and childish face made her seem a mere baby, with her victimization all the more tragic as a result, the former *Partridge Family* (ABC, 1970–1974) star Susan Dey played Valerie. Not only was Dey at least a few years older than Blair, but her appearance was hardly juvenile. Her tall, willowy figure, angular features, and mature, measured voice made her seem a woman in contrast to Blair's girlishness. The sexual threat Dey's Valerie faces thus does not have the same kind of moral urgency as does that faced by Blair's Chris Parker.

Cage without a Key, along with the other sex-themed TV movies of the 1974–75 season, furthered the discourse of young people's sexual endangerment, even if it did not have the same kind of immediate cultural and regulatory impact of its predecessor, *Born Innocent*. However, the broadcast of this film and others like it in the same season as *Born Innocent* illustrates that the latter film was not an exception — made-for-TV movies of the mid-1970s regularly represented sexually endangered youth. While *Born Innocent* may have been a significant catalyst for the institution of family viewing, it was part of a much larger trend in made-for-TV movies that family viewing sought to alter.

Protecting Endangered Youth: Family Viewing

The U.S. Congress had been pressuring broadcasters and the FCC about TV sex and violence, and in particular about its effect on youth, throughout the early 1970s, and these pressures were mounting in the summer and fall of 1974. A few months before the broadcast of *Born Innocent*, the House Appropriations Committee joined the Senate's Communications Subcommittee in prodding the FCC to protect America's youth. They were not satisfied with the commission's slow response to the demands for reform of the Action for Children's Television (ACT), nor were they happy with the ongoing presence of sex and violence on the air. Thus, in June 1974, Congress threatened punitive action against the FCC if it failed to submit a report by 31 December 1974, "outlining specific positive actions taken or planned by the Commission to protect children from excessive programming of violence and obscenity."[47]

The FCC quickly responded to these congressional demands, but it did so in ways that left responsibility with the broadcast industry. The commission's first action was to compel broadcasters to cut back the number of commercial minutes per hour in children's programming, but the onus for regulating children's TV was left on the industry.[48] Then, the FCC chair, Richard Wiley, used a similar tactic in pursuing the other major regulatory concern about television content, its sex and violence. Preoccupied with the children's television issue and increasingly pressured after the September broadcast of *Born Innocent*, Wiley began a campaign to convince the networks to institute a self-regulation system to better control the sex and violence on the airwaves. In an October 1974 speech to the Illinois Broadcasters Association, he warned that governmental action might be required if industry self-regulation did not have sufficient impact. In particular, he called for "intelligent scheduling, appropriate warnings, and perhaps even some kind of industry-administered rating program."[49] Wiley admitted the FCC's limited authority here, given the government's inability to interfere with broadcast content under the First Amendment. Still, he proceeded to meet with executives from the Big Three networks to discuss the issue of sex and violence. Eventually, Arthur Taylor, the president of CBS, wrote to the NAB, suggesting that a new scheduling policy be added to the NAB TV Code that would set aside the first hour of prime time for "family viewing," which was generally understood to mean programming without violent or "adult" (read: sexual) material. With the other networks in agreement, the NAB TV Code Review Board approved the amendment in February 1975, with the board officially passing it in April.[50] The revised code extended family viewing to the "access" hour preceding prime time as well as the first hour of prime time (7 PM to 9 PM EST).

The code amendment offered no specific definition of "family viewing," leading to much speculation within the television industry as to what would and would not be permitted for the upcoming 1975–76 season. Stockton Helfrich, the director of the NAB TV Code Review Board, asked the members of the board to fill out a survey with their thoughts on what was and was not acceptable content. For instance, the board was asked, "How do you define 'sexual connotations'?" and offered the options of: "A) Romantic interpersonal relationships; flirtation/courtship and B) Overt sexuality; petting; implied sexual actions; etc." The survey then attempted to define further the specific criteria by which to allow or disallow sexual material: "A) No sexual allusions whatsoever; B) Nothing too advanced for children under 12; or C) No 'spelled out' reflections of sexual concepts; handling allowing inference based on individual viewers' experience."[51] The NAB's efforts to regulate television's sexual content forced the Code Review Board to define the kind of sex permissible on television and, by implication, the version of the new sexual culture considered safe for America's youth.

As vague as the NAB TV Code Review Board's survey options were, they do reveal certain tendencies in the television industry's new guidelines for representations of sex suitable to the family hour and the young viewers presumed to be watching at that time. For example, the line between implied and overt sexual references was a matter of some significance to industry content regulators, as implied references might safely escape the understanding of younger audience members. When CBS's program practices chief, Tom Swafford, asked some of his network colleagues for their input on the survey, they made comments such as "Blatant & overt sexual material should be avoided in the family hour. However, vague references may be acceptable depending upon the situation. The youthful audience will accept Rhoda's tirade at Myrna for 'dating' prospective clients as just that . . . dating. The older audience can read between the lines & get the true significance."[52] From this executive's perspective, sexual allusion and suggestiveness were allowable, as long as they could *potentially* be read otherwise, particularly by the "youthful audience." None of Swafford's colleagues at CBS had a problem with romantic relationships being represented during the family hour; more problematic were sexual involvements that did not conform to conventional heterosexual monogamy. Dick Kirschner, Swafford's colleague who mentioned the Myrna story line in his questionnaire, also indicated that such topics as abortion, the pill, and prostitution would be inappropriate under the new policy, all subjects that challenged procreative heterosexuality.[53] Thus, the obviousness of the sexual references, as well as their degree of conformity to the most conventional of practices, were important indicators of acceptability. The subjective nature of these determinations, however, kept networks and producers on edge as they prepared for the 1975–76 season.

The networks were especially cautious about the material they allowed during prime time's "family hour" for the first episodes of the 1975–76 season. One episode of CBS's *Mary Tyler Moore Show* spin-off, *Phyllis* (1975–77), provides a case in point and demonstrates the ongoing centrality of representations of youth sexuality amid the attempts at regulation of youth viewing. In this episode, Phyllis's teenage daughter, Bess, goes on an overnight ski trip with friends and Phyllis comes to believe that Bess has spent the night with a boy. The narrative revolves around Phyllis's consternation over what she thinks Bess has done and how she might talk to her about it. The program was to end with Phyllis and Bess actually having a mother-daughter talk and Phyllis gleefully realizing afterward, "She didn't do it!" As originally written, the punch line was to come with Phyllis's double take a moment later. "Unless she lied," Phyllis was to wonder as the episode ended. At first, CBS refused to air the episode at all. Given the panic around young people and sex surrounding *Born Innocent*, the matter of teenage sexuality would likely have seemed forbidden material for the family hour, even when the subject was treated humorously. However, under protest by the show's producers, who held great clout with the network due to the success of programs such as *The Mary Tyler Moore Show*, CBS ultimately allowed the episode. Still, they did require one change — the last line had to be cut. The episode had to end with Phyllis's relieved assertion of "She didn't do it!" No double take, no commentary on the fragility of the mother-daughter relationship, no teenage sex, no punch line.[54] If teen sexuality were to exist at all during the family hour, it would only exist in the negative.

Conflicts such as this one, in which creative decisions were compromised in order to meet the presumed criteria for family viewing, were just the sort of interference the industry's creative personnel feared when the policy was instituted. As a result of these fears, the Writers, Directors, and Screen Actors Guilds, along with several production companies and individual producers (most prominently, Norman Lear and his Tandem Productions) filed suit against the FCC, the Big Three networks, and the NAB, charging that the family hour policy violated the First Amendment because the industry was coerced into adopting it by the FCC. The lawsuit had a chilling effect on network efforts to censor programming, so the kinds of changes CBS demanded of *Phyllis* would not last long. When, in November 1976, Judge Warren Ferguson of the U.S. District Court decided in the plaintiffs' favor, determining that the government had overstepped its bounds in having any part in broadcast content regulation, the family hour policy was removed from the NAB TV Code. The code's power to regulate any program content was thus defused, although the networks all declared that they would continue to follow the policy as a matter of their individual standards.

The Made-for-TV Movie and Endangered Youth:
After Family Viewing

The family viewing policy was the culmination of attempts to regulate young audiences' exposure to "adult" TV content both violent and sexual in the early 1970s. Multiple parties, including the government, citizens' groups, and industry insiders, would continue to try to control what young people could see on television throughout the decade (as well, of course, to the present day). However, because family viewing was relatively short-lived as an official policy, the TV industry's collective efforts to self-regulate were stymied. Also, because the policy was struck down due to the government's violation of the rights of free speech, Congress and the FCC scaled back their efforts at controlling television content. Yet these retreats from official regulation did not mean that concern over the exposure of children and teenagers to the new sexual culture had abated. Television of the 1970s remained intricately embroiled in moral panics around young people and sex; *Born Innocent*'s narrative of youthful innocence lost to sex-themed violence continued.

While *Born Innocent*'s initial impact on the issue of young people and potentially objectionable content seemed to take place in the realm of TV industry and government regulation, in fact the film's influence on the discourse of young people's sexual endangerment would be longer lasting in the realm of fictional representation. From the movie's initial broadcast in the fall of 1974 onward, made-for-TV movies regularly dealt with young people — almost always young women — endangered by or through sex. The moral panic around young people and the new sexual culture played out in a subgenre of the sex-themed made-for-TV movie, pairing moralizing condemnation with audience-grabbing titillation in ways much like *Born Innocent*'s combustible combination of the two.

Family Viewing Makes Its Mark: 1975–76

As short-lived as it was, the family viewing policy did have an impact on the kinds of made-for-TV movies produced and aired, at least for the 1975–76 season. Family viewing affected made-for-TV movies in two key ways during this season. First, the networks greatly reduced the number of ninety-minute movies they scheduled, leaning more heavily toward two-hour pieces while rather drastically reducing the total number of movies on the air. Second, the networks scheduled no sex-themed films, although violence-centered crime stories and dramatizations of real-world events appeared regularly. These shifts are revealing of the intersection between regulatory policy and profit-driven decision making, as well as the special sensitivity surrounding representations of sex (even more so than violence, the networks' choices suggest).

Until the mid-1970s, the majority of made-for-TV movies were ninety minutes long, in keeping with the format pioneered by ABC's *Movie of the Week*. The turn away from the ninety-minute movie in the 1975–76 season was driven by the convergence of two events: Fred Silverman's move from CBS to ABC and the institution of family viewing. Silverman had never been a fan of the ninety-minute made-for-TV movie; his programming style focused instead on series and on two-hour movies crafted and promoted as special events.[55] Silverman's preferences had led CBS to program the fewest movies of the Big Three during his reign there. As the new president of ABC Entertainment, he greatly reduced the number of TV movies on the network, especially ninety-minute features.[56] Because ABC was the leader in made-for-TV movies and the innovator of the ninety-minute format, the other networks followed its changes to the form. In addition, because two-hour films were seen as more prestigious products with higher production values, they cost considerably more than the ninety-minute versions and thus none of the networks were willing to license as many two-hour pieces as they had ninety-minute ones.

The institution of family viewing also affected the turn away from ninety-minute features. During the early 1970s heyday of ABC's ninety-minute *Movie of the Week*, the network often programmed two movies back-to-back in a given night, filling all three hours of prime time. But the typical ninety-minute made-for-TV movie traded in exploitable subject matter that was no longer appropriate for family hour scheduling. These ninety-minute features would thus need to be programmed after the family hour (9 PM EST), taking up the later part of the three-hour prime-time block. This meant that the networks could not schedule violence-heavy action shows at 10 PM, but neither could they schedule these shows at 8 PM because of family hour guidelines.[57] The ninety-minute movie thus became a scheduling problem in addition to being an inappropriate content problem.

The drastic reduction in sex-themed movies was also closely related to the family viewing policy and, I argue, to the disturbing blend of sex and violence in *Born Innocent* and the other sex-themed made-for-TV movies of the 1974–75 season. I have found no comedic or dramatic sex-themed made-for-TV movies in the 1975–76 season, at least in the ways that sex had previously been handled in TV movies. Especially noticeable was the lack of films dealing with rape, prostitution, or teenage sexuality—all themes touched on in movies of previous seasons.[58] At the same time, the networks seemed to have little problem with violence-laden fare. ABC aired such films as *Murder on Flight 502* (21 November 1975) and *The Killer Who Wouldn't Die* (4 April 1976). All three networks ran movies based on real-world violent crime, including *Helter Skelter* (CBS, 1 and 2 April 1976), about the cult leader Charles Manson, *Death Scream* (ABC, 26 September 1975), based on the murder of Kitty Genovese in New York City, and *Guilty or Innocent: The Sam Sheppard Murder Case* (NBC, 17 November 1975). Most of these were two hours or longer and were considered higher quality productions than the old ninety-minute made-for-TV films, but they still dealt with violent crime in ways not necessarily commensurate with the family viewing climate. The noticeable drop in sex-themed movies for the 1975–76 season, without an accompanying drop in violent tales, is quite telling of the sensitivity to sexual themes in particular in the era of family viewing. Yet the sex-themed made-for-TV movie did not permanently disappear from the TV schedule. Indeed, as of the 1976–77 season, the networks revived the sex-themed TV movie and resurrected the discourse of sexually endangered youth.

The Return of the Sex-themed Movie

The return of the sex-themed made-for-TV movie and its discourse of sexually endangered youth in the 1976–77 season illustrates the ultimate ineffectiveness of the family viewing policy as a block to sex and violence in TV programming. Even when the networks continued with a de facto policy of family viewing for the first hour of prime time, made-for-TV movies (which now typically aired at 9 PM EST) wallowed in the kinds of representations of youth under sexual threat that had helped instigate family viewing and the overall regulatory furor concerning young viewers' exposure to potentially damaging TV content. While the institution and eventual demise of family viewing seemed to dampen some of that regulatory furor, many politicians and citizen groups continued to challenge the appropriateness of TV's sex and violence for America's children. How and why, then, were the networks willing to program potentially offensive movies as soon as the 1976–77 season?

In addition to the ultimate unenforceability of family viewing and, by implication, any kind of institutionalized measures for TV content regulation, I see three key reasons why the networks willingly returned to the sex-themed made-for-TV movie in 1976–77. First, made-for-TV movies continued to be a great value, delivering impressive ratings for manageable cost. Production budgets for theatrical releases averaged $4 million in the mid-1970s, while the two-hour made-for-TV movie cost about $775,000. In the 1975–76 season, the networks typically could license a made-for-TV movie for about 30 percent less than they could lease a theatrical one.[59] In addition to being a much more economical choice, made-for-TV movies often garnered ratings equal to—and occasionally even higher than—feature films.[60] Of course, to make the networks' ongoing preference for TV movies work, those movies had to draw audiences consistently. By the second half of the 1970s, networks and producers had settled on some sure-fire strategies to attract viewers, many of which relied upon exploitative elements such as young people in sexual danger. As the producer Frank von Zerneck explained, the network involvement in the production process tended to revolve around one key issue: "Is it going to be a movie they can exploit[?] Will it get an audience[?] Will it have footage that they'll be able to put into a trailer to entice people to watch it[?]"[61]

These imperatives led producers and networks to focus heavily on the movies' titles, *TV Guide* descriptions and advertisements, and opening scenes. As the producer and former ABC executive Deanne Barkley explained, "For the TV movie, there is no word of mouth. Execution is irrelevant. You have only one shot at the audience."[62] Industry wisdom, backed by market research, argued that titles, descriptions, promotions, and openings were most effective in drawing viewers when they trafficked in sexual suggestion. As one CBS executive explained, "You want to hint at sex but not make it too explicit . . . if you combine it with violence, you're golden."[63] Paul Klein, the former programming chief of NBC, who coined such 1970s TV labels as "jiggle" and "kiddie porn," contended that "the very best title [for a TV movie] you could ever come up with would be 'Diary of a Rape.' "[64] Klein's pronouncement was an apt descriptor of many TV movies of the era, apt because the title he chose indirectly referenced both youth and sexual danger. As the standard provenance of the teenage girl, "diary" could easily signify the hidden — and potentially illicit — world of youthful femininity while "rape" could signify both sex and violence. Similarly, the producer Frank von Zerneck demonstrated the ideal *TV Guide* description in this summation of his 1978 film, *Katie: Portrait of a Centerfold* (NBC, 23 October 1978): "*Centerfold*, the story of a girl who becomes a centerfold, and how that wrecks her life."[65] A description like this one suggests youth (the "girl" who becomes the centerfold), sex (the sexual objectification that "centerfold" implies), and danger ("wrecks her life" in unspecified, but presumably harmful, ways). Klein's imagined "Diary of a Rape" title and von Zerneck's potential *TV Guide* description epitomized a certain subgenre of the sex-themed 1970s made-for-TV movie, one that took up the discourse of young women's sexual endangerment. The power of this discourse as an audience draw helped resurrect the sex-themed made-for-TV movie once the regulatory panic that surrounded the family viewing policy had subsided.

A second reason that the networks willingly — even eagerly — returned to the sex-themed made-for-TV movie as of the 1976–77 season was that the form had finally gained a measure of respectability that could usefully deflect attention from the network's more exploitative entries. Although individual films had been critically lauded from the earliest days of TV movies, it wasn't until the 1975–76 season (the season the networks stayed away from the sex-themed film) that films produced for television began to be taken seriously on a wider scale. In this season, the networks followed the path of British broadcasting by broadening the fact-based docudramas they had aired all along to include representations of respected historical figures and events. ABC's *Eleanor and Franklin* (11 and 12 January 1976) won nine Emmy awards and set a precedent for future efforts at historical fiction while the network's twelve-hour *Rich Man, Poor Man* (February and March 1976) proved the critical and ratings power of the miniseries-length "novel for television."[66] The overwhelming success of *Roots* (ABC) in January 1977 further proved to the networks and to television's critics that the medium could provide original, "quality" fare as good as—if not better than—many of the day's theatrical releases.[67] As Elayne Rapping has argued, these developments allowed TV movies to be "used as cultural capital in television's battle for serious attention."[68] Because miniseries and certain movies began to receive so much serious attention in the mid-1970s, the many *other* made-for-TV movies that filled the networks' schedules could attract much less notice and much less negative publicity. The networks could safely return to the sex-themed made-for-TV movie because they had more respectable fare to better balance their reputations in the eyes of viewers, critics, advertisers, and government regulators.

Although these economic and public relations-driven factors help to explain the networks' return to the discourse of sexually endangered youth in made-for-TV movies from the 1976–77 season onward, the third reason that this subgenre returned to the airwaves had to do with the movies' ability both to amplify and to mollify ongoing anxieties about youth sexuality. This discourse continued in the tradition of such movies as *Born Innocent* and *Cage without a Key* by representing the dark and dangerous side of contemporary young women's sexual liberation. While those earlier films saw a violent lesbian sexuality as the nadir of teenage girls' newfound sexual freedom, later made-for-TV movies featuring endangered youth more often represented the perils of heterosexual sex, at least as it was experienced by the underage prostitutes, centerfolds, and hitchhikers—many of them victims of rape or attempted rape—who populated these films. At the same time, this second wave of tele-films shared the earlier films' combination of the titillating and the cautionary, the exploitative and the educational, all the while capitalizing on the day's moral panic around young people's exposure to the new sexual culture.

The Danger Resumes: Sex-themed
Made-for-TV Movies, 1976–1981

The second half of the 1970s saw a range of sex-themed made-for-TV movies. Some of these centered on adult women's sexual troubles, including such films as *Secrets* (ABC, 20 February 1977), *Sharon: Portrait of a Mistress* (NBC, 31 October 1977), *A Question of Love* (NBC, 26 November 1978), *Anatomy of a Seduction* (CBS, 8 May 1979), *Portrait of a Stripper* (CBS, 2 October 1979), *Love for Rent* (ABC, 11 November 1979), and *Portrait of an Escort* (CBS, 8 October 1980). Elayne Rapping has argued that this sort of made-for-TV movie is invariably "about the lives of women who have crossed the line of bourgeois respectability but nonetheless are presented as conventional in their love for their children, their implied or explicit longing for a more conventional female life, and their struggles—sometimes successful, sometimes not—to escape their lifestyles."[69] She argues that the appeal of these films, especially for women viewers, is in watching the heroine act out "old-fashioned sexual rebelliousness" as well as in watching her overcome her troubles and reject her sexually rebellious lifestyle in favor of a normative femininity of "love, marriage, and motherhood."[70]

Rapping's analysis of this brand of sex-themed made-for-TV movie well captures the contradictory meanings such films offer, their exciting representations of sexual liberation most often counterposed with more traditional images of sexuality and femininity. Rapping includes some made-for-TV movies with younger protagonists in her analysis, as well, mentioning *Dawn: Portrait of a Teenage Runaway* and *Katie: Portrait of a Centerfold* along with the "portrait" films about adult women.[71] In contrast, I am setting these films apart from the many sex-themed entries that featured grown women, despite certain similarities in their titles and in their narrative trajectories. Because the discourse of young people's sexual endangerment was so pervasive in television regulation and representation in the 1970s these movies warrant their own treatment, apart from the equally fascinating tales of adult experiences with the new sexual culture.

I have identified at least eleven made-for-TV movies that featured sexually endangered youth between the 1976–77 and 1980–81 seasons (see table 2).[72] Together with the films in this category from the early 1970s, these movies re-

TABLE 2 Made-for-TV Movies Featuring Sexually Endangered Youth

Title	Network	Air date
Born Innocent	NBC	10 September 1974
Sarah T: Portrait of a Teenage Alcoholic	NBC	11 February 1975
Hustling	ABC	22 February 1975
Someone I Touched	ABC	26 February 1975
Cage without a Key	CBS	14 March 1975
Dawn: Portrait of a Teenage Runaway	NBC	27 September 1976
Nightmare in Badham County	ABC	5 November 1976
I Want to Keep My Baby	CBS	19 November 1976
Little Ladies of the Night	ABC	16 January 1977
Alexander: The Other Side of Dawn	NBC	16 May 1977
Black Market Baby	ABC	7 October 1977
Forever	CBS	6 January 1978
Are You in the House Alone?	CBS	20 September 1978
Katie: Portrait of a Centerfold	NBC	23 October 1978
Diary of a Teenage Hitchhiker	ABC	21 September 1979
Fallen Angel	CBS	24 February 1981
No Place to Hide	CBS	4 March 1981

inforced the notion of America's youth being under sexual threat. In addition to the stories they told, these movies also reminded viewers of the dangers for young people who were exposed to the new sexual culture by carrying parental guidance warnings in their promotions, their *TV Guide* listings, and before the films themselves. While this practice was clearly a product of the regulatory pressures that had peaked with the family viewing policy, it was also of a piece with those regulatory pressures. Notices like "Intended for mature audiences. Parental discretion advised," in the *TV Guide* ad for *Dawn* or "Due to mature subject matter, parental discretion is advised," in the magazine's ad for *Little Ladies of the Night* (ABC, 16 January 1977) reiterated the discourse of sexually endangered youth, even as they sought to protect (and, potentially, to appeal to) young viewers.[73]

Most of the films featuring sexually endangered youth continued *Born Innocent*'s formula of social realism paired with salaciousness, attempting a sort of balance between education and exploitation, much like the classical exploitation cinema of the earlier twentieth century. Most of them also resolved their stories by returning the wayward adolescent protagonist to a conventional family setting, either with her parents, a newfound nuclear family, or a monogamous, heterosexual relationship, all of which offered her protection from the sexually liberated society.

The sexually liberated society was represented in different ways in each of these TV movies, but the films had in common a sense of the menace this society held for America's youth — in particular for adolescent girls and young women. For example, Dawn's walk down Hollywood Boulevard with "Cherry Bomb" on the soundtrack is actually her second trip down the infamously seedy strip. She also walks the street when she first arrives in Los Angeles and we see this world through her eyes, shots of its sexual openness juxtaposed with takes of Dawn's shocked reactions. As she leaves the bus station, a man in a suit brushes past her and she is noticeably disturbed. As she crosses the street, a man on a motorcycle gestures for her to get on and she hurries past him. As she walks, she sees a man covered in tattoos, a midget, and an effeminate hippie-type coming out of the International Love Boutique; Dawn's eyes widen in surprise. From Dawn's point of view, we see words such as "Massage," "Nudity," "Girls," and "Pussycat" on the storefront signs that surround her. In the distance, a movie marquee advertises *Deep Throat* and *The Devil in Miss Jones*, those icons of 1970s hard-core pornography. At the corner of Hollywood and Vine, a bald, middle-aged white man pulls up in a convertible and asks, "Want a ride?" Moments later, several black men talk to Dawn, trying to block her way. She then passes two young girls, one of whom is visibly pregnant. The sequence ends with Dawn crouched in an alley after being mugged. The message of the sequence is clear: Dawn has entered a dangerous, licentious world where men seek to exploit her sexually; her fate is to wind up pregnant, destitute, and alone.

All of the made-for-TV movies that center on sexually endangered youth represent the post–sexual revolution society in similarly menacing ways. In *Little Ladies of the Night,* the runaway teen Hailey Atkins is lured into prostitution by a smooth-talking black pimp named Comfort who promises to love her and take care of her. Hailey's lost innocence is primarily represented through the change in her appearance and demeanor over the course of the film (a transformation Dawn also undergoes). When one of Comfort's more experienced prostitutes coaches Hailey, she still looks like a kid; her hair is in a ponytail, she is dressed in jeans and a t-shirt, with a sweatshirt tied around her waist. Toward the end of the film, she is hardened, corrupted by the sexually exploitative world. She wears hot pants, a glittery top, and heavy make-up, she smokes, she says "ain't," she boldly kisses a john in front of York, the former pimp turned cop who is trying to save her.

The pimps in both *Dawn* and *Little Ladies* serve as representatives of the sexually loose society and its particular threat to youth. Their one-word names (Swan and Comfort, respectively) sound as if they were chosen for their cuddly appeal to young girls. Their slick ways — nice cars, fashionable clothing, stylish apartments, and smooth talk promising love and security — lure the girls into their sleazy worlds. The fact that Comfort is black even further signifies the sordidness of Hailey's situation, given the damaging history of white America seeing black men as white women's sexual predators. In fact, the presence of black characters in the underworlds of several of these films may likely have been read as further proof of the corruption of the young white protagonists' virtue. For instance, even though Dawn's pimp, Swan, is white, the prostitute who first brings Dawn to Swan is a young black woman named Frankie Lee. Similarly, in *Katie: Portrait of a Centerfold*, the photographer who shoots Katie's nude centerfold is a black man. Ultimately, the ubiquitous whiteness of the girls whose innocence is lost in these films makes it seem as if *white* innocence in particular is in peril — and that black prostitutes, pimps, and other members of the sexually free society are key participants in the white girls' downfalls.

Sex spells doom for the young runaways-turned-prostitutes in films such as *Dawn* and *Little Ladies*, but the threats of the sexually open society pervade more seemingly benign environments, as well. In *Are You in the House Alone?* (CBS, 20 September 1978), the Osborne family has moved to the small town of Oldenfield for its safety, but Gail Osborne, a high school student, is raped by her best friend's boyfriend while she is babysitting. Similarly, *Diary of a Teenage Hitchhiker* (ABC, 21 September 1979) depicts the sexual dangers for young, middle-class white women who use hitchhiking as an everyday form of transportation. Julie, the film's seventeen-year-old protagonist, and her girl-friends all hitch rides with threatening men. One friend, Kathy, is raped and beaten; another, Dana, is killed. Although all of the men who pick up these girls are represented as potentially threatening, the biggest danger they face is represented not by a driver but by his car, a large black vehicle that blindingly reflects the sun in its metallic wheels and shiny, pointy, phallic tailpipe. This car appears three times in the film, twice as threats to Julie and once as a danger to two anonymous hitchhiking girls. After the car picks up these girls, we see its massive wheels roll over their torn clothing, a telltale sign of their tragic fate. In these ways, the men who pick up hitchhikers in their menacing cars are clear symbols of the sexually dangerous society. However, the girls themselves are also meant to signify the sexually open world. One of the girls picked up by the evil black car wears a t-shirt reading "X Rated," thereby marking herself as sexualized prey. Julie's single friend, Kathy, is pregnant (she miscarries as a result of being attacked while hitching), the girls joke around about which of them is still a virgin, and Dana declares that the smart response to an impending rape is either to "let him have what he [wants]" or "Tell 'em you have vd!" In this film, the girls' attitudes, behavior, and clothing signal the new sexual culture as much as do the external sexual threats they face.

Diary is one of the few films featuring young people's sexual endangerment that places some of the blame for their troubles with the young women themselves. Still, the placement of blame remains ambiguous here, wavering between the girls, their out-of-touch parents, and an immoral society (one that sells "X Rated" t-shirts to teens). The sexually endangered youth in other films are even more explicitly depicted as innocent victims, with external forces, often elements of the adult society, leading them to harm. The runaways-turned-prostitutes in *Dawn, Alexander: The Other Side of Dawn* (NBC, 16 May 1977), and *Little Ladies* have troubled home lives that drive them to the streets. The promises of love, protection, and security their pimps offer are hollow substitutes for needs that are supposed to be filled by their parents. The protagonists in other films in this cycle are also represented as victims. The innocent and modest Katie McEvers in *Portrait of a Centerfold* is driven into the porn industry out of financial desperation and a naive desire for stardom. The virginal and pious Ann Macarino of *Black Market Baby* (ABC, 7 October 1977) is tricked into an unwed pregnancy through the scheming of a corrupt lawyer running a baby-selling racket. Although the characters' actions (for example, Katie agreeing to pose nude or Ann sleeping with Steve) often lead to their troubles, those actions are portrayed sympathetically, as products of their innocence, not of their lack of morals.

While the films surely held appeal for young viewers eager for sympathetic representations of their generation, they were also framed as warnings for par-

THE GIRL BY THE SIDE OF THE ROAD

You've seen her standing there. Thumb out.
Smiling. There are thousands like her all over
America. And you've heard about what
happens to some of them when they get
into the wrong car. This movie is about
one of these kids. And about her family.
But it could be about your family.
Where is your daughter tonight?

Diary of a Teenage Hitchhiker

CHARLENE TILTON · KATHERINE HELMOND · KATY KURTZMAN · DICK VAN PATTEN

A WORLD TELEVISION PREMIERE

ABC FRIDAY NIGHT MOVIE 8:00 PM 2

9 Display ad for *Diary of a Teenage Hitchhiker*, TV Guide, 15 September 1979, A-129.

ents. Made-for-TV movies have long been considered women-targeted programming. Network wisdom argued that women made the decisions about
what to watch on TV in the 1970s, unlike the male prerogative that pre-
vailed when it came to theatrical movie-going; thus TV movies were designed
with "female appeal."[74] This "female appeal" included promotional tactics designed to attract adult women, in particular mothers, to the stories of sexually
endangered youth. For example, the *TV Guide* ad for *Diary of a Teenage Hitchhiker* described "the girl by the side of the road" and declared, "This movie
is about one of these kids. And about her family. But it could be about your
family. Where is your daughter tonight?" (see figure 9). The ad included pho-
tos of four of the film's actors: Charlene Tilton, who played Julie, Katherine
Helmond and Dick Van Patten, who played her parents, and Katy Kurtzman,
who played her younger sister. Julie's friends and the older man she dates
played roles at least as large, if not larger, than her family, but the decision to
focus the ad on the parent figures was surely one calculated to appeal to parent viewers. Certainly, Tilton, Helmond, and Van Patten were well-known TV

actors and so showcasing them in the film's promotion was a logical move. However, the choice to cast Helmond and Van Patten as Julie's parents, as opposed to lesser-known actors, illustrates how significant the parent figures were for the movie's audience appeal. Also, the fact that Kurtzman's photo is included in the ad demonstrates the network's effort to emphasize the family issues in the story, since Kurtzman was not a well-known performer and her character is a rather minor one in the actual film.

In addition to the parental guidance labels often applied to the films, the stories they told cautioned parents about their own complicity in their children's endangerment. In *Are You in the House Alone?*, Gail's parents are too busy with their own problems for her to tell them about the menacing notes and phone calls she has been receiving, which, it turns out, come from her future rapist. In *Little Ladies of the Night*, Hailey's overly attached father and emotionally removed mother host a cocktail party while their daughter wanders the streets of Los Angeles in the rain, homeless, destitute, and alone. When Hailey calls home and asks if she can return, her mother says no because "Everything's been so wonderful between us since you've been gone." In *Alexander: The Other Side of Dawn*, we learn that Alex left home when his father refused to support him unless he worked on the family farm. Because Alex wants to draw instead of farm, he heads to Los Angeles for art school, only to end up a street hustler. Like Hailey's mother, Alex's mother tells him not to come back home when he calls and asks to return. In addition, when Alex attends a rap session at a gay youth center, the young men talk about the ways their fathers failed them by rejecting their homosexuality. In movie after movie, the adults' poor parenting practices have left the young people vulnerable to the horrors of society in the aftermath of the sexual revolution. The stories thus served as warnings to the parents in the audience who were already on guard against their children's exposure to television's new sexual culture.

The films' representations of poor parenting may have offered cautionary messages to real-world parents, but these representations may also have appealed to real-world teens seeking to blame parents for their own troubles (even if those troubles were not nearly as dramatic as those of the on-screen youth). The films tended to portray the young people's plights sympathetically, blaming parents or the sexually corrupting society for their losses of innocence. Even though the movies often carried parental guidance warnings and addressed parents in their promotional materials, they were also clearly designed to appeal to young viewers. The same *Diary* ad that asked, "Where is your daughter tonight?" also depicted a full-length photo of a young woman's back as she thumbs a ride. Her white short-shorts and her tube top matched the fashion of the day, and the film's title was written in a girlish script. Because these movies had young protagonists, producers cast well-known teen stars such as *The Brady Bunch*'s Eve Plumb (*Dawn* and *Alexander*) and Christopher Knight (*Diary*), *Dallas*'s Charlene Tilton (*Diary*), and others such as Mariel Hemingway (*I Want to Keep My Baby*, CBS, 19 November 1976), Stephanie Zimbalist (*Forever*, CBS, 6 January 1978), and Kathleen Beller (*Are You in the House Alone?* CBS, 20 September 1978, and *No Place to Hide*, CBS, 4 March 1981). Young viewers may have taken the same cautionary messages from the films as did their parents, but they were also more likely to take pleasure in seeing young people living sexually adventurous lives, even if those lives sometimes caused them harm.

To Warn and to Arouse: Made-for-TV Movies as Exploitation Pictures

The combination of the titillating and the cautionary in the appeal of these movies functioned much like the "classical" exploitation cinema of the earlier twentieth century, including the movies' ultimately reactionary response to the society's changing sexual mores. As Eric Schaefer has argued, "Far from expressing a radical social agenda, [classical exploitation] films offered a fundamentally conservative prescription for American life in the twentieth century."[75] Schaefer points out that exploitation films were typically "fueled by moral panic," such as the white slavery scare of 1913 or fears of venereal disease in the later teens.[76] The moral panic around young people's exposure to the new sexual culture fueled this subgenre of the sex-themed made-for-TV movie in ways very similar to the sex hygiene or vice-centered exploitation films Schaefer analyzes. In these earlier films, "the city was an ominous place for young women," it was a "territory of predators who preyed upon single, usually young females."[77] However, instead of allowing this titillating content to offer audiences an imagined alternative to the strictures of bourgeois society, the classical exploitation films—and the 1970s made-for-TV movies—used titillation to serve up cautionary provisos about the changing culture.

The promotion of the TV movies featuring sexually endangered youth

10 Display ad for *Little Ladies of the Night, TV Guide,* 15 January 1977, A-40.

heavily referenced the exploitation film tradition. The *Little Ladies of the Night* ad in *TV Guide* included the headline: "IF YOU ARE A CONCERNED PARENT, YOU OWE IT TO YOURSELF TO SEE THIS MOTION PICTURE" (see figure 10). The ad for *Nightmare in Badham County* (ABC, 5 November 1976) announced, "SLAVERY IS NOT A THING OF THE PAST!" followed by slightly smaller text reading, "The sadistic sheriff knows it. The psychotic warden knows it. But two girls, alone in a women's prison learn it the hard way" (see figure 11). In keeping with the made-for-TV movie tradition of attracting audiences with shocking or suggestive titles, descriptions, and opening scenes, the display ads promoting many of these films used overblown language to communicate their panicked warnings and intimations of sex and violence.

As much as the networks willingly employed these exploitation tactics to draw audiences, they constantly struggled to justify the movies' sometimes scandalous subject matter and to protect themselves against criticism by the FCC, affiliated stations, advertisers, and the viewing public. Thus, the film's producers walked a careful line between promising the networks attention-

11 Display ad for *Nightmare in Badham County*, TV *Guide*, 30 October 1976, A-106.

grabbing content and reassuring jittery executives of their films' appropriateness for the "family" medium. For example, the executive producer Douglas Cramer scrambled to reassure ABC's finance executive, Mark Cohen, that the rough footage he had seen from *Nightmare*'s foreign distribution version would never be submitted for broadcast. Cramer described the footage as "shoddy," "really vulgar," "tacky and tawdry," and assured Cohen that the footage "in no way represented something [he] would care to have anyone consider something [he] either approved or condoned."[78] Cramer's disapproval of the footage was no doubt somewhat put on for the network's benefit, as he would later distribute a home video version of the film that included nudity and explicit language. Even though Cramer had to make this extra effort to mollify the network about *Nightmare*'s potentially shocking content, ABC executives were interested in the film, at least in part, for that very potential. The ABC executive Brandon Stoddard found the film's "white slavery aspect" one of its most compelling features, one that would distinguish the movie from other women-in-prison pictures.[79]

The networks' desire to have it both ways—to reap the ratings benefits of exploitation while retaining respectability and avoiding a *Born Innocent*-like outcry—helped keep the TV movies featuring sexually endangered youth teetering between the titillating and the cautionary. As Len Hill, ABC's one-time vice-president in charge of made-for-TV movies, justified *Diary of a Teenage Hitchhiker*, "Certainly in the promo there were aspects designed to appeal to the excitement and entertainment interest of the audience. In the subject matter itself, there were values beyond that."[80] In meeting these dueling network desires, producers rooted their movies in real-world social problems and negotiated with writers, actors, and network executives to tell stories that fit their more licentious elements under a banner of social responsibility. Thus, Douglas Cramer pitched *Dawn* to NBC as "an honest, authentic, tasteful, and yet deeply moving picture" on the "serious current problem of teen-age runaways" and documented his seriousness with newspaper clippings and reports of the scriptwriter's extensive research.[81] He consulted with Newton Dieter of the Gay Media Task Force for *Alexander* and struggled with how to deal with Alex's experiences without too explicitly representing or referencing gay male sexual activity.[82]

The classical exploitation cinema also attempted to balance the titillating and the cautionary, and a key tactic for doing so was the square-up, "a prefatory statement about the social or moral ill the film claimed to combat."[83] Such square-ups were common to the TV movies featuring sexually endangered youth, as well. In addition to the warnings in ads for films such as *Diary*, some films included a square-up at the movie's start. For instance, *Little Ladies of the Night* begins with a voice-over proclaiming, "This is Hailey. She's a runaway. The number of teenage kids who run away from home in this country each year numbers close to 1 million. It has become a major social issue. The story of their life on the street is not a pretty one. But it's one our society must cope with. This film is a warning to teenagers. And to you parents. Because you don't want to find your kid here."[84] In addition to warning parents and addressing teens, this square-up prepared viewers for the somewhat scandalous content to come and, even more importantly, provided a socially responsible justification for that content.[85] Schaefer points out that by the late 1950s, sexploitation films no longer employed the square-up because such educational justification was no longer necessary in a changed economic, social, and moral climate. By that point in U.S. history, he argues, male sexual desire had become economically legitimate.[86] By the 1970s, that desire would become even more economically viable—and socially acceptable—with the mainstream-ing of hard-core pornographic film. Yet 1970s made-for-TV movies still found the square-up a useful, even an essential, technique, one that could buttress the authenticity and social value of their titillating displays. The persistence of this strategy in television after it lost its utility for feature films demonstrates the television industry's anxiety about its social legitimacy and its investment in being considered a family medium, suitable for all ages, even when airing exploitable material.

The 1970s TV movies featuring sexually endangered youth also defused their controversial potential by resolving their narratives in ways conventional to much commercial television. In this respect, these films follow the same for-mula that Rapping identifies for the made-for-TV movies dealing with "adult" sexual issues, returning their heroines to bourgeois respectability. For ex-ample, Katie McEvers leaves Hollywood and her life in the porn industry be-hind when she discovers that her boyfriend, a former athlete, does not love her but is using her in his ongoing quest to sleep with every centerfold. *Little Ladies of the Night* ends with Hailey giving up prostitution and rejoining the nuclear family, in this case that of one of the detectives who helps her.[87] While the conclusion of *Dawn* leaves the teen still struggling to rid her life of pros-titution, its sequel, *Alexander*, ties up both films by allowing Dawn and Alex to leave L.A. together. They plan to marry and start a new life, one more in keeping with conventional morality.

Both *Dawn* and *Alexander* deliberately move toward this resolution; the characters' romance competes with their lives as prostitutes as the central focus of the narratives. The films carefully construct that romance, including its sexual element, in traditional ways, differentiating this kind of sex from the sex-for-hire that corrupts and endangers both young people. In fact, the scene in which Dawn and Alex first make love was described as "all-important (climactically and conceptually)" by the film's executive producer, Douglas Cramer (see figure 12). Both he and NBC executive Joe Taritero agreed that the scene needed to be "as poetically expressive and pictorially tasteful an artistic representation of the action as possible."[88] Although it would be more explicit than either Dawn's or Alex's sex scenes with paying clients, it needed to be markedly different from those scenes in tone and style. After all, this scene would help to set up the loving, monogamous, heterosexual romantic rela-

12 Dawn (Eve Plumb) and Alex (Leigh McCloskey) make love, *Dawn: Portrait of a Teenage Runaway*, NBC, 27 September 1976. COURTESY DOUGLAS S. CRAMER COLLECTION, AMERICAN HERITAGE CENTER.

tionship that would ultimately resolve both film's narratives, thus shooting and editing it expressively, tastefully, and artistically was crucial to the movies' conventional happy ending and to this subgenre's effort to offer exploitation-style pictures in TV-friendly form.

Yet as often as the made-for-TV movies featuring sexually endangered youth sought to return their young protagonists to more respectable circumstances by film's end, they rarely had altogether happy endings. In fact, such films often concluded with the suggestion that the problem of young people's sexual endangerment had not been solved, even if the film's protagonist had found a more wholesome life. In this respect, these films did not necessarily follow the path of the movies Rapping discusses, in which the sexually beleaguered heroines ultimately embrace conventional love and marriage and bourgeois respectability is thus restored. For instance, *Diary of a Teenage Hitchhiker* ends with Julie learning her lesson about hitching and embarking on a romance with her new boyfriend, Ron. But the final shots of the film are of girls continuing to hitchhike — including Julie's little sister, Trish. At the end of *Alexander*, Dawn and Alex hop on a bus to their new life, having escaped the seedy underworld of Hollywood, but we see another young man getting off a bus at the same time, seeking a better life in Los Angeles but surely headed for his sexual undoing. And at the end of *Katie*, another innocent young woman seeking fame as a model moves into Katie's former apartment and takes a call from the *Center Girl* magazine editor who roped Katie into the porn world. Such endings further reinforced the discourse of sexual endangerment, instigating even more anxiety for the parent-viewer, but they also offered more potential for titillation in keeping with the exploitation film tradition. Despite the films' moralizing messages, viewers could imagine that young people would continue to get themselves into sexually compromising situations in defiance of both traditional morality and conventional understandings of childhood. Even in their final moments, the somber warnings of the made-for-TV movies featuring sexually endangered youth wallowed in prurient pleasures.

Resolving the Discourse of Sexual Endangerment

By the 1980–81 season, the networks had begun to scale back on the made-for-TV movies centering on sexually endangered youth. However, CBS aired two movies early in 1981 that served as last gasps of the subgenre. The more significant of the two, *Fallen Angel*, aired during the February ratings sweeps period and helped CBS to place first in the network ratings race for that month.[89] This tele-film took the form to new extremes with its tale of a preteen girl who falls prey to child pornographers. A twelve-year-old, Jennifer Phillips is the youngest protagonist of the 1970s TV movies featuring sexually endangered youth. Jennifer is a troubled child; her father has recently died and her mother has already found a new boyfriend. Jennifer is charmed by a kids' softball coach, Howard Nichols, who is also a child-porn casting director, a pedophile, and a clear father substitute. Jennifer gradually sinks deeper and deeper into his world until she is rescued by her mother just before Howard would have molested her, but not before she has posed nude multiple times.

The story and stock characters would have been familiar to any viewer who had seen similar made-for-TV movies in recent years, but *Fallen Angel* takes this wave of the discourse of sexual endangerment to its peak. First, Jennifer's age makes her victimization all the more threatening; the sexually loose culture has reached beyond teens and young adults to harm children in this movie's worldview. Second, the film is relatively explicit about the sexual danger Jennifer and the other children face. The opening scene takes place on a child-porn movie set, and we learn that the young girl involved is pregnant by Howard. Later on, we watch Jennifer's frightened face as Howard convinces her to remove her bathing suit for the camera. These suggestions of adult-child sexual activity broach taboos not previously explored in the made-for-TV movie, giving the film's titillating and cautionary messages more intensity than previously seen.

The third way in which *Fallen Angel* took television's discourse of sexual endangerment to its most extreme was in its reference to television as a factor in the dangers of the new sexual culture. While previous films had referenced such cultural markers as hard-core porn theaters, adult bookstores, and disco music, *Fallen Angel* included television in that mix. For example, one of the signs of Jennifer's vulnerability to pedophiles, according to the police detective Jennifer's mother turns to for help, is her propensity for watching a lot of television. The television is often on at Jennifer's house and at the apartment Howard keeps for his young models. In Howard's initial play for Jennifer's attention, he references popular female sex symbols, first Olivia Newton-John and then Farrah Fawcett-Majors. As he snaps Jennifer's picture, he teases, "Bet you photograph exactly like Olivia Newton-John," and after he shoots it he claims, "Not even close to Olivia Newton-John. Farrah Fawcett." When he leaves that first encounter, he says, "See you around . . . Angel," the pet name he will call her throughout the film. While "Angel" is not solely a reference to the sex symbols of *Charlie's Angels*, it inevitably evokes that association, especially coming so soon after the reference to Fawcett-Majors. Lastly, the film hints that television is complicit with the threat to youth in its ending voice-over. The voice-over is the closing statement of the prosecuting attorney at Howard's trial, but its remove from the visual image of the attorney as she speaks makes it more like a square-up than a piece of the diegesis. After listing statistics about kids running away from home, committing suicide, and ending up in mental hospitals, the voice-over warns, "Many children rarely relate to their parents, the adults in their community, or the adults on television. And into this void walks the pedophile, the child lover. . . ." While the movie offers other explanations for Howard's behavior and the children's vulnerability to it (mostly problematic parenting), its suggestion that television is one of the dangers — or at least an indication of the dangers — that children face asserted the medium's role as a threat to youth as well as a site for the representation of that threat.

As much as *Fallen Angel* represented the final peak of its subgenre, made-for-TV movies did not give up sexual themes with the close of the 1970s. The imagined audience appeal of such exploitable material means that it will likely appear on television indefinitely. But the TV movies dealing with young people and tapping into adult anxieties about the next generation began to take on a wider range of themes as of the early 1980s. Teens in tele-films began to join cults (*Blinded by the Light*, CBS, 16 December 1980), take drugs (*Angel Dusted*, NBC, 16 February 1981; *Desperate Lives*, CBS, 3 March 1982), and get eating disorders (*The Best Little Girl in the World*, ABC, 11 May 1981). Teens in TV movies still got into some sexual danger during this time, but the wider diversity of troubles they faced helped make television's discourse of sexual endangerment less narrowly focused. In addition, the increasing power of the religious right in efforts to reform TV content began to make concerns about TV's impact on young people less the provenance of adult society at large and more the battle-ax of special interest groups.

The discourse of young people's sexual endangerment pervaded two mutually reinforcing sites in the 1970s: made-for-TV movies and regulatory debates around TV content. The family viewing policy and the regulatory uproar that surrounded it suggested that exposure to sexual and violent television would lead to harmful sexual and violent behaviors in America's youth. Made-for-TV movies that told stories of young people under sexual threat represented the consequences of those behaviors. Both discursive sites — the regulatory and the representational — perpetuated a moral panic around children, teens, and the sexual revolution. Both discursive sites suggested that only heightened vigilance on the part of adults could protect the young from the licentious society.

Yet in the very act of watching these made-for-TV movies, children and teens could subvert that adult vigilance and control. Because part of the adult world's effort to shield young people from the new sexual culture involved keeping them from sex-and-violence-themed television, watching that sort of television was one way that kids refused to mind the strict boundary between childhood and adulthood. As Pam Brownell's and Lisa Stewart's interest in

The Runaways' song "Cherry Bomb" from *Dawn* suggests, if and when those kids watched the made-for-TV movies featuring sexually endangered youth, they could vicariously experience "adult" knowledge through the films' protagonists. While the movie's scare tactics might have deterred young viewers from their own explorations with "adult" sexuality, it is also possible—indeed likely—that young viewers found Katie's or Dawn's or Alex's or Julie's or Ann's or Jennifer's experiences liberating. Despite the hardships they suffer, these characters all manage to strike out on their own in some way. They break away from parents, from school, from typical teenage peers and their pressures and often come out of their travails stronger and freer and happier. Katie exuberantly rides off on the back of her friend Madeleine's motorcycle, headed for a new life in New York City. Dawn and Alex happily board a bus to their future, entwined in each other's arms. Julie leaves her parents' home to train with a famous sculptor and pursue a romance with Ron. Ann walks away from the deceptive Steve, cradling the baby she will proudly raise on her own. Even young Jennifer, now thirteen, stands up to Howard and testifies against him, reclaiming her body and her sexuality. Yes, these characters' involvements with the sexually loose society endanger them and, yes, the films do suggest that these dangers cannot be easily removed. But for the youth audience of the 1970s, the sexually open society was full of exciting possibilities, and television's made-for-TV movies allowed them an early glimpse into that scary, but promising, new world.

— 4 —

SYMBOLS OF SEX
TELEVISION'S WOMEN AND SEXUAL DIFFERENCE

On an average school day in 1977, six fourth-grade girls gathered together to answer a question posed to them by an inquiring journalist. Their answer was unanimous and they shouted it out with emphatic gusto. "Far-rah Fawcett-Majors!" they yelled, in answer to the open-ended question, "If you could be anyone in the world, who would you want to be?" One girl explained her choice: "Because she's pretty," while another offered more specific reasoning: "Because she looks like my Barbie doll." In a poll of one thousand students that same year, these six girls joined with hundreds of other girls between the ages of six and eighteen to choose Fawcett-Majors as the famous person they would most like to be.[1] Young girls were not alone in their adoration of the winged-haired actress. Countless girls and women attempted to adopt her gravity-defying hairstyle and, by the summer of 1977, her first poster had set a sales record, with 8 million copies papering bedroom walls (see figure 13). Meanwhile, in the same poll in which girls overwhelmingly chose Fawcett-Majors, grade school and teenage boys chose her husband, Lee Majors, the star of the *Six Million Dollar Man*, as the person they'd most like to be because, according to one respondent, "I'd sure like to come home to *her* every night."[2]

13 Farrah Fawcett-Majors, circa 1976. PHOTOFEST.

While Farrah Fawcett-Majors was arguably the most celebrated example of television stardom in the 1970s, she was one of many women who drew such adoration. During the decade, a range of female performers engaged the public's attention and fascination. Along with Fawcett-Majors's *Charlie's Angels* co-stars, Kate Jackson, Jaclyn Smith, and Cheryl Ladd, series regulars Angie Dickinson, Teresa Graves, Lynda Carter, Lindsay Wagner, Suzanne Somers, Catherine Bach, Lydia Cornell, and Loni Anderson were joined by popular guest stars Charo, Barbi Benton, Judy and Audrey Landers, Roz Kelly, and the ubiquitous Dallas Cowboys Cheerleaders to make television host to the largest number of so-called sex symbols in the medium's history. Their predictable presence in a variety of television genres, from the sitcom to the action-adventure series, earned the phenomenon a litany of derogatory labels —jiggle TV, T and A television, smutcom, mammary madness, sexploitation, and girlie show, to name a few. As some of the most visible symbols of television's turn to sex, these women were central to television's new sexual culture. Through these stars and the characters they played, television of the 1970s represented sex and the new sexual culture as rooted in sexual difference, the newly contested notion of woman's essential difference from man. Sexy young women could symbolize sex because they could stand in for that fundamental difference, a difference that enabled and justified heterosexuality while perpetuating traditional gender roles.

When the female sex symbol first became a major feature of prime-time television, she was both popular and controversial because she often seemed to *transcend* traditional gender roles; she seemed to be very much "of the moment," the moment of women's liberation. Some of the most prominent of these TV characters—like the Angels or Lynda Carter's Wonder Woman— were engaged in distinctly nonfeminine pursuits. They solved crimes, hunted down criminals, and adeptly used weapons and their own physical strength to accomplish their goals. They were thus one way the television industry sought to make itself seem current. No longer would television's female characters be stuck in the kitchen or on some playboy's arm. Now they could have careers, could get into—and out of—dangerous circumstances, and still be as pretty as ever. Television's emphasis on the women's physical attractiveness was one key way that traditional gender roles were reiterated. But it was the combination of the conventionally masculine and the conventionally feminine in these characters that spoke to the question of sexual difference, of woman's difference from man and the degree to which that difference was natural as opposed to social. This question was central to the women's liberation movement and debates over it, to the television industry's struggle over what kinds of representations of women would be acceptable to the public, and to the television audience's conflicted responses to the medium's new female character type. Indeed, TV's sex-symbol women allowed viewers to accept *and* reject the ideas about sex and gender up for debate in the era of women's liberation and the sexual revolution.

Debating Difference: Feminism, Anti-feminism and the Debate over Sexual Difference

The women's liberation movement had such a large impact on U.S. culture of the 1970s because the movement's claims challenged the received wisdom, the "common sense" of many people's daily lives. Central to that common sense was the notion that men and women are different. For many, this difference was evident not only in men's and women's bodies, but also in their behaviors, their thoughts, their interactions with the world—indeed, in the very essence of their beings. When feminists began to question the supposed naturalness of that difference and to suggest that this supposed difference had led to women's oppression, they struck at the heart of many people's senses of themselves and their world.

The feminist challenge to the notion of sexual difference came from both radical and mainstream factions of the movement, each with their own take on difference, its impact on women's subordination, and ways to combat it. Radical feminism tended to follow the path laid by the French feminist Simone de Beauvoir in the 1950s. Beauvoir saw the identification of women with their bodies and thus as different from men as one of the root strategies of patriarchal oppression.[3] Radical feminists of the 1970s updated Beauvoir's perspective by echoing the link between biology and women's social role and by calling for the elimination of sexual difference as a cultural category.[4] More mainstream discourses of women's liberation, in particular the campaign around the proposed Equal Rights Amendment, assisted the widespread understanding of feminism as erasing, or at least refusing to acknowledge, all differences between men and women. Although the ERA ultimately failed to gain the necessary number of state ratifications to be added to the U.S. Constitution, it was a major rallying point for feminist organizing, accounting for a vast increase in feminist allegiance.[5]

Despite this wave of feminist affiliation, the ERA and the more radical feminist stances that rejected sexual difference faced severe opposition both inside and outside the women's movement. Within the movement, the refusal of sexual difference on the part of radical feminists led to disputes over which women could rightly be counted as feminists, which women could rightly be said to have rejected sexual difference. Anne Koedt, a writer and an activist in the women's movement, told of "women being told they could not be trusted as feminists because they wore miniskirts, because they were married . . . or because they wanted to have children."[6] Lesbian members of the movement were sometimes distrusted as feminists, in part because of straight feminist distaste for the butch and femme sex roles they saw as carrying over from patriarchal society into some lesbian relationships.

Ongoing activism by lesbians and by straight feminists who were uncomfortable with radical feminism's censure of insufficient sex and gender ambiguity helped develop a strand of feminism that endorsed the opposite extreme of the radical feminists' refusal of sexual difference. These feminists insisted on woman's fundamental difference from man and emphasized the nurturing and romantic aspects of women's sexuality in contrast to the aggressive, genitally-focused sexuality they attributed to the opposite sex.[7] Cultural or "difference" feminism gets its name from its insistence on, and celebration of, a separate woman's culture that validates the female body, feminine experience, and the feminist power to be found in those spheres.[8] Woman's difference from man underlies all cultural feminist thought, and often that difference is seen as natural and biological, with women's reproductive functions as a central, heralded part of their difference.

Yet the challenge to the movement's rejection of sexual difference came from *anti*-feminists, as well. The most vocal and powerful of the anti-feminist constituencies were the many women who devoted themselves to opposing stridently the movement that attempted to speak for them. Most often, this opposition took the form of anti-ERA activism, but undergirding the anti-ERA platform were claims about sexual difference, claims that rejected the radical and mainstream feminist stances on difference and that passionately argued that the differences between men and women should not only be preserved, but celebrated. Organizations such as STOP ERA, founded by the right-wing activist Phyllis Schlafly, as well as groups such as Women Who Want to Be Women, Happiness of Womanhood, and Females Opposed to Equality, fought for a recognition of sexual difference as the foundation of human experience. Such groups declared that pro-ERA feminists were "women-who-want-to-be-men," and that their push for a unisex world would rob women of important protections.[9]

Although the anti-ERA groups had a distinct political purpose, they also had a significant impact on many Americans, largely because their endorsement of a fundamental, irrevocable, and beneficial sexual difference resonated with many people's heretofore unquestioned beliefs about sex and gender. For example, Mary Donnelly, a fifty-nine-year-old Catholic housewife and an anti-ERA activist, expressed the pull many must have felt between feminism's potential and its problems for the notion of fundamental sexual difference: "I have three daughters so of course I want equal rights for them. I just don't want them saddled with having to be like a man."[10] For Donnelly and many others, the women's movement offered some exciting opportunities, but it also threatened the way she understood herself and her world. The debate over sexual difference within the women's movement, between the movement and its detractors, and across the society complicated the question of women's and men's proper roles — both in the real world and on television. As a participant in this debate that was eager, as always, to please a wide audience, the television industry would seek to balance the promise of women's liberation with the security of immutable sexual difference. In the process, television's New Woman would become a sex symbol, and the medium would lay yet another path to the new sexual culture.

Programming Difference: Seeking the New Woman

As cultural figures who helped the American public deal with its uncertainty over the women's movement, its impact on women's social roles, and its implications for the question of sexual difference, television's female sex symbols were as central to many people's senses of sex and gender in the 1970s as were the feminists, anti-feminists, and commentators who publicly debated such matters. But the sex symbol's arrival on television — and especially her immense popularity mid-decade with the near-simultaneous appearance of *Charlie's Angels*, *Wonder Woman*, and *The Bionic Woman* — was the product of years of negotiation within the television industry over just what kind of female characters audiences would accept and welcome. In the 1970s, television's representation of women changed, allowing women to lead action-adventure series and to take on conventionally male tasks in those series. Fashioning these women leads as sex symbols was both a deliberate strategy to make them publicly palatable and a logical outgrowth of the society's conflicted feelings on the questions of sexual difference and the new sexual culture.

Changing the Television Woman

As television historians have shown, representations of women on American television in the medium's first two decades had some definite limits, even though many characters frequently transgressed those limits. From Lucy's schemes to enter show business (*I Love Lucy*, CBS, 1951–57) to Samantha's shortcuts on housework (*Bewitched*, ABC, 1964–72), television's women characters regularly sought ways out of their roles as wives, mothers, or girlfriends, but remained steadfastly — and mostly happily — fixed in those roles.

The occasional female character who took up an unconventional career or who remained single was more an anomaly than a rupture in television's typical gender representations.[11] By the late 1960s, however, the television industry was beginning to consider a more marked change in these representations. Such change gradually moved forward in response to the transforming social climate. However, the TV industry was not motivated simply by the persuasiveness of the women's movement's rhetoric. Instead, networks and producers were motivated by specific economic pressures that the women's movement indirectly intensified.

From its earliest days, the U.S. commercial television industry has eagerly targeted women as a primary audience for its programming and, most importantly, for its sponsors' goods.[12] With the more sophisticated audience measurement tools of the late 1960s, market research determined that eighteen- to forty-nine-year-old women were the most desirable television audience because they were the demographic segment with the most disposable income and the segment that made most household buying decisions.[13] However, the increased value of the eighteen- to forty-nine-year-old women's audience was somewhat problematic for advertisers and broadcasters because the burgeoning women's liberation movement shook up traditional ideas about how to market to women.[14]

These industries began to recognize the problem with their traditional methods through a wave of criticism directed at their gender-related policies and politics. The National Organization for Women initiated charges of unfair employment practices against two major TV stations and the U.S. Commission on Civil Rights released a series of reports condemning the television industry for problematic hiring and promotion.[15] The Screen Actors Guild conducted a study that tallied the inferior numbers of female versus male actors on TV.[16] Meanwhile, women working in TV news were increasingly vocal about the problems they encountered in getting, and keeping, their jobs.[17]

Perhaps even stronger was the agitation around television's representations of women in fictional programming and in advertising. In 1970, *TV Guide* asked, "Is television making a mockery of the American woman?" and gave voice to various feminists who said the answer was yes.[18] In 1974, Stewardesses for Women's Rights published a position paper entitled "The Myth of the Great Playmate in the Sky" and charged National Airlines (with its "Fly Me!"

campaign) along with Continental Airlines (with its "We really move our tail for you" spots) of sexist advertising that seriously impaired airline safety.[19] Academics also joined in the criticism, as with a 1975 conference under the auspices of the National Science Foundation that explored the portrayal of women in the media and resulted in Gaye Tuchman, Arlene Kaplan Daniels, and James Benet's 1978 collection, *Hearth and Home: Images of Women in the Mass Media.* Addressing all of these concerns, NOW's Image of Women in the Media Committee repeatedly met with executives from the three networks to discuss programming standards, the depiction of women characters, and the elimination of sexually discriminatory language.[20]

Made aware of the problems their practices posed for a society changed by women's liberation and thereby for the much-desired target market of young women, the media industries began to ponder how best to market to the liberated New Woman.[21] As the trade journal *Marketing/Communications* reported in 1970, "Advertisers and their agencies, more than ever before, are having to reevaluate the traditional concepts on which they base their communications to women."[22] By 1975, the National Advertising Review Board commissioned the "Report on Advertising Portraying or Directed to Women." The report argued for advertiser sensitivity to women's changing roles, not only for the industry's sense of social responsibility, but as a profit-generating business practice. As the report pointed out, it is a "counter-productive business practice to try to sell a product to someone who feels insulted by the product's advertising."[23] Thus, by 1975, the advertising and marketing industries had, in some senses, accepted the fact that the consumers to whom they attempted to sell their products had become more "liberated" and that their strategies in reaching those consumers needed to change as a result. Television producers and networks were coming to a similar realization, and representations of women in programming began to change, as well.

The New Woman Comes to Television

American network television's first attempts to introduce the liberated New Woman character in the 1970s were in situation comedies. One of the earliest and most famous was *The Mary Tyler Moore Show*, which debuted in September 1970. Moore portrayed a single woman in her thirties who relocated to Minneapolis at the end of a long love affair and got a job as a TV news producer. The now-infamous tale behind Mary's incarnation as a single woman fresh off a break-up was that CBS executives forbade the show's producers from making her a recent divorcée. After this setback from their initial plan, as the writer-creator Allan Burns has remarked, "Finally, it occurred to [the producers'] male-chauvinist minds that a girl could be thirty, unmarried and have a past involving men."[24] Mary's status as a single career woman was a decided change from most sitcom representations of the past, yet many critics have argued that the series ultimately offered only a "compromised and contradictory feminism" and that Mary's New Woman qualities were tempered by her more traditional " 'girl-next-door' sweetness."[25]

This combination of liberated New Woman and old-fashioned girl-next-door were frequently cited in contemporaneous discussion of the character, Mary Richards, and the woman who portrayed her, Mary Tyler Moore. Both Marys were seen as appealing to men and to women, but neither was characterized as a sex symbol. As one critic wrote of Mary Richards/Mary Tyler Moore, "Men, whose taste in women runs from Tammy Wynette to Gloria Steinem, think she would make the perfect girlfriend. Women like the fact that she's the star without being a sex queen or a loser."[26] Mary was attractive both to stand-by-your-man types and to pro–women's libbers. She was a woman with power, but that power was not gained through her sex appeal. As CBS's vice-president of programming, Perry Lafferty, described her, "I think it's her vulnerability that makes her particularly appealing. Little girl lost. Also, she's beautiful and all that without being threatening."[27] Lafferty's description of Moore as the anti-Steinem (who was seen as beautiful *and* threatening) situates her squarely within the period's debates over sexual difference. For while Mary was considered attractive, and thus indisputably feminine, her feminine attractiveness was not the source of her power. Her sexual difference was a pre-1970s, pre–women's movement, pre–sexual revolution kind of difference, distinct from maleness yet not a difference that defied outright the women's movement attempts to make men and women the same.

The popularity of *The Mary Tyler Moore Show* encouraged the creation of other sitcoms with women leads. In addition to *The MTM Show* spin-offs *Rhoda* (1974–78) and *Phyllis* (1975–77), less successful attempts included *Funny Face* (CBS, 1971), starring Sandy Duncan, followed by *The Sandy Duncan Show* (CBS, 1972); *Shirley's World* (ABC, 1971–72), featuring Shirley Mac-

Laine; *Diana* (NBC, 1973–74), starring Diana Rigg of *The Avengers*; *Fay* (NBC, 1975), with Lee Grant; and *Karen* (ABC, 1975), starring Karen Valentine. Along with the MTM family of shows, a few other sitcoms with woman protagonists did well in the 1970s. Among them were *One Day at a Time* (CBS, 1975–84), *Alice* (CBS, 1976–85), and *Maude* (CBS, 1972–78). *Maude* starred Bea Arthur as a hot-tempered, opinionated, middle-aged liberal living with her fourth husband. In a variation on the "vulnerable" and attractive Mary Tyler Moore or the "charming" and "energetic" Sandy Duncan, Bea Arthur had a deeper voice, grayer hair, more pronounced facial lines, and a larger bodily frame than the typical sitcom lead. As she explained, the show was "trying to break the mold of the situation comedy, where the mother is always small and sweet."[28] Arthur and *Maude* also broke the sitcom mold by offering an unapologetic, leftist take on social issues, among them alcoholism and, in the series' most (in)famous episodes, abortion. In instances like these, *Maude* went further than the more tentatively feminist series such as *The Mary Tyler Moore Show*. Arthur's age and body exempted her from sex-symbol status in the eyes of Western patriarchy, yet some of the publicity around the series carefully positioned Arthur as a "lady," and even made clear that her relationship to her husband was ultimately quite traditional. As Arthur described it, "Gene [her husband] calls the shots in any situation."[29]

Made-for-TV movies joined sitcoms as an early 1970s TV form that began to experiment with new roles for women. Producers and networks developed a number of TV movies that featured so-called "liberated" women, many of which doubled as pilots for potential new series. Some, such as *The Feminist and the Fuzz* (ABC, 6 January 1971) dealt overtly with women's liberation, but did so comedically. Others addressed the movement more indirectly, offering representations of women that played with the boundaries of sexual difference. For example, the producer Douglas Cramer pitched *Strongarm*, which featured a school teacher-lady wrestler, to ABC in 1972.[30] Keeping with the women-in-traditionally-male-sports theme, in 1973 Screen Gems developed a movie titled *The Dandelions*, which was based on a real-life team of "lady football players." The company was hopeful about ABC's interest in the project, largely because the ABC executive Barry Diller had been so enthusiastic about *Strongarm* the year before. As the Screen Gems executive David Goldsmith remarked, "Diller's intrigued and titillated by the concept of women performing in male roles."[31]

The titillation factor was, of course, an important element in the TV sex-symbol phenomenon, and it was clearly part of the TV industry's thinking about the New Woman character from the outset. Just as would later be the case with the Angels and other TV sex symbols, "lady" wrestlers and football players were seen as intriguing characters because they crossed over the previously unassailable line differentiating women from men. The catch or hook with these characterizations was the persistence of femaleness and femininity even as women took on these conventionally male roles. Here, TV audiences could find humor (imagine the "lady" football player borrowing a male player's razor to shave her legs) as well as reassurance. For even in the newly mixed-up world in which women were acting more and more like men, characters like these could reassure viewers that fundamental sexual differences would ultimately prevail.

Even with the above efforts to reimagine television's female characters, the networks and the producers who hoped to sell series to them remained uneasy about certain kinds of women's roles, especially action-oriented, leading roles. Wonder Woman's slow journey from comic books to television illustrates this hesitancy well. In June 1973, the producer Douglas Cramer mentioned the idea of a Wonder Woman series to Art Frankel of Screen Gems, "since she seems to be the forerunner for Woman's Lib and more timely than ever."[32] Frankel's colleague at Screen Gems, John H. Mitchell, was open to Cramer's exploration of the project, but he had doubts about its potential. As he wrote to Cramer: "I would call your attention . . . to the singular lack of success and believability attendant to any creative efforts in the past that have involved a woman private eye. It is very difficult to make believable a woman in real physical jeopardy."[33] Much like others in the TV industry, Mitchell felt that action-oriented series with women leads had little chance for success, that the public was either uninterested in or unwilling to accept a woman in such an active, and conventionally male, role.

Cramer's idea for a Wonder Woman series was further delayed by the fact that Warner Bros. already held the rights to the character and was producing a TV movie featuring the superheroine for the 1973–74 season (*Wonder Woman*, ABC, 2 March 1974). In the film, which is set in the present-day 1970s, Wonder Woman's alter ego, Diana Prince, leaves her Amazon Island home to help out in the "world of men." She works as a secretary for a government intelligence officer, Steve Trevor, who knows of her secret identity and sends her on a counterespionage mission. Diana/Wonder Woman catches the villain through her cunning and physical skills and happily returns to her quasi-secretarial work. Warner Bros. was ultimately dissatisfied with this pilot and eventually partnered with Cramer to produce a new pilot, set in the 1940s of the comic books, which would lead off the mid-1970 series (*The New, Original Wonder Woman*, ABC, 7 November 1975). Still, the studio's earlier impulse to fashion Wonder Woman as a contemporary working woman was in keeping with network tendencies at the time, as two other pilots that aired the same season *did* turn into regular series.

Police Woman (NBC, 1974–78) and *Get Christie Love!* (ABC, 1974–75) incarnated the New Woman in series television as both heroic in the face of jeopardy and as distinctly female. Because their leads were already established sex symbols, these series furthered the TV industry's tendency to make women characters in conventionally male roles palatable by emphasizing their feminine attractiveness. Publicity for Angie Dickinson and Teresa Graves highlighted their femininity, assuring audiences of their fundamental difference from men and defusing any associations with anti-difference feminism. For example, Dickinson openly rejected any sense of responsibility to "the women's cause" and scoffed at statements she made earlier in her career about wanting to be an actress instead of "a pinup girl or a sex queen."[34] "Right now," she claimed in 1975, "I'm very happy being a sex symbol."[35] When her co-star Earl Holliman spoke about Dickinson's "different kind of femininity" in 1977, he referred to the fact that, while she insisted on doing some of her own dangerous stunts, she was also "so vulnerable you want to put your arm around her to protect her."[36] Holliman's comments constructed Dickinson as not completely out of touch with the advances of the women's movement (after all, she did some of her own stunts) while simultaneously portraying her as traditionally and as helplessly feminine as possible. She was clearly not one of those "women-who-want-to-be-men."

Much of the press coverage of Teresa Graves, the star of *Get Christie Love!*, focused not on her potential as a black feminist icon (as the first black woman to star in her own hour-long dramatic series) but instead on her religiosity, making her seem a very traditional woman. As a recently converted Jehovah's Witness, Graves had included in her series contract time off for religious meetings and provisions against her character having to tell direct lies, kill anybody, or use profanity, and the press was fond of reporting on these stipulations.[37] Yet despite the modesty required by her convictions, Graves was still constructed as a sex symbol. In a *TV Guide* article, for example, Graves's manager explained that "the mere sight of Teresa walking on a stage is going to give somebody the feeling that sex is there. Teresa just looking like a girl is sexy. . . . She doesn't have to play sexy to be sexy. It's nature's accident."[38]

Because both series put their sex-symbol leads in the typically male part of police detective, they carefully marked the characters as women. In addition to working undercover in stereotypically feminine roles, dressing in street clothes, not uniforms, and being treated as "lady cops" by criminals, both characters have rather deferential relationships with their male supervisors. Pepper has a friendly, flirtatious relationship with hers and Christie is treated as a daughter by her protective boss, Captain Arthur Ryan. Audiences were regularly reminded of the anomalousness of the women's work. For instance, Christie's first boss, Lieutenant Matt Reardon, wryly remarks of Christie in "Market for Murder" (11 September 1974), "She's one of my best men." Though such a line confirmed Christie's status as a New Woman working successfully in a man's world, it also served as a reminder of her inescapable sexual difference. Because the pronoun "she" was fundamentally incongruous with the noun, "men," it was clear that Christie was no man; in fact, she was quite the opposite.[39]

With these series breaking through the barrier against women as leads in action-oriented, hour-long television, programs such as Cramer's version of *Wonder Woman* and *Charlie's Angels* would turn the TV sex symbol into a mass phenomenon. The television industry's effort to revise the medium's representation of women into a mass-market version of the New Woman influenced by women's lib began to pay off mid-decade with these new series. Television's female characters could now embody a New Woman who symbolized women's sexual difference from men even while taking on conventionally male roles. She could be the ideal emblem of the new sexual culture.

The "A-mazing Amazon": Wonder Woman

The producer Douglas Cramer's interest in creating a Wonder Woman series was an explicit attempt to capitalize on the character's long association with female power. The psychologist William Moulton Marston created Wonder

Woman, an Amazon princess who came to the United States to assist the war effort, in 1941, blending nicely with the "Rosie the Riveter" brand of feminism soon to be popularized on the U.S. home front. Marston believed that, psychologically speaking, boys and girls needed a strong feminine archetype and that the popular comics provided nothing but "blood-curdling masculinity."[40] This belief motivated Marston to create a character whom he described as having "all the allure of an attractive woman but with the strength also of a powerful man."[41] As he wrote to the comics historian Coulton Waugh, "Frankly, Wonder Woman is psychological propaganda for the new type of woman who should, I believe, rule the world. There isn't enough love in the male organism to run this planet peacefully. Woman's body contains twice as many love generating organs and endocrine mechanisms as the male. What woman lacks is the dominance or self assertive power to put over and enforce her love desires. I have given Wonder Woman this dominant force but have kept her loving, tender, maternal and feminine in every other way."[42] From her very beginnings, Wonder Woman was not only a figure of female power, but a figure whose power stemmed from her female body. She was a liberated New Woman who was clearly identified *as* a woman; her difference from men was fundamental to her identity.

Wonder Woman's history as a model of feminine strength, not to mention her Amazon origins, made her an appealing figurehead for 1970s feminists. The Amazon myth was regularly referenced in the literature of the women's movement, most often in cultural feminist work that looked to woman's sexual difference as a source of power.[43] Wonder Woman herself appeared on the cover of the first regular issue of *Ms.* magazine with a headline trumpeting "Wonder Woman for President."[44] *Ms.* also edited a collection of Marston's Wonder Woman comics in 1972, including an essay on "The Amazon Legacy" by Phyllis Chesler. The Feminist Health Centers featured the superheroine in a poster advocating women's control over their own healthcare. Here, Wonder Woman brandished a plastic speculum over a small, cowering physician made to represent the nearly all-male practice of gynecology and women's ability to triumph over it.[45] Her iconicity as a symbol of feminine power was even appropriated by anti-feminists, in particular one woman who triumphantly referred to the anti-ERA activist Phyllis Schlafly as "Our Wonder Woman."[46] Though a longtime feminist symbol, Wonder Woman was easily adapted to anti-feminist ideas about sexual difference. After all, Wonder Woman found her power in her female essence, and anti-feminists such as Schlafly argued for the sanctity of that essence.

Douglas Cramer's contention that Wonder Woman was a "forerunner to Women's Lib" was thus evident in the way that the character was taken up by various 1970s interests eager to find a recognizable symbol of the New Woman. His persistent interest in the project—and his awareness of the character's feminist roots—paid off when Warner Bros. agreed to produce a second pilot with him.[47] The movie went into production in March 1975, two years after he initially introduced the idea, and after he had developed several other Amazon-oriented projects.[48] Cramer suggested to Warner Bros. that they give up the idea of modernizing the story, as the 1974 movie had done, and instead set the series in 1942, the original setting for the comics. While this version would take on a somewhat campy tone, it would not go as far in that direction as a version of the story that *Batman* (ABC, 1966–68) producer William Dozier had pitched to the networks for the 1967–68 season (a project on which Cramer had worked, as well).[49] This version would also differ from the 1974 pilot in its casting, especially in the casting for Wonder Woman herself. The 1974 film starred petite, blond Cathy Lee Crosby, but Cramer wanted a star who looked like the comic book Wonder Woman: "She should be built like a javelin-thrower, but with the sweet face of a Mary Tyler Moore."[50] Envisioning a lead who would have some of the same feminine, yet liberated, appeal of the sitcom heroine, Cramer "discovered" a former Miss World USA, a relative unknown named Lynda Carter who stood at five feet, nine inches tall (though the publicity at the time always claimed she was six feet), with long, black hair, blue eyes, and an "impressive size 38" chest for which Wonder Woman's gold eagle-encrusted bustier would be designed.[51]

Though the TV movie performed well in the ratings, ABC was hesitant about scheduling the series. The network had already decided to spin off Jaime Sommers, also known as the Bionic Woman, from *The Six Million Dollar Man*. Her series was scheduled to begin in January 1976 and ABC hesitated about over-programming superhero shows. Very likely, the network also was hesitant about airing a second action-adventure show with a woman lead. *Get Christie Love!* had failed by the summer of 1975 and many in the industry remained unconvinced that the public would welcome these powerful women characters. CBS, eager to pick up *Wonder Woman* should ABC drop it, ended up driving ABC to order two more "try-out" episodes. (CBS likely had two motivations here: one was an attempt to find more kid-friendly fare for the family hour; the other was an attempt to tap into the market for an action series with a New Woman in the lead, as NBC was still carrying *Police Woman* and ABC was to carry *The Bionic Woman*). These try-out episodes aired on ABC in April 1976 and were ratings successes. When NBC, in the summer of 1976, announced that it would pick up *Wonder Woman* should ABC decide not to continue with it, ABC finally committed to the show, ran a few more episodes sporadically throughout the fall, and began airing the series on a regular basis in December 1976.[52] At the end of the 1976–77 season, ABC decided to drop the show, but CBS was quick to step back in and claim the series in which it had long been interested.[53]

Although both the ABC and the CBS versions of the series made Carter's Wonder Woman a sex symbol, they were significantly different from one another in many ways, not least of which were their representations of the New Woman and her affinity with the ideals of the women's movement. The ABC version was the more faithful of the two to the original comic, both in its World War II setting and in its overtly feminist message. Here, Wonder Woman went undercover as Yeoman Diana Prince, U.S. Navy Intelligence, working with Major Steve Trevor to defeat the Nazis. Her Amazon origins played a recurring role, as Diana would occasionally make trips home to Paradise Island. Though Wonder Woman's primary mission in these episodes was to help the United States in its battle against the Nazis and thus to preserve freedom for all, she consistently made *women's* freedom a priority. For example, in the series pilot, Wonder Woman fought against Marcia, Steve Trevor's secretary and a Nazi spy. When she finally captured Marcia, she tried to convince her that the Nazi way was the wrong way. She appealed to Marcia's sense of gender solidarity: "The Nazis don't care about their women . . . any civilization that does not recognize the female is doomed to destruction. Women are the wave of the future and sisterhood is [thoughtful pause] stronger than anything."[54]

When the series moved to CBS, the setting was updated to the 1970s and Diana became a government intelligence agent. In her identity as Wonder Woman, Diana no longer had to save Steve from recurrent danger and no longer made trips home or referenced her Amazon past. In fact, she transformed into Wonder Woman less and less frequently, sometimes even dispatching the bad guys as Diana. She was thus more like a contemporary crime-fighting career woman — à la Charlie's Angels — and less like the mythical Amazon heroine championed in feminist lore. She also moved away from her feminist status by being presented as even more of a sex symbol. In this version, Carter's hair was longer, looser, and wilder and the Wonder Woman costume revealed even more skin, with a lower-cut bustier and higher-cut legs (see figures 14 and 15). The changing lyrics to the two versions' credit sequences aptly illustrate these shifts. In the first version of the series, the jazzy theme song proclaimed, "All the world is waiting for you / *And the power you possess* / In your satin tights / Fighting for *your* rights / And the old red, white, and blue!" In contrast, the second version of the series initially featured these lyrics: "All the world is waiting for you / *And the wonders that you do* / In your satin tights / Fighting for *our* rights / And the old red, white, and blue!" (emphases mine). A third version of the theme song during the CBS years would remove the lyrics altogether, leaving only the catchy "Wonder Woman!" refrain. The shift away from references to Wonder Woman's power or her fight for her *own* rights demonstrates the decreasing presence of explicitly feminist rhetoric over the series' run.

While the two versions had these important divergences in their representations of the New Woman and her feminist allegiance, both incarnations endorsed the idea of woman's fundamental sexual difference from man. In both, Diana's/Wonder Woman's differences from men are what make her special; in fact, they are the source of her power. As she explains in "Fausta, the Nazi Wonder Woman" (28 April 1976), her strength is a product of her upbringing on Paradise Island. At this Amazon sanctuary, "unhampered by masculine destructiveness," the women of the island develop their minds and their physical skills. Thus it is the quality of the women-only community that awakens the power within the female body. Wonder Woman's power additionally comes from her tools, also products of her Amazon homeland. As illuminated in "The Feminum Mystique" (6 and 8 November 1976) her bullet-deflecting bracelets are made from a rare material called feminum, found only in the mines of Paradise Island. Buried deep within the island, the feminum is a compelling metaphor for the power buried within the female body. It is a power valued not only by women but by the men who fear its potential and attempt to control it. As Diana explains to her mother about the Nazis' invasion of Paradise Island, "It's the feminum they want." The feminum is used

14 Wonder Woman (Lynda Carter) in costume, season 1, ABC, "Pilot," *Wonder Woman*, 7 November 1975.

in this episode to explain men's need to dominate women and women's right to resist domination. Much like cultural feminist assertions of women's essentially powerful nature and their historical explanations for the disappearance of matriarchy at the hands of a vengeful patriarchy, "The Feminum Mystique" and *Wonder Woman* overall defined woman as one with her sexually differentiated body and sought to celebrate that connection.

Sexual difference was also at issue in the series' representations of villainous women. Fausta, the Nazis' powerful woman spy, was marked as a very different kind of woman than Diana/Wonder Woman. Unlike Diana, who deliberately uses her androgynous military uniform to hide her essential femaleness (a femaleness that ultimately bursts out when she changes into Wonder Woman's skimpy, cleavage-baring costume), Fausta wears her suspenders and necktie proudly, as evidence of her manlike strength (see figure 16). Not fooled by Fausta's masculine garb, Wonder Woman senses her opponent's inner female and appeals to it repeatedly. Noticing the sexist treatment Fausta receives from the Nazi colonel, Kesselman, Wonder Woman tells her she is too intelligent to be taking orders from "that man." When she and Steve are held captive by the Nazis, Wonder Woman again attempts to connect with

15 Wonder Woman in costume, season 3, CBS, "Hot Wheels," *Wonder Woman*, 29 September 1978.

Fausta's inner woman: "I appeal to your womanhood. Do you want children growing up under tyrants like Kesselman?" Drawing upon women's reproductive potential as their common bond, Wonder Woman effectively converts Fausta from a necktie-wearing Nazi to an Allied freedom fighter, "an example to women all over the world who want to be free."

Even in the CBS version of the series, when Diana/Wonder Woman made many fewer explicit references to women's liberation, the sexually ambiguous villainess reappeared. In "Amazon Hot Wax" (16 February 1979), for instance, the singer Barbi Gordon is not only in cahoots with the other blackmailing villains who risk national security, she is also suspiciously like her brother and singing partner, Jeff. Barbi and Jeff dress in matching unisex outfits (pants, vests, and so forth) even when off-stage (see figure 17). Their curly hair, cut just above their shoulders, is also similar and the two stand at roughly the same height. Barbi is clearly the more dominant of the two siblings, as she pulls naive Jeff along on their unscrupulous missions and chastises him for protesting their involvement in illegal activities. Thus, Barbi is yet another inappropriately sexed and gendered villain whom Wonder Woman has to defeat.

A third way in which sexual difference was an ongoing issue in the series

16 Fausta (Lynda Day George), "Fausta, the Nazi Wonder Woman," *Wonder Woman*, ABC, 28 April 1976.

was in Diana's/Wonder Woman's relationships with men. Though, in many ways, the programs' insistence on sexual difference had a feminist motivation, it also served to reinforce the primacy of heterosexuality in male-female relationships and in a true femininity. Diana's relationship with Steve is the most frequent example of this. Diana develops a crush on Steve soon after his plane crash lands on Paradise Island in the pilot episode and Steve lusts after Wonder Woman on a regular basis. Thus, their interactions are tinged with hints of heterosexual romance from the very beginning. In "The Feminum Mystique," for instance, Diana, thinking of Steve, describes men to her visiting sister, Drusilla, who has never met a man before. Diana dreamily relates, "Oh, they're like children, they're like gods, they're like geniuses ... and fools. They are all things," as a close-up of her face reveals her delight. Although Diana and Drusilla were raised to distrust men and their difference from women, one of the lessons Diana learns from her work in the United States is that men's sexual difference is not all bad. In fact, she learns that men's difference from women is what makes them such fascinating and likeable creatures. In *Wonder Woman*, sexual difference is kept from being the kind of lesbian separatist difference espoused by some cultural feminists through its links to hetero-

CHAPTER 4

17 Villainous siblings Barbi (Sarah Purcell) and Jeff (Judge Reinhold), "Amazon Hot Wax," *Wonder Woman*, CBS, 16 February 1979.

sexuality. While Wonder Woman values women for their essential femaleness, she also learns to value (at least some) men for their essential maleness, a celebration of sexual difference more in keeping with anti-feminists than with cultural or "difference" feminists.

In the CBS version of the series, Diana's relationships with men are even more overtly tied to heterosexuality (though her crush on Steve fades), taking on a sort of "battle of the sexes" flirtatious banter. For instance, in "Hot Wheels" (29 September 1978), Diana works with police inspector Tim Bolt, a hothead who resents the interference of two women (Diana and Wonder Woman) in his attempts to catch a ring of car thieves. When Bolt and Diana realize they are forced to work with each other, Bolt apologizes for his outburst about her interference. He claims, "I take it all back. Except the female part. You are most definitely female," as he gazes approvingly at Diana. Bolt's and Diana's sexual difference (and sexual attraction) is a repeated theme in the episode. In fact, the staging of the above scene emphasizes their status as attracted opposites, with Bolt and Diana facing each other, centered in the frame (see figure 18). Their difference is emphasized when Steve Trevor sends a paper airplane between them, rupturing the scene's sexual tension and highlighting

18 Tim Bolt (Peter Brown) and Diana (Lynda Carter) argue in front of Steve Trevor (Lyle Waggoner), "Hot Wheels," *Wonder Woman*, CBS, 29 September 1978.

the characters' difference. In addition, their hostile yet flirtatious banter includes references to Bolt's attempt to get his "man," the head of the car-thief ring, and Diana's attempt to get her "lady," a hood ornament that contains within it top-secret missile plans. In episodes like this, sexual difference is not so much a rallying point for feminist organizing as it is the "spice" that makes life in the co-ed workplace more exciting. Even when Diana/Wonder Woman disparages sexist male behavior, both she and the series overall suggest that men's imperfections are individual, not products of a patriarchal society, and that they ultimately serve to make relations between the sexes more interesting.

Publicity around Wonder Woman's portrayer, Lynda Carter, also emphasized her sexual difference. Despite the program's obvious children's audience, there was widespread agreement in the popular press on Carter's sex-symbol status. In fact, *TV Guide* structured one article on the program around its dual appeal to nine-year-olds and their fathers, who were "impelled to steal peeks" as if surreptitiously gawking at a porn magazine.[55] While Carter protested the characterization, claiming, "I'm determined to make it on my talent, not my bosom," her adherence to ideals of traditional femininity kept her from coming across as a feminist icon.[56] For example, she was regularly quoted as happily submitting to the will of her manager/husband, Ron Samuels: "[It's] soooo much fun to have someone to take care of me, to fight my battles, to see that everything gets taken care of."[57] Carter was thus easily characterized in patriarchal, objectifying terms, in terms that reinforced her difference from men and that focused on her dependence and her body. She was not quoted as endorsing Wonder Woman's feminist potential, nor was she represented as an independent career woman. In fact, the discourse around Carter as sex symbol and as traditional woman helped to contain the potential for reading the *Wonder Woman* series as a feminist parable.

In the representations of Carter and her on-screen alter ego as well as in the ABC and CBS versions of the series, sexual difference was an ongoing theme. Sometimes it served anti-feminist ends, as in the characterizations of Carter as a submissive sex object. At other times, the discourses of sexual difference served explicitly feminist goals. As Barbara Corday, co-writer of "The Feminum Mystique" explains, "Barbara [Avedon, Corday's co-writer] and I were actively involved in consciousness-raising groups and all of that sort of thing and . . . that whole part of our lives influenced everything that we wrote."[58] Believing in Wonder Woman as a feminist character, Corday and Avedon created the myth of the "feminum" and forever instituted a metaphor for female power in the Wonder Woman story. Whether represented by Wonder Woman crusading for the rights of women, by Diana Prince celebrating the idiosyncrasies of men, or by a young Lynda Carter, spilling out of her revealing costume in a pin-up poster, women's sexual difference from men was central to *Wonder Woman*. The significance of this difference as it both grew out of and participated in the battles over sexual difference in the culture at large was amplified by the fact that *Wonder Woman*, especially in the CBS version, was in keeping with the period's other action-adventure series with sex-symbol women in lead roles. Especially influential in Wonder Woman's transformation into a 1970s secret agent working undercover as a pop singer, disco dancer, and skateboarder was one of the era's most popular series, *Charlie's Angels*.

Charlie's Angels

While most women stars of action-adventure series in the 1970s were constructed as sex symbols, the unabashed ways in which the *Charlie's Angels* producers and stars, as well as the journalists who covered them, celebrated the Angels' sex-symbol status was unprecedented. It drew the series an extraordinary degree of attention from both fans and detractors and made the program an emblem of television's treatment of women and of sex. *Charlie's Angels* grew out of the same industrial context of pressure to represent and target the New Woman as did *Wonder Woman* and its predecessors. Like *Wonder Woman*, the series was not automatically accepted by the networks. In 1974, the producers Aaron Spelling and Leonard Goldberg pitched an adventure show called *The Alley Cats* to ABC. Their proposed series would feature three beautiful young women (named Allie, Lee, and Catherine) as private detectives. ABC's Michael Eisner and Barry Diller rejected the proposal, with Diller opining, "Three beautiful girls running around doing male things, chasing criminals. It's not believable. It's terrible. Forget it."[59] Though Diller had reportedly been intrigued by the prospect of young women "running around doing male things" when Cramer pitched his ideas for movies about a lady wrestler and lady football players, he was less enthusiastic about this new proposal, perhaps caving in to the pressure from other industry executives to reject women leads in action series as just too preposterous.

Spelling and Goldberg, however, had substantial clout with ABC as producers of hit series such as *The Mod Squad* (1968–73) and *The Rookies* (1972–76). The network had already agreed to give them money toward a pilot they would develop with the actor-producers Robert Wagner and Natalie Wood. When Wood and Wagner agreed to co-produce the *Alley Cats* pilot, Spelling and Goldberg had the financial backing they needed. They also brought in former *Rookies* star Kate Jackson as the series lead. Unhappy with the series title and premise, Jackson suggested that the women be called "angels" and that they never meet their mysterious boss.[60] With a title change to *Harry's Angels*, Spelling and Goldberg brought the project back to ABC, where Fred Silverman was now president of the Entertainment division. Unlike Eisner and Diller, Silverman loved the premise and agreed to air the pilot, now renamed *Charlie's Angels*. The movie's impressive performance in March 1976, along with Silverman's support, gained the series a place in the prime-time schedule for the 1976–77 season.

The program quickly acquired a wide audience, regularly reaching 59 percent of all the television sets in use during its time slot. Within the first few weeks of its first season, it ranked fourth among all programs in urban areas, seventh among college graduates, and first with adults overall.[61] But the series was as controversial as it was popular. It became a scapegoat for all television sex to those groups seeking to regulate TV content, as well as being a target of feminists and a source of derision for many. The feminist Judith Coburn called the show "one of the most misogynist . . . the networks have produced recently . . . it perpetuates the myth most damaging to women's struggle to gain professional equality: that women always use sex to get what they want, even on the job."[62] Even Farrah Fawcett-Majors admitted, "Gloria Steinem doesn't like us, for sure."[63] Journalists covering the series regularly dismissed it as so much fluff; TV Guide even called it "TV's first prime-time girlie show" and mocked the show's stars as air-headed prima donnas.[64] It didn't help that the program's producers openly, even proudly, admitted to the show's exploitative nature. The executive producer Aaron Spelling remarked, "Anyone who thinks these girls are really private detectives is nuts," and his partner Leonard Goldberg added, "We love to get them wet, because they look so good in clinging clothes."[65]

In official publicity and in critical responses, the Angels were clearly constructed as sex symbols; in fact, they were often presented as being nothing *but* sexual objects. Despite such discourse, however, the series itself regularly engaged with issues of women's equality and even advocated a mainstream feminist, ERA-style version of women's liberation. The premise of the series, that the three women have gone to work for Townsend Investigations because they were so unfulfilled in their exasperating police department jobs as paper-pushers and crossing guards made the police department's discriminatory practices seem absurd and outdated. Yet as many critics have pointed out, audiences learned the Angels' back stories through the introductory credit sequence, narrated by Charlie Townsend, who patronizingly refers to them as "little girls" and paternalistically explains that he "took them away from all that." In addition, the credit sequence featured the women in a series of objectifying poses involving skimpy swimwear and hair tossed glamorously through the air. These kinds of contradictions permeated the program's premise. As Susan J. Douglas has argued, they "exploited, perfectly, the tensions between antifeminism and feminism."[66] The Angels answered to an unseen male boss, but they were most loyal to each other. They regularly found themselves in jeopardy, but they relied only on their own skills and on one other for rescue.

Individual episodes evidence this contradiction as fully as does the program's premise. Some episodes made explicit statements about women's equality and the absurdities of women being differentiated from men. For instance, in "Angels Go Truckin'" (19 September 1979) Kris (Cheryl Ladd) criticizes Maggie, the owner of the Venus Trucking Company (which employed only women drivers) when the Angels discover that she had been her own company's saboteur: "You really blew it. You could have proved once and for all that women can do anything men can do." Maggie answers that her whole career in the trucking industry has done just that—and that the Angels' efforts to uncover her misdeeds have proven women's abilities in yet another area—crime-solving.

While the series sometimes took these steps toward endorsing an equal rights version of feminism, the program also made light of feminist stances. For example, in "Target: Angels" (27 October 1976), the Angels speculate about why someone is trying to kill them and Jill (Farrah Fawcett-Majors) sarcastically comments, "Right, he's a male chauvinist who wants us out of the private eye business." In "Angels on Wheels" (22 December 1976), Kelly (Jaclyn Smith) encounters a shirtless muscle-man of an apartment manager who tries to keep her from searching the apartment of a dead roller derby player. When she attempts to distract him by suggesting he pose as "stud of the month" for the magazine she is using as her cover employer, Red responds angrily with, "Forget it. You Gloria Steinem–type broads turn me off. Just because a guy's put together right, you think he doesn't have a brain in his head! You know, I get real tired of being looked at like nothing but a sex object!" This humorous role reversal suggests that feminist complaints of sexual objectification had become so commonplace as to be redundant, so predictable as to be easily dismissed. Red's version of feminism ignores the differences between men and women as victims of oppression, equating the sexes as similarly subject to objectifying treatment. Though Red is a laughable character and the audience was thus not expected to accept his views as truth, the man appears genuinely offended and his characterization of Steinem-like feminists suggests that too much feminism leads only to reverse discrimination.

These contradictory stances on feminism point to one way in which

Charlie's Angels both responded and contributed to the sense of confusion over the goals of the women's liberation movement in the 1970s. Would this movement ultimately help most women or would it deprive perfectly contented women of their standing as wives and mothers? Would its result be a kind of reverse discrimination or would it resolve into more respectful treatment for both sexes? Perhaps most pressingly for *Charlie's Angels* and its sex-symbol stars, would the women's movement insist that men and women were fundamentally the same? *Charlie's Angels* addressed itself to this very question, making the Angels' difference from men the focus of the series.

As is evident from the discourses surrounding the show, the Angels' physical difference from men was central to the program's publicity and media hype. But it was also central to the program's narratives. Nearly every episode found the Angels taking on undercover identities and, like their predecessors on *Police Woman* and *Get Christie Love!*, those guises took the form of stereotypically feminine roles. Thus, in "Lady Killer" (24 November 1976), Jill goes undercover as a waitress and centerfold for the *Feline* clubs and magazine, a thinly veiled *Playboy*. In "Angel Flight" (5 October 1977), Kris and Kelly go undercover as stewardesses-in-training and in "Pretty Angels All in a Row" (28 September 1977) they pretend to be beauty pageant contestants. In "Game, Set, Death" (4 January 1978), Kris poses as a professional tennis player while Sabrina (Kate Jackson) and Kelly play a fashion designer and a model, respectively. In "Pom Pom Angels" (1 November 1978), Kelly and Kris take on the guise of professional cheerleaders. The list is endless, as nearly every episode featured such disguises and showcased the Angels' bodies in the process (see figure 19).

As objectifying as the disguises were, however, they were carefully identified as disguises; in other words, they were different from the Angels' everyday appearances and their "true" selves. Thus, when Kris goes undercover as a wannabe porn star ("Catch a Falling Angel," 23 January 1980), she wears a low-cut blouse, tight skirt, and big, curly hair, a decided contrast to her normal look of slightly wavy hair and modest blouses, slacks, and skirts. Even when in her disguise, she does not appear as sexually objectified as other women more legitimately working in the porn industry, such as the producer's busty secretary, who wears a revealing red halter top. The Angels' relatively conservative appearance is also emphasized in "Homes, Sweet Homes" (30 Janu-

19 Kelly (Jaclyn Smith) and Kris (Cheryl Ladd) go undercover in the locker room at a stewardess training school, "Angel Flight," *Charlie's Angels*, ABC, 5 October 1977.

ary 1980), when Tina, the possessive girlfriend and assistant to a crooked real estate mogul, wears a red skirt suit with a high leg slit (which she purposefully uses to expose her thigh) and a black camisole with a plunging, heart-shaped neckline. We later see Kelly also dressed in the potentially provocative colors of red and black, but her version is very different from Tina's. Kelly's black slacks and turtleneck, paired with a red blazer, are a distinct contrast to Tina's ensemble, just as Kelly herself is meant to be a much more wholesome version of the sexually attractive career woman.[67] Thus, while public discourse around the series highlighted the Angels' skimpy wardrobes and bodily display, such get-ups were not nearly as omnipresent as the discourse suggests.[68] When the characters did wear revealing attire, it was usually with a sort of eye-rolling acquiescence to the temporary absurdities their job demanded. Certainly, viewers could tune in for the pure spectacle of the women's bodies, but they could also have seen such moments as insignificant within the program's larger narrative focus.

The Angels' success as detectives was at least as predicated upon how they *used* their femininity and their femaleness as it was upon their appearance.

20 Kelly, Sabrina (Kate Jackson), and Kris go undercover as members of a women's football team, "Angels in the Backfield," *Charlie's Angels*, ABC, 25 January 1978. WISCONSIN CENTER FOR FILM AND THEATER RESEARCH.

For example, the Angels catch the truck of stolen pharmaceuticals in "Angels Go Truckin' " because Kris's CB identity, the sassy, charming, sweet-talking "Angel Eyes," has so enthralled the surrounding male truckers that when she asks for their help they bombard the airwaves with their responses. Similarly, in "Target: Angels," Jill distracts a cab driver by flirting with him so that Kelly can hijack his cab to chase the bad guys. "Lady Killer" ends with Sabrina and Kelly saving the murderer Paula from jumping off a ledge by empathizing with her plight as a now physically scarred former centerfold. Acting as a maternal figure to Paula, Sabrina even cradles her in her arms, assuring her that she can be well again. The Angels' femaleness not only allowed them access to a range of settings reserved for women only; their sex and their gender provided them with skills and abilities unlike those available to men.

As central as their femininity and their femaleness were to their work, the Angels also spent significant time taking on traditionally male roles, keeping with the day's spirit of role-reversal liberation. In "Angels Go Truckin'," Tiffany (Shelley Hack) and Kris become truck drivers. In "Angels in the Backfield" (25 January 1978), all three join a women's football team (figure 20).

And in "Stuntwoman Angels" (28 February 1981) they work as stuntwomen.[69] They also exhibited skills most often associated with men. Kelly lands an airplane in "Angel Flight" and Kris shoots and kills the villain in "Angel Baby" (16 November 1977). Of course, the women's employment as private detectives was itself a reversal of traditional roles. Whatever role they took on, be it the more common stereotypically feminine roles or the newfangled "women in men's roles," most important was their status as women. As women, they were able to penetrate situations men cannot, whether they were situations common to the traditional woman, like beauty pageants, or situations more fitting for the New Woman, like truck driving school. Traversing the available female roles as they did, the Angels transcended categories such as traditional and new. They were fundamentally women, and that fact is what allowed them to solve their cases and to succeed in the man's world of private detection.

The Angels' fundamental femaleness and its relationship to their identities as liberated women carried over into the media hype around the show's lead actresses. The stars were all constructed as sex symbols, though Kate Jackson frequently eluded the characterization and both Shelley Hack and Tanya Roberts (Jackson's replacements over the show's last two seasons) were not around long enough to become major stars. Because Fawcett-Majors, Jaclyn Smith, and Cheryl Ladd each had little acting experience when they began their roles (in contrast to Kate Jackson's previous series role), they more readily fit into the sex-symbol image offered in the press coverage of the series. Fawcett-Majors, Smith, and Ladd had worked as models and acted in bit parts and each had been featured in seductive television commercials, among them Fawcett-Majors and Ladd for Ultra-Brite ("The Sex Appeal Toothpaste") and Smith for English Leather cologne ("There are men and there are men, *you know* what I mean," as she coyly lowered her eyelids). Each was heralded as a sex symbol in her own way — Fawcett-Majors as the unexpected superstar, Smith as the reluctantly sexy "good girl," and Ladd as the down-to-earth girl-next-door. While Fawcett-Majors's status received the most attention, each woman's sexual appeal was regularly examined.

The *Charlie's Angels* stars were frequently asked to comment on their roles as sex symbols and their reactions, at least as represented in the popular press, included bemused acceptance, outright denial, and bewildered defensiveness. While sex symbols of the past may have been represented as feeling flattered or embarrassed or pleased with their categorization, the television sex symbols of the 1970s had a much more problematic relationship to the term. By the time of *Charlie's Angels'* debut in the mid-1970s, the women's movement had effected substantial changes in American life, among them a general awareness that labels such as "sex symbol" were objectifying and sexist. As a result, it was increasingly difficult for any woman in the public eye to openly embrace such a label. To do so would be to appear ignorant of the vast changes the movement had wrought and to contradict her own status as a serious career woman. Yet the stars of *Charlie's Angels* (and their handlers) knew better than to pretend that their sexual attractiveness was not a key part of their show's success. Consequently, coverage of the actresses continually attempted to negotiate the stars' status as sex symbols with their identities as liberated New Women.

Sometimes the actresses refused the sex-symbol moniker because of its exploitative associations. As Smith explained, "I really hated it when they said we were sex exploitation," and as Ladd reasoned, "If the ratings go down, they put you in a bathing suit. I intend to have some long talks with the writers."[70] Such remarks were often tempered by justifications for the show's reliance upon sex appeal, justifications based in the women's natural femininity. Fawcett-Majors argued, "One of the things women are blessed with is their femininity and their intuition. Maybe we use it a little on the show, but I don't think it's wrong."[71] Meanwhile, Smith rationalized, "Granted we use our femininity. Men like to turn on TV to see pretty girls. I like men to open doors in real life. We are not supercops."[72] These sorts of explanations relied upon a sense of fundamental sexual difference that the actresses (along with the reporters who interviewed them and the publications that printed their remarks) could assume they shared with their audiences and readers. Since so many voices of the 1970s, from cultural feminists to anti-feminists, insisted upon a natural difference between the sexes, the expression of that difference by the *Charlie's Angels* stars was of a piece with that broader discourse.

At times, the actresses defended the series and their sex-symbol status by insisting that everything about their characters and their work was in keeping with feminist goals. Smith explained that she did not feel exploited and would not stay with the series if she did. "I don't really understand the feminists," she claimed. "After all, we're in charge. We go ahead and concentrate on doing our jobs."[73] Although it is not clear whether Smith was referring to the actresses or to their on-screen counterparts, she voiced an awareness of feminist principles and found no discrepancy between them and her work. When Cheryl Ladd attended an ERA fundraiser in 1979, she insisted, "I think ERA and *Charlie's Angels* do go together. . . . [The series is] not just pretty ladies. We don't act like dummies and bimbos on the show. *Angels* shows that women can function in a man's world." She also verbalized what had by then become the ERA's widely accepted message: "I want my daughter to know she can be bright and she can expect to do whatever she wants when she grows up. I am a supporter of human rights and it's appalling to me that women don't have opportunities."[74] Because Ladd's assertions of the show's feminist potential were buttressed by her active involvement in a feminist cause, her defense of the series rings truer than Smith's. But my aim is not to assess the veracity of the actresses' claims. Instead, I am arguing that, even in the publicity around the *Charlie's Angels* stars, the women's movement was an ever-present issue. Because the question of sexual difference and its relationship to feminism was so hotly contested at the time, it was possible in popular discourse to link the series to the movement in one instant and understand the program as the nadir of patriarchal oppression the next.

Representations of the actresses' personal lives in the popular press further situated the series at the center of the controversy over the women's movement and the role of sexual difference within it. Unlike their defenses of the program and their status as sex symbols, the actresses' comments about their personal lives tended to emphasize traditional sex roles. Because most of these stories appeared in white, middle-class women's magazines such as *McCall's* and *Ladies' Home Journal*, they understandably featured tales of the stars' romantic relationships and understandably accented those aspects of their lives that would best match the lives of the magazines' readers. Still, the presence of such stories alongside the actresses' remarks about feminism and their status as sex symbols suggests that each informed the other, most clearly in their assertions of women's essential sexual difference.

All of the "Angels" spoke glowingly of marriage and motherhood, insisting that these parts of their lives were more significant than their careers. Fawcett-Majors, described as "*reverentially* married" to Lee Majors, reportedly insisted upon an early evening cut-off time for her *Charlie's Angels* workday in order to prepare dinner for her husband.[75] Underlying this traditional understanding of gender roles was a sense of immutable sexual difference. Fawcett-Majors explained that, while her husband would come home from work, have something to eat, and "flop" into bed: "I do women's work. I take off my nail polish, figure out a menu for tomorrow, maybe clean a room. In the morning I get up an hour and a half earlier than Lee and clean and get food ready and do half a dozen other chores. I've done a lot of work by the time that limousine rolls up at 5:30."[76] Not only by representing herself as a multi-tasking housekeeper, but also by assuming the naturalness of such a role as "women's work," Fawcett-Majors was able to fit easily into many women's notions of themselves and their social roles, especially in relationship to men. Despite her sex-symbol status, her female fans could reason, she was a woman just like them. Similarly, when Jaclyn Smith married the actor Dennis Cole midway through the series run, her "old-fashioned" values were emphasized even more strongly than they were during her single days. *Ladies' Home Journal* repeatedly stressed her prioritization of her marriage above her career: "Family, religion, and morality are what I'm all about" and "The show isn't my main concern. My primary interest is my husband, my family and my home." The story ended with, "To Jaclyn Smith, *Charlie's Angels* takes a back seat to her husband, her home and having a child."[77] Such discourse worked not only to offer the *Journal*'s readers an icon with which they could identify, but also to counteract any of the more feminist-influenced ideas about women's roles suggested by the series.

The representations of Cheryl Ladd's and Kate Jackson's personal lives in the popular press were less blatant attempts to assure readers of the actresses' traditional roles despite their careers and their status as sex symbols. Ladd's marriage to the actor David Ladd was sometimes represented as surprisingly liberated. Because Cheryl's working hours were longer and more consistent than her husband's, he spent more time caring for their daughter, even bringing her to the *Charlie's Angels* set to visit her mother at work. The women's magazines, while complimentary of David's efforts, were quick to assert Cheryl's devotion to her family, even relating a story of David's demand at the start of their marriage that Cheryl not work. Cheryl explained that she agreed, even though she wanted a career, so as to reassure him of her love. She insisted that his demand was "*not* chauvinistic," despite his admittance that it was.[78] Instead of highlighting David's changed attitude as a positive adaptation to the times, the magazines accented Cheryl's willingness to sacrifice for her marriage.

Kate Jackson, who was unmarried throughout her tenure on the show, was depicted as even less traditional than Ladd. She bucked the stars' tendency to assert their fundamental sexual difference by claiming, "I don't have to be validated by having a man on my arm, as if to say I might be successful but I'm still a woman."[79] Jackson also refused to wear bathing suits and other skimpy attire on the air and thus Sabrina and Jackson were not as marked as sex symbols as were the other Angels. Her resistance to conventional heterosexual femininity made Jackson a lesbian fan favorite and, perhaps to avoid the suggestion that Jackson herself was a lesbian, the coverage of her personal life attempted to assert her heterosexuality and her fundamental sexual difference. Gossip about her romantic attachments to actors such as David Soul, Warren Beatty, and Nick Nolte appeared alongside claims by Jackson that she planned to get married within two years because she so wanted to have children.[80] Still, there was no denying that Jackson did not fit the same sex-symbol mold as the other Angels. In that respect, it was not as necessary for women's magazines to convince their readers that she was just like them. As long as her heterosexuality was confirmed, the readership of *Ladies' Home Journal* could see Jackson as more invested in the New Woman lifestyle than the other Angels, but not see her as especially threatening to their own ways of life. Few in the *Charlie's Angels* audience could identify with the Angels as sex symbols, but many could identify with them as women, both traditional and new, who understood themselves as fundamentally different from men. Even though Jackson's image challenged traditional femininity, the fact that she did not embrace the sex-symbol label ultimately made her brand of femininity more obtainable than that of her co-stars, even for those viewers who saw their lives in more conventional terms.

As celebrities and as fictional characters, the Angels demonstrated that the New Woman was still a woman; that the changes brought by the women's movement would not alter the fundamental fact of sexual difference. However, the ultimately pro–sexual difference stance of *Charlie's Angels* was not only a TV industry ploy to place attractive young women in revealing outfits as they went undercover as centerfolds and pageant contestants (though there is no doubt that this was the case). The pro–sexual difference attitude of *Charlie's*

156   CHAPTER 4

Angels was both a product and a constituent of the debates over sexual difference in the broader culture. Thus, when the organizer of a national conservative women's group explained, "It's a great advantage being female. I get away
with things I could never do if I were a man!" and Phyllis Schlafly argued that
her ideal "Positive Woman," "wants to be treated like a woman . . . she knows
that her chance for success in a man's world is increased by requiring men to
treat her like a woman," they were echoing the lesson of *Charlie's Angels* as
well as providing the program with a premise that would resonate with much
of its audience.[81] As we have seen, it was not only anti-feminists who voiced
these beliefs about the benefits to women in distinguishing themselves from
men. By the late 1970s, in particular, cultural and liberal feminists alike were
embracing sexual difference as the key to liberation, or at least no detriment
to it. In 1978, Betty Freidan, the founder of NOW, would reveal that "Feminists all over the country have admitted to me that they enjoy looking pretty
and dressing up," and the journalist Blair Sabol would confess that the "ass-
shaking talent" of the singer and perennial TV guest star Charo reminded her
of how far women had come: "What's wrong with having it and flaunting it?"[82]
While it is possible to read these stances, as well as *Charlie's Angels* itself, as a
backlash to the anti-difference rhetoric of the radical feminists, it is also worth
considering them as conflicted expressions of a world in which it was less and
less clear whether or not women's difference from men was ultimately good
for women, for men, or for the feminist movement. In this respect, the series
can be seen as a New Woman representation engaged with the women's movement and the questions it raised, even if that engagement ultimately resulted
in a nonfeminist embrace of fundamental sexual difference.

The Proliferation of the TV Sex Symbol

The tremendous success of *Charlie's Angels* inspired all three networks and
multiple producers to duplicate the phenomenon of young women symbolizing sex. While most of these efforts failed, a new batch of sex-symbol women
did appear on-screen in the later 1970s and early 1980s. These representations fell into two general camps: attractive young women in action-oriented,
conventionally male roles and attractive young women as comedic figures.[83]
The latter would have the longer-lasting success and the TV sex symbol would
thereby vacate the action-adventure genre until the 1990s. Whether they were

unabashed Angels clones or the newer, comic style of TV sex symbol, television's post-*Angels* women of the 1970s continued to symbolize sexual difference but to do so in much less conflicted ways than had the blockbuster series. In other words, now that programs such as *Charlie's Angels* and *Wonder Woman* had proven the viability of women in conventionally male roles, television made it seem as if such battles had been won both on-screen and in the real world. Television's female sex symbols no longer had to fight for their rights; they seemed beyond such matters. Nor did they serve as the same kind of scapegoats or fantasy figures for viewers. The TV sex symbols of the late 1970s were not only post-*Angels*, they were unambiguously post-feminist. By picking up the New Woman trend where the Angels had left it, these representations suggested that the questions of women's rights and of sexual difference were now resolved. The TV sex symbol could now embrace her label instead of coyly waffling over it.

Imitating *Charlie's Angels*

All three networks sought to find the next *Charlie's Angels* by developing series, testing pilots, and scheduling series and movies in imitation of the Angels' sexy-young-women-in-action-adventure formula.[84] While none of these efforts were successful in any substantial way, their failure to capture favorable audience ratings helps illuminate what made *Charlie's Angels* so compelling and how television's handling of the female sex symbol had changed by the late 1970s.

One major indicator of a project's attempt to ape *Charlie's Angels* was its emphasis on the female characters' sexual difference. This difference was marked in three main ways in these texts. First, the female protagonists in conventionally male crime-fighting roles used their femininity to succeed. For instance, in *The Hunted Lady* (NBC, 28 November 1977), the police officer Susan Reilly (Donna Mills), who is on the run to escape conviction for a murder she did not commit, pretends to be an air-headed tart to get information from a crooked hotel owner. In *Wild and Wooly* (ABC, 20 February 1978), which was set in the Southwest at the end of the nineteenth century and the beginning of the twentieth, Liz (Chris DeLisle) pretends to give in to the warden's advances so as to steal his keys and break herself and three others out of a women's prison. And in *S.H.E.* (CBS, 23 February 1980), the security hazards expert Lavinia Kean (Cornelia Sharpe) gets a suspect's fingerprints by luring him into placing his hands on her bare flesh while she is clad in a revealing bathing suit.

This emphasis on the characters' sexual attractiveness was further highlighted through their juxtaposition with more masculinized women, much like some of the nemeses of the Angels and Wonder Woman. *S.H.E.*'s villains put Lavinia under the guard of Fanya, a former Olympic hopeful who "failed the chromosome test" and was thus kept from competing. Fanya's large body, martial arts-style robes, sumo wrestler-style topknot, and faint moustache make her almost unrecognizable as a woman. Not only is Fanya inappropriately gendered, she is inappropriately sexed; her very body fails to count as female. Placed next to the rail-thin, glamorous Lavinia (who still manages to best the much more powerful Fanya), Fanya's inability to be sexually differentiated and Lavinia's perfect embodiment of sexual difference come to the fore. A similar, but less extreme, example occurs in the climactic scene of *The Oklahoma City Dolls* (ABC, 23 January 1981), when the protagonists' women's football team plays their big game against the Minneapolis Maids, who are larger and tougher, with shorter hair and more dour facial expressions, than the slim, pretty Dolls.

The third way that the projects that came after *Charlie's Angels* emphasize their characters' sexual difference is by heterosexualizing the women, making clear their difference from men by highlighting their sexual involvements *with* men. In *Cover Girls* (NBC, 18 May 1977), Monique (Jayne Kennedy), the fashion model and spy, says a suggestive good-bye to a man who alludes to "last night," while her partner Linda (Cornelia Sharpe) finds herself falling for Russell Bradner, the suave criminal she is investigating. In *The Dukes of Hazzard* episode entitled "Luke's Love Story" (16 March 1979), the series regular Luke Duke becomes romantically involved with a female race-car driver (played by Roz Kelley, formerly known as the Fonz's race-car-driving girlfriend Pinky Tuscadero on *Happy Days*) who follows up her declaration, "Racing does not threaten my femininity at all," with a passionate kiss for Luke. These instances emphasize the characters' fundamental sexual difference by equating femininity and heterosexuality, making each a precondition for the other.

In all of these ways, the series, pilots, and TV movies featuring sexy young women in conventionally male, action-oriented roles clearly copied *Charlie's Angels*. Yet most of them failed to capture the earlier program's conflicted sensibility about women's roles in a society changed by feminism. Take the case of NBC's *Cover Girls* as an extended example. While *Cover Girls* seemed to have all the right ingredients—beautiful stars, glamorous clothing and settings, undercover work, car chases, guns, and even some humor—the pilot took for granted the women's status as fashion models-spies. Viewers received no explanation for how Linda and Monique got into the spy business (which came first—modeling or spying?) and thus the characters seemed equally at home on display as sexual objects and on the go as crime-fighters. Despite the discourse around *Angels* that suggested otherwise, those TV women were private detectives first and foremost, and they participated in sexual objectification (admittedly, without much protest) as an aid to their detective work, not as an equally significant occupation.

Cover Girls also moved beyond its predecessors' sexualized displays of their stars' bodies by attempting to titillate viewers with the suggestion of erotic involvement between the two leads. An early scene in their apartment features Monique laying on the sofa on her stomach, seemingly naked, with Linda perched next to her, massaging her shoulders and arms. When Linda turns Monique over, we see she is draped in a towel. Their conversation proceeds through shots of each woman over the other's shoulder, with Linda still hovering above the reclining Monique, in keeping with the love scene coding. This scene is followed by what might have read as a post-coital dressing scene, with Monique slowly pulling her nylons up around her thighs and a sweater over her head before zipping up her jeans. This obvious attempt at titillation was not completely foreign to *Charlie's Angels*. The infamous first season episode, "Angels in Chains" (20 October 1976), put the three women in prison, subject to the menacing leer of Maxine, the guard who orders the Angels to open their towels so she can spray their naked bodies with disinfectant. But "Angels in Chains" was the exception rather than the rule for the program; the characters were very rarely put in situations so blatantly exploitative.

Cover Girls also differed from *Charlie's Angels* in its range of representations of the New Woman. In certain respects, *Cover Girls* offered a more diverse range. Monique is African American, and the models'-spies' photographer is also a woman. However, Jayne Kennedy, the actress playing Monique, is light-skinned, with Caucasian features, and her racial identity is never remarked upon. In addition, Monique is, inexplicably, the junior member of the *Cover Girls* team; her white partner regularly directs her, and thus the two are differentiated by status as well as by race. As a third woman to help the program match the Angels' threesome, Ziggy, the photographer, has the potential to be an alternate version of the New Woman character that might have made *Cover Girls* progress beyond *Angels*'s limited vision of post-feminist womanhood. But Ziggy, played by Ellen Travolta, is a somewhat comedic figure, bumbling around with her cumbersome camera equipment, and is thus not an equivalent third. Instead, her presence invites a comparison between her and the models-spies she photographs. Along with her boyish nickname, Ziggy is markedly less feminine than Monique and Linda. Although she is thin, she is not tall and willowy; although she is not unattractive, she is no sex symbol, either. Ziggy has short hair, wears little obvious make-up, and dresses in fitted pants and jackets. Although she comfortably pals around with the models, she is clearly not one of them. Other than providing brief comic relief, her function in the narrative is unclear. She doesn't know that Monique and Linda are spies, so she is, by default, left out of the plot's real action (and because she is behind the camera, she is left out of most of the shots showcasing the models at work, too). In the world of *Cover Girls*, a woman must be a spy *and* a model to achieve narrative significance; being a liberated New Woman who works in a conventionally male profession such as photography is not enough.

In this respect, *Cover Girls* denies the impact of the women's movement and its challenges to the question of sexual difference more so than does *Charlie's Angels*. In *Angels*, Kate Jackson's character, Sabrina, is the Ziggy equivalent. She typically does not take on the "sexy" undercover assignments, more often working behind the scenes or in gender-neutral roles. She does not wear revealing clothing and Jackson did not pose for a scantily clad pin-up poster, as did her co-stars. Yet, unlike Ziggy, Sabrina is an equal member of the *Angels* team; indeed, she is its de facto leader. Although she was not as contrasted with her co-stars as Ziggy/Travolta was with hers, Sabrina/Jackson was undeniably different from the other Angels. While neither Jackson nor Sabrina offered a substantial challenge to the conventions of real-world femininity, in *television*'s world of sexual difference, Jackson/Sabrina *was* a real alternative — a New Woman figure who was not a sex symbol, whose difference from men was not the fundamental justification for her work in a typically masculine profession, and whose deviation from pin-up-girl status did not detract from her narrative significance.

This discussion of *Cover Girls* and its differences from *Charlie's Angels* is not meant to elevate *Angels* above its problematic status as a New Woman representation rooted in immutable sexual difference. After all, *Cover Girls* was only a pilot for a series that was never picked up by its network — and a not particularly well-made pilot at that. But the movie does embody the tendencies of most of the post-*Angels* attempts to capitalize on the trend of sex-symbol women in action-oriented roles. Its unquestioned adherence to a notion of woman's fundamental sexual difference — and to the benevolence of that difference for women's roles in a post–women's lib, post–sexual revolution society — leaves behind the slight ambivalence over the issue of sexual difference and its impact on women's social roles that helped make *Angels* such a cultural touchstone. Where *Angels* offered audiences a space to negotiate ideas about women, men, and the difference between the two, *Cover Girls* and its ilk saw the debate as already settled.

The New, Comedic TV Sex Symbol

Because the *Cover Girls*-style *Angels* imitators failed to capture the public's interest, it might seem as if the TV sex symbol was no longer a viable figure once some of the controversy over the women's movement had settled down. However, the TV sex symbol's late-1970s resurgence as a comedic character suggests something different — that television's representation of sexual difference became completely divorced from the ideals of the women's movement. Now, the TV sex symbol did not even need to use her femininity and her femaleness to succeed in a man's world; instead, she could be a vacuous innocent unaware of her sexual powers, the butt of suggestive jokes or the eye candy for narratives in which she was not a driving force. Characters such as *Three's Company*'s Chrissy Snow (Suzanne Somers), *Too Close for Comfort*'s Sara Rush (Lydia Cornell), *The Dukes of Hazzard*'s Daisy Duke (Catherine Bach), and *WKRP in Cincinnati*'s Jennifer Marlowe (Loni Anderson) were all likable, even admirable, but they did not typically take on male roles or challenge sexism. They did wear revealing clothing and serve as objects of lust for

21 Daisy Duke (Catherine Bach) flirts with Deputy Enos, "One-Armed Bandits," *The Dukes of Hazzard*, CBS, 26 January 1979.

male characters. And their portrayers did pose in minimal attire for pin-up posters, cementing their status as sex symbols.

The comedic sex symbols continued their predecessors' tradition of emphasizing, even celebrating, women's fundamental difference from men. This was accomplished most obviously in the visual presentation of the characters. The introduction of the characters in the series' pilot episodes is telling in this regard, for these episodes instructed viewers on the characters' roles in the series. For instance, in "One-Armed Bandits," the first episode of *The Dukes of Hazzard* (26 January 1979), Duke cousin Daisy first appears in a scene at the Boar's Nest, the local bar where she is a cocktail waitress. She has long, full, wavy hair and wears tight, revealing clothes—a camisole top, spike heels, and her trademark short-shorts. Daisy figures most prominently in the episode when she is taken to jail and her cousins attempt to break her out. A scene of Daisy in her cell begins with a shot of her legs in the foreground, with Luke and Deputy Enos in the background. As the scene closes in on a shot-reverse shot sequence between Daisy and Enos, we see Daisy over Enos's shoulder. She leans over her bent, bare leg, and the leg, framed by cascading hair, takes up the right two-thirds of the frame (see figure 21). While we also learn in this

22 Sisters Sara (Lydia Cornell) and Jackie Rush (Deborah Van Valkenburgh), "Pilot," *Too Close for Comfort*, ABC, 11 November 1980.

episode that Daisy is feisty and fearless, that she rejects the advances of the overbearing men in the Boar's Nest, and that she is devoted to her family, the overt display of her body (and the fact that she is the only regular female character) makes her stand out from the rest of the ensemble and better enables her to symbolize sex and the new sexual culture.

The introduction of Sara Rush in the pilot episode of *Too Close for Comfort* (11 November 1980) similarly emphasizes the character's body and her sexuality. We first see Sara clad in a towel, one hand tucking it in, the other hugging her torso, resulting in a posture that emphasizes her breasts (see figure 22). Sara appears as her sister Jackie (wearing a more modest robe) accuses her of stealing a guy she has been dating. Although Sara protests that she did no such thing, that "When it comes to personality, I just happen to be a 10," Jackie delivers one of the episode's (and the series') first punch lines: "When it comes to personality, you *happen* to be a 36C!" Throughout the episode, Sara literally bounces as she enters scenes, a perfect embodiment of the "jiggle" TV label.

For these characters, sex appeal was a defining characteristic; it drove their narrative purpose and justified their presence in ensemble casts. In part, this narrowness of character was a result of the comedic genres in which they appeared. Yet, sex and gender politics were also to blame. Whereas the action-adventure representations typically used the women's status as sex symbols to "balance" their conventionally male pursuits and assure viewers of their fundamental femaleness, the comedic representations had no such imperative. These characters were not typically engaged in any activities that challenged conventional sex and gender norms. And in the rare instances in which they did, such as when Daisy becomes a police officer in *The Dukes of Hazzard*'s "Officer Daisy Duke" (1 February 1980), those activities did not extend beyond one episode and were connected to the women's movement only in the most tenuous of ways (that is, Daisy is considered for the job because of a government order that the department be an equal opportunity employer).[85] Within these fictional worlds, gender inequities were not a problem and the women's movement was only the occasional subject of a joke.

Along with their status as sex symbols, these characters also embodied stereotypically feminine traits such as innocence or air-headedness. In this respect, they were often infantilized just as they were sexualized, a move that devalued them in multiple ways. For example, *Three's Company*'s sex symbol with the little girl name, Chrissy, would regularly bounce up and down in excitement or anxiety, her jiggling breasts moving along with the child-like, flopping pigtails worn in various configurations on top of her head. Her innocence was especially marked when she would try to be seductive. In "Coffee, Tea or Jack?" (16 May 1978) Chrissy attempts to lure her platonic roommate Jack away from Susan, a curvaceous flight attendant (played by Loni Anderson) who keeps loving and leaving him. Chrissy clumsily runs into the local bar, the Regal Beagle, clad in a slinky red dress. After taking a minute to pose herself in a "sexy" way—which comes off as awkward and silly—she comes up behind Jack and whispers, "Hi" (see figure 23). The hilarity intensifies from here—she asks, "Whaddaya say, you and me?" and gives Jack an exaggerated, open-mouthed wink; she sways her hips and knocks Jack off his chair; she tries to slink out of the bar, but wears only one shoe and ends up hobbling away. Chrissy's attempt to use her sexual appeal is a colossal failure, but the laugh track erupts throughout the scene. The bit is tailor-made for the new, comedic sex symbol. It displays Chrissy's voluptuous body and it works as comedy because it juxtaposes her sexual innocence with her sexual attractive-

23 Chrissy (Suzanne Somers) tries to distract Jack (John Ritter) from his date, Susan (Loni Anderson), "Coffee, Tea, or Jack?" *Three's Company*, ABC, 16 May 1978. WISCONSIN CENTER FOR FILM AND THEATER RESEARCH.

ness. Chrissy acts like a little girl *trying* to be seductive and that is why her actions are so funny. This infantilization of the TV sex symbol removes her ever further from empowerment and ever closer to longtime, sexist stereotypes.

The fact that it is Chrissy, not the third roommate, Janet, who takes on the task of luring Jack away is also significant, for it is emblematic of another key way the comedic sex symbols were characterized. These women were frequently paired with another female character, one who was not unattractive but who was not a sex symbol, either. The sex and gender of these characters was not suspect; they were clearly female, feminine, and heterosexual (unlike Fanya in *S.H.E.* or the Minneapolis Maids in *The Oklahoma City Dolls*). And yet they were clearly different from their sex-symbol counterparts, different in a way that made them less central to the series' comedy and less popular with audiences. Take *WKRP*'s Jennifer and Bailey as an example. As the only two women to work at WKRP, Jennifer and Bailey are constructed as opposites. From their names (the most popular female name of the 1970s, Jennifer, versus the gender-ambiguous Bailey) to their bodies (Jennifer's platinum blonde locks, curvaceous figure, and glowing make-up versus Bailey's straight, dark

CHAPTER 4

blonde hair, thin, athletic frame, and large glasses), their jobs (Jennifer is the station's receptionist and thus interacts with the public, while Bailey is the behind-the-scenes director of traffic and continuity, consumed with tedious details) to their personalities (Jennifer is bold and a bit haughty, Bailey is meek and shy), they embody the sex symbol/not a sex symbol options for women.

In the two-part episode, "For Love or Money" (17 and 24 September 1979), Bailey gets up the courage to ask the DJ Johnny Fever out to a movie, only to be stood up. As she slowly realizes that Johnny is not going to show, she sits at her desk, takes off her glasses, fluffs her hair, and engages in a mock-date conversation with a mirror, trying out, for just a second, what it might be like to cross over to the sex-symbol side. Eventually, Bailey finds out that Johnny is at Jennifer's apartment instead of being with her and she is crestfallen, thinking he has chosen the sex symbol over her. Although Johnny is merely borrowing Jennifer's apartment to impress an old flame, the setting of Johnny's rendezvous emphasizes the difference between Bailey and Jennifer. This difference is further amplified because Jennifer has jetted to Washington, D.C., for dinner with "the Admiral" while Bailey must deal with Johnny's rejection. Bailey and Johnny end up going on a date of sorts and, at the station the next day, the sleazy sales manager, Herb Tarlek, facetiously asks Bailey, "How's your sex life?" When she replies, "Great!" happy about her potential romance, Herb is startled, turning to Les with, "She's kidding, right?" Herb's question was meant to be a joke—everyone at WKRP knows Bailey has no sex life; Jennifer is the one with the dashing suitors. Even though this episode— and the joke on Herb—suggests that Bailey may develop a relationship with Johnny, the more powerful force is the sitcom's recurring situation, the one that Herb references with his joke. As the series continues, so do the differences between Jennifer and Bailey, the sex symbol and not the sex symbol, along with the latter's nonexistent sex life.

Be it Jennifer and Bailey, Chrissy and Janet, or Sara and Jackie, these female dyads shifted the focus of television's sex-symbol representations away from the differences between men and women and toward the differences between women. While a more varied roster of female representations is, in theory, the kind of thing that feminists would applaud, the fact that the comedic sex symbols were so often contrasted with one other woman encouraged a simplistic division between women as sex symbol and not, with the "nots" defined primarily in the negative.[86] This shift in focus also suggested that the question of sexual difference had been settled, that American culture was no longer preoccupied with debating the women's movement's challenge to the supposedly inherent differences between men and women. However, despite television's efforts to take a fundamental sexual difference for granted, that debate was far from resolved. Although progress had been made, the purported differences between men and women were still used to hold women back, to limit their participation in public (and private) life, and feminists continued to fight against such inequalities. The comedic sex symbols helped take that debate off the popular cultural table, giving the dominant, anti-feminist, pro–sexual difference side an edge because no other side was given voice.

The history of the female sex symbol demonstrates one central mode through which television of the 1970s constructed the new sexual culture—embodying that culture in young, attractive women whose fundamental difference from men was at times up for debate but was ultimately affirmed. In the process, the television industry found a way to bring the New Woman character to the airwaves without losing its mainstream audience or its adherence to rather conventional gender representation. At the height of the TV sex symbol's popularity, in the heydays of series such as *Wonder Woman* and *Charlie's Angels*, these symbols of sex teetered between the anti– and pro–sexual difference stances that resonated throughout the feminist movement and between the movement and its detractors. Although this precarious positioning would not last long, it was television's ability to use these characters to negotiate those tricky sex and gender politics that helped make TV's sex symbols matter so much to so many. By symbolizing not only sex, but also much of the turmoil embedded in the term, television's women played an important part in shaping the impact of the sexual revolution and the women's movement on Americans' everyday lives.

— 5 —

SEX WITH A LAUGH TRACK
SEXUALITY AND TELEVISION HUMOR

In 1975, Peter Tripp was faced with a dilemma. In a return appearance as a contestant on CBS's *Match Game*, the host, Gene Rayburn, posed him this puzzle: "A giant turtle tried to 'blank' a Volkswagen."[1] Tripp's task was to fill in the blank and, in so doing, to match his answer with as many of the responses offered by the six celebrity panelists as possible. Tripp was under pressure. His competitor, an executive secretary named Toni Escalese, had already gotten one match, while he had none in this final round. As was typical of *Match Game*, the previous questions had been similarly silly riddles. However, none of this day's puzzles had the same potential as this line about the turtle and the Volkswagen. The panelists' most common answer to a previous question, the story of a woman who told her doctor, "I swallowed an orange pit and now I have a tiny orange tree growing out of my 'blank,'" was "navel," an amusing rejoinder that drew much audience laughter. Tripp's response to the riddle of the turtle and the Volkswagen, however, drew the biggest guffaws of the day. His quiet, almost embarrassed answer, "make love," sent the studio audience, Rayburn, and the celebrity panelists into fits of giggles, cheers, and applause. The celebrity panelists offered similar terms, which allowed them to riff on the program's rampant sexual subtext. The sarcastic comedienne Brett Somers quipped, "You can mate, baby, without marrying, and I'm the one that's here to tell you," while the guilefully prim and proper Betty White obliquely referenced anal sex by cautioning, "Not with the engine in the rear!" Tripp found himself at the center of a quintessential *Match Game* moment, a moment when the program's sexual innuendo and double entendres edged toward more explicitly sexual references. Rayburn loved it. The panelists loved it. And the audience loved it. The moment provided the release to which *Match Game*'s ubiquitous sexual tension inevitably built.

With its humor structured around the evocative "blank," *Match Game* epitomized another key aspect of television's new sexual culture in the 1970s. By using comedy to reference sex suggestively, television managed to participate in the more sexually open culture in a relatively safe form. In many respects, humor was the ideal way for such a mainstream, commercially funded industry to handle the sexual revolution. By dealing with sex in this way, television programs were able to seem current, in touch with the changing society and comfortable with those changes, while attempting to keep within the boundaries of acceptable TV content nonetheless. The fact that the sex in television's sexual humor was nearly always suggested rather than overtly stated was important to the TV industry's claims of family-friendly propriety. Indeed, the comedy in TV sex comedy often arose from what was left *un*said, and thus it could be difficult to label as explicitly sexual. The risqué parts were almost always generated in the viewer's mind; television simply led the way by setting up a situation, a punch line, or a reaction that the viewer could then complete by drawing upon his or her knowledge of the new sexual culture. *Match Game*'s suggestive "blank" may have epitomized this brand of humor, but many other instances fit this formula, as well. From the one-liners of *Laugh-In*'s party scenes to the shenanigans of *Three's Company*'s roommates, from the prudish bluster of *All in the Family*'s Archie Bunker to the finger-snapping magnetism of *Happy Days*' Fonzie, 1970s television winked at its audience, inviting them to share in the sexually suggestive joke.

Although all of television's sexual humor in the 1970s was suggestive rather than explicit, that suggestiveness took on different forms across the decade. While the early years saw some attempts to use references to sex for pointed social commentary, by mid-decade television's comedic construction of sex became silly, trivial, and juvenile, the stuff of embarrassed giggles and surreptitious peeks. No matter the sexual material that television took on, whether it was women's sexual satisfaction, youth sexuality, homosexuality, the rejection of marriage, or the proliferation of promiscuity, television's silly sensibility made all kinds of sexual change seem not so radical after all. By the mid-1970s in particular, television's sexual humor defused much of the sexual revolution's revolutionary potential, reiterating the centrality and normality of conventional heterosexual monogamy.

Still, humor is not so easily contained and thus television's sex with a laugh track was read in a wider range of ways than its dominant tendencies might suggest. When pressure groups ranging from the National Federation for Decency to the National Gay Task Force took issue with television's sex comedy, their protests often emphasized the most radical bits in the medium's "family-friendly" tales, giving those representations more revolutionary power than they might otherwise have held. In addition, some series' experimentation with genre and narrative style, some on-screen talent's experimentation with performance, and some producers' experimentation with non-network distribution led to comedic treatments of sex that veered away from the simply silly and moved toward more politically charged laughs. In these ways, television's sexual humor retained some of its radical potential, even while offering a rather conservative take on sexual change.

Developing a Sense of Sexual Humor

The snickering suggestiveness that made up the bulk of 1970s TV sex comedy developed throughout the decade, arguably reaching its peak in the middle and late 1970s with such programs as *Three's Company*, *The Love Boat*, and *Match Game*. But sexual humor had been an element of American television since at least the late 1960s.[2] Sex jokes began to make regular appearances in variety shows (such as *The Dean Martin Show*) in the 1960s and in sitcoms (such as *M*A*S*H*) by the early 1970s.[3] Most of these sexual references were more suggestive than overt. They also framed sex as one of many social issues up for comedic commentary. In this way, the sexual revolution took its place alongside the civil rights movement, the women's movement, and the war in Vietnam as contemporary matters that, when referenced, could appeal to the young, urban, affluent audience increasingly valued by the networks.

Burlesque-style Sexual Humor: Comedy-Variety Shows

One of the first ways that sexual humor entered into 1970s television was in comedy-variety shows, and much of this humor kept with a very broad, slapstick, late-burlesque style.[4] While this style of comedy-variety was common throughout U.S. television history, sex-themed humor became a feature of the style only as of the late 1960s.[5] For example, in *The Sonny and Cher Comedy Hour* (CBS, 1971–74), the married hosts' mutual ribbing tended to play off of their contentious relationship and thus sex was an occasional topic. In the opening segment of their 20 March 1972 show, Sonny makes fun of Cher's prominent nose as she silently fumes. He laughs at his own cleverness, remarking, "Boy, I'm getting her tonight!" Cher responds, with her trademark deadpan expression, "That's what you think," and Sonny's face falls, his overblown ego deflated as the audience laughter is now directed at him instead of with him. Sex-themed humor sometimes appeared in the program's sketches, as well, as in Cher's burlesque-style "Vamp" numbers, in which a standard chorus ("She was a scamp, a camp, and a bit of a tramp / She was a V-A-M-P / Vamp!") strung together verses and accompanying skits about powerful, seductive women throughout history (for example, Eve, Calamity Jane, Queen Nefertiti). The "Vamp" verses and skits regularly included sexual allusions and gags, such as Cher's line in a verse about the bank robber Bonnie Barlow, "Bonnie really showed him how to load his gun" (20 March 1972). While the suggestive tenor of this sexual humor would reappear throughout the 1970s, on the whole Sonny and Cher's brand of comedy tended toward "cleaner," nonsexual laughs.[6]

Some of the sex-themed humor in comedy-variety shows was more topical, making reference to the youth counterculture or the increased visibility of gay men in the wake of the Stonewall uprising and the active gay rights movement. Skits and jokes about gay men appeared on comedy-variety programs such as *Sonny and Cher, Laugh-In, The Tonight Show* (with Johnny Carson), *The Dean Martin Show*, and Bob Hope's specials. This kind of humor frequently had an anti-gay or homophobic cast, as in a November 1970 special in which Bob Hope derided "Sissy Power," his derogatory label for gay liberation.[7] Some of the gay jokes were more ambiguous in their intention. In the 10 November 1969 episode of *Laugh-In*, guest Carol Channing commented on the government's plan to "legalize" homosexuals with "Oh, darn! Now I'll have to take mine down to City Hall and register them." And in the series' first episode (22 January 1968) hosts Dan Rowan and Dick Martin joked about the supposed gayness of Tiny Tim, the falsetto-voiced singer who appeared on their show. Rowan remarked, "Well, it kept him out of the service," to which Martin replied, "I bet the *Army* burned *his* draft card."[8] Though the joke depended upon the stereotypical association between homosexuality and effeminacy, it also managed to critique the draft and the military's intolerance for homosexuals, complicating the humor's sexual politics.

As these examples illustrate, the sex-themed humor in comedy-variety shows occasionally engaged in social and political commentary and in that respect sex-themed jokes were no different from these shows' many other bits centered on contemporary social issues. *Laugh-In* was as likely to play off of civil rights or anti-war protests as it was gay rights or the sexual revolution. When *Laugh-In*'s producers created *Turn-On* for ABC, however, they focused almost exclusively on sex as a comedic subject. In fact, the longest segment of the first — and only — episode (5 February 1969) featured the word "SEX" flashing on the screen while performers Tim Conway and Bonnie Boland made faces at the camera just under the sign, as if flaunting the program's blatant sexual wallowing.[9] Another skit featured a woman desperately trying to get her chosen item out of a candy vending machine. The product she so desperately wanted, displayed alongside the Hershey Bars and Milk Duds, was labeled "The Pill." The program's risqué humor led to outraged viewer responses, including that of the Senate Communications Subcommittee, which questioned ABC executives about the program's propriety.[10] Although *Laugh-In* was considered a boundary-pushing show, *Turn-On* was especially controversial because the boundaries it pushed were almost exclusively sex-related.

Sex as Social Commentary: CBS's Early 1970s Sitcoms

The appearance of sex-themed comedy in sitcoms of the early 1970s followed in the tradition of the topical humor of the comedy-variety show, but it refrained from the near-exclusive focus on sex that got *Turn-On* into so much trouble. Instead, the sitcoms of the early 1970s that engaged in sexual humor used sexual openness as another symbol of the changing times, right alongside more forthright attitudes toward race relations, the generation gap, and women's liberation. This use of sexual humor for social and political commentary appeared primarily in CBS's new slate of socially relevant sitcoms. For instance, on *All in the Family*, Mike's and Gloria's unfettered mutual desire was a frequent source of humor. Their playful behavior (such as their game of Gloria running into Mike's arms and straddling his body with her legs) and Archie's disgust with their openness often inspired jokes. In the pilot episode (12 January 1971), Archie catches Mike and Gloria sneaking upstairs and cracks, "Used to be the daylight hours were reserved for the respectable things in life." Archie's reaction to the younger generation's sexual expressiveness functioned primarily to draw attention to and comment on the much-discussed generation gap. When Gloria says to Archie, "Your whole generation's afraid of sex," she references an ongoing, politically charged theme of the show, a theme expressed even more often through Archie's bigoted attitudes toward people of color.

The liberal mind-set of *All in the Family*'s creator, Norman Lear, led to story lines with explicitly political purposes, particularly surrounding the acceptance and tolerance of difference. In this vein were gay-themed episodes, including the first season's "Judging Books by Covers" (9 February 1971), which well exemplifies *All in the Family*'s use of humor for politically charged morality lessons. Archie is convinced that Mike's and Gloria's friend Roger is gay and he unleashes a string of anti-gay epithets in his typically outrageous fashion. Though it turns out that Roger is not gay, despite his effeminate demeanor and his fondness for England ("England is a fag country!" Archie declares), Archie discovers that his own drinking buddy, an ex-football player, is. The audience and Archie (to a lesser extent) learn that gay men are just like everybody else and that it is wrong to judge people by outward appearance.[11] Lear instituted similar lessons in his other series. In each case, the sex-related humor functioned mainly to teach liberal lessons about the dangers of stereotyping. Audiences were sometimes invited to laugh at the intolerant characters (such as Archie) and sometimes at the eccentricities of the "different" characters (such as those of the bickering gay couple, Gordon and George, in *Hot L Baltimore*, ABC, 1975), but they were always invited to learn a lesson in tolerance. In the Lear oeuvre, it was not so much sex that was supposed to be funny, but instead the clash of the more sexually open world (including out gay men) and more traditional, outdated values.

The early years of CBS's *M*A*S*H* also used sexuality to comedic and political ends, in this case with sexual humor as a counter to the program's representation of the horrors of war. At the 4077th, the field medical unit in which
the series was set, sex was a favorite pastime of the military personnel. The
significance of sex in this setting was strikingly illustrated in the pilot episode's opening moments (17 September 1972). Shots of doctors and nurses
rushing to the care of incoming wounded soldiers are juxtaposed with a shot
of a female nurse, hurriedly adjusting her clothes as she exits a tent labeled
"Off limits to male personnel" (see figures 24 and 25). She is soon followed out
of the tent by a man, also adjusting his uniform, as the plaintive strains of the
program's instrumental theme song, "Suicide Is Painless" connect the scenes
of suffering with those of hanky-panky in this darkly comedic moment. Much
like the 1970 feature film on which the series was based, the sexual shenanigans of the base's personnel played some part in every episode, at least in the
show's early years. Just as these joyful encounters offered the characters a salve
for the wounds of battle, so too did they offer *M*A*S*H*'s viewers a respite
from the program's biting anti-war commentary. However, *M*A*S*H*'s social
commentary covered more than just war. Even though the program's Korean
War setting was an obvious stand-in for Vietnam, the fact that the series was
set in the 1950s allowed for a contrast between the innocence of the 1950s and
the seen-it-all knowingness of the 1970s.[12] The critic David Marc describes the
political stance of the show and its variation across its run in terms of this
cross-decade incongruity. He argues that, in the early years, Hawkeye was "a
sixties hero in a seventies sitcom set in the fifties," a character whose liberal
outlook functioned to critique the conservatism of the 1950s.[13]

These ideas can be applied to the program's stance on sexuality, as well.
Though in the early years the program never took sex seriously in and of itself,
it was frequently used to poke fun at and even to critique outright not only the
horrors of war but also the uptight morality associated with the 1950s. This is
well exemplified in the characters of Major Frank Burns and Major Margaret
"Hot Lips" Houlihan. The two carry on a torrid affair for years. Most episodes
have at least some reference to their passionate involvement, regardless of the
wife Burns has left stateside, and Houlihan's past affairs with various military
higher-ups play a part in multiple episodes. At the same time, however, these
two are the most prudish, most judgmental, most morally rigid characters

24 AND 25 First a woman, then a man, leave the tent in an attempt to hide their "off-limits" fooling around, "Pilot," *M*A*S*H*, CBS, 17 September 1972.

on the show—they constantly attempt to foil Hawkeye's and Trapper's plans for subversive fun and insist upon upholding military protocol to an absurd extreme. Thus, Burns and Houlihan stand in for the hypocrisy of 1950s-style morality; their characterization as such pits the sexual liberation of the late 1960s and early 1970s against the sexual repression of the 1950s. The early years of *M*A*S*H* used sexual humor in multiple ways, putting that humor to work in social and political commentaries. In many of CBS's sitcoms of the early 1970s, sex was not used to generate laughs for laughs' sake; instead, this form of sex-themed humor commented both on the politics *of* the sexual and on political matters *beyond* the sexual.

Counter-programming Sex as Social Commentary: ABC's *Happy Days*

*M*A*S*H*'s skewering of old-fashioned morality or the traumas of war would peter out over the course of the series, with the program's humor becoming more centered on the characters as flawed individuals than as emblems of their times or circumstances. Marc argues that, with the end of the Vietnam War, "interpersonal relationships shoved American foreign-policy issues to the textual margins; a sixties revisionist history of the fifties gave way to a seventies revisionist history of the sixties."[14] He contends that a 1970s-style emphasis on individualism and personal growth overtook the political radicalism of the 1960s as the primary attitude of the show. The same might be said of the program's take on sex, which became less radical and more personalized as the series overall became more melodramatic. This is especially evident in the fates of Burns and Houlihan. Houlihan's marriage and divorce, Burns's departure from the show, Houlihan's humanization, and her eventual tender one-night stand with Hawkeye stripped the characters of their symbolic status as the embodiment of 1950s sexual hypocrisy and, in the process, changed the program's comedic sexual commentary.[15]

The fact that *M*A*S*H* underwent this transformation away from the use of sexual humor as social and political commentary as the 1970s progressed is telling of the general direction of TV sex comedy across the decade. As part of the heated climate of network competition and as an artifact of American culture at large, television's sex-themed comedy began to shift by the mid-1970s toward a less politicized form of humor that trivialized the changes engendered by the sexual revolution, the gay rights movement, and the women's movement. One of the first new series to shift the tenor of television's sexual humor was ABC's *Happy Days*. The transformations in this program's sex comedy in the first few years of its run illustrate how TV's sex with a laugh track developed the silly, juvenile tone that would come to define the decade.

Once CBS's new sitcoms began to dominate the Nielsen ratings, both NBC and ABC sought ways to draw audiences away from the number one network. One of ABC's first efforts in this regard was *Happy Days*, which debuted in January 1974 and offered a total rejection of the topical humor, sexual and otherwise, found in CBS hits such as *All in the Family* and *M*A*S*H*. A family sitcom set in the 1950s, *Happy Days* in its first season focused on teenage Richie Cunningham learning life lessons, often from his father, Howard. Designed as a comedic version of the wholesome family drama *The Waltons* (CBS, 1972–81), *Happy Days* originally relied upon nostalgia for a family life in the style of *Father Knows Best*.[16] Like the kids on actual 1950s sitcoms, Richie and his friends got into various kinds of trouble, only to be rescued and taught a valuable lesson by their parents (almost always Richie's father). In this respect, the early episodes were the complete opposite of the CBS shows, where the patriarch (read: Archie Bunker) was hardly in a position to offer moral instruction. Still, *Happy Days* was not an exact replica of a 1950s sitcom, since some of the trouble Richie got into was the result of his sexual curiosity. For example, in "Richie's Cup Runneth Over" (29 January 1974), Richie and his friend Potsie get drunk at Potsie's cousin's bachelor party, where they excitedly ogle Verna LaVerne, the woman who jumps out of the cake and performs a song-and-dance number for the partygoers. Another early episode features Richie and Potsie sneaking into Eddie's Pink Palace, a strip club where they hope to see the legendary Bubbles McCall ("The Skin Game," 5 March 1974). In these episodes, the boys often find out that the sexually exciting world they imagine to be just beyond their reach is in fact rather tame. For example, Verna LaVerne remains clothed throughout her number and becomes Richie's maternal protector when she drives the drunken teenager home after the party. In such plots, not only is the boys' innocence preserved, so too is a sense of the 1950s as a more sexually naive time.

However, in the 1974–75 season, when CBS scheduled *Good Times* (1974–79), a Normal Lear production, opposite *Happy Days*, the ABC executives and the show's producer, Garry Marshall, agreed that the Eisenhower-era show needed some kind of contemporary updating in order to compete. (*Good Times* represented the lives of an inner-city African American family and featured the comedian Jimmie Walker in the pivotal and popular role of teen-age son J. J.) Marshall gradually began to include Richie's friend Fonzie in more and more of the episodes.[17] The rebellious hoodlum character tested positively with audiences; his black leather jacket (which ABC only gradually allowed, fearing he appeared too much a criminal), irreverent attitude and, perhaps most compellingly, his prowess with women were his most marked features. Fonzie's appearances during this season often emphasized his Lothario-like pull, but his vast knowledge of women and sex remained more the forbidden territory that Richie and his pals sought to enter than the organizing logic of the series. In many episodes, Howard Cunningham still stepped in to give Richie advice and even, on occasion, to give Fonzie advice. In "Fonzie's Getting Married" (21 January 1975), for example, Howard recognizes Fonzie's supposedly virginal fiancée as a stripper he saw at a hardware convention. When Richie and Howard break the news to Fonzie, he is crushed (as one of the main guidelines on his list of qualities required in a marriageable girl is virginity and, as a stripper, Maureen is apparently not sufficiently virginal). Much as Howard often did for Richie, he here comforts Fonzie, offering him his middle-class homilies on love and marriage.

The more significant transformation in the show occurred in the 1975–76 season. When Fred Silverman joined ABC he concurred with the current management's thinking about the character of Fonzie and he pushed Marshall to make him even more central to the show.[18] The program also changed in this season by switching from a one-camera shooting style to a three-camera style, a production method that allowed for a studio audience. The studio audience, the centering of Fonzie, and a third element—a broader style of comedy—combined to transform *Happy Days* into a top ten and, eventually, number one hit. Even more significantly, the program adopted a different stance toward sex and toward the source of authority on such matters. Placing the Fonz at the center of the show placed a character that was sexually experienced and proud of it at the program's heart. This meant that Fonzie's sexual exploits were regular sources of suggestive humor. In "Jailhouse Rock" (21 October 1975), for example, he hangs out at a train station where Elvis is rumored to be passing through because he knows it will be a great "chick scene," full of broken-hearted girls who fail to meet Elvis and need comforting. At the end of the episode, Fonzie tells his friends about the experience. He relates that the girls had ripped off their clothes in anticipation, but Elvis did not show. Fonzie assures his pals that the girls didn't mind because "It wasn't for nothing. I was there! And believe me, nobody left unhappy, if you get my drift!" In addition to Fonzie's sexual adventures becoming a focal point for the program's humor, so too did Richie's (and his friends') sexual experiences, even if they rarely had the same success as Fonzie. Richie sang his signature song, Fats Domino's suggestive "Blueberry Hill," whenever he "scored" with a date. And Richie's little sister Joannie salaciously relished every snippet of her brother's "grown-up" adventures, approvingly declaring in "The Other Richie Cunningham" (7 October 1975), "Richie, I'm proud of you. You're not a nerd, you're an *animal!*" in response to her assumption that he made an aggressive pass at a girl. While there was never any confirmation in the *Happy Days* world that the characters were actually having sex, the humor was designed to suggest that they were—or at least to make the viewer unsure as to whether or not they were. This sort of humor came increasingly to the fore from the 1975–76 season onward.

Perhaps even more significant was the shift in the program's voice of authority along with the centering of Fonzie and the increase in sexually suggestive humor. This shift helped make the series more a participant in the new sexual culture of the 1970s than a 1950s nostalgia trip. Beginning with the 1975–76 season, Fonzie's advice, insights, and attitudes became the source of authority in the show. The "Father Knows Best" wisdom of Howard Cunningham disappeared; Howard became another of the characters who lacked the know-how that Fonzie possessed. Though Howard sometimes made gestures toward asserting his authority, the audience was typically shown that Fonzie in fact knew best. At the end of "A Date with Fonzie" (11 November 1975), for example, Howard believes Fonzie over Richie when Fonzie explains the compromising position in which the Cunninghams discovered Richie and his date (Shirley Feeney, soon to be spun off in *Laverne and Shirley*). Though it was actually quite innocent, Fonzie confidentially tells Howard that Richie was "about to get her" after a tussle, hence their position prone on the floor. Howard does not lecture Richie on proper behavior, nor does he chastise him for lying (Richie has actually told the truth about the incident). Instead, Howard takes Fonzie's story as the truth: "That's my boy!" he beams with pride. No longer the moralizing father of the 1950s, Howard accedes authority to the sexually accomplished Fonzie and heartily approves his son's presumed sexual experimentation.[19] Part of the humor of *Happy Days* lay in the fact that even the 1950s dad recognized the power of the younger, more sexually experienced figure, that the sexually freer morality of the 1970s had displaced the repressive stance of the 1950s.

These changes in the show's sexual humor in its first few years marked an industry-wide change in network dominance as ABC rose to the number one ratings spot. They also marked an industry-wide change in the role of sex in TV comedy. Now, suggestive sexual humor would move to the center of TV narratives. While this humor was topical in its dependence upon the audience's knowledge and acceptance of contemporary sexual attitudes and behaviors, it was not paired with social commentary and criticism. Unlike the early *M*A*S*H*'s take on 1950s sexual morality, *Happy Days* took no stance on the hypocrisy of prudery or the pleasures of sex as an antidote to the inhumanity of war. On this show, sex was funny because it was *there*, being referenced on TV and acknowledged by all of the characters—young and old, male and female—as a fun fact of life. When Mrs. Cunningham asked her husband if he was feeling "frisky," the laugh track erupted. When Fonzie snapped his fingers and girls came running, the laugh track erupted. When Richie growled, "I found my thrill / on Blueberry Hill," the laugh track erupted. The embellished studio audience was laughing at the relatively forthright way that sex was being referenced, taking adolescent pleasure in getting the joke after so many years of silence about sex, especially on TV. The sexual humor that would follow *Happy Days* would continue this trend, making the new sexual culture safe for television and the American mainstream in the process.

Producing Television's New Sexual Humor: *The Love Boat*

The turn in television's sexual humor that accompanied *Happy Days*' rise to ratings success was the product of specific TV industry manipulations and of a more diffuse, less deliberate shift in American culture at large. Both causes contributed to television's use of sexual humor to make potentially radical changes, among them the increasing acceptance of gay sexuality and the celebration of promiscuity, seem not so radical or threatening to traditional beliefs and practices. We have already seen how network competition led ABC to highlight sex in its programming, and a key means through which it did so was sex-themed comedy. The specifics of that comedy's take on sex, in particular its light-hearted, giggling humor laden with double entendres, both drew from and contributed to a broader cultural stance on sex that defused some of the more controversial aspects of the sexual revolution and the social movements (such as gay liberation and women's liberation) that were associated with it.

Derisively labeled "Lust Bucket," "Leer Boat," and "Floating Foreplay" by its critics, ABC's Saturday night hit, *The Love Boat*, was a key instance of the sexually suggestive humor of the late 1970s.[20] The program's production history is telling of the deliberate ways this brand of sexual humor was constructed. The one-hour show's formula included multiple stories in each episode, each of which featured differently aged characters facing some kind of love-related conflict. Most often, these stories revolved around romantic and sexual relationships, but family relations and friendships factored in on occasion. Although the amount of comedy varied among each episode's three stories, the entire series had a light-hearted tone and made liberal use of a laugh track. A revolving door of guest stars played the ship's passengers, with a regular cast of crewmembers providing week-to-week continuity. As was much of ABC's fare of this era, the program was designed to be family-friendly, although it was also intended to entice viewers with suggestions of sex.

The show's executive producers, Aaron Spelling and Douglas Cramer, strove throughout *The Love Boat*'s early years to include just the right amount of sexual suggestiveness. They sought to keep with their own senses of what made a successful show, as well as responding to ABC's demands for sexy fare. Spelling believed that successful TV sex comedy depended upon avoiding "too much blatant sex." This was not just a matter of meeting standards of acceptable TV content; instead, it was a matter of what was actually funny. Spelling insisted that humor came from *holding off* on sex and he thus ordered that the sex in his productions be more suggestive than overt.[21] While suggestive reference to sex was already a television staple, Spelling's orders along these lines helped to institutionalize such an approach to sexual humor in 1970s television.

Spelling shaped *The Love Boat*'s construction of sex in a range of more specific ways, as well. For example, he vociferously vetoed several suggestions for more glamorous sets on *The Love Boat*'s ship, particularly one for a co-ed exercise room, where men and women could flirt while using "interesting machines," not because of costs but because an "exercise room is *not* sexy!" Spelling preferred instead the idea of a sauna, where towel-clad men and women could interact.[22] Instead of being an arbitrary choice resulting from Spelling's personal proclivities, such a decision likely resulted from Spelling's interpretation of the new sexual culture and his sense of which elements of that culture would be appealing and familiar for viewers. By 1978, bathhouses such as Plato's Retreat in New York City had already been converted from centers of gay sex to pleasure domes for heterosexual couples, where a $25 entrance fee could buy access to a sauna as well as an orgy-ready "mat room."[23] While such places were certainly unconventional, they were not as challenging to heterosexual monogamy as were the gay bathhouses that preceded them. Whether deliberately or not, Spelling's image of *The Love Boat*'s sauna was in keeping with an increasingly commercial, increasingly mainstream fixture of the sexual revolution, the heterosexual bathhouse.

As *The Love Boat*'s executive producer more directly involved with production, Douglas Cramer also contributed to the show's handling of sex. Cramer followed Spelling's lead in his efforts to hold off on "blatant sex" and worked to balance sexual suggestiveness with wholesomeness. Like Spelling, he recognized the need to reference the new sexual culture. Thus, he asked of Gordon and Lynne Farr, the program's hands-on producers, "Do we have enough titillating, purely sexual stories?"[24] He regularly considered each episode's three plots in relation to one another, making sure that youth and sex were prominently featured in at least one. For instance, he asked of upcoming episodes, "Do *any* of the first six hours have a *love* story for Julie [the ship's young, pretty cruise director]? *Let* the poor girl get laid—please!!"[25] Yet Cramer and his staff were also well aware that "purely sexual stories" were problematic for a series, a network, and an industry that prided themselves on offering family-friendly fare. Thus, the sexual titillation that was so central to *The Love Boat*'s appeal was necessarily couched in light-hearted humor. Indeed, humor and sex were understood to be two sides of the same coin. As Cramer commented on an upcoming episode, "What this beautifully emotional script needs most is FUN-HUMOR-LAUGHS-SEX!"[26] Included in the equation of humor and sex was a sort of old-fashioned morality in which sex, while fun, was never frivolous. Instead, it was always connected to heartfelt emotion, to the "love" of the program's title. Thus, Cramer qualified his call for "purely sexual stories" as "naturally" including "heart and depth."[27]

Cramer so fully believed that *The Love Boat*'s combination of sexual openness and old-fashioned values was a "natural" fit and not an inherent contradiction that he was thrown by a letter he received from Dennis Blackhurst, a man who identified himself as both an attorney and a father of five daughters. Blackhurst wrote to complain that he was "continually embarrassed" by the sexual content when he watched a recent *Love Boat* episode with his daughters and that he would keep them from watching future episodes as a result. Although Cramer at first considered ignoring the letter, he found himself bothered by Blackhurst's claims, in particular because he believed that Blackhurst must have turned the TV off before the end of the episode, thereby missing the "*decent* resolution of the stories"—the teenagers considering sex realized they were too young and the adults in the other two stories ended up in monogamous, loving relationships.[28] Cramer decided to send Blackhurst a letter, along with a script of the episode in question. In this correspondence, he did not deny the program's sexual content, but he did insist that "we always point out that sex carries with it a responsibility, and that sex is not love."[29] The fact that Cramer took Blackhurst's criticisms seriously enough to respond to and that he defended the series by insisting that its version of the new sexual culture actually adhered to traditional values illustrates the precarious balance between suggestiveness and wholesomeness attempted in much TV sex comedy of the late 1970s.

Cramer's efforts to sustain this balance were somewhat short-lived, as ABC asked *The Love Boat*'s producers for more and more sexual content as the series entered its third season.[30] Cramer's notes on a fall 1979 script draft are telling in this regard. He began by commenting, "Six months ago, this would have seemed an A+ show—now, I ask (as ABC will) does it have enough *hot sizzle*? Can we tune up the sexuality of the stories? . . . I've made some leering suggestions . . . and bear in mind the request for the jacuzzi in every show!" His "leering suggestions" included eliminating the t-shirts the characters Ben and Sally were wearing as they sat up in bed together and having the two kiss and slide down onto the bed at the end of the scene. In a later scene, he suggested that Ben and Sally be wearing bathing suits on deck "or in *hot tub*—best of all!!" He noted places where many of the characters might be dressed in swimsuits, or where couples might kiss.[31] His comments included no mention of the "heart and depth" he had sought in the past. Concurrent with Cramer's input, *The Love Boat*'s production staff met in October 1979 to devise additional changes "designed to make the show 'sexier.' " The producer Gordon Farr reiterated Cramer's note about the obligatory jacuzzi scene in every episode and the producers planned to include more young women in revealing attire as extras. Even the Pirate Lady statue in the Pirate's Cove lounge was scheduled for a make-over! The line producers were instructed to make sure that scenes on the Lido Deck (by the pool) and in the ship's spa (Spelling's sauna come to fruition) emphasized the "attractive young people."[32] But the specific ways those young people may have been selected reveal much about the strategies through which network television was shaping definitions of sex and sexual attractiveness.

A few months before the October 1979 efforts by *The Love Boat*'s producers to increase the program's sexiness on ABC's orders, the producer Gordon Farr wrote to Spelling and Cramer about what he termed a "potentially explosive situation" on the series, a situation that had been ongoing since the show's debut. Farr described the "directives," "suggestions," "advice," and "comments" delivered to the show's directors about the use of black performers. In effect, the directors were being pressured to "isolate or de-emphasize" black players. The directors, as well as Farr himself, were "shocked" by these requests and distinctly displeased with following them. Farr warned Spelling and Cramer that the situation had to change, that if these directives got out, the show would be destroyed. In his memo, Farr never made clear the source of these directives, but his wording suggests that the pressure was coming from ABC. Because he seems to have been informing Spelling and Cramer about the situation, it does not appear to be something they had ordered. Whomever was the source of this order to de-emphasize black performers, the end result was a program with a slew of young, attractive, *white* extras and few to any blacks. Surely the isolation of black characters that Farr referenced made it likely that those blacks who did appear were rarely filmed near whites, and that even black guest stars (of which there were a small but noticeable number) did not interact with white guest stars and certainly did not have romantic or sexual involvements with them. For example, in a story titled "Mike and Ike" (21 October 1978), the African American guest stars Bill Davis Jr., Marilyn McCoo, and Todd Bridges play old friends of the black bartender (and regular cast member), Isaac Washington. Their characters interact solely with Isaac, the only African American crew member, and their story involves Davis's Mike Sr. getting back in touch with his son, Bridges's Mike Jr., after being distracted by his newfound success as a businessman. Not only did this story stay away from romance and sex (instead dealing with familial love), but its characters were restricted to interactions with other black characters only.[33] Like much television of the period, *The Love Boat* was an overwhelmingly white show. While problematic in its own right, the racial politics of *The Love Boat*'s writing and casting also affected the way that the program represented sex, with nonwhite characters basically excluded from the sex-themed laughs. Although ABC's vision of the show seemingly involved an increase in blatantly sexual material, a liberalization of content, these steps also constricted television's take on the new sexual culture, making it available to some and not to others.

Mainstreaming the Revolution:
De-radicalizing Gayness and Promiscuity

Television networks, producers, and directors made many specific and deliberate choices in the medium's comedic representation of sex, choices that helped turn the seeming risks of more liberal content into "safer," less objectionable material. Yet, as Spelling's preference for the bathhouse-like sauna as a sexy new *Love Boat* set suggests, those choices were also influenced by broader cultural forces, forces that worked upon and through TV executives, creators, and audiences to encourage certain meanings and discourage others. The de-radicalization of the sexual revolution as the 1970s progressed—a process that involved a turn away from the ideals of social movements such as gay liberation or the youth counterculture and toward a more mainstream, commercialized take on sex—both contributed to and drew from television's increasingly apolitical brand of sexual openness.

Creating a Gay Character: *Soap*'s Jodie Dallas

One way in which television comedy of the later 1970s increased its sexual openness and decreased its sexual radicalness was in its handling of homosexuality. By the later part of the 1970s, gay characters and themes had begun to play a different sort of role in TV comedy. Instead of serving as the butt of derisive jokes or an occasion for lessons about tolerance, gayness began to stand in for the new sexual culture, or at least one element of it. The presence of gayness as a theme or as a suggestive allusion allowed sitcoms such as *Three's Company* or joke-intensive games shows such as *Match Game* to seem contemporary and bold while avoiding the controversy that often accompanied representations of explicitly gay characters. When an out gay character did appear, as in the case of *Soap*'s Jodie Dallas, the network and the show's producers found themselves in a comedic quagmire, uncertain how to build jokes around such a character without slipping into moralistic tolerance lessons or old-fashioned anti-gay humor. *Soap*'s struggles with its gay character and other less controversial instances of gay-themed content demonstrate the ways that 1970s television made this potentially radical subject the stuff of silly, nonthreatening laughs.

The controversy around *Soap* began before the show even aired. In the spring of 1977, months before the program's scheduled fall debut, ABC previewed the first two episodes for its affiliates, as well as for Newton Dieter, the director of the Gay Media Task Force, an "information and research group" that saw itself as a resource for the broadcast networks as they began to include representations of gays and lesbians in programming.[34] When word of the program's sex-saturated humor reached the press, religious groups began to agitate against the show, protesting the inclusion of the gay character as well as the romantic triangle between the middle-aged, married Jessica Tate, her twenty-something daughter, Corinne, and a male tennis pro. These religious groups were outraged over the program's irreverent attitude toward all things sexual, including rumored plans for Corinne to sleep with a Catholic priest. They deluged ABC with protest letters and, as a result, seventeen affiliates refused to air the first two episodes, forty-seven more scheduled them an hour later than the network feed, and multiple advertisers withdrew their sponsorship.[35]

As if this sort of controversy weren't damaging enough, gay rights activists also protested the series. Newton Dieter's relationship with the networks was more cooperative than confrontational; thus, while he expressed some displeasure with *Soap*'s stereotypical representation of a "limp-wristed" gay man who dressed in women's clothes and was considering a sex-change operation, he made no outright objection when he previewed the first two episodes. He did recommend that the character drop his sex-change plans and instead become a militant gay liberationist, a device that would allow the program to maintain its satirical, insult-driven comedy, but that would make Jodie a fuller participant in the family's squabbling and would no longer offend the gay community. ABC responded to Dieter by promising that changes in Jodie's character were already planned; the network claimed that Jodie was going to drop the sex-change idea, become a stronger figure, and begin a relationship with a nonstereotypical gay man. This assurance momentarily appeased Dieter, but not the more radical National Gay Task Force (NGTF). The NGTF was wary because of the public statement of Fred Silverman, the president of ABC Entertainment, that "Jodie was going to meet a girl and find there are other values worth considering." Silverman's statement came in the wake of protests by the religious right and pull-outs by affiliates and advertisers and was a clear attempt to salvage the show, which still had not aired. The NGTF media director, Ginny Vida, saw Silverman's statement as "an effort to pacify the homophobes" and the organization took its objections to the pages of *Variety* with an ad denouncing ABC's "gay 'Stepin Fetchit.' "[36]

Soap finally debuted on 13 September 1977, without any immediate changes to the Jodie character.[37] In the first two episodes, the episodes that had caused such a ruckus, Jodie is indeed the embodiment of a gay male stereotype. In the credit sequence, he fastidiously spreads cream cheese on a bagel, lips pursed, pinky finger in the air. The first time we see the character he is posed in the kitchen doorway, hands braced on the frame, with a campy smirk on his face. He enters the room singing, "Oh, what a beautiful morning," and his stepfather, Burt, refers to him as a fruit. Jodie is clearly coded as effeminate and as very much the opposite of his macho brother Danny. Danny is muscular, in tight jeans and a tank top, with fashionably feathered hair; Jodie is slight and nerdy, in a jacket and tie and short hair. Danny slumps in his chair, legs spread wide; Jodie sits up straight, legs daintily crossed. The gay male caricature continues in the second episode (20 September 1977), when Jodie wears his mother's pink dress and blonde wig and announces that he is thinking of getting a sex-change operation (see figure 26). After these two episodes, however, the Jodie character begins to change rather dramatically.

26 Jodie tries on his mother's dress, Episode 2, *Soap*, ABC, 20 September 1977.

First, in Episode 3 (27 September 1977), Jodie stands up to Burt, requesting, "Just think of me as a person." Burt has a long monologue in response, in which he talks through his thoughts about "this gay business." In his typically bumbling, twitchy fashion, Burt goes on about how, when he was growing up, "gay meant happy," and how it used to be easier on "us" (straight people) when "you" (gay people) were in the closet. Burt ends up reluctantly agreeing to try to be nicer to Jodie; he even shakes his hand, although he is clearly uncomfortable doing so. *Soap* regularly included pathos amid its comedy, but this scene is played mostly for laughs. The source of the humor is no longer Jodie's mincing about; it is Burt's inability to handle Jodie's gayness, the clash of an old-fashioned sensibility with sexual-revolution-style openness.

From this point in the series onward, Jodie's sexuality is never the joke, although it lands him in situations and conversations that generate laughs. By Episode 8 (8 November 1977), Jodie forces Danny to accept his gayness, by Episode 10 (22 November 1977), Jodie decides not to have the sex-change operation (he was only doing it to hold onto his boyfriend, a football player), and by Episode 16 (10 January 1978), the credit sequence has been shortened, and Jodie's breakfast-table preening has been cut out. In many ways, the Jodie that populates the vast majority of *Soap*'s episodes is a multi-dimensional, nonstereotypical representation; however, his gayness becomes less and less significant to his identity. Many of his story lines include involvements with women, involvements that are romantic and/or sexual to varying degrees. He is not "converted" to heterosexuality, but his sexuality becomes more and more ambiguous. While it was possible to read this as an especially radical move (rejecting all categories of sexual identity), it also functioned to make Jodie's gayness more palatable to anti-gay forces *and* less offensive to gay activists. The character's sexual ambiguity left him open to a divergent range of readings. As "liberated" as *Soap* was about sexuality, its problems with the recurring gay character and its innovative development of that character as a result demonstrate the limitations of television's ability to make the new sexual culture fully revolutionary.

Winking at Gayness and Promiscuity: *Three's Company*

Broadcast just before *Soap* on ABC's Tuesday night line-up was *Three's Company*, the program that was often cited as the epitome—or nadir—of late 1970s TV sex comedy. While the sitcom's handling of sex drew plenty of opposition (for example, from the religiously motivated National Federation for Decency), it also helped make the show extremely popular. *Three's Company* placed among the top twenty rated shows until its final season on the air, landing in the top three for several seasons. The sitcom was premised upon its three main characters, Jack, Janet, and Chrissy, sharing a Southern California apartment as they juggled their work and dating lives. The roommates saw their arrangement as a perfectly innocent way to live cost-efficiently, but much of the program's humor was based in the fact that many other people assumed their relationship was more a sexual than a financial three-way. Though this confusion created many comedic mishaps with dates, parents, and employers, the roommates' set-up was most problematic for their relationship with their landlord, Stanley Roper. At first, Mr. Roper refused to let Jack live with the two women, so the roommates devised a ruse to get him to agree. They led him to believe that Jack was gay, thus ensuring the innocence of the roommates' relationship. *Three's Company* was able to use references to gayness to signify its sexual knowingness without falling into *Soap*'s dilemma of trying to represent an actual gay character.

Much of the program's humor came from the fact that Mr. Roper constantly suspected that Jack was straight and constantly schemed to expose his true identity. This situation was able to recur because many an episode concluded with Jack, Janet, and Chrissy convincing Stanley, yet again, of Jack's gayness. For example, in "Cyrano de Tripper" (8 November 1977) Mr. Roper mistakenly thinks he has seen Jack and Chrissy kissing. His suspicions (and libido) are further aroused when Janet talks to him about Jack (who is a chef) secretly cooking dinner for Chrissy and her date, Michael. Of course, in the suggestive style laden with double entendres that is the norm of late 1970 TV sex comedy, she never explicitly refers to the fact that he is cooking, nor that Chrissy has a date in the apartment. Instead, she refers to Jack and Chrissy being busy in the apartment and says things such as "[Jack] lives there and he can do the job" and "I would've loved to have stayed and watched," which Mr. Roper interprets as further evidence of these young people's sexual deviance. Both infuriated and excited, he dashes upstairs. By this point, Chrissy's food-snob date has discovered that Jack, not Chrissy, has done the cooking and he and Jack are together in the kitchen, comparing recipes. When Chrissy wails, "He stole my date!" and Mr. Roper sees Jack and Michael (wearing an apron) deep in conversation about the "dashiest dash of tabasco" in the stuffing, he is assured of Jack's gayness yet again.

Though Jack often deliberately "plays" gay to convince Mr. Roper, nearly as often the landlord is convinced by inadvertent circumstances. Thus, while the program plays upon stereotypes of gayness — Jack girlishly fluttering his eyelashes at Roper — it also suggests that gayness and straightness are impossible to determine by surface appearances. Jack's passion for cooking (a conventionally feminine activity) is matched by his passion for women, but Roper's mind is made up about Jack's identity on the basis of whichever characteristic Jack displays at any given moment. Although Jack's mugging generates plenty of laughs, much of the humor revolves around Roper's confusion, a mocking of an old-fashioned sexual politics that saw gayness and straightness as mutually exclusive categories. Still, Stanley Roper is no Archie Bunker. When Archie was confronted by any kind of nonconventional sexuality — from a gay buddy to an unmarried straight couple who live together — he railed against it, using every expletive the censors would allow to denounce the deviant behavior. Despite his outward insistence on propriety, however, Stanley is a dirty

27 Stanley Roper (Norman Fell) offers his trademark smirk, "Chrissy's Date," *Three's Company*, ABC, 11 October 1977.

old man. He gawks at a sunbathing Chrissy through binoculars in the show's credit sequence, he hides pornographic magazines in his toolbox, and he takes lascivious delight in the possibility of Jack's straightness ("What were those three *doing* in that apartment?") *and* in the possibility of Jack's gayness. Whenever Roper delivers a suggestive zinger about his wife, Helen, or thinks he has found definitive evidence of Jack's sexuality, he turns toward the camera, offering a self-satisfied leer, a lecherous smile of prurient glee, as the laugh track erupts (see figure 27).

As Roper knowingly turns toward the audience in these reaction shots, we are invited to laugh at both his easy titillation and his old-fashioned notions. We know better—we know that Helen's quips about Stanley are more stinging, and more frequent, than are his about her. We know there is not necessarily anything sexual between the roommates and we know Jack's true sexual orientation. We also know that Roper's mind is the most sex-obsessed place of all, that more goes on in there than anywhere else in the on-screen world. Here is where the program's sexual openness is closed off, its stance on matters such as gayness and promiscuity de-radicalized. As much as the audience is invited to share Roper's dirty thoughts—that's how we get the joke, after all—and as much as the audience is encouraged to take pleasure in the many sexual references, we never see the characters engage in any sexual activity, other than occasional kissing scenes. In fact, for all their sexual suggestiveness, they seem rarely—if ever—to have sex.[38] They certainly do not have gay sex; the refutation of Jack's gayness (or any character's gayness) is a given for the viewers, if not for Mr. Roper. Ultimately, all of the desires expressed by the main characters are strictly heterosexual, except perhaps for Mr. Roper's titillated response to Jack's supposed gayness. And Roper's impotent sexuality (his wife, Helen, constantly complains of how little he satisfies her) is hardly a model of a more open, more flexible sexual identity.

If anything, Roper's sexuality is part of the comedy *because* of its impotence; Roper's leering is humorous because the audience knows how ineffectual he really is. Indeed, much of the so-called sex comedy depends upon the audience's certainty that all of the characters are rather chaste. We know that Jack is not sexually involved with his female roommates; nearly every episode makes light of his mock sexual passes and Janet's and Chrissy's inevitable rejections of them. Entire episodes revolve around the roommates teaching an overly aggressive Lothario or seductress a lesson. In "Chrissy's Date" (11 October 1977), Jack and Chrissy find out that her new boyfriend, Lloyd, is actually married, and they threaten to expose his philandering to his wife. Similarly, in "Janet's High School Sweetheart" (29 November 1977), Janet learns that her old crush, Peter, is only after one thing—one thing she has no intention of giving him. Because the characters' prudery was so central to so many plots, indeed, so central to the entire series, the sexual suggestiveness around which *Three's Company*'s humor revolved served rather conservative ends. The characters lived in a post–sexual revolution world but their values and their actions remained safely ensconced in a more innocent past.

Promiscuity and the Comedic Game Show

A similar blend of the innocent past and the sexual culture of the present marked the comedy of some of the era's more salacious game shows, such as *Match Game* and *Three's a Crowd*. The former was the longer-running series, having begun on NBC daytime in the 1960s.[39] In 1973, after a three-year hiatus, CBS brought the program back to daytime and between 1975 and 1981 a second version of the show, *Match Game PM*, was sold in first-run syndication. Both 1970s incarnations of the show had the same format: two contestants competed to match the answers of the six celebrity panelists in their own responses to the questions. The questions featured a suggestive "blank" that the participants had to fill in, often elaborating upon a double entendre already present in the question. Although sexual humor and an awareness of the sexually open times were part of the program's premise, traditional attitudes toward sex were regularly asserted. For example, most of the questions dealt with hypothetical, married characters (e.g., "The magician's wife was upset because . . ."), perpetuating the idea that sexual raciness was permissible if within the bounds of marriage. Also supporting this traditional notion were many of the panelists' typical answers. Thus, in the question about the turtle that "blanked" the Volkswagen related at the beginning of this chapter, many of the panelists answered "marry" as a euphemism for "have sex" or some other, more explicit phrasing, as if marriage and sex were synonyms. While *Match Game*'s distinctiveness depended upon the sexual suggestiveness of its humor, the kind of sex referenced in many of these jokes was more conventional than revolutionary, more safely located in the boundaries of marriage and heterosexual monogamy than in the "new," sexually open promiscuity.

Even the outrageous game show *Three's a Crowd* often reified traditional sexual morals. As a product of Chuck Barris's game show empire, *Three's a Crowd* placed contestants in potentially embarrassing situations and sought to expose their sexual secrets. The program pitted secretaries (all of whom were women, usually young and single) against wives — the wives of the secretaries' male, typically middle-aged bosses. In the game's first round, the host, Jim Peck, asked the husbands/bosses a series of questions, all related to sex, some more overtly than others: "How many days a week are you in a sexy mood?" "What is the sexiest item of clothing your secretary has ever worn for you?" "What is your secretary's bust size and what is your wife's bust size?" After Peck posed these questions to the men, they were joined by the secretaries. The secretaries would then answer the same questions (for example, "How many days a week is your boss in a sexy mood?"). For every match between the secretary's answer and her boss's, the "secretary" team would earn a point. The program reached its climax, however, when the wives came out. As did each secretary, each wife would answer the questions. Peck would then call upon first her husband, then her husband's secretary, to reveal their answers. If the wife's answer matched her husband's, the "wife" team scored a point. Whichever team scored the most — the secretaries or the wives — would get to split the one thousand dollar prize. But the real hilarity of the show came in the moments when the wives and the secretaries compared their answers. Though this comparison had no impact on the score of the game, it was the focal point of the show. Thus, when Tina Cardozza, Art Cardozza's wife, found out that her husband and his secretary, Judy, had both described Judy's tight sweater that she wore without a bra in answer to "What is the sexiest item of clothing your secretary has ever worn for you?" Tina half-indignantly, half-jokingly exclaimed, "You had to add 'without a bra'!"

Three's a Crowd's humor was supposed to arise from the clash between the new, sexually open society and the conventional morality associated with marriage. Often, however, this presumed clash failed to materialize. For example, for the comedic premise to work, the audience needed to assume that the husband might very well be sleeping with the secretary *and* that the wife knew about this, or at least suspected it, and was closely monitoring the secretary's responses (as well as her husband's) as a result. Both the swinging single secretaries and the philandering husband/bosses stood in for the new sexual culture, while the more suspicious and defensive wives were representative of an older, more conventional sexual sensibility. The program was structured to bring the old (the wives) in conflict with the new (the secretaries) and to watch the link between the two (the husbands) alternately squirm and gloat.

Several features of the participants' behavior, however, disrupted this formula, leaving impressions of a less radically altered society than the premise suggested. For instance, not all of the husbands seemed to understand their role as cheating husband and lecherous boss. When asked, "Other than a kiss, what sign of affection are you most known for?" the husbands responded with their signs of affection to their wives. The men's automatic reference to their wives instead of their secretaries suggested that they had no sexual involvement with their secretaries. And many of the questions innocently presumed the same; for example, to the men, "If you were single, why wouldn't you date your secretary?" Certainly, these pretensions to innocence helped to make the show's racier moments all the more risqué, as if the producers had no intention of things taking such a salacious turn, as if the contestants' sexual adventurousness was beyond the producers' knowledge. Still, this presumption of marital fidelity in some of the questions and responses made the contestants' marital ties seem solid and monogamous. Like *Match Game, Three's a Crowd* depended as much upon an assertion of old-fashioned heterosexual monogamy as it did upon references to the new sexual culture. No matter who won, the wives or the secretaries, the husband's/boss's patriarchal privilege remained intact.

Across game shows and sitcoms, daytime and prime time, much of television's sex with a laugh track in the 1970s reified traditional values, affirming their "normality" in a period of vast sexual change. In the inimitable style of U.S. broadcast network television, the sexual revolution was simultaneously given voice and silenced, flaunted and ignored. Even though much of the sexually suggestive TV comedy of the middle and late 1970s was excoriated for being inappropriate, tasteless fare, the dominant messages about sex offered through these laughs affirmed heterosexuality, monogamy, and premarital chastity as norms and relied upon such "new" developments as gayness and promiscuity as comedic foils. The new sexual culture was good for a laugh precisely because it was so clearly deviant, so fully other than television's traditional world.

Beyond the Laugh Track: Uncontainable Sexual Humor

Even while the most visible instances of television's sexual humor ultimately upheld conventional morality, their reliance upon the "deviant" challenges of the new sexual culture required that those challenges be represented. Because those challenges were so often presented comedically and thus ambiguously, they were sometimes able to go further, to push more boundaries, than were representations of sex in other areas of television. Also, because these representations generated such controversy, they garnered the reputation of being more transgressive than they actually were. The very groups that protested against these programs so loudly helped to make them emblems of the new sexual culture in ways the programs may not have on their own.

Protesting Sexual Humor: The Religious Right

Throughout the 1970s, multiple religious groups protested television's new sexual content, going so far as to compel advertisers to pull their sponsorship from particular shows under threat of consumer boycotts. These groups placed enormous pressure upon the television industry and upon the medium's instances of sexually suggestive humor. Such groups offered broad characterizations of the medium as sex-and-sin-saturated and in so doing they helped to make television's handling of sex seem especially salacious.

Although such groups would achieve their greatest public prominence in the late 1970s, at the height of the adolescent turn in sexual humor, religiously motivated pressure groups were active throughout the decade.[40] Although certain specific cases were widely publicized (such as the National Council of Catholic Bishops' protest against the *Maude* episode about abortion), the Reverend Donald E. Wildmon's National Federation for Decency (NFD) made a name for itself in the wake of the clamor around *Soap*. Taking note of the *Soap* protestors' impact on advertisers, Wildmon set out to pressure program sponsors as a means of reforming content. A 1978 NFD survey named Sears as the sponsor with the third-largest number of commercials on shows with "explicit" sex. As a result, Sears withdrew its sponsorship from *Three's Company*, among others. Sears denied that its actions were in direct response to the NFD's boycott threats, but the company was surely reacting to the climate of concern over television morality publicized through the NFD and other religiously motivated groups.

These efforts had an impact on public attitudes toward television sex, as well, at least as determined in surveys conducted by major ad agencies. These surveys found that the general public was particularly uncomfortable with "ideas and behaviors which seem to threaten their existing concepts of [the] family institution," such as homosexuality and "mate swapping."[41] As a result of such findings, ad agencies began careful screenings of all programming during which their clients might advertise; companies totally dedicated to such screening services even began to appear.[42] These screening processes were particularly problematic in the case of sex-themed comedy, since the suggestiveness embedded in the genre made it difficult to determine what was and was not to be considered offensive.

When the National Federation for Decency teamed up with the Moral Majority, another right-wing, Christian fundamentalist group, to form the Coalition for Better Television (CBTV) in 1980, major advertisers became even more wary of sponsoring sexually suggestive shows. Procter and Gamble's chairman, Owen Butler, announced that his company had withdrawn sponsorship from more than fifty programs and that CBTV was "expressing some very important and broadly held views." [43] By the spring of 1981, advertisers had begun to withdraw 5 to 8 percent of their commercial sponsorships (a large increase from the average of 1 to 2 percent advertiser pull-outs in previous seasons). [44] In 1982, when the Moral Majority left CBTV, the organization began to lose some of its influence. But religiously motivated protests of TV sex comedy had already achieved their most powerful impact. The threat of advertiser withdrawals was an important jolt to television economics, yet the religious groups' effect on specific constructions of TV sex was minimal. Most significant was the role of these groups in labeling 1970s TV as shamelessly, immorally, and embarrassingly wallowing in sex. This reputation helped television and its sex-themed comedy to seem a radical component of the sexual revolution, a conduit for the new sexual culture's entrance into the American home. According to these self-appointed guardians of decency, television and the new sexual culture were equally guilty partners in immorality.

Challenging Conventions of Television and Sexuality: Game Show Humor

The controversy around television's sexual humor incited by the religious right certainly helped give TV sex comedy a more radical edge than it might have acquired on its own. Yet some instances of 1970s TV sex comedy challenged television's typical take on the sexual revolution in ways that resisted the de-radicalizing impulse of most television humor. Through particular comedic performances, through experiments in genre and narrative form, and through alternative distribution channels, multiple instances of 1970s TV sex comedy offered a version of the new sexual culture that truly recognized and championed the changed society.

Despite their repeated assertions of monogamous heterosexual marriage as the norm, the sexually charged game shows *Match Game* and *Three's a Crowd* contained moments of subversion that suggested an irreversible change in the "normal." On *Match Game*, this subversion was regularly evidenced in the performance of the celebrity panelist Charles Nelson Reilly. With his oversized glasses, decorative ascots, quick wit, and bitchy barbs, Reilly embodied the stereotype of the effeminate "queen" who reveled in camping it up. His caustic repartee with his fellow panelist Brett Somers was a regular feature of the show's humor, as were his intimations of gayness. Unlike the explicitly gay character Jodie Dallas, and unlike the fictional Jack Tripper, who pretended to be gay, Reilly was a real person who was the subject, not the object, of many jokes. As campy as Reilly could be, he was not usually the butt of the joke; instead, he *made* the jokes, often at the expense of traditional sexual morality. Reilly functioned to "queer" the show; his innuendo-tinged answers to the already-suggestive "blanks" hinted at a nonstraight sexuality that the other participants and the studio audience found hysterical and rather lurid.[45]

Reilly's queer presence was particularly noticeable in contrast to the sometimes hopelessly straight contestants. For example, a male contestant answered a riddle about a magician bringing his "blank" to bed with him. His response, "magic wand," failed to gain him any matches (most of the panelists answered "assistant"). As the host Gene Rayburn was surveying the panelists, however, Reilly announced, "Now I get it!" to great laughter and applause. In so doing, Reilly queered the meaning of the contestant's answer, which had been, in its initial form, merely a poor choice, not a sexual allusion. Throughout the rest of the episode, Reilly pushed the "magic wand" metaphor, offering it up as an answer to every question, drolly delighting at the double entendre, a reference to male anatomy that became queer when uttered repeatedly, and with great pleasure, by Reilly. The audience's excitement at this shtick was rooted in its ability to "get" Reilly's joke. Because members of the audience were familiar with his campy persona, and because they were living in a post–sexual revolution culture in which gay sexuality was a newly prominent matter of public discussion, viewers could reveal their trendy comfort with some of the more racy features of the new sexual openness by laughing at Reilly's gag. The same could be said of the allusions to homosexuality on *Three's Company*. However, *Three's Company* had to resolve each episode with an assertion of Jack's heterosexuality (and his female roommates' chastity) in order to allow for the return of the misunderstandings that would propel the next episode's narrative. *Match Game* required no such return to stasis. Gags such as Reilly's "magic wand" joke did not get recuperated and viewers did not necessarily leave the show reminded that heterosexuality was still safely dominant.

Some of the performances of *Three's a Crowd*'s wives also functioned to challenge the conservative tendencies of the game show's take on the new sexual culture. Although the show was designed to place the wives in the position of woman scorned, newly confronted with her husband's philandering, the contestants did not always play the roles they were assigned. Instead of reacting with outrage to how well the secretaries knew their husbands, the wives often were playfully willing participants in the suggestion of nontraditional sexual entanglements. For example, one wife, when asked what was the strangest or funniest thing that either she or her husband had asked the secretary to do, responded, "Well, I once asked Roberta to go out on a date with us." Roberta's earlier answer to this question was an embarrassed refusal to get into details about the kind of club her boss and his wife invited her to attend. With the wife's response, the host Jim Peck and the audience were confronted with the suggestion that she was at least as much a sexual swinger as was her husband or his secretary, possibly even more so, given her interest in some kind of swingers' or group sex club. Another wife told Peck, in response to a question about her sex drive, "Frankly, we've been having a problem about that, but I don't think it has much to do with my sex drive. It's more that he couldn't—you know, carry it out."[46] She thus reversed the sexual scrutiny of the question onto her husband's sexual inadequacy, making her the active sexual agent to her husband's sexual object. Such attitudes suggested that the wives were as willing to go along with the promiscuous culture (or with the program's pretensions to it) as were the husbands and the secretaries. Without an outraged wife to stand in for old-fashioned values, the conflict that structured the show was neutralized and the husband's power to surreptitiously sleep with two women was diminished. Such moments made the sexual revolution seem more disruptive than anyone had thought; after all, even the wives were in on it. These moments offered instances of sexually suggestive comedy in which women's sexual liberation was the new norm and men's sexual dominance was a relic of the past. Despite its regressive premise, *Three's a Crowd* allowed for just this sort of comic reversal, wherein television's new sexual culture offered something truly new.

Challenging Conventions Through Serialized Storytelling

Women's sexual freedom was given voice elsewhere on the television schedule, as well, primarily in two fictional comedy series—*Soap* and *Mary Hartman, Mary Hartman*—that challenged the sitcom form just as they challenged traditional sexual values. *Soap*'s serialized narrative structure was a first for the sitcom and a near-first for prime-time television, as well, in the years before the ascendancy of *Dallas* and the prime-time soap opera. All members of the Tate and Campbell families around whom the series revolved grappled with sexual dilemmas and, as a result of the program's serialized narrative, these dilemmas held a complexity and a sense of character specificity that sitcom-centered sexual humor typically avoided. Much like other instances of 1970s TV sex comedy, *Soap*'s humor relied upon the clash between its characters' promiscuous behavior and their attempts to appear to conform to conventional sexual morality. Jessica Tate's affair with her tennis pro, Peter Campbell, is a case in point. The naive Jessica is wracked with guilt over her liaison with Peter; she imagines that she has broken the heretofore unblemished marital bond she shares with her husband, Chester, who has in fact long been a relentless adulterer. She determines to break it off with Peter for the sake of her marriage but ends up sleeping with him again. Even though she has felt great sexual pleasure with Peter (she admits to her sister, Mary, that she "likes it," something she never realized before), she resolves to commit to her marriage instead. Jessica's competing desires, as well as her naiveté about sex, marriage, and Chester's fidelity, are sources of much humor. The comedy arises from the disjoint between Jessica's ideas of traditional sexual morals and the reality of her promiscuous life (not to mention her husband's).

Yet *Soap* did more than just poke fun at the clash between sexually "free" attitudes and behaviors and more traditional ones. The program also suggested that the freedoms of sexual liberation brought an important benefit to some of the characters' lives. The likable, if remarkably naive, Jessica's sexual awakening through her affair is presented as a positive step for her, as is Mary's assertiveness in pursuing a remedy for her husband Burt's impotence. When the primary women characters, Jessica, Mary, and Jessica's daughters, eat ice cream and talk openly about sex in various episodes, the program again allows for an expression of female sexual desire not often found in prime-time television of the 1970s and not entirely expected for such a comedy-heavy show.[47]

Soap's narrative form also allowed for challenges to television comedy's typical take on sexual change in its blending of humor and pathos. The moments of pathos kept the outlandish stories, including the tales of sexual promiscuity, from serving solely as instigators of adolescent giggles. Instead, the serialized stories and emotional range gave the program's representations of sexual liberation a gravity and thoughtfulness that most TV sex comedy lacked. For instance, Jessica's remorse over her affair with the tennis pro is amplified when she finds out that her daughter, Corinne, is involved with him, as well, and she tearfully apologizes to Corinne for her behavior. Similarly, Danny Dallas's homophobic refusal to acknowledge his brother Jodie's gayness melts when Jodie passionately insists that Danny recognize him as gay and as the same person he has always loved. Danny and Jodie's heartfelt embrace at the end of this scene, as well as Jessica's talk with Corinne and numerous other such instances, changes television's typical stance on the freedoms brought by the sexual revolution from one of puerile titillation to one of sincere reflection. These moments are possible precisely because of *Soap*'s revisions to the sitcom form, revisions that borrowed serialized storytelling and extended scenes that were more about character exploration than plot advancement from daytime soap operas. Indeed, *Soap*'s creator, Susan Harris, has claimed that the ability to "have scenes about nothing that moves the story forward" was a key benefit of *Soap*'s unconventional narrative style.[48] It was also central to the program's unusual take on sexuality. As Jason Mittell has argued, *Soap* stood apart from its contemporaries in that "instead of normal sitcom endings reinstating the status quo, the last scenes . . . typically [posed] unresolved dramatic conflicts and [elicited] melodramatic emotional responses of suspense and pathos."[49] Through its serialized narrative and blend of comedy and melodrama, the most controversial and derided of ABC's sex comedies in fact generated many thoughtful observations on the benefits and drawbacks of the new sexual culture.

Mary Hartman, Mary Hartman (MH, MH) also used serialization and a blend of humor and pathos — along with an alternate distribution strategy — to tell its stories of life after the sexual revolution, and it resulted in a TV sex comedy that embraced sexual change instead of denying its significance. Its producer, Norman Lear, pursued the unconventional path of first-run syndication for the series after all three broadcast networks elected not to purchase it.[50] Even though the program was thirty minutes long and contained comedic elements, the narratives were wholly serialized and were stripped in a five-day-per-week schedule. *Mary Hartman*'s odd structure made many station owners reluctant to buy it. At its January 1976 premiere, 70 to 80 stations carried the show, but its fast ratings success encouraged another 30 to join in seven weeks into the run. By the second season, beginning in September 1976, the show was appearing on 125 stations nationwide.[51]

Mary Hartman, Mary Hartman's brand of sex-themed humor was a surprise hit because the show was different from most TV sex comedy, not only in its distribution and its narrative structure, but also in its tone, style, and subject matter. Lear envisioned the show as a satire, with commercial television as its target, in particular television advertising and the populist programming, such as daytime soaps, in which much of it appeared.[52] But Lear also constructed the show as a commentary on class and gender politics in the era of the sexual revolution, in other words as a newer, more radical version of his hit CBS sitcoms. By employing typical soap opera conventions but setting them within a working-class community instead of the middle- and upper-class enclaves more typical of daytime drama, the series pointed out the mismatch between our television fantasies and our everyday lives. By exploring Mary's dissatisfaction with her life as a wife and homemaker, the creators sought to address the feelings sweeping the nation in the wake of the women's movement.[53] In addition to politicizing some of the soap world's concerns in these ways, the program also mocked some of the soaps' formal conventions through an overuse of melodramatic organ music, elaborate pauses at the end of scenes without much dramatic import, and shoddy sets, shaky camera work, and generally on-the-cheap production values. At the same time, however, MH, MH paid homage to the soaps' most compelling elements. With the experienced soap writer Ann Marcus at the helm, the series was built upon the tribulations of interpersonal relationships and the kind of character development made possible by a serialized narrative structure.[54]

One of *Mary Hartman*'s strongest continuities with and departures from daytime soaps came in the program's treatment of sex. Like soap operas, sexual relationships were a primary concern in the MH, MH world — marriage, divorce, adultery, pregnancy, and romantic love received extensive attention. But *Mary Hartman* treated these themes with a comedic and politicized twist seldom found in daytime (see figure 28). For example, the series begins with Mary clearly dissatisfied with her husband Tom's sexual interest in her. We find out that they have not had sex in five weeks and that both are deeply disturbed by it. Their reactions to this situation propel many of the show's story lines and offer pointed, humorous commentary on the new sexual culture.

28 Greg Mullavey (as Tom) and Louise Lasser (as Mary) in *Mary Hartman, Mary Hartman,* syndicated. COLUMBIA PICTURES TELEVISION/PHOTOFEST.

Mary, convinced by her voracious consumption of TV soaps, commercials, and *Reader's Digest* that it is her wifely duty to remedy the situation, visits the library to check out a stack of sexual self-help books—*You and Your Climax*; *It's Your Body: Do It—A Guide to Erotic Pleasures*; *343 Ways to Improve Your Marriage*; *Orgasm and You*. She later hires a sex therapist (who turns out to be a sex surrogate), tries out a personal growth therapy called STET (a parody of the 1970s therapy trend EST), and eventually sleeps with the man who pursues her throughout the series, the police officer Dennis Foley. Tom has an affair with the divorcée Mae Olinsky, from whom he fears he has contracted a venereal disease, nearly sleeps with the sex surrogate, and cruelly blames Mary for his own sexual problems. Both Mary and Tom waver between their commitment to the values of conventional marriage and their involvement with the new sexual culture. Mary in particular is attracted to the liberation, sexual and otherwise, that she suspects may be hers in this age of the women's movement and sexual freedom. For example, in the first episode (6 January 1976), Tom rejects Mary when she comes on to him in bed. He claims, "Every time I feel like doing something, you do it first . . . It kills everything." When Mary protests that *Reader's Digest* says things are different these days, Tom

CHAPTER 5

cuts her off, insisting that he must initiate their sexual relations. He insists that she "Act like a woman!" to which she queries, "And do nothing?" Tom's response is his attempt to reassert a pre-liberation stance on sexuality: "That's right. Stay put. And then when I feel like doing it, I'll do it. But I don't feel like doing it when you're doing it." The scene ends with a close-up of Mary's face as she wonders, to the camera, "Wait a minute . . ." while both the incongruity and the sexism of Tom's words slowly dawn on her.

Mary's and Tom's sexual problems are further highlighted by the unbridled sexual expressiveness of many of the other characters, from the blissful marriage of their friends and neighbors Charlie and Loretta Haggars, to the sexual adventures of Mary's promiscuous sister Kathy, and even to the sexual eccentricity of Mary's Grandpa Larkin, also known as the Fernwood Flasher. Thus, when Loretta and Kathy chattily compare their impressive orgasmic responses in front of her, we see that Mary is disturbed by her failure to achieve the same level of sexual freedom.

Much of the sexual material in the series is not strictly comedic. Tom's and Mary's problems, for example, are represented as truly painful for them. For example, in the tenth episode (17 January 1976), Tom even tears up as he asks Charlie, "You ever feel like you just don't got it anymore?" Still, the show's satirical nature gave every moment a comedic edge. Mary's absurd appearance and demeanor — her little-girl look, complete with braids and pinafore, and her remarkably unaware naiveté — are humorous in and of themselves, as is Loretta's unflagging, innocent cheerfulness in the face of any adversity. The show contained its share of double entendres and innuendo-heavy jokes, particularly in the lyrics to Loretta's autobiographical country songs (for example, "It Feels So Good When You Feel Me"). With no laugh track, however, these sexual allusions do not become the stuff of embarrassed tittering. Instead, the sex jokes are more ambiguous — sometimes it is difficult to tell if they are jokes or not. In addition, and as *Soap* would soon do as well, *Mary Hartman* mixed humor and pathos to such an extent that the distinction between the two was often blurred.[55] Even the most heartfelt dramatic moments contained a tinge of irony. For example, when Tom and Mary argue about their sexual problems and Mary tells Tom she understands that his "sexual power is diminishing," he angrily responds, "I do *not* want your understanding!" In return, Mary poignantly remarks, "That's funny. Because the one thing I want in this world is your understanding." To Tom's frustrated, "Why? What don't I understand? What? What?" Mary despairingly notes, "You wouldn't understand." While the emotions in this scene are intense and genuine, Tom's and Mary's awkward miscommunication and Mary's typically circular reasoning (for example, her comment to a caller, "I can't talk now, I'm on the phone") turn the tone just slightly away from straightforward drama and slightly toward absurdist satire.

MH, MH's forthright handling of sexual material earned it a place among other instances of TV sex comedy as a subject of protest and as an object of moral condemnation. Complaints by citizen groups about the racy content got the program canceled in Richmond, Virginia, and Salt Lake City, Utah. In Seattle, a suburban housewife staged a moderately successful campaign to get advertisers to pull out of the show.[56] When Cleveland's WJW-TV switched the program from 11:30 PM to 7:30 PM in February 1977, a coalition made up mostly of religiously affiliated groups vigorously objected to the move, placing an ad in the *Cleveland Plain Dealer* and generating an estimated ten thousand letters and phone calls.[57] Much as with the religiously motivated groups campaigning against *Soap* and other instances of television's sexual humor, these sorts of controversies helped emphasize *Mary Hartman*'s radical take on the sexual revolution.

Despite (or perhaps because of) these protests, MH, MH found a substantial audience. In the major markets of Los Angeles and New York, it captured a larger share of viewers than did the CBS stations' late evening newscasts (against which it was scheduled).[58] Many of the show's fans were particularly enamored of the program's politicized stance. For example, Shelley Fields, a thirty-three-year-old schoolteacher in Oakland, California, expressed her admiration for the series to her local station by declaring, "I am involved in the women's movement and theater and from that point of view I want to say 'right on'!"[59] *Mary Hartman*'s non-network scheduling, its unconventional narrative structure, its off-beat tone, and its earnest effort to grapple with the implications of the sexual revolution turned out to be more compelling than off-putting for many viewers, suggesting that television's typical comedic take on sex was not necessarily Americans' only way of understanding the sexual revolution. In *Mary Hartman*, these viewers found a comedic handling of 1970s sexual culture that spoke effectively to their own senses of the changing world, revealing both its absurdities and its glories without diminishing the serious significance of those changes.

Assessing TV's Sex with a Laugh Track

Because comedy has long been a staple of American television entertainment, and because the comedic treatment of sex was one major way that the medium constructed the new sexual culture, television's sex with a laugh track is exceptionally revealing of the medium's tendencies when it comes to social change. Although politically charged humor earned a place on-screen by drawing substantial ratings, network competition, the parameters of the sitcom genre, regulatory and sponsorship pressures, and a neoconservative turn in the culture at large shifted television's comedic take on sex away from the political and toward the silly and juvenile as the 1970s progressed. In American television's distinctive way, sex-themed comedy for much of the 1970s managed to reference such newly acceptable subjects of public discussion as homosexuality and promiscuity while simultaneously denying these arenas of experience any credibility or permanence. Most often, matters such as women's sexual expression, nonstraight sexual orientations, or non-, pre-, or extramarital sexual involvements could be the butt of jokes or suggestive allusions, but could not have an ongoing, fully realized existence on-screen. Still, the ambiguity of meaning at the center of much humor, and especially at the center of sexually suggestive humor, allowed for moments when the post–sexual revolution culture was an undeniable TV presence. As one of the central elements of television's new sexual culture in the 1970s, the comedic treatment of sex made TV seem up-to-date and old-fashioned at the same tumultuous time.

FROM ROMANCE TO RAPE

SEX, VIOLENCE, AND SOAP OPERAS

The difference between rape and romance is a very thin line.
—NEW YORK STATE ASSEMBLYMAN JOSEPH F. LISA, 1972

Rape is not a crime of irrational, impulsive, uncontrollable
lust, but a deliberate, hostile, violent act of degradation
and possession.—SUSAN BROWNMILLER, 1975

Among the 14 million viewers who attended the romantic wedding of Luke Spencer and Laura Webber Baldwin in November 1981 were many who had also witnessed Luke's dramatic rape of Laura two years earlier. Those fall 1979 viewers of ABC's increasingly popular daytime soap opera, *General Hospital*, saw a drunk, lovesick Luke, convinced he was about to lose his life, force the married, seventeen-year-old Laura onto the dance floor of the deserted disco he managed. As Luke sank to the ground, pulling Laura with him, those viewers watched the dizzying multi-colored disco lights fly by, the camera tilting and panning aimlessly around the walls of the disco, Luke and Laura just beyond the bottom of the frame. As Luke kissed Laura and dragged her to the floor, those same viewers heard her cries, her protests, her "No"s. They also heard, with increasing volume, the thumping bass, echoing horns, and synthesized drum machine of Herb Alpert's hit single, the instrumental "Rise," the record Luke chose to play as mood music for his disco-themed rape. *General Hospital*'s viewers would hear the strains of "Rise" for months thereafter in the program's daily episodes; the music became the audio cue for Luke, Laura, and their audience of millions to repeatedly relive the rape.

Nearly a year later, at a soap opera festival in St. Louis, *General Hospital*'s fans cheered and applauded as Anthony Geary, the actor who portrayed Luke, took to the stage. Geary had become the most popular actor in soaps within that year, regularly placing in the top ten actors in *Daytime TV* magazine's monthly readers' poll. By October 1980, he was receiving one hundred fan letters a day and *Daytime TV* could proclaim, "There's no doubt about it. Tony Geary . . . is definitely the most popular actor on daytime TV, judging by the mail he receives."[1] Thus, in many ways, the zealous reaction of the St. Louis fans was not unexpected. Nor was it surprising when one woman broke through the crowd to present her idol with a gift — an award presumably intended to honor Geary for his compelling performance. Inscribed, "To Luke — America's Most Beloved Rapist," the award testified not only to Geary's popularity, but also to the significance of his character's act of rape in the minds of at least some of his fans.[2] Luke's rape of Laura was central to Geary's success, to the characters' status as daytime's first "supercouple," and to their wedding's capture of over 50 percent of the viewing audience and the highest daytime soap opera ratings ever.

In deeming Luke "America's Most Beloved Rapist," Geary's St. Louis fan was, in fact, selecting Luke out of at least eighteen other rapist or attempted rapist characters in U.S. daytime soap operas between 1978 and 1981. During these years, all three broadcast networks and at least ten different shows featured rape story lines, the highest concentration of such plots in the history of U.S. daytime television. Scarce to nonexistent before the 1970s, rape stories became standard fare in daytime serials during the decade, steadily building to the virtual explosion of rape plots at decade's end. Not all of the soaps' rape stories were as controversial, or as successful, as *General Hospital*'s, but the sheer volume of representations of rape in a genre that had avoided such plots before the 1970s, as well as the diversity of the representations, make these stories a highly notable instance of television's handling of sex and the new sexual culture in the 1970s.

These rape narratives offered audiences a way to negotiate long-standing views of rape as motivated by sexual desire and the newer, feminist-generated conception of rape as inspired by hostility and power. In these stories, sex is constructed as alternately pleasurable and dangerous and often as a confusing blend of the two. Unlike the discourse of sexual endangerment in made-for-TV movies and regulatory debates, soap opera rape plots were not expressions of moral panic. Instead, they were examinations of the intensity of feeling associated with sex, and the problematic situations of the women and men who were overcome with that intensity. Although daytime's attention to rape was part of the soap genre's new embrace of social issues, rape stories adhered to time-worn conventions of soap storytelling. While such conventions sometimes compromised the revolutionary potential of these narratives, they also allowed for an attention to the complexities of the new sexual culture that few other of television's representations of sex achieved.

What Is Rape? Defining Sexual Violence

The multitude of rape stories appearing in daytime soap operas contributed to an outpouring of media discussion on the subject during the 1970s. Throughout the decade, mainstream magazines and newspapers devoted more and more pages and column inches to rape.[3] Similarly, U.S. broadcast network news programs went from covering three rape stories in 1969 to covering forty stories in 1978.[4] This was accompanied by a rise in fictional rape representations in prime time, especially in detective series such as *Baretta* (ABC, 1975–78), *Charlie's Angels* (ABC, 1976–81), *Hawaii Five-O* (CBS, 1968–80), and *Starsky and Hutch* (ABC, 1975–79).[5] Rape stories were an appropriate fit for a ratings-greedy industry eager to exploit sex and violence, but the change in the degree of media attention accorded to rape was also occasioned by developments in the real world, namely, substantial increases in the number of rapes reported to law enforcement. According to FBI statistics, 27,100 rapes were reported nationwide in 1967, while 51,000 were reported in 1973 and 82,088 in 1980.[6] These numbers were only a percentage of the rapes actually committed (the FBI estimated that there were at least three times this amount), but they are notable because they indicated the vast increases in the number of women willing to report the crime.

This newfound openness about rape was largely due to the activities of the anti-rape movement, a mostly feminist endeavor that had a major impact on the handling of rape cases by the justice system. Feminist anti-rape efforts took on several forms in the first half of the 1970s, including the creation of activist groups and the publication of anti-rape tracts. After two 1971 rape "speak-outs" organized by the New York Radical Feminists and NOW's formation of a National Task Force on Rape, women's anti-rape groups organized into the Feminist Alliance Against Rape in 1974.[7] A series of explicitly feminist anti-rape books appeared in the same period.[8] Most famous was the 1975 release, *Against Our Will*, in which the author, Susan Brownmiller, proclaimed that rape was "nothing more or less than a conscious process of intimidation by which *all men* keep *all women* in a state of fear."[9] She thus argued that rape was at the very foundation of patriarchy; it was the violence upon which women's subjugation to men depends. She explicitly denied that rape was motivated by sexual passion, insisting instead that understandings of rape as seduction, as uncontrollable sexual urge, function to perpetuate rape's violence in that they blame women for their supposed sexual vulnerability and ambivalence.[10]

The assertion that rape is motivated by hostility, not by sexual desire, became a rallying point not only for radical feminist thought but also for more mainstream anti-rape discourse.[11] Such discourse appeared in multiple sites, from psychological studies to women's fashion and home-making magazines, where the ideas were wholly endorsed. For example, in a 1976 issue of *Harper's Bazaar* readers were told, "Rape is not a sexual crime. Rape is a crime of violence like a mugging or battery, and has its roots not in lust or uncontrollable passion, but in hostility and hatred of women."[12] Anti-rape activism led to substantive changes in rape legislation and investigatory practices, but its more widespread impact was in changing the *terms* through which many Americans understood what rape was. The insistence that rape is a crime of violence, not an act of sexual passion, fought against the logic that had kept rape out of public discourse and rape victims away from psychological and judicial reparation. Maria Bevacqua contends that this altered definition of rape was the most important element of feminists' anti-rape ideology of the 1970s: "The assertion that rape is violence provided feminists with a whole new framework in which to analyze rape, to remove blame from victims, and to develop a convincing argument to gain acceptance for their claims."[13]

Yet as powerful as the feminist effort to change public understandings of rape was, long-standing prejudices, myths, and fantasies continued to associate rape with men's sexual desires and women's sexual allure. The fact that these myths were often perpetuated by participants in the justice system—police officers, attorneys, jurors, and judges—continued to impose obstacles on women's efforts to bring rapists to justice. As one juror explained in 1974, "Unless her head is bashed in or she's 95 years old . . . there's a suspicion . . . that she led the guy on or consented."[14] Such sentiments and their ongoing public circulation left many confused about the true meaning of rape. When a 1974 study of college and professional women asked whether they had been raped, many replied, "I don't know."[15]

The debate over how to define rape was further confused by widespread uncertainty about the boundaries (or lack thereof) of sexual permissiveness. As some anti-rape feminists transformed into anti-pornography activists, as questions of homosexual rape, date rape, and marital rape came to the fore, and as racial inequalities continued to affect which accused rapists were convicted and which rape victims were believed, a definitive answer for the meaning of rape remained elusive. After a decade of anti-rape activism, many Americans were still unsure whether a man could rape his wife, whether women provoked rape by their dress or demeanor, whether rape was motivated by sexual passion or by violent hostility. In a period of simultaneous openness about, and wariness of, sexual liberation, it was still possible to argue, as did one reader of *U.S. Catholic* magazine, that "there is a high correlation between the rise in rapes and the laxness in moral standards of dress today. The way some women bounce around half exposed these days, it's surprising there aren't *more* rapes." Yet, in the pages of the same publication, another reader could insist, "It is a myth that only promiscuous women get raped, that women ask to be raped by their style of dress or behavior, or that no woman can be raped against her will."[16] A third participant in the same reader forum could ambivalently claim, "Although it is true that rape is not solely a crime of lust, in many cases it certainly is—and could be prevented."[17]

By 1979, when these women expressed their conflicting perspectives, much had changed in rape laws and in the treatment of rape victims, and much had changed in public understandings of rape, as well. However, consensus on the meanings and motivations of rape remained elusive as the 1970s drew to a close. It was at this time of confusion and conflict over the meaning of rape that so many television soap operas took on the issue. In so doing, television both drew from and contributed to the new sexual culture's understanding of sexual violence, generating a forum within which distinctions between sex and violence, passion and aggression, romance and rape would be debated.

Rape Comes to Daytime: 1960s and Early 1970s

The smattering of soap opera rape plots before the late 1970s and the nineteen different rape story lines between 1978 and 1981 may have been important elements in television's construction of sex, but they did not offer a univocal message about the meaning of rape.[18] All of these narratives adhered to basic conventions of soap storytelling, relating the experiences of individual characters and using rape as a catalyst for interpersonal conflict.[19] But they had differing degrees of affinity with the anti-rape movement and differing degrees of clarity in their definitions of rape. From the earliest tales of nonconsensual sex in the mid-1960s to the flurry of rape plots at the end of the 1970s, soaps told three kinds of stories about rape. The first kind, what I am calling the "old-fashioned" rape plot, describes the earliest attempts to include nonconsensual sex in soaps, although it persisted in some stories of the late 1970s, as well. This kind of rape story was strictly apolitical, with no reference to the anti-rape movement (a movement that was virtually nonexistent when many of these story lines aired) and little recognition of the confusion around the meanings and motivations for rape. These fictionalized rapes were not always motivated by lust, but they were often the result of a tumultuous romantic relationship and the man's resulting intensity of feeling. In contrast, the second kind of story took on a political and pedagogical mission, seeking to educate audiences about the crime and its ramifications for victims and perpetrators. While such stories still adhered to the conventions of soap storytelling, they also sought to make a point about rape, arguing that the woman involved was completely blameless and that a society that thought otherwise was in need of change. In these cases, writers and producers purposefully endorsed an understanding of rape as motivated by violence as opposed to passionate lust, thus directly engaging with real-world rape discourse. The final class of stories combined these approaches, depicting rapes with complicated motivations and exposing audiences to the rapists' and the victims' perspectives. These plots tended to offer an ambiguous message about rape, failing to side clearly with either the notion of rape as sexual passion or of rape as violent attack. To a greater extent than the other two kinds of stories, they blurred the line between real-world experiences of rape and fictional ones. This category of rape story, best exemplified by *General Hospital*'s Luke and Laura plot, drew the largest and most impassioned audiences to daytime.

The "Old-Fashioned" Rape Plot

Before the pressures to draw younger audiences to daytime began in the late 1960s, television soap operas continued a tradition in place since the heyday of radio serials in the 1930s, a tradition of focusing on "women's concerns" such as family relations and domestic life.[20] By the mid-1960s, a few soap operas began to broaden the troubles that befell their heroines by exposing them to the dangers of rape, but these stories did not treat rape as a social issue. In fact, the nonconsensual sexual encounters faced by these characters were not typically labeled as rape. Instead, they were identified as traumatic experiences that complicated the characters' marriages and that set off a sequence of further troubles. In the mid-1960s *The Guiding Light*, *General Hospital*, and *Another World* each aired a story line in which a woman was raped by her husband and became pregnant as a result.[21] The men's actions in these three stories were represented as hostile; they were not motivated by inflamed sexual desire but by a desire to punish or control their wives. Thus, while sexual attraction was not presented as a primary motivator, an intensity of feeling related to an intimate relationship was. In this respect, rape was another destructive choice made by a soap character, on a continuum with such relationship-complicating actions as deception and adultery.

The violent husbands on *General Hospital* and *Another World* were rather villainous characters even before the rapes, but the story of *The Guiding Light*'s Mike Bauer was somewhat different. Because Mike was not the immoral figure that both *General Hospital*'s Tom Baldwin and *Another World*'s Danny Fargo were, the show's writers and producers had to provide him with a motivation for his attack on his wife, Julie, that would be forgivable later on.[22] However, because marital rape was not considered a crime in the 1960s, and because rape in general had yet to undergo the critical exploration that would seek to dissociate it from sexual passion, having a non-villainous main character who rapes his wife was not especially untenable. As long as his actions could be explained as a poor choice, made under great emotional duress, Mike Bauer could—and would—continue to be a pillar of the Springfield community for years to come.

Mike Bauer's rape of his wife, Julie, on the 10 August 1964 episode of *The Guiding Light* is the first instance of rape in the history of U.S. daytime drama, as far as I have been able to identify. At this point in the story, the couple has been married for a year and are parents to a baby girl, but neither is especially happy with their situation. Julie has told Mike that she wants to leave him and Mike, drunk and angry, has awakened Julie late at night to insist she stay. "You are my wife and Hope is my baby and you are not going to leave me," he declares. According to the script, Julie feels a sense of mounting panic as Mike grows more and more insistent. They continue to argue and Julie attempts to leave the room to check on Hope, but Mike puts his hands on her shoulders, reminding her, "You're my wife." When she asks him to let her go, he insists, "You're going to try to love me, Julie, you're going to try." As she struggles to get away, he grabs her and takes her in his arms; the scene fades out. In a scene set the next morning, he apologizes for "last night." Julie says, "You don't have to apologize, Michael, I am still your wife," but Mike assures her that "last night will never happen again."[23]

Mike and Julie soon separate, but Julie discovers that she is pregnant as a result of that night with Mike. Mike, believing the child has been fathered by Julie's new love, Alex Bowdon, accuses Julie of infidelity. It is only when Julie miscarries, in an early 1965 episode, that Mike realizes the truth of the baby's paternity. His memories of that night come back to him as he admits, "I . . . I forced myself on her. She told me she was going to leave me and I . . . I got angry. I . . . I sort of went crazy."[24] The story plays heavily on Mike's remorse and anguish from this point on, but his guilt and his friends' and family's reactions to it center more on his unfair accusations about Julie and Alex than on the rape. On-screen, the event is never referred to as a rape, and the characters move on to new troubles.

Mike's accusations about Julie and Alex motivate much of the conflict experienced by these characters in the latter part of 1964 and the beginning of 1965, and thus they have a significant function within *The Guiding Light*'s narrative. Of course, Mike's denial that the baby could be his was an essential, causal element in this chain of events and, thus, his denial of the rape was also an essential element. In order to make this denial feasible, the GL writers had to characterize Mike as a man who, "from the moment after he forced himself on Julie, wanted to forget the incident. He looked on it as a totally animal abandonment of himself and that, coupled with the fact that he was drunk at the time, [had] allowed him to pretty well block it out of his mind."[25] Mike's pain was supposed to explain his heated accusations of Alex and Julie, as if he were using the accusations to avoid facing his own shameful actions, as if Julie's reputed infidelity were much worse than his actual assault. His "confession" after the miscarriage (a confession he makes to Alex, not to Julie) not only makes rape a matter to be settled between men but also functions as the beginning of Mike's salvation. Here, he recognizes that his actions were as shameful as Julie's supposed infidelity and, as a result, the character begins to be redeemed.

No greater penance is required of Mike for several reasons. First, nonconsensual sex between married people was not considered a crime; second, the rape factored into the soap narrative mainly as a cause for future events (the pregnancy and Mike's accusations about Alex and Julie); it was not a source of major conflict in its own right. The *Guiding Light* creators had to have a character as central as Mike (the son of the town matriarch Bert Bauer) regret such socially denigrated behavior, but they did not have to have the more peripheral character of Julie experience any aftereffects beyond the pregnancy and Mike's accusations about Alex. Indeed, the rape was significant emotionally more for its impact on Mike than on Julie. The rape thus provided an unusual narrative catalyst, helping to drive Mike and Julie apart and Julie and Alex together, but also causing a central male character to grapple with his intense feelings about his own behavior and about his wife. This intensity of feeling associated with rape was common across the different categories of the soaps' rape stories of the 1960s and 1970s. However, this first instance of a soap opera rape plot was different than later rape stories in the relative lack of significance of the rape itself in the lives of the characters, and especially in the life of the woman. Before the sexual revolution and the anti-rape movement had their full impact, Mike's actions were represented as shameful, but not violent or criminal, and their effect upon Julie was depicted as hurtful but not especially damaging or enraging.

Two other rape stories of the late 1960s and early 1970s tread similar ground, but they furthered the intensity of feeling involved in the rapes by explicitly invoking the characters' feelings of sexual passion. Even more so than the old-fashioned rape plots on *Another World*, *General Hospital*, and *The Guiding Light*, these stories used rape to depict a romantic relationship gone so far as to exceed the boundaries of social acceptability. Because these stories depicted rapes between men and women who were not married to one another, but who did have some kind of involvement, the rapes were even more illicit than those in the earlier stories. Without the parameters of marriage to define the characters' relationships, the overwhelming sexual passion they experience is both more deviant and more motivated by uncontrollable desire.

The rapes on *Days of Our Lives* and *Love Is a Many Splendored Thing* occurred within stories of unrequited love and frustrated sexual passion. Like *The Guiding Light*'s Mike Bauer, the men who committed rape in these stories were established and well-liked members of their on-screen communities and, as a result, the shows' writers had to build a justification for their actions into the stories. In some ways, these justifications were easier to establish than was Mike Bauer's, since Bill Horton and Mark Elliott both acted out of an overwhelming romantic attachment to the women they raped.

In 1968, *Days of Our Lives*' Bill Horton raped his sister-in-law, Laura, with whom he was deeply in love. Although Laura and Bill had been planning to marry, Bill, a surgeon, had left town in anguish over a career-crushing hand injury. In Bill's absence, Laura marries Bill's brother, Mickey, only to have Bill return to Salem, hoping to reconcile. Bill rapes Laura in a drunken bout; she becomes pregnant and passes off the child as Mickey's. As in the earlier rape plots, this rape and the pregnancy it generates serve as rich narrative catalysts: in 1972, Laura reveals the truth of her son's parentage to a medical board in order to save Bill's career; in 1974, Mickey and Laura divorce, allowing Laura to marry Bill; in 1976, Mickey finally finds out that the child is Bill's son, not his. For eight years, the ramifications of the rape guide Mickey's, Laura's, and Bill's story lines. Bill is allowed to retain his status as a romantic leading man; his marriage to Laura is represented as a triumph of true love. Thus, William J. Bell, the head writer of *Days of Our Lives*, had to justify Bill's actions, and he did so using logic similar to the justification used by the writers of *The Guiding Light* regarding Mike Bauer—a description of the character as being overwhelmed with feeling. But he also questioned the meaning of rape and its applicability to this scenario. Responding to a letter from a viewer who identified himself as a minister and expressed concern about the moral fiber of the show (particularly its "illicit sex indulgences" like rape), Bell explained: "As for Bill Horton and his relationship to his sister-in-law—in my own mind I seriously question whether the act was truly rape, as Laura herself has recently questioned. But certainly there can be no doubt that Bill has suffered deeply and gravely, personally and professionally, for that one drunken act that was borne out of his deep love for a woman. Please don't misunderstand, I don't for a moment condone what Bill did—but I hope you'll agree that Bill was not his normal, rational self at the time."[26]

Citing Bill's remorse, his drunkenness, and his abnormal state, Bell found a way to justify the rape—or at least to justify Bill's place as a sympathetic character despite the rape. Unlike the explanation of *The Guiding Light* writers, however, Bell also turned to Bill's love for Laura (and Laura's for Bill) as reasoning for the rape. Though he was clear to state his disapproval of Bill's actions, he also attributed them to Bill's "deep love," a love that, in this case and in Bell's mind, made the rape an act of sexual passion. Thus, while the 1960s story lines on *The Guiding Light*, *General Hospital*, and *Another World* featured marital rapes committed by hostile husbands attempting to control their wives, the *Days of Our Lives* story line invoked a notion of rape as a sexual act, motivated by love rather than hostility.

Similar motivations propelled Mark Elliott's rape of his sister-in-law, Iris Garrison, on *Love Is a Many Splendored Thing* in 1972. In this case, however, it was not Mark's love for Iris, but his love for her sister (his wife, Laura) that inspired the rape. After suffering through their share of problems, Mark and Laura are gradually making their way back to each other when Mark goes on a drinking binge in an effort to forget their troubles. In the 9 February 1972 episode, Mark arrives at Iris's door, expecting to find Laura there (she has already gone home); instead, he finds Iris. In Mark's drunken haze, however, Iris appears to him to be Laura. He declares his love for her, his need for her, "You're my wife. I love you . . . I love you . . ." as he kisses her passionately, "overpowering her in a crushing embrace," "[putting] her down on the couch and [pinning] her body with his own."[27] Though Iris struggles against him, Mark's insistent, "I can't wait for you any longer. I've got to have you . . . now!"

and his physical strength prove too much for her.[28] He rapes her and passes out, remembering nothing the next day. Later, when he does remember, he is extremely distraught, desperately wishing, to Iris, "If there only were a way to correct mistakes, erase incidents. When I think of what I did, of how I acted towards you that terrible night. . . ."[29] Mark and Iris both suffer as a result of the rape, as they feel that they must hide the event from their respective spouses. Predictably for the old-fashioned rape plot, Iris becomes pregnant as a result of the rape, which further complicates the situation and becomes the focus of the story.

Because the writer Ann Marcus constructed the rape as "accidental" (she refers to it this way repeatedly in her notes), there was not as much need to exonerate Mark as there was for the writers of *The Guiding Light* and *Days of Our Lives* to exonerate their respective rapists. And because marital rape, as defined legally, did not exist in 1972, had Mark done the same with Laura as he did with Iris (thinking she was Laura), Marcus and the other *Love* staff might not have felt the need to explain his actions any more so than did the writers of the marital rape story lines in the other shows. Marcus envisioned Mark's passionate "taking" of Laura/Iris as akin to Rhett Butler's ambiguous rape of Scarlett O'Hara in *Gone with the Wind*—without the woman's explicit consent, but motivated by lust and the man's inherent understanding of the woman's true needs.[30] In fact, Marcus expended more effort justifying why Iris was not telling her husband, Spence, the truth about her pregnancy than in getting Mark off the hook for rape.[31] In these ways, the LIAMST rape plot of 1972 was much like the rape story lines of the 1960s—the characters did not explicitly refer to the events as rape, both the men and the women involved were punished to some extent (but not via the criminal justice system), the rapists' motivations were generally justified, if not excused, and the inevitable, resulting pregnancy took the focus away from the rape itself. As in many of these early stories, rape was a dramatic plot device that demonstrated the intensity of the characters' passions and led to an unwanted pregnancy that perpetuated the ramifications of the rape into future plots.[32]

While the representation of rape as a romantic, if misguided, act of passion may be disturbing to our contemporary conception of the horrors of rape, it is important to recognize the context within which these stories appeared. There is no doubt that those women who experienced rape themselves were well aware of the violence and hostility involved, but even they may not have been cognizant of the systemic injustices and inequalities that support and, some might argue, encourage rape. Before the feminist anti-rape movement successfully intervened in public discourses of rape, and before that same movement agitated for changes in rape laws and investigatory procedures, the stories of rape told in daytime soaps were in keeping with those stances toward rape that were sympathetic to the victim (as opposed to blaming her for "asking for it"), but that saw the act more as an unfortunate expression of an individual's intense emotions than as a socially sanctioned wrong deeply rooted in a patriarchal disregard for women. Before books such as Susan Brownmiller's *Against Our Will* became a bestseller, before rape laws were revised, and before mainstream discussion of rape recognized the feminist position, an apolitical and — sometimes — romanticized conception of rape could easily be found in romance novels, in Hollywood's cinematic classics, and in television soap operas.

Rape as a Social Issue

CBS's cancellation of *Love Is a Many Splendored Thing* in March 1973, along with its cancellation of *Where the Heart Is* (CBS, 1969–73) the same month, signaled the beginnings of a shift in the daytime television industry, a shift that would, over the course of the decade, displace both CBS and soap producer Procter and Gamble from their longtime berths at the top of the daytime ratings. These two soaps were among CBS's newer entries in the genre. Although both had begun in the late 1960s, they tended to adhere to many of the same storytelling principles that continued to drive longer-running CBS serials such as *The Guiding Light* and *As the World Turns*. But CBS's newer entries did not hold up against their seniors; nor did they manage to compete effectively with the younger shows on other networks. While *LIAMST* had dropped the interracial romance on which the serial was initially premised in response to pressures from CBS affiliates and had adhered to old-fashioned storytelling in its 1972 rape plot, ABC's *One Life to Live* and *All My Children*, also begun in the late 1960s and early 1970s, eagerly embraced race relations, the Vietnam War, and abortion as story fodder.[33] ABC saw attention to these issues as an ideal way to draw young viewers, a strategy that was beginning to pay off in the early 1970s.

Increasingly threatened by the other networks' incursions into the daytime TV ratings and increasingly aware of the difference in tone, style, and subject matter between its soaps and newer fare on other networks, CBS debuted *The Young and the Restless* in 1973. *The Young and the Restless* was CBS's attempt to diversify (away from Procter and Gamble), to draw young audiences, and to keep up with the pace and content of the other networks' soaps. Along with the program's more glamorous look and its focus on youthful romance, one of the primary strategies *The Young and the Restless* used to mark itself as a new kind of soap was its early adoption of a rape story line, a rape story line very different from the old-fashioned rape plots of previous years.

One of the serial's first stories focused on beautiful, young Chris Brooks. In this story, Chris is a virgin, in love with a handsome medical student, Snapper Foster, and bristling at her father's disapproval of their relationship. Snapper, raised by a single mother and struggling to get through school, loves Chris deeply but is not entirely satisfied with her, given her insistence on "saving herself" for marriage. When Chris's wealthy father finds out about Snapper's sexual relationship with Sally McGuire and eagerly reveals the truth to Chris, Chris leaves Snapper and, eventually, the sheltered security of her parents' home, eager to break free from old ties and to "find" herself. Chris feels dissatisfied with her parents' protective, upper-middle-class world and unsure about her own moral convictions regarding premarital sex. She is no longer certain that these old-fashioned ways are right for her. When she meets nice, polite George Curtis at a neighborhood bar and agrees to let him walk her home, however, he forces his way into her apartment and rapes her. In the succeeding six-month story line, Chris slowly recovers from the trauma, presses charges against Curtis, suffers through a trial in which Curtis will go free, and eventually marries Snapper.

Chris's story was different from earlier rape plots in many ways. Unlike the long-term characters that became rapists in the 1960s and earlier 1970s, Chris's rapist, George Curtis, was an incidental character, a day player hired for the run of the story only (ironically enough, the actor was Anthony Geary, who would go on to portray a much more sympathetic rapist, Luke Spencer, on *General Hospital*). Also unlike these earlier stories, Chris's relationship with her rapist was insignificant to the long-term narrative development of the serial (that is, he was not her husband) and she did not become pregnant as a result of the rape. This was a story line much better matched to the feminist anti-rape agenda because it represented rape as a violent crime, not an act of sexual passion. It also illustrated the hurtful and disrespectful treatment rape victims often faced from the justice system. As Bill Bell, the creator and executive producer of *The Young and the Restless*, described the story, "I think it's going to hit a lot of people between the eyes . . . in a court of law she was stripped naked, so to speak, bared her soul, bared all the intimate details, and yet the man is going to be let go, and this happens all too often."[34] Bell's agenda, at least as publicly documented, was clear: he wanted to alert his audiences to the real-world trauma of rape, including the unjust treatment of rape victims and their attackers. As the former head writer for *Days of Our Lives*, and the creator of that show's Bill and Laura passionate rape story of 1968, Bell's shift in focus well illustrates the changing public discourses of rape, as well as the changes in permissible subject matter for soap storytelling.

This treatment of rape as a social issue, steeped in anti-rape discourse that defined the act not as an expression of passion but as a violent crime, was new to daytime in 1973, and still not especially widespread across American culture. Perhaps because of the persistence of myths about rape at this time (as well as a history — albeit short — of a very different kind of rape story in soaps), not all of *The Young and the Restless*'s audience read the tale as Bell intended.[35] Trish Stewart, the actress who portrayed Chris, received a lot of audience mail saying that Chris had "asked for it" by putting herself in such a vulnerable position.[36] Because the character had recently chosen to live on her own, was questioning the prohibition against premarital sex, patronized a bar, and allowed a man to walk her home, these viewers saw her as inviting the attack. Implicit in such a perspective is the assumption that rape is motivated by sexual desire, that Curtis was "naturally" responding to Chris's inviting signals, to her virtual announcement of her sexual availability. Despite its intended meaning, this more politically motivated rape plot failed to communicate unequivocally a conception of rape as aggressive, hostile, and uninvited.

When *The Young and the Restless* took on another rape story a few years later, it was at least partly motivated by a desire to rectify the problematic readings some viewers made of the first story. According to the actress Trish Stewart, "one of the reasons for doing the second rape story in the plot line was so there would be no way anybody could make the accusation that there was provocation on the part of the victim. . . . This time there could be no doubt. There was no way to blame the victim."[37] The second rape plot resembled the first in many ways. The victim in the 1976 story was Chris's sister, Peggy, and she faced many of the same consequences that Chris had faced a few years earlier. Both Chris and Peggy suffered through an unsuccessful trial, both Chris and Peggy had sexual problems afterward, and neither Chris nor Peggy got pregnant. In all of these ways, both stories differed from the old-fashioned rape plots on other shows.

The creators of The Young and the Restless tried a slightly different approach in this second attempt to instruct viewers on the trauma of rape. Unlike Chris's experience of acquaintance rape, Peggy is raped by a man she has never met. Because this kind of rape was more easily assimilated into the anti-rape activists' assertion that rape is an act of violence, Peggy's story had a better chance of winning audience sympathy and of forwarding a definition of rape as a hostile attack perpetrated upon the woman. Yet the demands of soap storytelling, which require characters and events to be entwined in multiple ways so as to propagate future narrative developments, made Peggy's rape as much about Chris as about Peggy. Ron Becker rapes Peggy because he thinks she is Chris (Peggy is in Chris's apartment at the time). He seeks to hurt Chris because she has been working with his wife at a legal aid clinic. Nancy Becker has been trying to get Ron acquitted of what she believes to be a false rape charge, but Chris remains suspicious of him, and Becker takes out his rage at Chris through the rape. Although this does not detract from the story's ability to paint rape as an act of violence, it does shift some of the focus away from Peggy's experience (Chris continues to be embroiled with the Becker family when she takes in Nancy and Ron's daughter), and it does suggest that Ron was motivated by something Chris did, even if that something was not specifically sexual. Still, because this story aired once the anti-rape movement had achieved more widespread attention and support, and because Peggy's status as innocent victim was incontrovertible, this story more readily fit into an anti-rape discourse insisting that rape was not a product of men's sexual desire or women's sexual allure.

About nine months after Ron raped Peggy, however, The Young and the Restless saddled the young character with another rape; this time perpetrated by her new husband, Jack. Peggy's reluctance to get sexually involved with Jack takes a vicious turn in May 1977 when he refuses to take no for an answer. Instead of using this story line to further explore the meaning of rape, in this case between a husband and wife, *The Young and the Restless* ends up suggesting that Peggy is somewhat to blame. In talking with a psychiatrist, Peggy realizes that she wants to have a relationship with Jack more akin to a father-daughter bond than that between husband and wife. She comes to believe that it was not necessarily the (first) rape that had generated her sexual uncertainties but her unresolved father issues instead. In recognizing this, Peggy takes on some of the responsibility for her problematic marriage and thus for Jack's "loss of control."[38] Although marital rape was still not socially or legally recognized as such, which may in part explain the inconsistency of the serial's stance, *The Young and the Restless*'s story about Jack's treatment of Peggy defused some of the earlier story's potential to intervene in the soaps' construction of rape in a progressive way. The vagaries of the mid-1970s rape stories of *The Young and the Restless* demonstrate both the increasing acceptability of treating rape as a social issue and the ongoing obstacles to doing so.

Rape in Vogue: Soap Opera Rape Plots, 1978–81

Among the nineteen rape stories airing on all three networks and at least ten different soaps between 1978 and 1981 were stories that replicated the formulae of earlier rape plots, in particular the old-fashioned rape story and the rape as social issue story debuted on *The Young and the Restless* (see table 3).[39] In addition, this period also featured daytime's most (in)famous rape tale, that featuring Luke and Laura on *General Hospital*, a version that did not easily conform to either of the other two modes of representing rape in daytime television. Although many of the late 1970s rape narratives had traits in common with earlier such stories, the changes that befell the daytime TV industry and public conceptions of rape over the course of the 1970s, as well as the overwhelming volume of such plots in a four-year time span, make these instances worth examining in their own right. To what extent had the changes in the daytime TV marketplace affected the way that the soaps handled rape? How had the reforms, both practical and rhetorical, to public thinking about rape changed the soaps' rape plots? And why was this subject so compelling for so many soap producers, as well as so many soap viewers, at this particular historical moment?

TABLE 3 Rape Stories on Daytime Television Soap Operas, Early 1950s–1981*

Characters	Show	Date
Mike Bauer rapes his wife, Julie	The Guiding Light (CBS)	10 August 1964
Danny Fargo rapes his wife, Missy	Another World (NBC)	1966
Tom Baldwin rapes his wife, Audrey	General Hospital (ABC)	Late 1960s
Bill Horton rapes his sister-in-law, Laura Horton	Days of Our Lives (NBC)	1968
Mark Elliott rapes his sister-in-law, Iris Garrison	Love Is a Many Splendored Thing (CBS)	10 February 1972
George Curtis rapes Chris Brooks	The Young and the Restless (CBS)	1973
Virgil Paris rapes Ginger Kurtz	Somerset (NBC)	1973–74
Phil Brewer rapes Diana Taylor	General Hospital (ABC)	1973–74
Ron Becker rapes Peggy Brooks	The Young and the Restless (CBS)	1976
Roger Thorpe rapes Rita Stapleton	Guiding Light (CBS)	11 October 1978
Ray Gardner rapes Ruth Martin	All My Children (ABC)	1978
Larry Atwood rapes Julie Williams	Days of Our Lives (NBC)	1978
Carolee Simpson is raped	The Doctors (NBC)	1978–79
Phil Higley rapes Eileen Simpson	Another World (NBC)	1978–79
Hank Robinson rapes Carol Stallings	As the World Turns (CBS)	January 1979
Roger Thorpe rapes his wife, Holly	Guiding Light (CBS)	6 March 1979
Luke Spencer rapes Laura Baldwin	General Hospital (ABC)	5 October 1979
Brad Vernon rapes his sister-in-law, Karen Wolek	One Life to Live (ABC)	November 1979
Elliott Lang rapes his estranged wife, Betsy	Love of Life (CBS)	1 February 1980
Billy Clyde Tuggle rapes his wife, Estelle	All My Children (ABC)	1980
Duke Lafferty rapes Morgan Richards	Guiding Light (CBS)	1980–81
Plot and character details unknown	Texas (NBC)	1981
Kellam Chandler rapes Marlena Craig	Days of Our Lives (NBC)	1981

* This list excludes attempted rapes and story lines in which I am uncertain whether a rape occurred.

By the late 1970s, mainstream American culture had felt the impact of the feminist anti-rape movement. However, the continuing power of many myths about rape, alongside the permissive mind-set characteristic of America's new sexual culture, kept any kind of consensus on the meaning of rape at bay. The ongoing debate over the meaning of rape, paired with the possibilities and constraints of soap storytelling, made this flurry of tales compelling viewing. Because the context out of which these stories emerged was so conflicted, the many soap plots of the late 1970s did not offer a singular message about the significance of rape in the new sexual culture. If anything, the soaps' rape stories contributed to a construction of sex as both pleasurable *and* potentially dangerous. In the world of daytime TV, sex was an increasingly ambiguous experience and, in that respect, may have more closely approximated many people's conflicted feelings about the new sexual culture than many other of television's sex-themed tales.

The Return of the Old-Fashioned Rape Plot: *Love of Life*

The Young and the Restless's intervention in the soaps' rape narratives had a significant impact on the rape stories to follow. Many of the rape plots at the end of the 1970s followed this social issue orientation. Because of this, the old-fashioned rape plot, in which rape is not treated as a social or political issue, in which some form of intense emotion leads to rape, in which the rape inevitably leads to a pregnancy and the pregnancy becomes the focus of future story lines, was much less common than it was when the 1970s began. Still, such stories continued to appear, testifying to the ongoing power of problematic rape myths in the society overall and to the usefulness of the old-fashioned rape plot to the soaps' form of serialized storytelling. Despite the intervention of *The Young and the Restless*'s rape stories, at least three other soaps featured rape plots in this old-fashioned, depoliticized vein between 1973 and 1976.[40]

Although trends in daytime dramatic storytelling began to veer toward a more explicit address of social issues by the end of the 1970s, at least one of the nineteen rape plots airing in this period adhered to the older formula. Tellingly, however, CBS's long-running *Love of Life* (1951–80) was cancelled before its attempt to participate in the rape-on-soaps trend could be resolved. In the program's last episode, airing 1 February 1980, Betsy Lang faints at the murder trial of her longtime love, Ben Harper, just before delivering the testimony that may save him from conviction. Ben is on trial for assaulting Betsy and, in the process, killing her unborn child. Though Betsy and Ben have, in fact, been victims of a boating accident that led to Betsy's miscarriage, Betsy's estranged husband, Elliott, has pursued the charges against Ben because Betsy had been carrying Elliott's child. Elliott believes that Ben had a motivation to harm Betsy and the baby because of the baby's paternity, especially since Betsy and Ben had been finding their way back to each other after a time apart. Although this story might easily have been a tale of consensual, if misguided, sex, instead it was constructed as a rape story. The child Betsy lost had been conceived when Elliott raped Betsy on the night of their wedding anniversary, just as she was trying to finalize their divorce.

The head writer, Ann Marcus, had been brought to *Love of Life* not long before; CBS hoped that she could revive the failing drama but didn't give her much of a chance before canceling it. In an attempt to appeal to disaffected viewers, Marcus drew upon a story idea much like the plot she had used in *Love Is a Many Splendored Thing*'s final months, when Mark Elliott raped his sister-in-law, Iris Garrison, thinking she was his wife, Laura, and impregnating her (Iris) in the process. As she had done with Mark, Marcus represented Elliott's actions as being motivated by sexual passion. Elliott hopes and fantasizes that Betsy is coming to see him that night to ask for a reconciliation. He prepares for a romantic evening, complete with candles and champagne, which he liberally imbibes while waiting for Betsy to arrive. When, despite his attempts to woo her, Betsy explains that she has come to expedite their divorce, Elliott embraces her, kisses her "passionately but harshly," and proclaims, "I want to hold you and touch you . . . make you come alive!"[41] Elliott later denies that the encounter was rape because he and Betsy were still married and because, he claims, she only got what she deserved. The *Love of Life* writers imagined that, because of her shame, Betsy initially would not tell anyone about the rape. They planned that she finally would explain to Ben what had happened, but that she would refuse to go through a sensational trial. Much like the story in *Love Is a Many Splendored Thing* and the other pre- and early 1970s rape plots, it was the pregnancy, Ben's and Elliott's reactions to it, and Ben's subsequent murder trial that would become the focus of the story, not Betsy's experience of the rape or its aftermath.

The rape was an effective storytelling device in that it complicated Ben's and Betsy's reconciliation and heightened the tension between Ben and Elliott. Yet, as Marcus realized, she could have motivated the same developments with a consensual sexual encounter between Betsy and Elliott, especially if Betsy remained in love with Ben and merely "slipped" in a moment of passion with her estranged husband.[42] Indeed, a consensual "slip" would still have wrenched apart a central couple (Ben and Betsy), would still have launched a "who's the father?" paternity mystery, would still have reactivated a latent romantic triangle that had no clear resolution — all golden plot developments in soap storytelling. Yet Marcus chose to accomplish these ends by structuring the story around a rape.

It is difficult to determine exactly why Marcus made this choice, but we can make some logical assumptions. The fact that she and the show's producers decided to make the story center around a rape suggests that they saw rape as the more compelling dramatic situation. After all, they were rather desperately trying to save the show at that point and wanted to create the most engaging story possible. Using a rape plot allowed them to tap into the social issue trend visible on the other soaps, a trend that was drawing big audiences, and often the especially desirable young audiences, to those shows. Marcus clearly recognized this tactic as a last-ditch effort to transform the show into the newer, sexier kind of soap. She jokingly compared the story to *The Young and the Restless*, still seen by many as the premier example of the new trends in soap storytelling and style. Marcus facetiously suggested that Betsy could respond to Ben's remark about what a strange coincidence it was that one sexual act resulted in pregnancy by quipping, "Not if you watch 'The Young and the Restless'!"[43] Marcus saw *The Young and the Restless*'s emphasis on young characters, sexual situations, and social issues as an extreme of the new kind of soap, an extreme that may not have been entirely to her liking but that she recognized as the secret to success in the late 1970s daytime TV market.

Despite Marcus's efforts to give *Love of Life* the kind of compelling, sexy, heavy social issue image of some of the other shows, the rape plot she penned largely conformed to the characteristics of pre-1970s rape narratives. The unbounded sexual desire at the center of the story, motivating Elliot's actions, was closely in keeping with the early form of rape story. And the resulting ruckus over Betsy's pregnancy kept the focus on traditional soap opera concerns and away from matters of victims' rights, post-trauma counseling, and legal action. While the outdated nature of the narrative was surely not the sole cause of the soap's cancellation, its chronological correspondence with the serial's end (after nearly thirty years on the air) is a fitting symbol of the way the soaps—and attitudes toward rape—were changing.

The Social Issue Rape Plot

Many of the nineteen rape plots airing on daytime television at the end of the 1970s followed the example of *The Young and the Restless* and represented rape as a contemporary social issue. More than just considering the social ramifications of this individual trauma, however, these stories addressed the many problems faced by women who have been raped, critically exploring their encounters with the criminal justice system, medical and psychological authorities, and community sensibilities. These stories tended to be wholly unambiguous about the rapes they depicted—the women involved were not to blame; the male perpetrators acted out of hostility and violence, not sexual passion. Many soap writers had an explicitly didactic mission in developing these stories, finding ways to conform soap opera conventions to their social and political goals.

Daytime soap operas have a long history of didacticism, dating back to the instructions in morals, values, and household management embedded in the fifteen-minute radio serials so popular in the 1930s and 1940s. What was new about the pedagogical turn in the soaps' handling of rape in the late 1970s was the more overtly political nature of the lessons the serials taught. The anti-rape movement had made rape a political matter; however, the fact that the soaps' rape stories were products of the inescapably conservative context of advertiser-supported network broadcasting tempered the political messages these stories offered. Soap viewers were told that rape was a crime of violence, not an expression of lust, and that rape victims received unjust treatment by multiple segments of society, but they were not urged to link these injustices to women's unequal status under patriarchy.

One strategy that some soaps used to teach viewers about the horrors of rape was to subject a central female character, well-loved by viewers, to rape, and to make her rapist a more incidental—and expendable—peripheral character. Agnes Nixon, in many ways the founder of the soaps' turn to social issues with her work on *All My Children* and *One Life to Live*, designed such a story for *All My Children* in 1978. Nixon deliberately set out to debunk many myths about rape: "I've always known that since the dark ages, the attitudes are that nice women don't get raped. And I knew that wasn't true," and she did so by making the middle-aged matron and pillar of the community Ruth Martin the victim of rape.[44] Nixon wrote a story in which Ruth was robbed, beaten, and raped in a deserted parking lot by Ray Gardner, the long-lost biological father of her foster son, Tad. By centering the story around Ruth, Nixon emphasized that women of all ages and social standings are vulnerable, a common point raised by anti-rape activists who sought to deny that young, attractive, and sexually promiscuous women were rapists' targets, a denial that implicitly argued *against* a conception of rape as motivated by sexual desire. Nixon made it easy for audiences to condemn Gardner's actions as violent by making Ruth's status as victim completely unambiguous. This morally straightforward narrative came down clearly on one side of the rape as sex versus rape as violence debate — rapists (like Gardner) were evil men, victims (like Martin) were not to blame, and rape itself was a violent assault born of hostility and anger.

The head writer, Ann Marcus, designed a similar story for *Days of Our Lives* in 1978. She claimed that she wanted to deal with rape on *Days* "not only because it is a dramatic subject, but because I think that women who see it who have been victims of forced intercourse will maybe learn how to deal with it; or [will learn] that it isn't something they have to be ashamed of."[45] The victim in Marcus's story was Julie Williams, the wife of the nightclub owner Doug Williams and longtime heroine on the serial. Julie is raped by Larry Atwood, a nefarious businessman obsessed with her and out to sabotage Doug. Marcus painted Atwood as an irredeemable villain and worked to ensure the audience's empathy with Julie, making clear that she was a victim of a crime she did nothing to provoke. Marcus instructed that Julie was to get very angry at Atwood and to resist his advances vehemently. "She can be a very spunky, very spicy dame," Marcus wrote, "and we have to show it now." She described the "nasty" language Julie was to use in denouncing Atwood and her screams as he pushes her onto the couch.[46]

Although she does not report the rape to law enforcement, Julie does seek counseling and volunteers to work at a rape crisis center.[47] When Atwood is murdered and Julie is charged with the crime, however, the rape is finally addressed through legal channels. In fact, Julie's trial becomes the setting for the program's viewer education campaign. The psychiatrist Marlena Evans testifies to the problems rape victims face and the reasons more women don't report it. She criticizes the justice system for allowing defense attorneys to suggest that the woman's "bad reputation" has led to rape and debunks multiple other rape myths.[48] Through this testimony, the program voices a position in keeping with the now-mainstream anti-rape movement. Yet the soap stays away from a more avowedly feminist stance by having Marlena cite a well-known sociological study of rape as opposed to Susan Brownmiller's book or the many other feminist works on the subject. Because the anti-rape message avoids feminist assertions about patriarchal misogyny, because it is delivered by the sympathetic and admirable Marlena, and because Julie is represented as an innocent victim, *Days* offered a persuasive anti-rape message to viewers. In fact, the horror of Julie's experience so impressed itself upon the *Days* audience that some fans expressed great anger and resentment at the show for putting the heroine through such hell. As one distraught viewer wrote to Marcus, "Why did you have Larry Atwood go and RAPE Julie for. It made me ill to see it on daytime TV. When that is all I see on TV news and in the newspaper now" [*sic*].[49] This viewer's discomfort with the story line and its relationship to real-world issues evidences the story's power in its own right and as a relatively new approach to rape in daytime television.

The story of Julie Williams's rape is an especially significant development in the history of the soaps' handling of rape in the 1970s. It follows a very different path than that of the 1968 rape plot of *Days of Our Lives*, in which Bill Horton rapes his sister-in-law, Laura, because of his intense, unrequited passion for her. Thus, the 1978 story represents the rather dramatic shift in the ways this soap in particular and soaps in general handled rape over the course of the 1970s. Julie's story is also especially significant because of the involvement of the head writer, Ann Marcus. Marcus had designed the rape plot centered around passion and unrequited love on *Love Is a Many Splendored Thing* in 1972 and would go on to write another such story for *Love of Life* in 1979. In comparison to the *LIAMST* story, the 1978 *Days* story represented Marcus's conversion to the anti-rape movement's stance. However, her reversion back to the "old-fashioned" kind of rape storytelling the following year, in her work on *Love of Life*, suggests that the soaps' stances on rape are not attributable solely to the programs' head writers. Marcus's involvement in two very different soap stories airing so close to each other illustrates the many different forces that shape soap storytelling, including producers, networks, ratings standings, and target audiences. Even more telling, however, is the way these two different approaches demonstrate the ongoing ambivalence in American society's attitude toward rape in the wake of the sexual revolution and the anti-rape movement. Conceptions of rape as an act of sexual passion and as an outpouring of hostility coexisted in the late 1970s. And daytime dramas offered viewers a space to consider those seemingly opposing constructions.

Negotiating the Social Issue Rape Plot: *Guiding Light*

While "younger," non-CBS, non–Procter and Gamble soaps such as *All My Children* and *Days of Our Lives* featured social issue rape plots in the late 1970s, it was more unusual for Procter and Gamble's serials airing on CBS to take up such an overtly political stance. Thus, the two intertwined social issue rape stories airing on Procter and Gamble's *Guiding Light* in 1978 and 1979 marked some significant changes. As Procter and Gamble's longest running serial (begun on radio in 1937 and transferred to television in 1952), *Guiding Light* was foundational to the Procter and Gamble-CBS soap opera empire. The fact that it was *this* show that told not one, but two, stories about a rapist and the women he attacked, that it was *this* show that made the rapist a main character and that refused to excuse or explain away his behavior, that it was *this* show that argued that marital rape was indeed an act of violence and not the result of frustrated romantic passion, was quite telling of the transformations in daytime television's handling of sex in general and rape in particular. The production choices and viewer responses surrounding these stories reveal the complicated negotiations around such ground-breaking tales.

Guiding Light's first attempt to deal with rape as a social issue featured the villainous Roger Thorpe raping his former lover, Rita Stapleton, in October 1978. Roger's animosity toward Rita was clear from her first appearance in Springfield in 1977, when viewers gradually learned of their past together. When their affair was publicly revealed, Roger lost his wife, Peggy, who was horrified at his scandalous past.[50] As if this weren't enough reason for him to hate Rita, he also despised her because she was now romantically involved with upstanding Dr. Ed Bauer, his long time nemesis. Roger had always been a dark character, but viewers saw a new intensity to his nefarious ways throughout the fall of 1978. Indeed, in the days leading up to the rape, the *Guiding Light* writers and producers strove to depict Roger's enmity and Rita's growing fear while building audience suspense. In voice-overs and in conversation, Roger threatens Rita and expresses his resentment toward her. Just how he did so seems to have been a source of concern for the *Guiding Light* writers and the decisions they made greatly influenced the degrees to which Roger's rape of Rita appeared motivated by hatred versus sexual desire.

The original scripts for these days strove to indicate a sexual dimension to Roger's feelings for Rita, albeit a rather vindictive sexuality. Often, this was communicated through Roger's hostile references to Rita's "hot, sexy bod." Thus, on 6 October, Roger was scripted as referring, in voice-over, to Rita as "little Miss Bluefield Bod" (presumably referencing her posh hometown); on 9 October, as saying to Rita, "You must have used that hot, sexy little Bluefield bod overtime," and as describing Rita, to Hillary, as "a hot, juicy, little tart" and "a cold, calculating clever bitch."[51] Also on 9 October, Roger was scripted as saying, to Holly, of Rita, "It took all her wily ways and that hot little bod of hers," and, on 10 October, Roger was to refer, while talking to Rita, to that "perky little Bluefield bod of yours."[52] These lines functioned to establish the sexual nature of Roger's hatred for Rita. They were daring in their sexual allusions (particularly for a Procter and Gamble soap) and thus in keeping with the more overt sexual tenor of newer soaps such as *The Young and the Restless*, but they also conformed to the old-fashioned use of rape as a plot device. Roger's sexual feelings toward Rita, even if they were laced with hostility, implied a complicated mixture of motivations for the upcoming rape. In making clear that Roger found Rita sexually appealing these lines suggested that rape was related to the woman's appearance and the man's sexual reaction to it— a presumption that worked against the anti-rape movement's message.

This dialogue *would have had* that kind of impact—had it made it to air. However, none of the lines I cite above made it to the broadcast episodes. In each of these, the references to Rita's "hot bod" and to Rita as a "tart" or a "bitch" were crossed out of the script, with revised lines written in by hand. Thus, on 9 October, Roger said to Rita, "You must have used every little trick in your book but you won the big Chief of Staff," instead of the originally scripted, "You must have used that hot, sexy little Bluefield bod overtime . . . but you won the big Chief of Staff!"[53] The consistency with which this sort of dialogue was altered suggests that the revisions were motivated by the *content* of the lines, not the length of the script (as edited lines in these and other scripts seem to have been). Whether a last minute decision by producers, a demand of Procter and Gamble's, or a requirement of CBS standards and practices, Roger's feelings toward Rita and the threat he posed to her did not contain the degree of sexual jealousy and resentment they might have, had the lines remained as originally written. This change was important to the show's message about rape. Instead of supporting an ambiguous—if not outright false—notion of women's sexuality encouraging rape, these changes made clear Roger's hostility toward Rita, regardless of how she looked or whether he felt sexually attracted to her.

The rape itself was represented as a terrifying experience for Rita. Viewers saw Roger's body menacingly fill the frame as he approached her (after forcing his way into her apartment) and they heard her crying as the scene faded out. Immediately afterward, Rita cursed him, "Damn you, you raped me!" and threatened to go to the police, but Roger quickly reminded her of her questionable reputation, of their sordid past together, and of her lover Ed's likely disbelieving response should she tell him about the rape.[54] Roger's threats had their intended effect. Rita told no one about the rape for months, revealing the truth to her sister in February, and exposing Roger to the whole town only once he was tried for raping his wife, Holly, later in 1979.

Although Rita did not pursue Roger's punishment through the justice system and thus had more in common with 1960s soap opera rape victims than characters such as AMC's Ruth Martin, viewers were encouraged to empathize with her suffering. She had difficulty resuming sexual relations with Ed afterward and was emotionally distraught for months. While her anguish may have succeeded in winning viewers' sympathy and assuring her status as victim of a violent attack (as opposed to a love affair gone awry), her hesitancy in pursuing help made the story an incomplete version of the social issue rape plot. As one viewer from Skokie, Illinois, wrote to *Daytime TV*, "*Guiding Light* missed a perfect opportunity to educate viewers on the treatment of rape victims because the story didn't permit Rita to tell anyone. And if she doesn't go for help, how will people learn what treatment is available?"[55] Having seen rape-as-social-issue story lines on other soaps, viewers such as this one recognized that *Guiding Light* had not followed through with the formula. Rita was clearly a crime victim, but the show seemed to be lacking the other half of that story—the woman's resources for survival and the rapist's punishment. Thus, in toning down Roger's sexual motivations and depicting Rita's suffering, the serial followed the genre's new tendency to represent rape as violence, but in failing to follow through with the consequences of the crime the story lacked certain features of the typical issue-oriented "rape as violence" plot and key elements of the anti-rape activism of the day.

The serial's second rape-as-social-issue plot made a much more definitive statement on real-world rape and demonstrated *Guiding Light*'s (and Procter and Gamble's) full passage into the newest of the contemporary soap trends. *Guiding Light*'s head writers, Bridget and Jerome Dobson, based the story on the Rideout marital rape case, which had launched the issue of marital rape into public discourse.[56] The resulting story drew on Roger and Holly's past together and thus kept within the soap opera tradition of embroiling characters in relationships riddled with historical baggage, but it also borrowed from the Rideout case and the media hoopla that surrounded it, taking up the soaps' newer interest in representing real-world concerns.

Roger and Holly were romantically involved earlier in the 1970s, and she had become pregnant with their daughter, Christina. Because the unfaithful Holly was married to Ed Bauer at the time (the same man who would later be involved with Rita), she attempted to pass off the child as Ed's. When the truth of Christina's parentage came out, Ed and Holly divorced, but Ed remained Christina's primary father figure. Roger's hatred of Ed was largely rooted in Ed's relationship with Roger's daughter, not to mention his relationship with Holly. By early 1979, however, Roger and Holly had reunited, deciding to marry and raise their daughter together. Though Holly was initially charmed by Roger's apparently sincere desire to form a family with her and Christina, she soon realized that Roger was just as untrustworthy as ever. She suspected him of having affairs with two other women, and he proved unreasonably possessive of their daughter, especially where her stepfather, Ed Bauer, was concerned.

By late February 1979, the GL writers began to set up Roger's eventual rape of Holly. First, they had Roger attempt to coerce Holly into having sex when they have been arguing. Though Holly is clearly uninterested in sex in this scene, the writers made clear that she eventually accedes. As the script for the 26 February episode described Holly's feelings: "Holly feels she should give in. Roger is her husband, and she had such hopes for their marriage, but she hates this. Still, in the end, we should feel she is reluctantly submitting."[57] In the next episode, the morning after this sexual encounter, Holly's voice-over clarifies for the audience that she did consent, though unhappily: "I didn't want that. Why did I let him?"[58] When she attempts to talk to Roger about it, he declares that "a man has a right to certain things from his wife" and that "you're my wife, and when I want you, I don't want you turning me away."[59] The Friday, 2 March episode ended ominously, with Roger pulling Holly toward the bedroom and insisting, "You're my *wife*. You are going to start acting like a wife," with Holly's fearful face in close-up.[60]

Fans who tuned in again on Monday, 5 March found out that Holly had managed to avoid Roger's advances on Friday but that she had taken his threats seriously and was packing her bags, planning to leave him. He discovers her leaving and taunts her to stay, arguing that were he Ed Bauer she would never want to leave. Their argument continues in the next day's episode, during which it quickly escalates into violence. The rape scenes privilege Holly's perspective, to the extent of showing Roger through Holly's point of view, not merely through the over-the-shoulder shots typically used in soaps. The point-of-view shots receive even further emphasis by being shot with a hand-held camera, another stylistic anomaly for soap production. Roger menacingly moves toward Holly, toward the camera, and toward the viewer at once. The day's scenes underscore the rape's violence a final time when, after the actual rape, Holly — face bruised, blouse torn, arms clasped around her abdomen — makes her way out of the house, determined to leave despite Roger's attempts to keep her from doing so, despite the physical pain she clearly feels.

The program continued to emphasize the violence of Roger's act in the subsequent days, as viewers watched Holly seek medical attention and decide to press charges. On 7 March, Holly labels the act as rape, a bold gesture given the limited acceptance of marital rape as a possibility in the U.S. at this time. The recent changes in state laws regarding marital rape quickly became a part of the story line, as the attorney Mike Bauer informs Holly that their state has recently passed a law such that "a wife may charge her husband with rape, take him to court, and the case will be prosecuted just like other crimes of violence." Holly then repeats, "Violence . . . Oh, yes, it was violent."[61] Two days later, a rape crisis center worker explains to Holly that marital rape "usually happens out of the husband's need to . . . dominate, humiliate his wife."[62] All of these conversations convince Holly to press charges, an action that, as Mike Bauer explains to his brother, Ed, may make things difficult for Holly because "the awful fact is that some people look at a woman differently after that. . . . Some will think it happened because she invited it. . . . It's the way some people are. They think rape is a sexual act. It's not. It's an act of violence, of hostility."[63] Holly's case becomes the first test of the new marital rape laws in the state and she is subjected to the same intensity of media attention Greta Rideout faced, all of which allowed the program to emphasize the unfair treatment of women who have been raped and the potential for women to fight back despite these obstacles. Repeatedly, then, the program made indisputably clear its stance on rape, even marital rape, coming down definitively on the question of rape as violence versus rape as passionate sex and insisting on women's rights to recourse and revenge.[64]

Audience negotiations of the story line were mixed. Many read the story in keeping with its preferred rhetoric of rape as a crime of violence, accepting the notion that a husband could indeed rape his wife.[65] For other viewers, however, the length and complexity of the soap opera narrative and its characters' histories interfered with the writers' attempt to offer an unambiguous message. Thus, viewer Carolyn Blankenship wrote to the editor of *Daytime TV*: "I'm sorry any man feels as though he can get away with raping his wife or any woman! I think that's the lowest a man can sink to. But as far as I'm concerned *Guiding Light*'s Holly got exactly what she deserved by marrying Roger. She should have known better."[66] Drawing on her knowledge of the characters' back story, Blankenship insisted that Holly bear some responsibility for the rape. While her perspective was surely as shaped by the extratextual circulation of rape myths as by the soap's narrative, GL's long textual history made the story unintentionally ambiguous in certain respects.

This is even more evident in the case of one *Soap Opera Digest* reader, who angrily wrote to the magazine to complain about *Guiding Light*'s hypocrisy on the rape issue. This viewer pointed out that Holly's crusading attorney was the same Mike Bauer who had raped his wife, Julie, in 1964, in a story line that was never explicitly identified as a rape plot: "It irritates me to no end to see the contempt the writers of 'The Guiding Light' have for their viewers' intelligence. They now have Mike Bauer self-righteously prosecuting Roger for 'marital rape' when Mike himself was once guilty of the same thing. We are supposed to have forgotten that he raped his estranged wife Julie. . . . How things do change!"[67] The fact that Mike Bauer could be a hero fifteen years after he raped his wife might have been commensurate with the character's development given the "rules" of the soap genre, but it did not necessarily sit well with viewers who both remembered the past and lived in a society changed by anti-rape activism.[68] In naming Mike's 1964 rape of his wife *as rape*, something even the program's scriptwriters did not do when they originally wrote the story, this viewer's indignation reveals the ongoing, contested nature of rape discourse in the late 1970s, as well as the difficulty the soaps faced in presenting an unambiguous anti-rape message. Even though the social issue rape stories set out to teach a political lesson about rape in keeping with the anti-rape movement, these stories more typically served as sites of negotiation over the meanings and motivations of rape in a conflicted cultural context.

The Ambiguous Rape Plot: *General Hospital*'s Rape-Seduction on the Disco Floor

The most overtly ambiguous rape story of the late 1970s was Luke Spencer's rape of Laura Baldwin on ABC's *General Hospital*. This story line, and the romance between the two characters that succeeded it, helped to solidify *General Hospital*'s place as the number one rated daytime drama and to definitively reverse the longtime daytime ratings standings of the Big Three networks, as well as to confirm the appeal of the newer brand of soap storytelling for young viewers. The story combined the old-fashioned, apolitical rape plot with the issue-oriented rape story and offered an ambiguous message about the meaning of and motivation for rape in the process. As *General Hospital* told the tale, rape could be an expression of sexual passion *and* a display of hostility; the woman involved might indeed be truly victimized, but the man involved might also suffer. Ultimately, the soap suggested that rape is not so easily categorized as a sexual act or a violent one, a move that undermined the efforts of the anti-rape movement by allowing that rape can have a romantic or erotic dimension but that also spoke to the confusion and fear many Americans, particularly women, were feeling about this now highly publicized crime.

When Luke raped Laura in October 1979, *General Hospital* was steadily climbing in the ratings after nearly being canceled two years earlier. As *General Hospital*'s ratings rose and Luke and Laura's romance blossomed, the pair appeared on the covers of magazines such as *Newsweek* as daytime's first "supercouple" and journalists, network executives, the show's producer, and the actors found themselves trying to explain how a woman could fall in love with her rapist and, concomitantly, how audiences could embrace such a couple as a romantic ideal. The most commonly repeated explanation, then and to this day, has been that the writers and the show's executive producer, Gloria Monty, did not at first realize how strong the chemistry between Geary and Genie Francis, who portrayed Laura, would be. When they did, they scrambled to "rewrite" the rape as a seduction, a "choreographed seduction" in Monty's words.[69] Thus, Francis explained, "I played a rape victim for a year. . . . Then they realized that the chemistry between Tony Geary and me was something they couldn't ignore, and they turned everything around."[70] As recently as 1998, Geary repeated the same story: "It was played as a rape, desperate and dirty, and then there was a quick rush to rewrite it as a seduction."[71]

Though this version of events was told as early as 1981, the soap opera press, the GH producers, and the actors spoke about the story in more ambiguous terms in the two years between the rape and the characters' record-breaking wedding (see figure 29). The later explanations tended to insist that the rape was indeed a rape, with all its violence and suffering intact, which the producers had chosen to ignore or redefine after the fact. In contrast, the earliest comments on the story tended to qualify the *kind* of rape it was. Most common was the explanation that what transpired between Luke and Laura was an "acquaintance rape" and thus somehow less reprehensible than rape proper.[72] This sort of justification is nearly unintelligible from a twenty-five-year vantage point, during which time acquaintance rape has been identified as not only as serious a violation as stranger rape, but as the most common type of rape. Yet, in 1979 and 1980, when this explanation was set forth, acquaintance rape was only beginning to be discussed in the mainstream media and, as we have seen, many myths about rape continued to hold great power. Thus, labeling Luke and Laura's sexual involvement as "acquaintance rape" some-

how managed to soften the horror of what Luke had done to her, making their subsequent love affair more acceptable.

Other explanations performed a similar function. For example, *Soap Opera Digest* explained that the rape was "defended by Tony as unplanned and, by Genie, as subconsciously invited," a justification that, again, perpetuated rape myths by defining it as spontaneous, instigated by the woman, and, by implication, an act of sexual passion.[73] Similarly, in October 1980, Geary relayed Gloria Monty's characterization of the rape as "a rape like no one had ever put on TV before. No hitting, no slapping, no screaming. It would all be sensual."[74] The most reasonable way to understand not only how Laura could fall in love with Luke, but how millions of fans could fall in love with their romance, it seemed, was to understand rape as an intensely sexual, even romantic, event.

While the explanations of the story line by those involved in its production have varied over the years, they tend to suggest one of two things: that the program depicted the rape as a violent act, devoid of sexual connotation, and then sought to ignore this when producers decided to have the two characters fall in love, in effect denying the pain and suffering that accompany real-world rape *or* that the serial all along represented the rape as more motivated by sexual desire than by hostility, more an act of seduction than one of force, in effect not really a rape at all. My viewing of most of the scenes between Luke and Laura and between them and others from the day of the rape, 5 October 1979, into the following summer, when Luke and Laura went on the run from the mob and became an official couple, suggests a more complicated picture than any of the justifications for the story make clear.[75]

As I have described in the opening to this chapter, the rape itself was presented in a stylized sequence that emphasized the flashing lights and throbbing beat of the deserted disco where it took place. The event was thereby placed at the center of the new sexual culture, making the ultimate ambiguity of the rape a clear product of the sexually liberated times. In this episode, Luke, the manager of the Campus Disco, is drinking heavily, drowning his anguish over being ordered by his boss, the mobster Frank Smith, to assassinate a senator and, Luke reasons, likely face his own death in the process. Laura Baldwin, a waitress at the disco, Luke's friend, and the object of his undying affection, seeks to comfort him, asking what has him so upset. Laura and Luke have developed a friendship despite the fact that Luke had come to Port Charles to help his sister, Bobbie, sabotage Laura's relationship (now marriage) to Scotty, whom Bobbie wanted for herself. Luke soon began to fall for Laura and refused to help Bobbie any further. Laura, fond of Luke but devoted to her husband, repeatedly found herself trying to help her boss and friend. Thus, when Luke declares his love and drunkenly insists, "I'm not going to die without holding you in my arms just one time," she reluctantly agrees to dance with him. He soon escalates their physical contact, kissing her and pulling her to the floor. After a protracted shot of the disco lights, the scene ends. When it cuts back to the action, Laura slowly rises from the floor, shaking as she runs out. The scene ends with Luke crying into Laura's sweater, hauntingly asking, "Oh my God, what have I done?" as the musical theme that accompanied the rape rises in the background, this time eerily distorted.

Laura admits to her husband and family that she has been raped, but claims she does not know who raped her. She is treated at the hospital, has trouble relating to Scotty sexually, and attends a group therapy session at a rape crisis center as she recovers. In these ways, and much in keeping with the rape-as-social-issue stories airing on many other soaps, *General Hospital* sought to represent the trauma experienced by rape victims authentically. Yet the serial also followed in the tradition of the earlier generation of soap opera rape stories by having Laura keep secret the identity of her rapist and suffer for months under the burden of the lie. For the nine months succeeding the rape, she struggles over whether to tell her husband the truth and ultimately determines not to do so. Scotty eventually finds out by reading a letter Laura has written to Luke and this event precipitates Laura and Luke running away together. Though much of the story line revolves around whether or not Laura will tell Scotty, the problem is compounded by Luke's involvement with the mafia, Laura's knowledge of it (she accidentally overhears a conversation between Luke and the mobster Smith, and is discovered by Smith), and the fact that telling Scotty about the rape comes to include telling him about Smith's crime ring, an action that will place Scotty, Laura, Luke, and much of Port Charles in danger. These additional plot developments complicate the characters' motivations in dealing with the aftermath of the rape (for example, sometimes Luke pressures Laura not to reveal the truth about the rape so as to protect her and others from Smith), but from the time of the rape to July 1980, when Luke and Laura first go on the run, Luke, Laura, Scotty, and Bobbie repeatedly discuss the rape, debating whether it was, in fact, rape, and alternately challenging and supporting longtime rape myths.

For most of the nine months during which the rape was a major part of the story line, Luke fully admits his culpability. As he tells his sister, Bobbie, a month or so afterward, "I forced her to dance with me right out there on the disco floor and then I raped her. Yeah, I said rape. I took her as cruelly and as inhumanly as any woman was ever raped. And when I was finished with her, she was bruised, she was battered, and she was destroyed. So that's the truth, dear little sister. It was not a sleazy little affair, nor was it a fling, Bobbie — it was *rape.*" He repeatedly tells Laura that she can and should tell Scotty the truth, that she should make him "the heavy . . . because [he] was," that he knows it was rape and asks her forgiveness for it. As the repentant "bad boy" of the soap opera genre (and other mass-produced fantasies directed at women), Luke is represented as tortured by his actions — not only is the audience invited to experience his pain immediately afterward, but he flashes back to the rape more frequently than Laura, often exploding in anger or collapsing in tears at the memory. Alongside Luke's admissions of guilt are his proclamations of love, from the night of the rape ("Damn it, Laura, I'm in love with you!") to his pleas for forgiveness ("For loving you so much, too much") to his promises of devotion ("It'll always be you for me"). Luke's response has two effects, in addition to heightening his attractiveness as an unrequited lover: first, it confirms that the encounter was indeed rape; it corroborates rather than refutes Laura's claims. However, his response also suggests that rape may not always be *only* a crime of violence and hate, that it can be motivated by sexual desire, even romantic love, and that the insistence on rape as always the former and never the latter by a range of anti-rape activists may be incorrect. In this way, *General Hospital* was telling a more complicated rape story than its fellow soaps; however, that story was told, at times, at the expense of a clear anti-rape message.

The meaning of rape comes under even more scrutiny from Luke's sister, Bobbie, and Laura's husband, Scotty. Throughout the story, Bobbie challenges Laura's (and Luke's) claims of rape. She frequently refers to the "so-called rape," suggests that Laura "cried rape," and accuses her of teasing and tormenting men. Bobbie's doubts voice the suspicion with which rape victims are often met; Bobbie assumes that Laura must have invited Luke's advances and is only calling it rape after the fact because she knows to do otherwise would jeopardize her marriage. Bobbie's suspicions are rooted in her longtime resentment of Laura, both because of Bobbie's interest in Scotty and because of Bobbie's "wrong side of the tracks" background. After surviving an ill mother, an alcoholic father, and a stint as a teenage prostitute, Bobbie distrusts the privileged, sheltered Laura and believes any involvement she might have with Luke will only hurt him. But while Bobbie could be manipulative, she was also characterized as straight-talking and down-to-earth. As a sympathetic character, her perspective likely held some weight with audiences and thus, though it was clearly rooted in class-based tensions, Bobbie's response challenged the definition of the rape offered elsewhere in the program, serving to give the other characters pause, as well as unsettling audience understandings of the plot and the role of rape within it.

While Bobbie's response might have disturbed audience members' ideas about what transpired between Luke and Laura, Scotty's response worked to convince viewers that Luke was a much preferable, even an ideal, partner for Laura. Soon after the rape, Scotty urges Laura to go to the rape center for a group therapy session. While he is concerned about her well-being, he is particularly upset because Laura has been unable to have sex with him since the rape. At the session, Scotty admits his fear that *he* is capable of raping Laura (presumably due to his sexual frustration—another link between rape and sexual desire). Laura's angry response to him later on, when he demands that she let him into the bedroom, suggests that he is as guilty as her rapist of mistreating her.[76] This is the beginning of an important reversal—the sweet, heroic "good boy," Scotty, is gradually becoming less appealing, just as Luke's "bad boy" is becoming more so. For example, months later, when Laura finally works up the nerve to tell Scotty the truth about the rape, he falls asleep in the middle of her story, prompting Luke to ask incredulously, as he tries to stifle a laugh, "You were talking about being *raped* and he fell asleep?!" But Scotty's abusiveness as a husband (and Luke's idealness in comparison) become most clear when he finally discovers that Luke was the rapist. He instantly assumes that Laura had an affair with Luke, he says he hates her, he almost hits her, he throws her to the ground, he calls her a tramp. He also assumes that there never was a rape; "It wasn't rape at all, was it?" he challenges her. He insists to his parents that Laura was "yelling rape as a cover-up": "She lived with me for the last six months, pretending to be in love with me, pretending to have been brutally raped, when all along she'd been *seduced* by Luke and fallen in love with him!" Scotty redefines the rape as a seduction based on his assumption that Luke and Laura have been having an affair. Because fans knew that they hadn't, that both had suffered as a result of the rape and that Laura had kept the truth from Scotty as much in fear of Frank Smith as in defense of Luke, Scotty's response would likely have seemed unjustified, even cruel. When, in contrast, Luke was repeatedly pledging his love to Laura and was going to great lengths to keep her and the rest of the town safe, the program effectively worked to shift viewer allegiance from Scotty to Luke. Over the course of nine months, the serial made being raped by the passionate, loyal, and devoted Luke immensely preferable to being married to the abusive, distrusting, and unromantic Scotty.

Because Scotty had gradually become such an unappealing character, his claims about Luke, Laura, and the rape (mainly, that it wasn't a rape at all) were likely much less compelling to fans than were Bobbie's suspicions. But viewers had other reasons to question whether what had happened between Luke and Laura was indeed rape and, if it was, what that meant. Though Luke is most frequently devastated by his memories of the rape, occasionally his flashbacks are almost wistful—he seems to yearn for the way the rape tied Laura to him. When he is frustrated with Laura for acting jealous of his relationship with Frank Smith's daughter and yet still insisting that she loves her husband, he nastily suggests that she was to blame for the rape. "Both of us know you know how to say no," he snickers. "All you know how to do is tease a man, Laura. You never, ever deliver." And, after Laura admits her attraction for him and passionately kisses him, Luke taunts that she should now "go tell Scott that night in the disco was *rape*," intoning that she should well know that it was nothing of the kind. Laura's actions also suggest, at times, that what transpired between her and Luke may not have been rape. She flashes back to the night of the rape and remembers trying to help Luke, as if wondering whether he perceived her concern for him as an invitation to more intimate contact. She talks to each of her parents about feeling attracted to a man who is not her husband, again suggesting that she is questioning her own role in encouraging Luke's advances. Most significantly, she avoids reporting Luke to the police or identifying him as her rapist even to her friends and family; though her reasons for this are complicated (involving Smith's organized crime operation, among other issues) she mostly seems to be protecting Luke, taking on some responsibility for what happened between them.

Despite these contradictory moments, the characters are primarily represented, respectively, as injured victim and repentant rapist, at least until both Laura and Luke explicitly question the events of that October night, verbalizing their confusion. In June 1980, Bobbie confronts Luke, challenging him to definitively answer, "Was it rape or wasn't it?" Eventually Luke responds, painfully admitting, "I don't know; I honestly don't know." After insisting for months that he was indeed guilty of rape, Luke here begins to express doubts about his own experience and, perhaps most significantly, about the meaning of rape itself. Laura soon reveals similar thoughts. She tells Luke that she has lain awake all night wondering if it was really rape. She speculates, "Maybe I was just as much at fault as you were." By questioning whether it was truly rape, both characters confirmed the suspicions voiced by Bobbie and Scotty, in effect endorsing those myths that blame the woman for sexually arousing the man to rape.

Though these pieces of dialogue might seem to have offered the closest thing to narrative resolution one might find in a soap opera, concluding the rape portion of the Luke and Laura story with their mutual doubts that the rape was actually a rape, the narrative development of a soap is not so easily settled. Whether the story was intended to head in this direction or not, the nine months between the rape and Luke and Laura's official connection as a couple offered viewers an elaborate justification for the changes in the characters (for example, Scotty becoming a jealous and near-abusive husband, Luke becoming a tortured romantic hero, Laura loving Luke, not Scotty). As much as those months were spent justifying these changes, however, viewers who had been with the characters from the beginning knew that what had transpired between Luke and Laura was not identifiable as solely a violent attack or entirely an outpouring of frustrated passion. For these viewers, Luke's rape of Laura was both a rape and a seduction, a result of violence and of sexual passion, a disturbingly ambiguous act. Thus, the soap genre's ability to narrativize changes in character psychology over a span of time allowed the creators of *GH* to shift the parameters of the relationships between Luke, Laura, and Scotty, but that same ability to explore characters over time worked *against* the soap's authority to impose a single meaning on the catalyzing event.

Perhaps not surprisingly, the ambiguity of the rape story elicited a range of responses from *General Hospital*'s viewers, as well as from fans of the serial's competitors. While the viewer responses I have found do not seem to doubt that Luke raped Laura, they vary in their conceptions of what that plot point meant. The responses can be broadly characterized in two ways: those who approved of the story and those who disapproved of the story. Within each of these categories, viewers focused on different aspects of the program's discourses of rape, its appeals to young viewers, and its relationship to other soap opera rape plots.

Perhaps the strongest evidence of a reading of the story as a romantic fantasy can be found in the response of fans who attended Geary's 1980 appearance in a Fort Worth, Texas, shopping mall. Cries of "Rape me, Luke! Rape me!" emanated from the crowd, much as fans might more typically shout, "I love you!" or "Marry me!" to a celebrity sex symbol.[77] While it is easy to be horrified by such exclamations, it is more productive to attempt to understand their motivations. Much of the gender-specific fantasy such viewers found in the show was dependent on Luke's construction as an ideal romantic hero.

As the fan Marilyn Henry described Luke's appeal in an *Afternoon TV* article, "They *told* us [Luke] was a criminal type, a cheap, punk hoodlum with a mob background and they put him in surroundings to substantiate this, but they showed him buying up a poor newsboy's last papers, being loyal and kind to his sister, growing panicked when ordered by his gangster boss to commit a real crime. Most important of all, they let us see that his heart was being purified by love for a beautiful, good girl. This deep, hopeless love made it possible for us to excuse most of his antisocial behavior."[78] Amy Steppe of Johnson City, Texas, expressed a similar view in a letter to *Daytime TV*, "When Luke raped Laura in the disco, he showed so much pain, as well as the great love he possessed for Laura, that his performance haunted me for days."[79] This kind of fan adoration found in the rape story and in the Luke Spencer character reflects a sexual fantasy quite similar to that found in many romance novels of the same period. In extremely popular romances such as Kathleen Woodiwiss's *The Flame and the Flower* (1972) and Rosemary Rogers's *Sweet Savage Love* (1974) strong, handsome, secretly sensitive men rape feisty but innocent young women only to fall in love and live happily ever after. The novelist Daphne Clair argues that these stories—rape fantasies, as they are often labeled—"enable women whose greatest terror is rape to face it safely between the pages of a book."[80] Within the serialized format of daytime soaps, fans could relish in even further detail the *process* through which such a male character fell in love and was transformed.[81]

Rape fantasies were a frequent subject of discussion in 1970s discourses of rape, particularly in women's magazines and feminist books such as that by Susan Brownmiller. Many of these discussions dismissed the theories of Sigmund Freud, his follower Helene Deutsch, and their theories of female masochism, most often insisting that, while many women may have sexual fantasies that involve some form of rape, these women in no way desire to be raped in their real lives.[82] As Molly Haskell argued in the pages of *Ms.*, "These fantasies, containing neither violence nor unpleasantness, are something quite different from rape itself. . . . The male lead is not some seedy delivery boy with a knife lurking in a doorway, but Clark Gable or Robert Redford in the setting of her choice; he acts not out of hostility but out of desire; and the fantasy ends in euphoria rather than in night court."[83] By fantasizing rape as an act of (secretly or subconsciously) welcomed sexual desire, it is removed from the violence that makes it such a terrifying reality. Given the intensified discussion of rape in U.S. culture of the 1970s, and given the tension within that discussion between understanding rape as an expression of violence versus one of sexual desire, it is understandable that millions of *General Hospital*'s fans (particularly female ones) might have treasured a representation of rape that, they could believe, proved to be more fantasy than reality, more sexual than violent, more a product of love than of hate.

Another set of audience responses to the *General Hospital* rape story focused not on the program's fantasy element, but instead on the plot's fit with the rape-as-social-issue narrative appearing on other soaps at the time. Perhaps because there were so many such plots, and because anti-rape activism had become so prominent during the 1970s, certain GH viewers read the show's take on rape as another example of the soaps' contribution to real-world discourses of rape's motivations and meanings. To some considering the story from this perspective, the program's construction of rape as a torturous experience was admirable.[84] Yet other viewers noted a difference between the GH plot and the rape-as-social-issue story lines they were seeing on other soaps. These viewers disapproved of the Luke and Laura story because of its lack of adherence to the soaps' typical handling of rape and its consequent misfit with mainstream anti-rape discourse. For example, Pat Smith of Cincinnati, Ohio, praised the realism and rape-as-violent-crime message of *Texas*'s (NBC, 1980–82) rape story in comparison to *General Hospital*'s: "*Texas* is a great soap. Like *General Hospital*, it had a rape scene, too, but it showed what really happens to the girl. She was scared and hurt. She didn't fall in love with the rapist and chase after him."[85] Chicago's Angela Burns admitted that she was "a little upset with *General Hospital* for the way they handled the aftermath of Laura's rape. The idea that she'd feel anything but repulsion for Luke, the man who raped her, is sickening."[86] Audience members such as these welcomed the turn to social issues in daytime drama and, used to the lessons they taught, found themselves offended and distraught at *General Hospital*'s more ambiguous take on the motivations for rape.

Still others viewers disliked the ambiguity of the GH plot and its intimations about rape because it did not conform to the earlier generation of soap storytelling. Fans of the longer-running soaps, particularly those from the Procter and Gamble empire, disapproved of the soaps' turn to what they saw as sensationalized social issues to appeal to younger audiences. For example, an Altoona, Pennsylvania, viewer chastised *Soap Opera Digest* for its heavy coverage of *General Hospital* and the other ABC soaps, urging the magazine to spend more time reporting on the talented actors of *As the World Turns* instead of "this rapist with the moles on his face and hair like Bozo the Clown!"[87] Disgruntled with the eclipsing of her favorite, the traditional Procter and Gamble serial *As the World Turns*, this viewer used the ambiguity of Luke's actions as a rapist to disparage the show and, by implication, the turns to young viewers and different kinds of stories on ABC daytime overall. Meanwhile, the soap fan Ken Dowzycki speculated that the "young kids who like the junk that Luke and Laura do on *GH*" were keeping his favorite serial, *The Doctors* (NBC, 1963–82), at the bottom of *Daytime TV*'s reader's poll.[88] And a Georgia viewer blamed young people for making "a hero out of the rapist Luke" and pushing soap magazines to feature the "immoral type of soap" on ABC over more moral programs such as *Search for Tomorrow*.[89] To viewers like these, the turn to youth and sensationalized social issues in daytime television was objectionable; *General Hospital*'s Luke and Laura plot was the symbol of all that was wrong with the changed soap opera genre and the television industry that supported it.

A third kind of disapproval came from viewers who saw the combination of the program's failed social issue plot (and consequent failed anti-rape message) and its appeal to young people as a dangerous blend. This brand of criticism meshed well with the broader climate of concern over the effects of television and the new sexual culture on youth. For example, the viewer Susan Patterson asked in the pages of *Daytime TV*, "What kind of example do [Luke and Laura] set for all the young people who have made this show number one? Who knows how many boys have raped because Luke has become a sex symbol to impressionable young girls?"[90] Gloria Ransom of Grasham, Oregon, concurred with Patterson, approvingly citing the social issue rape plots on other shows, plots that had served to educate people about "the true nature of rape," particularly the myth that women really want to be raped and enjoy the experience. Characterizing *General Hospital*'s story as the antithesis of such praiseworthy plots in that Luke and Laura "*prove* that rape is an act of love or, at least, can lead to love!" Ransom found the greatest problem with *GH*'s rape message in the show's young audiences and the impact of this message upon them.[91] Its stance that rape is an act of sexual passion was disturbing to her in and of itself; in combination with the soap's young viewers, it was downright dangerous.

Viewer disapproval of the Luke and Laura story is understandable given the contentious social context of debate over the motivations for rape in the real world and the tumultuous TV industry context of changes in soap storytelling and style. Whether because the story line did not keep with the straightforward anti-rape message of the social issue plots, whether its sensational appeal to young people was eclipsing an older kind of soap, or whether the combination of the program's politics and its target audience was morally suspect, audiences had many reasons to reject the Luke and Laura story and all it represented. Just as significant, however, were the program's impassioned fans who found in the story a fantasy that acknowledged the debate over the motivations for rape in the real world but that applied the conventions of soap storytelling to that debate, resulting in an ambiguous depiction of sex and violence in the new sexual culture. Thus, when one teenage fan wrote to *Soap Opera Digest* defending her pleasure in the GH story, she argued, "I might be only 13, but I do know the difference between an act of love . . . and an act of violence."[92] It is unclear from her statement how she categorized Luke's rape of Laura. Was it an act of love? Or was it a gesture of violence? What was clear was her recognition of a difference between the two, a difference highlighted in the anti-rape discourse of the day and in the on-screen world of *General Hospital*. The controversy over the Luke and Laura plot drew from and contributed to the controversies around both the motivations of rape and the rules of the soap opera genre that occupied television audiences, the television industry, and the society within which they functioned during the 1970s.

Television's Most Unobtrusive Discourse of Sex

With nineteen different characters on ten different shows subjected to rape or attempted rape between 1978 and 1981, the daytime soap opera became a major site for the negotiation of discourses of sex and violence in the United States. Already a source of controversy for its prime-time images and themes, television once again found itself both a product and a constituent of changing understandings of sex and the new sexual culture. Assisted by developments in the daytime television industry that encouraged the inclusion of social issues and the targeting of young audiences, television's serials grappled with the meaning of rape in a period of increased sexual liberation and intensified anti-rape activism. While pushing for a revised conception of rape as a violent act, feminists and other activists encountered the kinds of long-standing myths, fantasies, and fears about rape that understood it as an act of sexual desire. Thus, when soap opera viewers watched Roger rape Holly on *Guiding Light* or saw Luke rape Laura on *General Hospital*, they reacted with all the passion, distress, and confusion they were feeling about rape and its role in the altered world of daytime dramatic storytelling.

The soap opera rape plots that characterized sex as a potentially dangerous, potentially violent, undeniably emotionally wrought experience offered one of the more conflicted takes on sex available in television of the 1970s. Because of the typically denigrated cultural status of soaps, making them even further below the country's "official" moral radar than even sitcoms or made-for-TV movies, daytime television of the 1970s managed to address one of the more disturbing matters raised in the post–sexual revolution society with a degree of complexity and ambiguity difficult to come by in the more high-profile world of prime time. While the ambiguity of some of the soaps' rape plots may have worked against the interests of the feminist anti-rape movement, it also offered soap viewers a forum in which they could slowly consider the ramifications of America's changed sexual landscape. In this case, television's construction of the new sexual culture recognized how confusing, contradictory, and complex sex had become in the changing climate of 1970s America.

conclusion

The new sexual culture of 1970s television changed Americans' relationship to the sexual revolution, securing some of its most significant gains while minimizing some of its more radical impulses. By translating the changes in sexual mores, beliefs, practices, and identities instigated by scientific developments, legal liberalizations, and a host of social movements into a commercially viable form, broadcast network television disseminated those changes to a wide public and shaped their meanings. Television offered its viewers a picture of sex and the new sexual culture in which teenagers had sexual desires and experiences, in which women took on conventionally masculine roles, in which gay characters and themes found tentative acceptance, in which sexual violence could be discussed and debated. Yet television's new sexual culture also deemed one of the most affordable and accessible forms of birth control and disease prevention unacceptable, it encouraged a moral panic over youth sexuality, it insisted that women taking on unconventional roles fit narrow standards of beauty, and it reinforced heterosexual marriage as a de facto norm. The commodification of sexual change under the auspices of network television sold a compromised and conflicted version of the sexual revolution to American audiences.

The specifics of television's new sexual culture were hammered out in negotiations among government and intra-industrial regulators, network executives and advertisers, program producers and performers, activist groups and audiences. Those negotiations produced constructions of sex that varied rather widely in their perspectives on the new sexual culture. Sometimes television's constructions of sex refused altogether the changes that characterized the sexual revolution. The efforts of government and intra-industrial regulators to keep X-rated films, ads with live, lingerie-clad models, and condom commercials off-screen kept television from embracing the new, more open, more "liberated" attitude toward sex that was evident in other cultural forms. But these efforts did not limit television's acceptance of the sexual revolution only by repressing certain representations. They also resisted television's involvement with sexual change by forwarding particular conceptions of sex: that any representation of sex on television should be appropriate for all ages; that women's bodies symbolize the most shameful, most "dirty" aspects of sex; that the proper purpose of sexual encounters is reproduction. At the opposite extreme of television's new sexual culture were representations that incorporated recent changes in sex-related beliefs and practices, openly grappling with the changing times. Some of daytime soap operas' numerous rape plots may have upheld traditional, pre-sexual-revolution values, but more of them either gave voice to the new, politicized anti-rape rhetoric or combined that rhetoric with conventions of soap storytelling to offer an extended exploration of the meaning of rape in a culture of sexual "freedom." Across television's diverse representations of sex and the new sexual culture was a range of ways the medium spoke to the sexual revolution and the changes it brought.

There were definite limits to the diversity of television's take on sex. Certainly, the new sexual culture that television offered supported capitalist interests, or at least did not oppose them. It did not directly address the most radical stances associated with the sexual revolution, and it may have actively denied those stances in certain respects. Television's offerings helped establish a new cultural sense, a "common sense" of American sexual culture that incorporated many emergent, somewhat "revolutionary" elements but typically required that they accommodate residual ways of understanding sex, as well. For example, television made women's new, more public, more gender-challenging roles contingent upon a fundamental sexual difference that suggested that the basis of American sex and gender relations would not be disrupted, no matter the surface changes.

This book has told the story of television's hegemonic incorporation of the potentially oppositional elements of the sexual revolution, of television's ability to nod to those oppositional forces while still servicing the dominant culture's interests.[1] Yet *Wallowing in Sex* has also revealed the ways in which television's new sexual culture of the 1970s functioned more benignly, perhaps even progressively, as a *forum* for the American mainstream's processing of the sexual revolution. This was a forum within which television creators and viewers, operating within larger economic and political constraints, could consider, question, comment on, and clarify the impact of the sexual revolution on their lives and those of their fellow citizens.[2] Looking at the period from this perspective, TV's female sex symbols can be seen as a site for the cultural processing of the women's liberation movement and its challenge to the concept of sexual difference. The stories of young people's sexual endangerment can be understood as a means of considering the impact of the sexual revolution on the American family. And the soaps' rape narratives can be remembered as a way to contemplate the motivations for sexual violence — and its effects — at a time when women were sexually "free" and relations between the sexes were purportedly more open than ever before. Ideological forces limited and shaped what this forum could consider and how it could explore those issues that were represented, but the multitude of representations of, allusions to, and discussions about sex in 1970s TV became a central site for the negotiation of just what role the sexual revolution would have in mainstream American culture from the 1970s onward.

In recent years, American television has continued to represent sex and sexuality in a range of ways, some in keeping with the more progressive outcomes of the sexual revolution, and some continuing to resist those challenges by asserting residual sex and gender hierarchies. Often, these seemingly opposing perspectives are embodied in a single representation. For example, gay and lesbian sexualities have become an increasingly significant presence, indicating the progress that has been made in the American mainstream's acceptance of nonstraight orientations. By the late 1990s, the gay, conventionally masculine Will Truman (*Will and Grace*, NBC, 1998–2006) could replace the pretending-to-be-gay effeminacy of Jack Tripper at the forefront of a hit sitcom. Despite this seeming progress, however, representations such as this often reinforce heteronormative values and eschew queer points of view, being more concerned with appealing to an affluent audience niche than with advancing sexual politics.[3] Similarly, women's autonomy and sexual sovereignty have received greater attention and respect, but they remain contingent upon norms of race, class, and body type. *Sex and the City*'s heroines can openly enjoy sex and bond with each other in discussions of it, but their liberation is predicated upon their whiteness, their upper-middle-class status, their thinness, and their conventionally feminine attractiveness. The conflicted versions of "liberated" sexuality proffered by 1970s TV have taken on different forms in the succeeding decades, but their fundamentally compromised, softened, and limited perspective on sexual change has persisted.

Just as with the broader societal changes in sexuality over the course of the twentieth century, American television's "sexual revolution" has not followed a path of ever-increasing progress but instead has played out — and continues to play out — in fits and starts, with small instances of change accompanied by backlashes and retreats. At moments, one tendency may seem to be winning out over others, as in the late 1980s and early 1990s when networks, advertisers, and producers became especially skittish about gay-themed material,[4] or in the late 1990s, when *Buffy the Vampire Slayer* showcased the powers embodied by young women, or in 2004 and 2005, when politicians reopened the question of regulating cable and broadcast indecency in the wake of the Janet Jackson Super Bowl scandal. The industrial, regulatory, and technological changes since the 1970s, which have led to a vast proliferation of television programming across the many networks of cable and satellite TV and into the cross-media platform of the Internet, have intensified and multiplied television's opportunities to represent sex, but they have not necessarily produced the breadth and depth of sexual representation that might begin to do justice to human sexual experience. Because television is primarily an entertainment medium, and one with a profit motive at that, it is perhaps unrealistic to expect TV to grapple fully with as complex and taboo-ridden a matter as sexuality. But this does not mean that those with an investment in sex and gender equity should shy away from criticizing and questioning television's sex-themed tales. For as the new sexual culture of 1970s television demonstrates, television's means of handling sexual change can play an important role in translating that change into the mainstream of American culture.

If television of the 1970s mediated the sexual revolution for mainstream American culture, then what has been its legacy? What are the long-term effects of the sexual revolution more generally, and of television's participation in it more specifically? What traces of the new sexual culture of 1970s television still exist? And what might those traces reveal about the lasting impact of television's take on the sexual revolution? Perhaps the greatest achievements of the sexual revolution are those dealing with women's sexuality and queer sexualities, both of which escaped longtime legal, psycho-medical, and social restraints as a result of the activist movements of the 1960s and 1970s. These groups still face substantial obstacles and oppressions, and the strides they have made remain frequently imperiled, but the circumstances for both have improved markedly since the 1970s. The hard work of activists and the everyday battles fought by many more are responsible for these improvements, but their efforts paid off in part because television helped make women's liberation and gay rights palatable to mainstream America. This deradicalization was a troubling loss, but one that has affected the history of sex and gender liberation since the 1970s. The contemporary state of sex and gender equity is thus in certain respects an outgrowth of the new sexual culture of the 1970s.

Traces of the new sexual culture of 1970s television continue to appear in multiple media forms, and their ongoing presence suggests their resonance with contemporary sex and gender politics. From the mass-produced products of 1970s kitsch to the more personal memories of individual artists, the new sexual culture of 1970s television is regularly cited and commented upon. Such remnants appear in VH-1's *I Love the '70s* specials, in the Fox sitcom *That '70s Show*, and in Hollywood's reimagining of series such as *Charlie's Angels* (2000, also *Charlie's Angels: Full Throttle*, 2003) and *The Dukes of Hazzard* (2005). The fact that it is this particular cultural moment, and these particular instances of television, that continue to receive attention indicates that the 1970s and its television still speak to American society's debates over sexuality.

Because of the important legacies the sexual revolution has left for women and nonheterosexuals especially, it is perhaps not surprising that the voices of women and of gay men appear frequently in the contemporary cultural products that reference 1970s TV, in particular those products that express personal perspectives on America's sex and gender systems. The work of the gay singer-songwriter Rufus Wainwright is one such product. Wainwright's citations of *Maude*'s Bea Arthur, *The Mary Tyler Moore Show*'s Rhoda, and the *Three's Company* theme song in his lyrics function as kitschy nostalgia, but they also provide a contrast with the more alienating and "adult" contemporary culture he also references.[5] Wainwright regularly remarks upon the changing sexual landscape (for example, "Men reading fashion magazines / Oh what a world it seems we live in / Straight men, oh what a world we live in"),[6] against which he contrasts the 1970s TV allusions. Unlike his more cynical commentaries on the present, the references to the 1970s evoke a sense of comfort and familiarity, a time in Wainwright's own life—and in that of American culture more generally—when sex had a different meaning, perhaps a more innocent one (at least as offered on television and as understood by the young Wainwright) but also one more open to possibility.

Similarly, the memoirist Augusten Burroughs remembers 1970s TV as the norm, the reality, against which he lived the surreal life of his troubled youth, as well as an important site in the shaping of his identity as a young gay man. His 1970s TV encounters with "admitted homosexuals" on *Donahue*, with Charles Nelson Reilly on *Match Game*, with Maude, with *One Day at a Time*'s single mother, and with the anti-gay activist Anita Bryant pervade his 2002 autobiography.[7] Burroughs does not claim that television helped him discover his identity; he remembers being perfectly aware of his gayness all along. Yet the many allusions to the sex-themed television of the 1970s make clear that television was intimately intertwined with his sense of self and his sense of the larger world. Burroughs leaves the impression that his queer sensibility was formed, in part, through his connection to television's new sexual culture.

Traces of the new sexual culture of 1970s television also appear in contemporary cultural productions by women, many of which offer takes on the female sex symbols of the 1970s quite different from Hollywood's. In a commentary broadcast on public radio, the schoolteacher Emily Wylie compares her initially idealized notion of the all-girls' public school in which she works to Wonder Woman's all-female Paradise Island. As a child, Wylie's favorite episodes were those in which Diana traveled to her Amazon homeland. Wylie envisioned teaching in an all-girls school as an opportunity to "produce some Wonder Women!" herself.[8] Although she does not use the word "feminist," she describes Wonder Woman's Paradise Island episodes as feminist fantasies (as opposed to, say, sexist displays of female flesh), and presents her work as a teacher of girls within that same feminist perspective, giving the 1970s series a more definitive, more progressive meaning than it might originally have held.

The female sex symbols of 1970s TV have been resurrected in overtly feminist cultural productions as well, many of which offer conflicted readings of the earlier texts. The Bionic Woman, Jaime Sommers, is the subject of a book of poetry by Julia Steinecke and an experimental documentary, *Bionic Beauty Salon*, by Gretchen Stoeltje.[9] In both, the creators critique the program's assumption that it is natural and beneficial for Jaime's body to be "rebuilt," both through "bionics" and more conventionally feminine beauty treatments. Both texts' authors find the beautiful, powerful Jaime compelling, and the means through which she is "awarded" her beauty and her power disturbing. Similarly, Jennifer Tillity writes of her lifelong love-hate relationship with Farrah Fawcett-Majors and *Charlie's Angels* in the third-wave feminist magazine, *Bust*.[10] She remembers, and regrets, the competition she felt with her childhood friends to determine which Angel each would be, and how the sex-symbol appeal of Fawcett-Majors's Angel, Jill, made her the most desirable. Although Tillity wants to celebrate the Angels as empowering role models, she sees their message as much more conflicted, and thus she is left trying to reconcile her earlier ambition to be an Angel with her present-day status as a feminist. The tensions between feminism and femininity posed by the TV sex symbols run throughout these contemporary feminist citations. Although they offer very different interpretations from the Hollywood-produced films, all of these iterations share an investment in the 1970s TV sex symbols as embodiments of the sex and gender politics of the 1970s *and* the present.

The many allusions to and dissections of 1970s television in our contemporary cultural field demonstrate that the new sexual culture it offered had the resonance and power to help shape ways of imagining sex and gender, at least through the end of the twentieth century and into the early years of the twenty-first. Although 1970s television was not the only force to have such power, it was an important one, and it continues to influence American sexual culture. That influence has been greatest among the generation of Americans, my own generation, that grew up in the 1970s and began to create the cultural productions I discuss here in their young adulthood. As a result, the legacy of 1970s TV is likely to fade as that generation ages, and as younger generations' mediated experiences of sex and gender replace that of the 1970s.

As a girl who played Charlie's Angels and Wonder Woman in her driveway, who re-enacted Love Boat departures from her basement steps, who learned about dating and rape and venereal disease and gayness in part from what she saw and heard on television, I was especially influenced by the new sexual culture of 1970s TV. Yet I still assert that its influence has been felt beyond the childhood memories of those of us who grew up watching television in the 1970s. *Wallowing in Sex* has illustrated how and why the world of the Angels and Wonder Woman, Captain Stubing and Julie McCoy, Jack Tripper and Chrissy Snow, Luke Spencer and Laura Baldwin, Charles Nelson Reilly and Brett Somers, Linda Blair and Eve Plumb was important to an entire culture's envisioning of a society changed by the sexual revolution. The women's movement, the gay rights movement, the de-articulation of sex and reproduction, the recognition of youth sexuality — these forces of change all passed through television on their way to mainstream America. Television's involvement helped keep them from achieving their most revolutionary potential, but it also helped thread small filaments of change into the fabric of American everyday life. For both of those reasons, American sexual culture will be forever altered by the repressive, paranoid, titillating, cautionary, empowering, silly, de-radicalizing, subverting, questioning, reassuring, involving world of 1970s TV.

—NOTES—

Introduction

1. Swanbrow, "Talking T-shirts," 12–13.
2. Allyn, *Make Love, Not War*, 234, 229, 238.
3. Greene, "Beyond the Sexual Revolution," 13, quoted in Allyn, *Make Love, Not War*, 271.
4. "Closed Circuit," *Broadcasting*, 8 August 1977, 5.
5. The concept of "common sense" and its negotiating function come from Antonio Gramsci: Gramsci, *Selections from the Prison Notebooks*. For cogent discussions of Gramsci's ideas and their applicability to media, see Williams, *Marxism and Literature*; Hall, "Gramsci's Relevance for the Study of Race and Ethnicity"; and Fiske, *Power Plays, Power Works*.
6. Koedt, "The Myth of the Vaginal Orgasm," 198–207.
7. D'Emilio and Freedman, *Intimate Matters*; Peiss, *Cheap Amusements*; Stamp, *Movie-Struck Girls*.
8. Chauncey, *Gay New York*, 9.
9. Bailey, *From Front Porch to Back Seat*; D'Emilio and Freedman, *Intimate Matters*.
10. Projansky, *Watching Rape*; Davis, "Rape, Racism and the Myth of the Black Rapist," 172–201.
11. While conventional thinking about the place of sex in struggles for power would argue that sex is either repressed or not, Michel Foucault has argued that social power is not best described as repressing sex but rather as *producing* it. Power produces different discourses, or conceptions, of sex and thereby exercises its influ-

ence. Thus, even when sex is constructed as dangerous or tasteless or inappropriate, it is not an independent entity that is being repressed but is instead a creative and productive discursive force that is used to distinguish people, bodies, and practices from one another and thus to deem some as normal and some as not. That is where the real power of discourses of sex lies. Foucault, *The History of Sexuality*, vol. 1, *An Introduction*.

12. For an overview of these developments, see D'Emilio and Freedman, *Intimate Matters*; Weeks, *Sexuality and Its Discontents*.

13. Bailey, *Sex in the Heartland*.

14. D'Emilio and Freedman, *Intimate Matters*, xv. For additional insights into this shift, see Heath, *The Sexual Fix*; Radner, "Introduction: Queering the Girl," 1–38.

15. Ehrenreich, Hess, and Jacobs, *Re-Making Love*. This is not to say that subordinated groups only benefited from the sexual revolution. As the case of women's sexuality demonstrates, there are many ways in which the sexual revolution placed new kinds of oppressions upon women. Gerhard, *Desiring Revolution*; Jeffreys, *Anticlimax*.

16. Allyn, *Make Love, Not War*; Heath, *The Sexual Fix*; Altman, *The Homosexualization of America, the Americanization of the Homosexual*.

17. See, for example, Bodroghkozy, *Groove Tube*; Radner and Luckett, *Swinging Single*; and Spigel and Curtin, *The Revolution Wasn't Televised*.

18. To analyze 1970s television in relation to its industrial, social, and audience contexts, I draw upon a wide range of source materials, some typical of media historians and some more unconventional. I rely heavily on archival sources and television trade press coverage, perhaps the most conventional of historiographic materials. At times, however, I use these resources in somewhat unconventional ways. Although the history I construct is one of large institutions, such as the broadcast networks, and of powerful individuals, such as the producer Aaron Spelling, it is often a history of small matters within the worlds of these institutions and individuals. I look to decisions about casting, about whether to use one phrase or another to describe an on-screen sexual relationship, about the display of a woman's body in a television commercial to help me paint a picture of exactly how the television industry created its version of the sexual revolution. Thus, script and memo marginalia are as important to my research as more "official" documents. I also draw on archival sources to help me revisit some audience encounters with television, in particular through audience letters, fan mail reports, and market research data. In addition, I turn to the popular press, particularly letters to the editor and first-person journalistic accounts, for additional insights into the connections between television and the broader social world of changing sexual mores. By

combining relatively standard resources such as archives and press coverage with materials as far-ranging as contemporaneous social scientific studies, high school yearbooks, and proceedings of congressional hearings, I seek to reconstruct the new sexual culture of 1970s television in as rich and full a way as possible, despite the impossibility of ever fully recapturing the past. Finally, this project is heavily indebted to the fact that I have been able to view most of the programming I write about, either through syndicated reruns, recent DVD releases, out-of-print videotapes acquired through on-line auctions, or private fan collections. My experience has convinced me of the necessity of preserving the past television programming that still exists so that it is available to future historians.

1. Kiddie Porn versus Adult Porn

1. "Third Try; Prime Time Race," *Forbes*, 1 February 1973, 48.

2. Quinlan, *Inside ABC*, 172.

3. Ibid., 173.

4. Schemering, *The Soap Opera Encyclopedia*, Appendix 2.

5. Bill Greeley, "Daytime Now 3-web Scramble," *Variety*, 1 December 1971, 29.

6. Arthur Lubow, "Soap Hits the Fan," *New Times*, 2 September 1977, 29; Herminio Traviesas, "They Never Told Me about *Laugh-In*," *Broadcasting*, 21 July 1980, 53. On the value of the youth audience beginning in the late 1960s, see Bodroghkozy, *Groove Tube*, 199–200.

7. Gitlin, *Inside Prime Time*, 206–7.

8. Ibid., 207. See Bodroghkozy, *Groove Tube*, 202, for an analysis of Woods's statement and an analysis of CBS's hypocrisy in its canceling of *The Smothers Brothers Comedy Hour*.

9. Bodroghkozy, *Groove Tube*, 205–7.

10. Harry Waters, "Rated PG," *Newsweek*, 11 September 1972, 76.

11. Pekurny, "Broadcast Self-Regulation, 212 and 247.

12. Harry Waters, "Out of the Closet: Depicting Homosexuality on Television," *Time*, 5 March 1973, 80; Capsuto, *Alternate Channels*.

13. From ABC's press release for the film, quoted in Capsuto, *Alternate Channels*, 80.

14. Goldenson and Wolfe, *Beating the Odds*, 337.

15. Bedell, *Up the Tube*, 54.

16. Ibid., 54–55; "Halcyon Days for ABC — and All TV," *Business Week*, 18 August 1973, 47–48.

17. ABC gained thirty new stations between 1968 and 1973 (in comparison to CBS's two and NBC's eleven), by offering higher than normal payments to stations willing to switch their affiliation. "Halcyon Days," 48; "Third Try," 49.

18. "Halcyon Days," 48, 54.

19. CBS held off on the made-for-TV movie business for a few more years. Edgerton, "High Concept, Small Screen," 116.

20. Edgerton, "High Concept, Small Screen," 121; Dwight Whitney, "Cinema's Stepchild Grows Up," TV Guide, 20 July 1974, 23; Patrick McGilligan, "Movies Are Better Than Ever on Television," American Film 5 (1980): 52; Goldenson and Wolfe, Beating the Odds, 333–34.

21. Judith Crist, "Tailored for Television," TV Guide, 30 August 1969, 8–9. See also Marill, Movies Made for Television for brief descriptions of all made-for-TV movies.

22. Goldberg describes this period in Goldenson and Wolfe, Beating the Odds, 247–49.

23. Les Brown, "Daytime's Cheerful Tearful," Variety, 29 October 1969, 52; "Network Daytime: More of a Horse Race," Television Age, 8 September 1969, 28.

24. Bill Greeley, "Daytime Now 3-web Scramble," Variety, 1 December 1971, 29.

25. Max Gunther, "Duel in the Sun," TV Guide, 13 May 1972, 6.

26. Ibid., 8.

27. Nixon, "Coming of Age in Sudsville," 61–70; Bob Knight, "Life to Live: A Pubservice Soaper Pegged upon Actual Drug Therapy," Variety, 22 July 1970, 33+. The soaps did occasionally deal with social issues before the 1970s, although these tended to center on illness and disease, unlike the 1970s stories, which took on more explicitly political and sexual issues.

28. "The High Drama of Network Daytime," Broadcasting, 13 December 1971, 23.

29. "Writing On: Irna Phillips Mends with Tradition," Broadcasting, 6 November 1972, 75. Ironically, Phillips had trained the purveyors the newer soap style, including Agnes Nixon and William J. Bell, the creator of The Young and the Restless, a new-fashioned soap that would debut in 1973.

30. Paul Denis, "The Latest News," Daytime TV, June 1973, 80.

31. Ellen Torgerson, "Heartache, Illness and Crime Do Pay," TV Guide, 8 July 1978, 14.

32. Paul Denis, "The Latest News," Daytime TV, November 1974, 10.

33. Paul Denis, "The Latest News," Daytime TV, May 1974, 6.

34. Judith Viorst, "Soap Operas: The Suds of Time March On," Redbook, November 1975, 62.

35. "Preface to notes on projected projection: Star-crossed lovers." Box 13, Production Files 1974–75, Search for Tomorrow, Ann Marcus Collection, AHC.

36. Edgerton, "High Concept, Small Screen," 118.

37. Dick Adler and Joseph Finnigan, "The Year America Stayed Home for the Movies," TV Guide, 20 May 1972, 8.

38. Dwight Whitney, "Cinema's Stepchild Grows Up," TV Guide, 20 July 1974, 22, 24.

39. Henry R. Bernstein, "Women Come on Strong in Newest Video Shows," Advertising Age, 24 September 1973, 23. On previous attempts at women leads in action-

oriented series, see D'Acci, "Nobody's Woman? *Honey West* and the New Sexuality," 73–94.

40. Henry R. Bernstein, "Women Come on Strong in Newest Video Shows," *Advertising Age*, 24 September 1973, 23.

41. Memorandum from Douglas S. Cramer to Bud Baumes, 7 June 1973. Box 1, File Folders—ASP Development, Douglas S. Cramer Collection, AHC.

42. ABC's other two female-led action pilots were *Brenda Starr*, featuring Jill St. John, and *Kiss Me, Kill Me*, starring Stella Stevens. The two aired back to back on 8 May 1976.

43. "The Man with the Golden Gut," *Time*, 5 September 1977, 51.

44. Silverman, "An Analysis of ABC Television Network Programming from February 1953 to October 1959."

45. Ibid., 125–26.

46. This success can also be attributed in part to the ratings performance of the winter Olympics, broadcast in early 1976.

47. "ABC-TV Wins in Prime Time and in a Big Way," *Broadcasting*, 25 April 1977, 38–39.

48. By the fourth quarter of 1978, typical thirty-second spots on ABC were going for $60,000, while those on CBS and NBC were selling for about $45,000. "NBC Plans Its Climb out of TV's Last Place," *Business Week*, 3 July 1978, 30. On ABC's top-rated shows, like *Charlie's Angels* and *Three's Company*, ads sold for as much as $200,000 a spot.

49. "Changing Priorities at Stodgy NBC," *Business Week*, 4 July 1977, 42.

50. Bedell, *Up the Tube*, xii.

51. James P. Forkan, "Will Writing Team Find Happiness?" *Advertising Age*, 5 October 1981, 3; "She's Behind the Biggest Bubble in Showbiz: Soap Operas," *People*, 4 January 1982, 44.

52. J. Loftus, "ABC Keeps on Packin' Daytime Dynamite," *Variety*, 30 December 1981, 29.

53. "How ABC Found Happiness in Daytime TV," *Business Week*, 24 August 1981, 62 and 64.

54. Bedell, *Up the Tube*, 142–43.

55. Ibid., 146.

56. Described by Garry Marshall, the creator of *Happy Days*, in Eliot, *Televisions*, 96.

57. Douglas Cramer notes in script K-64, 10 October 1979. Box 36, *Love Boat* Script K-64, Douglas S. Cramer Collection, AHC.

58. Memorandum from Gordon Farr to Aaron Spelling and Douglas S. Cramer, 15 October 1979. Box 35, *Love Boat*—Farr, Gordon and Lynne, Douglas S. Cramer Collection, AHC.

59. Bedell, *Up the Tube*, 205.

60. William S. Rubens, *Sex on Television, More or Less*, Association for Consumer Research, Chicago, 14 October 1977.

61. Bedell, *Up the Tube*, 204.

62. Dwight Whitney, "What Uproar over *Soap*?" *TV Guide*, 26 November 1977, 9.

63. Among these were several comedy-westerns with attractive women in lead roles: *Wild and Wooly* (20 February 1978), *Kate Bliss and the Ticker Tape Kid* (26 May 1978), and *The Wild Women of Chastity Gulch* (31 October 1982). Spelling's other efforts along these lines were *Beach Patrol* (30 April 1979) and *Sizzle* (29 November 1981).

64. James P. Forkan, "Sex, Multi-plots Spice up Pilot Series," *Advertising Age*, 27 March 1978, 2.

65. Bill Davidson, "*Black Sheep Squadron* Just Won't Play Dead," *TV Guide*, 15 July 1978, 28.

66. "The Year TV Turned to Sex," *TV Guide*, 6 May 1978, 7, 5.

67. Memorandum from Gordon Farr to Aaron Spelling and Douglas S. Cramer, 15 October 1979. Box 35, *Love Boat*—Farr, Gordon and Lynne, Douglas S. Cramer Collection, AHC.

68. J. Dempsey, "NBC Discovers the (Ratings) Joy of Sex," *Variety*, 14 December 1977, 37.

69. None of the networks aired sex-themed movies of the week in 1975–76. See chapter 3 for my analysis of this phenomenon.

70. Harry F. Waters, "Sex and TV," *Newsweek*, 20 February 1978, 57–59.

71. Richard M. Levine, "Cotton Mather's Last Stand," *New Times*, 20 February 1978, 66–67.

72. David Blum, "King of the Tube," *The New Republic*, 28 October 1978, 13.

73. Sally Bedell, "Silverman Outlines Strategy for Making NBC 'The Class Act,' " *TV Guide*, 30 September 1978, A-6, A-5.

74. Marvin Kitman, "New Man at NBC: Fred Silverman," *New Leader*, 11 September 1978, 22.

2. Not in My Living Room

1. Related by FCC Commissioner Robert Lee, U.S. Senate, Committee on Commerce, Subcommittee on Communications, *Federal Communication Commission Policy Matters and Television Programming*, 91st Cong., 1st sess. (Washington: U.S. Government Printing Office, 1969), 79.

2. I use the term "regulation" instead of "censorship" here and throughout this book for several reasons, in addition to those I enumerate in the text. First, I am following Michel Foucault's argument that a consideration of "censorship" emphasizes a repressive notion of power, and that power is more accurately described

as productive, instead of repressive, for the ways that it shapes our categorization of people and practices as opposed to merely refusing to categorize them. Foucault, *The History of Sexuality*, vol. 1, *An Introduction*, 17. Second, I seek to avoid the loaded connotations of "censorship" and its association with First Amendment violations. As Matthew Murray points out, most scholarly studies of broadcast regulation and/or censorship have fallen within positivist legal and social scientific paradigms that seek to "repair the existing system of regulation without evaluating the discursive limits to that system." I am not interested in judging the relative democracy of different regulatory or censorship efforts; instead I seek to analyze why, how, and to what effect regulatory measures were enacted. Murray, "Broadcast Content Regulation and Cultural Limits, 1920–1962," 2. Lastly, because "censorship" was a term employed frequently in the television regulation discourse of the 1970s, mostly by those in opposition to regulatory efforts (for example, producers opposed to the National Association of Broadcasters' family hour policy), I want to use different language to describe the much broader efforts I see as contributing to the shaping of television's sex discourse. See Hendershot, *Saturday Morning Censors*, especially 14–22, for a different approach to the regulation-censorship issue and her sense of the distinction (or lack thereof) between the two.

3. Coakley, *Rated X*, 28, 38, 39, 79, 86, 87, 152.

4. Wyatt, "Selling 'Atrocious Sexual Behavior,' " 105–32.

5. Robert E. Lee, *Self-regulation or Censorship in the TV Industry*, Association of Broadcasting Executives of Texas, 31 July 1969.

6. U.S. House of Representatives, Committee on Interstate and Foreign Commerce, Subcommittee on Communications and Power, *Subscription Television—1969*, 91st Cong., 1st sess. (Washington: U.S. Government Printing Office, 1969), 38–40.

7. U.S. Senate, Committee on Commerce, Subcommittee on Communications, *Amend Communications Act of 1934*, S.2004, 91st Cong., 1st sess. (Washington: U.S. Government Printing Office, 1969), 498–99.

8. Ibid., 360.

9. "How B'casters Answered McClellan," *Variety*, 3 December 1969, 26.

10. Frank Beermann, "*The Damned* a Hell-raiser for CBS as First X-rated Film on Network," *Variety*, 1 March 1972, 33.

11. Ibid., 68.

12. Addison Verrill, "The Surgery on *Damned*," *Variety*, 1 March 1972, 33. Some critics and station owners argued that these cuts made the narrative unintelligible and that the film was not worth showing on these grounds alone.

13. U.S. Senate, Committee on Commerce, Subcommittee on Communications, *Sur-*

geon *General's Report by the Scientific Advisory Committee on Television and Social Behavior*, 92nd Cong., 2nd sess. (Washington: U.S. Government Printing Office, 1972), 40–42.

14. Sanford Markey, "WEWS-TV to Air *Damned* This Week after Cleve. Council Voted 'X-pic' Ban; Other Blackouts and Reverberations," *Variety*, 8 March 1972, 34.

15. U.S. Senate, *Surgeon General's Report*, 200.

16. "Where Did the Rumor Start that Flooded CBS Offices with More Than 400,000 Pieces of Mail?" *TV Guide*, 28 July 1973, 8–9.

17. Ibid., 10 and "Legislators in Carolinas Move Toward Curbing X-rated Pix on TV," *Variety*, 11 April 1973, 39. The North Carolina state senate had a hearing on the matter but took no action. "Attorney Bricks It to FCC," *Variety*, 11 April 1973, 56.

18. "CBS and Affils Still Plagued with Letters on X Pix," *Variety*, 4 April 1973, 125.

19. "A Sour Look at Some TV Programs," *Nation's Business*, May 1973, 24.

20. "FCC: Closing in on Broadcast Smut," *Broadcasting*, 2 February 1970, 54.

21. F. Slover, "Advertisers Aplenty for Baby Blue Film Shows on Toronto's CITY-TV," *Advertising Age*, 9 April 1973, 78; "Blue Tube: Broadcasting of Mildly Salacious Movies on Canadian Television," *Time*, 9 April 1973, 54; Jack Batten, "X-rated Movies Come to Television," *TV Guide*, 10 February 1973, 20–21.

22. "Public's Upper Hand Forces Sex Off Air in Nevada Experiment," *Broadcasting*, 19 March 1973, 8.

23. "Touchiest Topic on Radio Now: Talk about Sex," *Broadcasting*, 19 March 1973, 118–19.

24. "Pastore Pushes FCC to Move Against 'Indecent' Programs," *Broadcasting*, 26 February 1973, 50; J. B. Roy, "Sex on the Airways: Congress Is Aroused," *Saturday Review of the Arts*, 7 April 1973, 70.

25. Jim Harwood, "Sex Boiling in Broadcasting," *Variety*, 11 April 1973, 39; "Sonderling Relents, Won't Battle FCC Over Sexy Show," *Advertising Age*, 30 April 1973, 39. The FCC had filed a notice of apparent liability against Sonderling, charging the broadcaster with obscenity and indecency in response to a listener complaint and the commission's own review of some *Femme Forum* episodes. In particular, the commission cited a February 1973 program dealing with oral sex that was presented in what the FCC termed a "titillating and pandering" manner. *Illinois Citizens Committee for Broadcasting v. Federal Communications Commission*, 169 U.S. App. D.C. 166; 515 F.2d 39 (1974).

26. Federal Communications Commission, 12 February 1975. "Memorandum Opinion and Order," appendix E, "Report on the Broadcast of Violent, Indecent, and Obscene Material," in *Federal Communications Commission Reports* 51 (Washington: U.S. Government Printing Office, 1976), 433. WBAI took the FCC to court over

the case, which eventually made its way to the U.S. Supreme Court. In 1978, the Court affirmed the FCC's decision.

27. John Revett, "FCC Fearful Loopholes Might Permit 'Sexy' Programs on TV," *Advertising Age*, 24 February 1975, 3.

28. Streeter, "Blue Skies and Strange Bedfellows."

29. "The Cable Blues," *Newsweek*, 9 April 1973, 83. The Syracuse station ran *Deep Throat*.

30. "Pastore Pushes FCC to Move Against 'Indecent' Programs," *Broadcasting*, 26 February 1973," 50.

31. Federal Communications Commission, "Report on the Broadcast of Violent, Indecent, and Obscene Material," in *Federal Communications Commission Reports* 51 (Washington: U.S. Government Printing Office, 1976), 424.

32. Neither the FCC nor Congress acted on issues of the visual depiction of obscene material until they began to deal with obscenity and pornography on the Internet in the late 1990s. In 1988, the FCC did not follow through with a Notice of Apparent Liability against KZKC-TV in Kansas City for the visual depiction of indecent material in a broadcast of the feature film *Private Lessons*.

33. Sally Bedell, "Too Hot to Handle?" *TV Guide*, 8 October 1977, 19–20.

34. U.S. House of Representatives, Committee on Interstate and Foreign Commerce, Subcommittee on Communications, *Cable Regulation*, 94th Cong., 2nd sess., 1976, 229–30.

35. As the president of Cox Cable said, "It is the kiss of death politically. We don't want to walk down the halls of Congress and hear them say, 'Here come the porno guys.'" Sally Bedell, "Too Hot to Handle?" *TV Guide*, 8 October 1977, 20.

36. U.S. House of Representatives, *Cable Regulation*, 235.

37. The case of *Midwest Video Corp. v. FCC*, 571 F.2d 1025 (D.C. Cir. 1978) determined that the FCC's requirement that cable systems carry access channels at all was outside the commission's jurisdiction, so cable systems no longer felt the need to be responsible for public access in the same way. This decision, along with the threat to sue Manhattan Cable by the producers of *Midnight Blue*, encouraged the cable system to drop its public access content standards. Hofbauer, "'Cableporn' and the First Amendment."

38. In 1979, the U.S. Department of Justice estimated that 77 percent of the television stations in the nation's top fifty markets and 93 percent of network-affiliated stations in the top fifty markets were code subscribers. R.L. Gordon, "U.S. Suits against TV Code Seen Self-regulation Peril," *Advertising Age*, 18 June 1979, 103. The three major broadcast networks (ABC, NBC, and CBS) were also code subscribers throughout the TV code's history.

39. Stations or networks that defied the TV code could lose the NAB's "seal of good practice," a relatively toothless enforcement measure.

40. For a brief description of some early 1950s bra commercials, see "Exquisite Form Girds for Girdle Ad Battle with NAB," *Advertising Age*, 8 December 1969, 36.

41. Memo from Stockton Helfrich to all TV code subscribers, 18 February 1970. Box 4, Binder "Subscriber Memos," NAB Collection, WSHS.

42. Echols, *Daring to Be Bad*, 93–94.

43. Douglas, *Where the Girls Are*, 160.

44. "Vassarette Push Aims to Counter Bra-less Trend," *Advertising Age*, 28 December 1970, 3.

45. "Big Letdown: Anti-bra Movement," *Newsweek*, 1 September 1969, 49–50.

46. For example, Exquisite Form Industries developed the No-Bra, the Maybe-Bra, and the Bye-Bye Bra. C. Lindsay, "Whither the Bra," *McCall's*, November 1969, 138.

47. Marilyn DeJong, "Only Her Bra-maker Knows for Sure," *Marketing/Communications*, December 1969, 33–34.

48. "Skip Your Bra—If You Have Super Shape, Say Peter Pan Ads," *Advertising Age*, 2 February 1970, 16.

49. "Exquisite Form to Defy Code on Scanties TV Ads," *Advertising Age*, 17 November 1969, 136.

50. Memo from Stockton Helfrich to all TV code subscribers, 18 February 1970.

51. "Exquisite Form Girds for Battle with NAB," *Advertising Age*, 8 December 1969, 36.

52. Memo from Stockton Helfrich to all TV code subscribers, 18 February 1970.

53. Television Code Board Minutes, May 1970. Box 4, NAB Collection, WSHS.

54. Douglas, *Where the Girls Are*, 140.

55. Marilyn DeJong, "Only Her Bra-maker Knows for Sure," *Marketing/Communications*, December 1969, 33.

56. "TV Ads (Male View)," *New York Times Magazine*, 18 June 1972, 4.

57. Correspondence of John T. Murphy to head of TV Code Committee, 1 October 1969. Box 4, TV Code Board Minutes, December 1969, NAB Collection, WSHS.

58. Correspondence of John T. Murphy to Stockton Helfrich, 24 October 1969. Box 4, TV Code Board Minutes, December 1969, NAB Collection, WSHS.

59. "Murphy Will Argue for Models in Lingerie Ads," *Broadcasting*, 17 November 1969, 48.

60. "Living Bras, of Sorts," *Time*, 15 May 1972, 80.

61. Judith Ramsey, "The Bra Question," *New York Times Magazine*, 31 August 1975, 30.

62. "TV Code Board Scrutinizing Personal-Product Ads More Intently," *Broadcasting*, 18 October 1976, 45.

63. "TV Code Board Stands Firm on Several Matters," *Broadcasting*, 25 April 1977, 34.

64. The suspension of the code was instigated in 1979, when the Department of Justice filed suit against the NAB, seeking to bar the organization from requiring commercial time standards (a maximum number of commercials per hour). In 1982, a U.S. District Court ruled that one of the NAB's time standards, limiting the number of products that can be advertised in a spot of less than sixty seconds, was illegal. This judgment effectively served as the end of the NAB's advertising standards. With its advertising standards gone, the NAB TV Code was practically eliminated, as the programming standards had been basically inactive since the family viewing decision in 1976. R. L. Gordon, "U.S. Suit against TV Code Seen Self-regulation Peril," *Advertising Age*, 18 June 1979, 1; "Little Change Expected in Wake of NAB Code Ruling," *Broadcasting*, 22 March 1982, 79.

65. Maurine Christopher, "TV Folk Wary of Sexier Ads, but See 'Em as Reflection of Times," *Advertising Age*, 26 May 1969, 94.

66. "Brickbats, Laurels for Ads with Women," *Broadcasting*, 30 August 1971, 44.

67. "Vulgar Sex Ads Demean All, Insult Consumer, Panel Finds," *Advertising Age*, 24 March 1975, 67.

68. "Lighthearted Celebration of National Condom Week," *American Druggist*, March 1978, 30.

69. M. D'Antonio, "How Men Feel Now about Contraceptives," *Glamour*, August 1978, 102.

70. Gordon, *Woman's Body, Woman's Right*, 421; and "Pill on Trial," *Time*, 26 January 1970, 60.

71. See, for example, Alice Lake, "Advice to Women Who Are Once-a-Month Witches," *Redbook*, April 1969, 178.

72. Robert W. Kinter, M.D., "What 'The Pill' Does to Husbands," *Ladies' Home Journal*, January 1969, 66, 68.

73. Gordon, *Woman's Body, Woman's Right*, 422.

74. "Poll on the Pill," *Newsweek*, 9 February 1970, 53; and Gordon, *Woman's Body, Woman's Right*, 422. In the 1980s, pharmaceutical companies attempted to revive acceptance of the pill, and the pill's hormonal doses were increasingly lowered so as to minimize the health risks.

75. This argument about men's assumption about women's use of the pill comes from Michael Castleton, the former director of the San Francisco Health Department's Men's Reproductive Health Clinic. D'Antonio, "How Men Feel Now about Contraceptives," 101.

76. Dan Kushner, "The Condom Comes Out of Hiding," *American Druggist*, January 1976, 26–27.

77. "How Changing Attitudes Affect Sales of Male Prophylactics," *American Druggist*, 1 July 1973, 35.

78. "Proselytizers for Prophylactics: Population Services, Inc. Promotes Condoms," *Time*, 7 December 1970, 97.

79. Kushner, "The Condom Comes Out of Hiding," 26.

80. "High Court Outlaws Curbs on Contraceptive Sales, Displays, Ads," *Drug Topics*, 1 July 1977, 7.

81. Kushner, "The Condom Comes Out of Hiding," 26.

82. D'Antonio, "How Men Feel Now about Contraceptives," 101.

83. For example, in 1969, only one publication of eighteen approached agreed to run a Youngs Drug Products' ad for Trojan condoms, but by 1976 such publications as *Parents*, *Ladies' Home Journal*, *Psychology Today*, and *Ms.* were carrying ads for a variety of brands. "In condoms, everything is changing . . . product, packaging, display, advertising," *American Druggist*, January 1976, 33.

84. Nancy Schwartz, "TV Films," 32.

85. Levine, "Having a Female Body Doesn't Make You Feminine," 39–58.

86. Storyboard by McCann-Erikson, 1971. Box 2, Exhibits: Agenda Item H — Personal products advertising, NAB Collection, WSHS.

87. "Canada OKs TV for Ortho," *Advertising Age*, 16 August 1971, 33; and "Major Ad Taboo Ends in Canada," *Broadcasting*, 9 August 1971, 31.

88. "Contraceptive Group Ready," *Advertising Age*, 17 June 1974, 128.

89. Maurine Christopher, "Freer Use of TV Sought for Male Contraceptives; Trojan on Two Stations," *Advertising Age*, 4 August 1975, 45.

90. Ibid, 45; "Change of Season: First Condom Commercial on KNTV," *Time*, 11 August 1975, 48–49.

91. Maurine Christopher, "Ohio Station Pulls Trojan Ads after News Preview," *Advertising Age*, 11 August 1975, 2.

92. Fred C. Poppe, "The Trojans Wars: A Beachhead in Broadcast Advertising," *Broadcasting*, 24 November 1975, 10.

93. Schwartz, "TV Films," 32.

94. "Positions Taken on Broadcast Contraceptive Advertising by Organizations Included in Code Authority's June 1976 Poll," March 1978. Box 1, Minutes of March 1978 TV Code Review Board Meeting, NAB Collection, WSHS.

95. Colby Coates, "Code Board Mulls Contraceptive Ads," *Advertising Age*, 29 May 1978, 54.

96. Rick Horowitz, "Should Contraceptives Be Advertised on Television?" *Channels* (October-November 1981), 65; correspondence from Joan Sprague, Girls Clubs of America, to Vincent Wasilewski, NAB, 22 July 1981; Society for Adolescent Medicine, "Position Paper on Media Advertising of Contraceptives," 20 March 1981; correspondence from William H. McBeath, American Public Health Association, to

Vincent Wasilewski, 10 April 1981. Box 4, TV Code Review Board Minutes October 1981, NAB Collection, WSHS.

97. Kaplan and Houlberg, "Broadcast Condom Advertising," 172.

3. The Sex Threat

1. Letter from Pam Brownell to Douglas S. Cramer and Letter from Lisa Stewart to Douglas S. Cramer. Box 21, *Dawn*—Composer/Music, Douglas S. Cramer Collection, AHC.

2. The lead singer, Cherie Currie, was particularly known for wearing lingerie on stage. The band suffered from a lack of credibility in rock and punk music circles during the 1970s, especially among those who disdained the band's teenage "bad girl" image as shameless exploitation. More recently, however, many musicians, particularly female rock acts, have cited The Runaways and band members such as Joan Jett as important early influences. See http://entertainment.msn.com/artist/?artist=129149 for a full band biography.

3. Letter from Brownell to Cramer.

4. Aries, *Centuries of Childhood*.

5. Spigel, "Seducing the Innocent," 190.

6. D'Emilio and Freedman, *Intimate Matters*, 159.

7. J. Gilbert, *A Cycle of Outrage*.

8. Quoted in Spigel, "Seducing the Innocent," 195.

9. See Rowland, *The Politics of TV Violence* for the long history of congressional interest in media violence and studies of media effects. See also Boddy, "Senator Dodd Goes to Hollywood."

10. "Congressmen Seek Probe of TV Violence," *Television Digest*, 8 July 1968, 5.

11. "Advertisers React to Violence," *Broadcasting*, 8 July 1968, 19; "TV Responds to Violence Charge," *Broadcasting*, 17 June 1968, 48.

12. "1968–69: The Nonviolent Season," *Broadcasting*, 19 August 1968, 23.

13. "TV Responds," 48.

14. U.S. Senate, Committee on Commerce, Subcommittee on Communications, *Federal Communications Commission Policy Matters and Television Programming*, 91st Cong., 1st sess., 1969, 2. For more on Pastore's proposals in this hearing, see "New Twist on Pre-screening," *Television Digest*, 31 March 1969, 3; "A Conversation with Television's Chief Censor," *TV Guide*, 23 August 1969, 6; and Baker and the Media Task Force Staff, "The Views, Standards, and Practices of the Television Industry," appendix III-K.

15. U.S. Senate, *Federal Communications Commission Policy Matters*, 1969, 336.

16. See ibid., 338–39 for Stewart's statement to the subcommittee.

17. Vance Hartke to John O. Pastore, 24 February 1969, reprinted in ibid., 378.

18. U.S. Senate, *Federal Communications Commission Policy Matters*, 1969, 343.

19. Ibid., 374.

20. Nixon's letter read, "I want you to know that I join you in supporting the proposed one-year study of the possible relationship between scenes of sex and violence on television and antisocial behavior among young people." President Richard Nixon to Senator John Pastore, 24 March 1969, reprinted in ibid., 517.

21. Ibid., 374.

22. Judith Crist, "Tailored for Television," in *TV Guide*, 30 August 1969, 8.

23. Ibid., 9.

24. See D'Acci, *Defining Women*, 135–36 for a useful critique of exploitation topics in television.

25. Gitlin, *Inside Prime Time*, 161.

26. Schulze, "The Made-for-TV Movie," 362.

27. Pekurny, "Broadcast Self-Regulation," 290.

28. Maurine Christopher, "NBC Boss Raps Sponsor Pullouts from 'Innocent,'" *Advertising Age*, 16 September 1974, 1.

29. John J. O'Connor, "TV: A Glimpse of Reality," *New York Times*, 18 September 1974, 83. Karl E. Meyer, "Television's Trying Times," *Saturday Review*, 16 September 1978, 20.

30. Pekurny, "Broadcast Self-Regulation," 290.

31. See, for example, John J. O'Connor, "TV: Girl Inmate Is Focus of 'Born Innocent' Film," *New York Times*, 10 September 1974, 83.

32. Unlike other movies I discuss, *TV Guide* did not carry an ad promoting *Born Innocent*. This is most likely because the networks tended to spend their promotional dollars on the made-for-TV movies that aired during ratings sweeps periods.

33. Gerald DiPego, *Born Innocent*, Revised First Draft, July 9, 1974. Box 12, Gay Media Task Force Collection, Carl A. Kroch Library, Cornell University.

34. The *New York Times* critic John J. O'Connor found the film worthwhile, though flawed. He claimed that it was "more interesting than most of the other fare . . . this first week of the new television season." O'Connor, "TV: Girl Inmate," 83. In addition, some people involved in the juvenile justice system found the film valuable. As O'Connor reported, one associate of a girls' detention center in Boston "felt that the movie would help instigate more desperately needed reform." John J. O'Connor, "When a TV Show Takes Itself Seriously, Viewers Tend to Become Upset," *New York Times*, 29 September 1974, 133.

35. Cowan, *See No Evil*, 69.

36. O'Connor, "TV: A Glimpse of Reality," 83.

37. Cowan, *See No Evil*, 78.

38. John J. O'Connor, "Warning: Violence on TV Is Dangerous to Your Health," *New York Times*, 3 November 1974, 171.

39. Marvin Lewis, interviewed on NBC News, 31 July 1978. Vanderbilt University Television News Archive. In 1978, a Superior Court judge awarded a non-suit judgment in the case, arguing that NBC's First Amendment rights protected the network from such a negligence claim.

40. Montgomery, "Gay Activists and the Networks," 115. Montgomery claims that gay activists had no impact on the film until its impending rebroadcast was announced. However, I found a revised first draft script dated July 1974 in the collected papers of the Gay Media Task Force, suggesting that this group was at least consulted about the film in the early stages of its production. DiPego, *Born Innocent*, Gay Media Task Force Collection.

41. Lesbian Feminist Liberation's Tayloe Ross, quoted in Les Brown, "Four Advertisers Drop Spots on Repeat of 'Born Innocent,'" *New York Times*, 25 October 1975, 59.

42. Les Brown, "NBC Plans Replay of 'Born Innocent,'" *New York Times*, 27 September 1975, 61.

43. Montgomery, "Gay Activists and the Networks," 114–20.

44. From what I have gathered about the edited rape scene, it may not even have read clearly as a rape. Instead it might have seemed to be a physical attack, but not a sexual one.

45. These films aired regardless of the uproar over *Born Innocent* and the subsequent institution of the family viewing policy, most likely because they were already scheduled and paid for by the networks.

46. See, for example, "Close Up," *TV Guide*, 22 February 1975, A-18; display ad, *TV Guide*, 22 February 1975, A-19; John J. O'Connor, "TV: Funny Lily Tomlin," *New York Times*, 21 February 1975, 63.

47. Cowan, *See No Evil*, 88.

48. Action for Children's Television was dissatisfied with this. Cole and Oettinger, *Reluctant Regulators*, 276–281. For another analysis of the ACT campaign, see Hendershot, *Saturday Morning Censors*.

49. Cowan, *See No Evil*, 93.

50. For a clear chronology of these events, see Geller and Young, "Family Viewing," 194–96. The FCC issued its *Report on the Broadcast of Violent, Indecent, and Obscene Material* in February 1975, supporting the NAB policy and fulfilling its responsibility to Congress to report back on these matters.

51. Memo from Tom Swafford to Messrs. Schneider, Wood, Kirschner, Currlin, CBS, 20 June 1975. U.S. House of Representatives, Committee on Interstate and For-

eign Commerce, Subcommittee on Communications, *Sex and Violence on TV*, 94th Cong., 2nd sess., 1976, 163–64.

52. Memo from Dick Kirschner to Thomas Swafford, CBS, 24 June 1975. U.S. House of Representatives, *Sex and Violence on TV*, 1976, 171.

53. Ibid., 169.

54. Producers Allan Burns and Larry Gelbart relayed this story at the House Subcommittee hearings in 1976. Ibid., 91, 141.

55. "TV Movies Decline," *Television/Radio Age*, 1 September 1975, 32. Silverman's propensity for series and specials is evident even in his master's thesis of 1959. Silverman, "An Analysis of ABC Television Network Programming from February 1953 to October 1959."

56. In 1974–75, ABC programmed thirty-seven ninety-minute movies and four two-hour films. In 1975–76, the network scheduled five ninety-minute movies and seven two-hour features. The other networks engaged in similar downsizing of their made-for-TV movie schedules. "TV Movies Decline," 32.

57. "TV Movies Decline," 32.

58. As I discuss in chapter 1, in the 1975–76 season, all three networks tried out pilots or series with women characters in traditionally male roles. Some of these, such as ABC's pilot for *Charlie's Angels*, drew on the female characters' attractiveness to present them as sex symbols. Perhaps this version of sex on TV was seen as "safer" in the wake of *Born Innocent* and family viewing.

59. Edgerton, "High Concept, Small Screen," appendix 1, 125.

60. The most frequently cited instance of a made-for-TV movie surpassing feature films in ratings was the 1979 broadcast of *Elvis* on ABC, which beat *Gone with the Wind* on CBS and *One Flew Over the Cuckoo's Nest* on NBC. McGilligan, "Movies Are Better Than Ever on Television," 51.

61. Stone, "TV Movies and How They Get That Way," 151.

62. Ben Stein, "Love, Rape, Highway, Diary: Have We Sold You, Dear Viewer?" *TV Guide*, 25 July 1981, 34.

63. Ibid., 35.

64. Ibid.

65. Stone, "TV Movies and How They Get That Way," 148.

66. Edgerton, "High Concept, Small Screen," 122–23.

67. As Gary Edgerton has put it, "The made-for-TV movie was indisputably realized with this mini-series, fulfilling with a vengeance its earliest promise of becoming a television 'special event' in 'longform.' " Ibid., 123.

68. Rapping, *The Movie of the Week*, xi.

69. Ibid., 106.

70. Ibid., 109–10.

71. Ibid., 106.

72. I determined which made-for-TV movies featured sexually endangered youth by reading through all of the entries in Marill, *Movies Made for Television*, for these seasons. Based on Marill's descriptions, I selected films that seemed to feature young people in some kind of sexually perilous circumstances. I further confirmed Marill's descriptions (and determined whether the films had ever been released on video) through Maltin, *TV Movies and Video Guide*. (Later versions of Maltin's guide do *not* include made-for-TV movies.) I acquired video versions of ten of the films (along with the five films from the 1974–75 season discussed earlier) through on-line auctions. Steven Tropiano kindly supplied me with a second copy of *Alexander: The Other Side of Dawn* when my copy was missing a key scene.

73. Display ads, *TV Guide*, 25 September 1976, A-71 and 15 January 1977, A-41.

74. Schwartz, "TV Films," 37. Critics have also classified made-for-TV movies as a women's genre in terms of the themes and issues such films tend to cover. See Rapping.

75. Schaefer, *'Bold! Daring! Shocking! True!'*, 216.

76. Ibid., 25.

77. Ibid., 256, 260.

78. Douglas Cramer to Mark Cohen, 24 September 1976. Box 46, ABC Correspondence, Douglas S. Cramer Collection, AHC. In the letter, the only detail about the footage Cohen saw that Cramer mentions is the poor quality of the editing, but I am surmising that the footage included material more explicit than typically allowed on U.S. network television. I have drawn this conclusion from Cramer's language (for example, "tawdry") and from the fact that the version of the film I have seen was clearly that intended for foreign distribution. It included nudity and explicit language that might have been easily edited out for the broadcast version.

79. Paraphrased in Douglas Cramer to Jo Heims, 23 April 1976. Box 46, Heims, Jo, Douglas S. Cramer Collection, AHC.

80. Auster, "If You Can't Get 'Em into the Tent, You'll Never Have a Circus," 13.

81. Cramer's opposition between "honest, authentic, tasteful" and "deeply moving" suggests a perceived difference between "quality" and entertainment value. Douglas Cramer to Stanley Robertson, 5 May 1975. Box 21, Teenage Runaway-NBC, Douglas S. Cramer Collection, AHC.

82. "From Newton Deiter," Box 4, Newton E. Deiter, Ph.D., and Handwritten notes, Box 9, Script Writer "Alexander," Douglas S. Cramer Collection, AHC. The Gay Media Task Force collection housed at Cornell University also has scripts for *Alexander* on file, indicating that Deiter had been consulted.

83. Schaefer, *"Bold! Daring! Shocking! True,"* 69.

84. *Diary of a Teenage Hitchhiker* also began with a square-up listing statistics of young women sexually assaulted and murdered while hitching in various cities.

85. Schaefer lists these as purposes of the classical exploitation film square-up, as well. *"Bold! Daring! Shocking! True!,"* 71.

86. Ibid., 338–39.

87. The fact that Garfield, the detective, is black is a twist on the stereotypical association between black characters and the sexually dangerous underworld in these films. In fact, *Little Ladies* comments on the stereotype of black men as pimps (a stereotype the movie perpetuates with the character of Comfort) when a panel of politicians asks York, the white pimp turned cop, why he (as a white man) became a pimp. York answers, "All white men are not born into money. It's not the color of a man's skin that sends him out into the street. It's not black or white. It's green." Although York's remarks point to the importance of economics, they also deny the systemic economic deprivation suffered disproportionately by African Americans. The inclusion of Garfield as a "good" black character to balance the "bad" Comfort is a strategy typical of mainstream media production by the 1970s.

88. Douglas S. Cramer to Joe Taritero, 26 May 1976. Box 21, Teenage Runaway-NBC, Douglas S. Cramer Collection, AHC.

89. The second film was *No Place to Hide* (4 March 1981). This film was not as clearly placed in the sexual endangerment subgenre; it was more a conventional thriller. However, at the very end of the film, we learn that twenty-year-old Amy Manning's stalker is her new husband, David, who, it turns out, seduced and married her with the intention of killing her and stealing her inheritance. This twist—paired with the fact that Amy is played by Kathleen Beller, the actress who played a similarly terrorized young woman in 1978's *Are You in the House Alone?*—confirms that young women are still threatened by meeting men in public settings and becoming sexually involved with them. The ending twist shows that the discourse of sexual endangerment still has cultural power, even while this movie's plot differs somewhat from others in the subgenre.

4. Symbols of Sex

1. Mary Susan Miller, "The Farrah Factor," *Ladies' Home Journal*, June 1977, 34.

2. Ibid., 38.

3. Beauvoir, *The Second Sex.*

4. See, for example, Firestone, *The Dialectic of Sex*, 83.

5. From a membership of 35,000 in the mid-1970s, the National Organization for Women grew to 250,000 members by 1982, largely due to support for the ERA.

Ryan, *Feminism and the Women's Movemen*, 73. For a cogent summary of the ERA's history, see Mansbridge, *Why We Lost the ERA*.

6. Koedt, "Lesbianism and Feminism," 255.

7. For a critique of this sort of essentialism, see Alcoff, "Cultural Feminism vs. Poststructuralism," 405–36; Echols, "The New Feminisms of Yin and Yang," 439–59, and "The Taming of the Id," 50–72.

8. The name "cultural feminism" is a label applied to this branch of feminism more frequently by scholars and historians than by the feminists themselves. While the so-called cultural feminists of the 1970s most frequently referred to themselves as radical feminists, I am reserving that title for those feminists who refused to acknowledge women's sexual difference from men and labeling as cultural feminists those feminists who reclaimed sexual difference as the basis of female power and feminist revolution. See Echols, *Daring to be Bad*, for an elaboration of this distinction.

9. For more on the discourse of anti-ERA activists, see Mathews and Mathews, "The Cultural Politics of ERA's Defeat"; and Marshall, "Keep Us on the Pedestal."

10. Klatch, *Women of the New Right*, 166.

11. See, for example, the female spy Honey West in her eponymous 1960s series. D'Acci, "Nobody's Woman?"

12. Spigel, in *Make Room for TV*, discusses the television industry's attempts to woo women to the medium and its advertised products in its earliest years. Women were also a key audience for U.S. broadcast network radio. See Allen, *Speaking of Soap Operas*. For a discussion of the continued emphasis on women as the main consumers for television advertising, see D'Acci, *Defining Women*, 65–67.

13. Morry Roth, "TV Being Shaped by Ad Pressures for Young Femme Demographics," *Variety*, 3 January 1973, 99.

14. Ralph Leezenbaum, "The New American Woman . . . and Marketing," *Marketing/Communications*, July 1970, 22.

15. "Setback for NOW Is Seen in Loss of Two Key Cases," *Broadcasting*, 7 April 1975, 76; and United States Commission on Civil Rights, *Window Dressing on the Set*.

16. "SAG Crusades: More Use of Women, Less Use of Reruns," *Broadcasting*, 11 November 1974, 40.

17. "New Breed: Female Reporters," *Newsweek*, 30 August 1971, 62. See also the kafuffle around the hiring of Barbara Walters to co-anchor ABC's evening news in 1976 (at a salary of $1 million). "Supersalaried Superstar: Eyebrows Are up Everywhere over Walters's High Price Tag," *Broadcasting*, 3 May 1976, 30.

18. Edith Efron, "Is Television Making a Mockery of the American Woman?" *TV Guide*, 8 August 1970, 8.

19. Bob Donath, "New National Ads Spark Attacks Against 'Sexist' Airline Campaigns," *Advertising Age*, 24 June 1974, 2, 74; "National Near NAB Okay for New 'I'm Going to Fly You' Ads," *Advertising Age*, 4 November 1974, 2+.

20. "NOW Asks Networks to Give Women a More Positive Role," *Broadcasting*, 22 September 1975, 59.

21. Andrew J. DuBrin and Eugene H. Fram, "Coping with Women's Lib," *Sales Management*, 15 June 1971, 20.

22. Ralph Leezenbaum, "The New American Woman . . . and Marketing," *Marketing/Communications*, July 1970, 22.

23. "Advertising Portraying or Directed to Women," *Advertising Age* 46, 21 April 1975, 72.

24. T. Johnston, "Why 30 Million Are Mad about Mary," *New York Times Magazine*, 7 April 1974, 30.

25. Dow, *Prime-Time Feminism*, 51. Taylor, *Prime-Time Families*, 124.

26. Johnston, "Why 30 Million Are Mad about Mary," 96.

27. Ibid., 30.

28. "Type Casting," *Newsweek*, 23 October 1972, 63.

29. J. Wilkie, "Beatrice Arthur, TV's Maude," *Good Housekeeping*, June 1973, 42, 44.

30. Memorandum from W. L. Baumes to Art Frankel via Douglas S. Cramer, 22 August 1972. Box 1, File Folders — ASP Development, Douglas S. Cramer Collection, AHC.

31. Memorandum from David Goldsmith to Joseph Goodson, 25 September 1973. Box 1, File Folders — ASP Development, Douglas S. Cramer Collection, AHC. As far as I have been able to determine, neither *Strongarm* nor *The Dandelions* actually made it to air, although I do not know what stymied their production.

32. Memorandum from Douglas S. Cramer to Bud Baumes, 7 June 1973. Box 1, File Folders — ASP Development, Douglas S. Cramer Collection, AHC.

33. Memorandum from John H. Mitchell to Douglas S. Cramer, 14 June 1973. Box 1, File Folders — ASP Development, Douglas S. Cramer Collection, AHC.

34. Sue Cameron, "Police Drama: Women Are on the Case," *Ms.*, October 1974, 104; and Digby Diehl, "Why Angie Dickinson Finally Decided to Join the Force," *TV Guide*, 4 January 1975, 24.

35. Diehl, "Why Angie Dickinson Finally Decided to Join the Force," 24.

36. Jane Wilkie, "Lucky Men! Male Actors and Female Costars," *Good Housekeeping*, January 1977, 74.

37. See, for example, "Will the Real Teresa Graves Please Stand Up?" *Ebony*, December 1974, 67.

38. Richard Warren Lewis, "Then Time out for Bible Study," *TV Guide*, 30 November 1974, 22.

39. Christie's racial difference was much less frequently remarked upon. However, the series began as an explicit attempt to capitalize on the blaxploitation film phenomenon of the early 1970s. In the pilot, Christie is a more cartoonish figure than in the regular episodes, fighting six men at once and tossing off her trademark phrase, "You're under arrest, sugar." In the first few months of the series, Christie retains some of these elements, particularly the trademark phrase. But when the series changed production hands and the cast was reworked midseason, Christie became much less of a stereotypical blaxploitation figure and more of a racially indistinguishable woman detective.

40. Quoted in Robbins, *The Great Women Superheroes*, 7. While comics publishers insisted that women leads had always failed (an interesting parallel to TV industry beliefs in the early 1970s), Marston convinced All American Comics, the sister company of DC Comics, to run a Wonder Woman strip in one of its magazines.

41. Quoted in Daniels, *Wonder Woman*, 22.

42. Ibid., 22–23.

43. See, for example, the journal *Amazon Quarterly*; Atkinson, *Amazon Odyssey*; and the following cultural feminist works: Daly, *Gyn/Ecology*; E. Davis, *The First Sex*; and Diner, *Mothers and Amazons*. The heading of my discussion of Wonder Woman borrows from Daly, who heralded the "A-mazing Amazon" in every woman in *Gyn/Ecology*.

44. *Ms.*, August 1972, cover.

45. Kimball, *Women's Culture*, 20.

46. Felsenthal, *Phyllis Schlafly*, x.

47. Cramer's files include a copy of the "Amazon Legacy" essay from the *Ms. Wonder Woman* book. Particularly significant for Cramer were the passages about Wonder Woman, for example: "Amazons wear bracelets as reminders of the slavery in store for women if they submit to men. Wonder Woman herself is the embodiment of the use of force for love, while men, wonderful or otherwise, represent the use of force for hate or evil." "Land of the Amazons," Box 32, Land of the Amazons Background, Douglas S. Cramer Collection, AHC.

48. *Land of the Amazons* and *Island of Lost Women* were two of these projects. "Land of the Amazons," Douglas S. Cramer Collection. "Island of Lost Women," Box 31, Island of the Lost Women Final Draft, 25 February 1974, Douglas S. Cramer Collection, AHC.

49. "Tele-scope," *Television Age*, 7 November 1966, 17. A full pilot was never created, though a four-minute presentation that has survived illustrates the concept behind the series. Dozier envisioned a campy series, much like *Batman*, with a mousy main character who changes into Wonder Woman to help save the world. A version of the presentation is available at http://wonderwoman.simplenet/ww1960.htm.

50. Bill Davidson, "From the Pages of Comic Books . . ." *TV Guide*, 29 January 1977, 25.

51. Ibid., 24.

52. Ibid., 26.

53. Fred Silverman, the president of ABC Entertainment, reportedly thought that the show's potential was just about tapped, which is why he did not renew it.

54. According to Cramer, ABC was not entirely comfortable with such overtly feminist dialogue, and he engaged in many debates with network executives over whether it was necessary for the character to make such statements. Douglas Cramer, DVD commentary, "The New, Original Wonder Woman," *Wonder Woman: The Complete First Season*, Warner Bros.

55. Davidson, "From the Pages of Comic Books, . . ." 24.

56. Suzy Kalter, "On Stage," *People*, 14 August 1978, 104.

57. Ibid.

58. Barbara Corday, phone interview by author, Madison, Wisconsin, 4 December 2000. Corday and Avedon's feminist agenda is clear in the project for which they would be best known, the CBS series *Cagney and Lacey* (1982–88), which featured two female cops without the sex-symbol labels of the 1970s series. Corday and Avedon first wrote a *Cagney and Lacey* script in 1974, initially envisioning it as a feature film. See D'Acci, *Defining Women*, for a history and analysis of *Cagney and Lacey*.

59. Bedell, *Up the Tube*, 135.

60. Hofstede and Condon, *Charlie's Angels Casebook*, 6.

61. "TV's Super Women," *Time*, 22 November 1976, 67.

62. Ibid., 69.

63. Charles Champlin, "Farrah Fawcett-Majors: An Unlikely Sex Symbol," *McCall's*, April 1977, 28.

64. Bill O'Hallaren, "Stop the Chase—It's Time for My Comb-out," *TV Guide*, 25 September 1976, 26.

65. Ibid., and "TV's Super Women," 69.

66. Douglas, *Where the Girls Are*, 213.

67. Douglas argues that the "bad women" the Angels encounter tend toward lesbian stereotypes ("a menacing, bull dyke dominatrix"). While they do encounter such women on occasion, another version of the "bad women" they encounter is the evil sexpot, a woman who performs heterosexual difference and sex-symbol status to excessive extremes. Both versions serve as contrasts to the Angels, whose sexual difference is ostensibly the appropriate kind for the New Woman. Ibid., 215.

68. According to Hofsted and Condon, only 32 of 109 *Charlie's Angels* episodes featured one of the Angels in a bathing suit or towel. Hofsted and Condon, *Charlie's Angels Casebook*, 289.

69. However, as Douglas has pointed out, even though this "cross-dressing" challenged conventional gender roles, it also emphasized the Angels' femininity. "Women in men's clothing look smaller than men in men's clothes, reminding us that women aren't as big and strong as men." Douglas, *Where the Girls Are*, 216.

70. Dwight Whitney, "Look Homeward, Angel," *TV Guide*, 23 April 1977, 10, and Dick Russell, "I Don't Want to Be an Image," *TV Guide*, 26 August 1978, 22.

71. Champlin, "Farrah Fawcett-Majors," 28.

72. Whitney, "Look Homeward, Angel," 10.

73. Champlin, "Farrah Fawcett-Majors," 28.

74. D. S. Davis, "Lass Named Ladd," *Saturday Evening Post*, October 1979, 74, 75.

75. Champlin, "Farrah Fawcett-Majors," 30.

76. O'Hallaren, "Stop the Chase," 30.

77. Stephen Decatur, "Jaclyn Smith: Wholesome Is Beautiful," *Ladies' Home Journal*, July 1979, 44.

78. Sheila Weller, "Cheryl Ladd: The Happiest 'Angel,'" *McCall's*, April 1978, 78. See also Patricia Miller, "Cheryl Ladd: Juggling Sanity and Success," *Ladies' Home Journal*, March 1979, 78+.

79. Penelope McMillan, "Kate Jackson: Rich, Famous—and Vulnerable," *McCall's*, September 1978, 104.

80. Ibid., and Stephen Decatur, "I'm No Real Angel," *Ladies' Home Journal*, February 1978, 86.

81. Klatch, *Women of the New Right*, 50–51; and Schlafly, *The Power of the Positive Woman*, 41.

82. Judy Klemesrud, "The Year of the Lusty Woman," *Esquire*, 19 December 1978, 33; and Blair Sabol, "Sexy vs. Sexist," *Working Woman*, June 1978, 74.

83. A few of the post-*Angels* TV sex symbols did not fit in either the action-adventure or comedic categories. These representations featured women in conventionally feminine roles, without any blending of the masculine and the feminine. Among these were the short-lived CBS series *Flying High*, about a trio of flight attendants (1978–79) and the made-for-TV movies *Dallas Cowboys Cheerleaders* (ABC, 17 January 1979) and *Dallas Cowboys Cheerleaders II* (ABC, 13 January 1980).

84. A subset of these attempts to imitate the success of *Charlie's Angels* featured women in conventionally male roles who were not necessarily sex symbols. While they did not share the Angels' glamour and sex appeal, they were indisputably feminine. Their femininity was often marked by their adherence to conventionally feminine attitudes (such as timidity or devotion to one's husband) and their conventionally feminine appearance (dresses, make-up, and so forth). Among the examples I have been able to screen that fit this template are *Wild and Wooly* (ABC, 20 February

1978), *Flatbed Annie and Sweetie Pie: Lady Truckers* (CBS, 10 February 1979), and *The Oklahoma City Dolls* (ABC, 23 January 1981).

85. In addition, the obstacles Daisy faces in her work are not due to her sex or gender, but instead to her family name. The sheriff and Boss Hogg are horrified at the idea of one of the authority-challenging Dukes joining the force and try to get rid of Daisy for that reason. Gender roles do come into play in the way that Daisy's cousins, Bo and Luke, follow her around and try to help her with her police work. Although the episode offers a thin attempt at asserting Daisy's competence on the job, Bo and Luke do more to catch the criminals than she does. The Duke boys' antics (especially on the road) were the centerpiece of the series; anything that happened to Daisy was window-dressing for the main, male characters' actions.

86. Occasionally, a third woman would guest-star on these shows and would represent a third type: the sex symbol who was *not* sweet and innocent. Among such characters was Loni Anderson's Susan on *Three's Company*'s "Coffee, Tea or Jack?" and the series' recurring character Lana Shields (Ann Wedgeworth). These were typically aggressive, unlikable characters, which is telling of television's (and mainstream culture's) bias against women who forcefully assert their own sexuality.

5. Sex with a Laugh Track

1. I have been able to view this episode of *Match Game*, along with many others, in syndicated repeats on the Game Show Network.

2. This chronology is, of course, highly debatable. For example, one might point to Milton Berle's cross-dressing antics on *The Texaco Star Theater* (NBC, 1948–53) as a very early example of sex-themed humor in U.S. television.

3. Sexual humor also appeared in *Love, American Style* (ABC, 1969–74, 1985–86) a comedy anthology series that would eventually feature a skit, "Love and the Happy Days" (25 February 1972), that would serve as a pilot for the hit sitcom *Happy Days*, which debuted in January 1974. *Love, American Style*'s multi-story format would serve as a model for another sex-themed ABC series of the 1970s, *The Love Boat*.

4. In labeling the comedy "late-burlesque" I am borrowing from Robert C. Allen's history of the form and am referencing the burlesque of the early twentieth century. See Allen, *Horrible Prettiness* for a sense of the changes in burlesque between the nineteenth and the twentieth centuries.

5. See, for example, such programs as *Your Show of Shows* (NBC, 1950–54) or *The Red Skelton Show*. The male comedians who headlined these programs tended to have spent their formative years performing in burlesque shows of the early twentieth century.

6. The relative lack of sexual humor in *The Sonny and Cher Comedy Hour* is made

apparent when that series is contrasted with the then-divorced couple's return to television in *The Sonny and Cher Show* (CBS, 1976–77). By the 1976–77 season, sexual humor laden with double entendres was standard TV fare and Sonny and Cher's new series was in keeping with that trend.

7. Capsuto, *Alternate Channels*, 65–66.

8. Ibid., 55.

9. McNeil, *Total Television*, 868.

10. U.S. Senate, Committee on Commerce, Subcommittee on Communications, *Federal Communication Commission Policy Matters and Television Programming*, 91st Cong., 1st sess. (Washington: U.S. Government Printing Office, 1969), 405–6.

11. I do not want to presume that all audiences read the program this way. As research on *All in the Family*'s audiences has indicated, many viewers identified with Archie and agreed with his homophobic, racist, and sexist views. See, for example, Vidmar and Rokeach, "Archie Bunker's Bigotry." Still, I would argue that the preferred reading of the episode is the one I offer and that many viewers took this meaning, even if they disagreed with it.

12. Even though the program's relevance to Vietnam seemed obvious to critics and lay viewers at the time and since, the producers of *M*A*S*H* would only vaguely acknowledge the show's relationship to the Vietnam War, tending instead to focus on the horrors of war generally. Gitlin, *Inside Prime Time*, 217; Bodroghkozy, *Groove Tube*, 233–34; Marc, *Comic Visions*, 192.

13. Marc, *Comic Visions*, 194.

14. Ibid., 196.

15. Marc cites the replacement of Trapper with B. J. Hunnicut and the feminist reworking of Hawkeye/Alan Alda as additional elements of the program's turn to character development over political commentary. Though the revision in the program's sexual morality is implied in Marc's argument, it is not his key point.

16. The creator, Garry Marshall, made the comparison to *The Waltons*, which was set in the Depression-era 1930s. See Bedell, *Up the Tube*, 113. Nostalgia for the 1950s was a prominent trend of popular culture of the 1970s, a trend that Daniel Marcus reads as a conservative backlash against the progressive social developments of the 1960s. Marcus, *Happy Days and Wonder Years*.

17. Bedell, *Up the Tube*, 113.

18. Ibid., 126.

19. Eventually, Fonzie's authority is taken to such an extreme that he virtually becomes a 1950s-sitcom-style father figure himself. He becomes a high school teacher, a substitute parent to his nephew Chachi, and the moral center of the *Happy Days* universe.

20. "Love Bloat," *TV Guide*, 5 June 1982, 30.

21. Spelling made these comments regarding a TV movie his company was developing titled *Love on Fire Island*. Reported in memorandum from Bob Stevens to Aaron Spelling, Douglas Cramer, Duke Vincent, Cindy Dunne, Norm Henry, and John Whelpley, 26 September 1977. Box 1, File Folders—ASP Development, Douglas S. Cramer Collection, AHC.

22. Handwritten comments from Spelling on memorandum from Lynne Farr to Douglas Cramer, 11 December 1978. Box 35, *Love Boat*—Farr, Gordon and Lynne, Douglas S. Cramer Collection, AHC.

23. Allyn, *Make Love, Not War*, 236–38; "Is There Life in a Swingers' Club?" *Time*, 16 January 1978, 53.

24. Memorandum from Douglas Cramer to Gordon and Lynne Farr, 22 June 1977. Box 35, *Love Boat*—Farr, Gordon and Lynne, Douglas S. Cramer Collection, AHC.

25. Handwritten comments from Cramer on memorandum from Lynne Farr to Lance Taylor, ABC, 16 January 1978. Box 35, *Love Boat*—Farr, Gordon and Lynne, Douglas S. Cramer Collection, AHC.

26. Douglas Cramer notes on script K-54, 10 April 1979. Box 36, *Love Boat* Script K-54, Douglas S. Cramer Collection, AHC.

27. Memorandum from Douglas Cramer to Gordon and Lynne Farr, 22 June 1977. Box 35, *Love Boat*—Farr, Gordon and Lynne, Douglas S. Cramer Collection, AHC.

28. Correspondence from Dennis P. Blackhurst to *The Love Boat*, 4 December 1979 and marginalia by Douglas Cramer on same. Box 35, *Love Boat*—Farr, Gordon and Lynne, Douglas S. Cramer Collection, AHC.

29. Correspondence from Douglas S. Cramer to Dennis P. Blackhurst, 2 January 1980. Box 35, *Love Boat*—Farr, Gordon and Lynne, Douglas S. Cramer Collection, AHC.

30. ABC's first place lead was beginning to erode, albeit slowly, at this point, which might have led to the network's demands for more sex on screen. Memorandum from Gordon Farr to Aaron Spelling and Douglas S. Cramer, 15 October 1979. Box 35, *Love Boat*—Farr, Gordon and Lynne, Douglas S. Cramer Collection, AHC.

31. Douglas Cramer notes in script K-64, 10 October 1979. Box 36, *Love Boat* Script K-64, Douglas S. Cramer Collection, AHC.

32. Memorandum from Gordon Farr to Aaron Spelling and Douglas S. Cramer, 15 October 1979. Box 35, *Love Boat*—Farr, Gordon and Lynne, Douglas S. Cramer Collection, AHC.

33. The *Love Boat* stories were always self-contained. They were written by different writers and directed by different directors, then cut together into an episode. However, the crew often interacted with characters from multiple story lines within one episode. In "Mike and Ike," Mike, Lenore, and Mike Jr. interact solely with Isaac.

34. Newton E. Deiter, "The Last Minority," 70; and Montgomery, "Gay Activists and the Networks," 63.

35. "If the Eye Offend Thee," *Time*, 26 September 1977, 53; and "Advertisers Feel Pressure on 'Soap,'" *Broadcasting*, 29 August 1977, 22, as well as brief discussions in Montgomery, *Target: Prime Time*; Cowan, *See No Evil*; and Gitlin, *Inside Prime Time*.

36. Montgomery, *Target: Prime Time*, 96–99; Montgomery, "Gay Activists and the Networks," 127–35; and display ad, *Variety*, 7 September 1977.

37. It seems that there were some changes made to at least the first episode, but they centered around scenes of Jessica and Peter, her tennis pro lover.

38. This is especially true for Janet and Chrissy. Jack's sexual activity is a bit more ambiguous, and we are nearly assured that their friend and neighbor, Larry—a swinging 1970s Lothario complete with exposed hairy chest and gold chains—has sex with different women on a regular basis.

39. The 1960s *Match Game* had a different format from the 1970s version, and it was not nearly as reliant on sexual humor. The 1960s version featured two three-person teams, each consisting of two contestants and a celebrity, who attempted to match each others' answers to such questions as "Name a part of a chicken." Holmes and Wood, *The TV Game Show Almanac*, 68–69.

40. Among such groups were the Leadership Foundation, Stop Immorality on TV (a subgroup of the Society for the Christian Commonwealth), Morality in Media, Citizens for Decency through Law, and the Churches of Christ's "Clean Up TV campaign." "New Group Mounts Grass-Roots Attack on Offensive TV," *Broadcasting*, 11 December 1972, 35; "Crusades for TV Morality on the Rise," *Broadcasting*, 18 December 1972, 37; John Revett, "Group Pressures FCC to Curb TV Violence, Sex," *Advertising Age*, 22 September 1975, 8; "FCC's Mailbag Groaning with Cries of Filth," *Variety*, 13 December 1978, 55.

41. "DDB Study Finds Public Wants Reins on Television Sex, but Shies Away from Total Censorship, Federal Controls," *Broadcasting*, 23 January 1978, 46.

42. "The Advertiser/Agency View," *Marketing and Media Decisions*, June 1979, 62.

43. Harry F. Waters and Frank Gibney Jr., "P and G's Move in a 'Holy War,'" *Newsweek*, 29 June 1981, 60.

44. Bernice Kanner, "How the Coalition Is Changing TV," *New York*, 28 September 1981, 26.

45. Alexander Doty defines a "queer" reading of a text as any reading that is non-, contra-, or anti-straight. It need not necessarily be aligned with a specific sexual identity, for example, gay. In fact, by defining "queer" in terms of what it is *not*, Doty and other queer theorists seek to disarticulate gender and sexuality from

one another, allowing for a more fluid understanding of identity. Doty applies this idea to television, arguing that much of U.S. television is ripe with potential queer readings. I am here reading Reilly along these lines. Doty, *Making Things Perfectly Queer*.

46. Michael J. Arlen, "Jim Peck's Cabaret," *The New Yorker*, 4 February 1980, 104 and 101.

47. I do not mean to suggest that *Soap* was the only comedy program at the time to offer this kind of commentary. In addition to the politically charged sexual humor on such series as *All in the Family* (still running across the decade), even a program such as *Three's Company* included some more oppositional moments. For example, Helen Roper's constant expression of her sexual frustration — her desire for sexual fulfillment and Stanley's inadequacy in meeting her needs — acknowledged women's sexuality (older women's sexuality, at that) in a way that encouraged the viewer to side with her over the adolescent sexuality of her husband.

48. Quoted in Mittell, *Genre and Television*, 170.

49. Ibid., 175.

50. ABC rejected *Mary Hartman* along with *All in the Family* in 1969. Although CBS picked up the latter series, it also declined to air *Mary Hartman* (although it did finance two pilot episodes). Lear gave NBC a chance at the show, but this network also turned him down, reportedly because NBC's daytime chief, Lin Bolen, thought the program mocked the female viewers of daytime TV. Harry F. Waters and Martin Kasindorf, "The Mary Hartman Craze," *Newsweek*, 3 May 1976, 61.

51. "Mary, Mary, Quite Contrary," *Time*, 23 February 1976, 50; "Fernwood Follies," *Time*, 18 October 1976, 64.

52. The program also satirized recent efforts to regulate TV content, such as the family viewing policy. For example, in an early 1976 episode, Mary's neighbor Blanche Fedders touts her organization, SMUT (Society of Mothers Upset with Trash), and its efforts to clean up the culture's corrupt "atmosphere." Blanche and her SMUT minions appear again when Mary is held hostage, insisting that television sex and violence have led to situations like this. Even Mary herself comments on the regulatory fray. When she is interviewed by a television reporter after she has escaped her captor, she asks, "Is this the family hour? This is a lot of violence for the family hour."

53. As Lear told his staff in a January 1976 story meeting, "I am convinced that every woman in America can plug into this because women are restless, sex morals have changed." *Mary Hartman, Mary Hartman* Writers Meeting Notes, 20 January 1976. Box 16, Production Files 1975–1976 *Mary Hartman, Mary Hartman*, Ann Marcus Collection, AHC.

54. I would argue that Marcus's prominent role in the series further confirms the

gentle, even admiring, tenor of *Mary Hartman*'s parody of the soap genre. Though Marcus was clearly eager to put her trenchant sense of humor to work in another genre (as soaps of the early 1970s had not yet recognized the value of humor), she was also a prolific and committed soap opera writer. See Correspondence from Ann Marcus to Charles B. Bloch, 25 August 1976. Box 16, Correspondence 1976, Bloch, Charles B., Ann Marcus Collection, AHC, for Marcus's own perspective on writing *Mary Hartman* versus writing daytime soaps.

55. In *Soap*'s mix of comedy and melodrama, the two tones were more distinctly separated from one another than they were in MH, MH.

56. "'Mary, Mary' Finds Out Some Parents Are Quite Contrary," *Broadcasting*, 11 April 1977, 51.

57. Ibid., 48; and Joseph H. Kraker, "Cleveland vs. 'Mary Hartman,'" *America*, 28 May 1977, 484–87.

58. "Mary, Mary, Quite Contrary," 23 February 1976, 50.

59. Correspondence from Shelley Fields to Channel 44, 22 January 1976. Box 16, Fan Mail *Mary Hartman, Mary Hartman*, Ann Marcus Collection, AHC.

6. From Romance to Rape

The first epigraph to this chapter is quoted in Martha Weinman Lear, "Q. If You Rape a Woman and Steal Her TV, What Can They Get You for in New York? A. Stealing Her TV," *New York Times Magazine*, 30 January 1972, 11. The second epigraph is from Brownmiller, *Against Our Will*, 391.

1. Bob Lardine, "Anthony Geary Is a Reformed J. R. in *General Hospital* but at Home He's Heaven on Wheels," *People*, 6 October 1980, 98; and "You the Viewer," *Daytime TV*, November 1980, 40.

2. Lardine, "Anthony Geary Is a Reformed J. R.," 98; and Eric Gelman and Janet Huck, "A Perfect Couple," *Newsweek*, 28 September 1981, 63.

3. In 1968, the *New York Times* carried 18 rape stories. In 1974, the paper carried 117 such stories compared to 105 such stories in 1978. Bevacqua, *Rape on the Public Agenda*, 123.

4. Ibid., 236, n. 10. In addition, Washington, D.C.'s WRC-TV aired a two-part local news special on rape entitled *The Lonely Crime* in 1972. Also in 1972, CBS broadcast a special news program called *Rape*. In May 1977, ABC aired a documentary called *The Rape Victims*. Ibid., 126.

5. See Cuklanz, *Rape on Prime Time* for a list of television series with rape plots 1976–80. Cuklanz makes clear that her list is incomplete and that it excludes made-for-TV movies and series that did not air in prime time.

6. Bevacqua, *Rape on the Public Agenda*, 150. The number of reported rapes did not increase at such a rapid pace after 1980.

7. Ibid., 102; and Alice Lake, "What Women Are Doing about the Ugliest Crime," *Good Housekeeping*, August 1974, 133.

8. New York Radical Feminists, *Rape*; Medea and Thompson, *Against Rape*; and Russell, *The Politics of Rape*.

9. Brownmiller, *Against Our Will*, 15.

10. Among the most controversial of Brownmiller's claims were her seeming equation of rape and patriarchy and her stances on lynching and interracial rape. Some argued that Brownmiller's discussion did not adequately address the racial imbalances in the punishment of black and white men on rape charges. Brownmiller discusses this criticism in *In Our Time*, 248–49.

11. Though Brownmiller was neither the first nor the only feminist to assert that rape was a crime of violence, she became the most widely recognized source for the statement. According to Maria Bevacqua, the point was made as early as 1948 by Ruth Herschberger. Bevacqua, *Rape on the Public Agenda*, 58.

12. Janet Kole, "Rape and What to Do about It," *Harper's Bazaar*, March 1976, 118.

13. Bevacqua, *Rape on the Public Agenda*, 58.

14. Lake, "What Women Are Doing," 134.

15. Shana Alexander, "A Simple Question of Rape," *Newsweek*, 28 October 1974, 110.

16. "Feedback," *U.S. Catholic*, February 1979, 14 and 15.

17. Ibid., 14.

18. In this section and throughout this chapter, I have done my best to identify all the rape story lines on all of the soaps airing at the time. While I have managed to piece together many of these story lines and their airdates, I cannot definitively claim that I have recovered all of them. My sources for this information are numerous and scattered, but among the most helpful have been story synopses from *Soap Opera Digest*, 1977–81; Schemering, *The Soap Opera Encyclopedia*; Schemering, "*Guiding Light*"; LaGuardia, *The Wonderful World of TV Soap Operas*; Zenba, "*Days of Our Lives*"; Irwin, "*The Young and the Restless*"; Poll, "*Guiding Light*"; Poll, "*As the World Turns*"; Poll, "*Another World*"; Warner, "*General Hospital*"; Warner, "*All My Children*." As cited throughout the chapter, archival sources were invaluable in pinpointing story and script specifics.

19. Charlotte Brunsdon asserts that "the ideological problematic of soap opera . . . is that of 'personal life' " and that this perspective functions not only to explore familiar institutions but also to "[colonize] the public masculine sphere, representing it from the point of view of the personal." Brunsdon, "*Crossroads*," 14–15. Laura Stempel Mumford concurs, adding that "public" issues, when they do come up in soaps, are "couched almost entirely in terms of the familial, romantic, and emotional relationships between characters." Mumford, *Love and Ideology in the Afternoon*, 41–42. I am arguing that, in the 1970s, U.S. daytime soaps made a more

concerted effort to deal with public issues, even if they were still viewed through the lens of the personal. In this respect, soap operas are little different from other fictional genres of U.S. commercial television.

20. Allen, *Speaking of Soap Operas*, 149.

21. Until the late 1970s, nonconsensual sex between married persons was not legally defined as rape.

22. On *General Hospital* in the 1960s, Tom Baldwin rapes his wife, Audrey, impregnating her and leading her to leave town. Tom continues to cause trouble for Audrey when she returns to Port Charles, claiming that their child has died, though she is secretly hiding him from Tom. Similarly, on *Another World*, the con man Danny Fargo rapes his wife, Missy, in 1966 when she tells him that their new marriage is a mistake. Though Danny is soon murdered, Missy discovers she is pregnant with his child.

23. *Guiding Light* script, 10 August 1964. Reel 57, Procter and Gamble Television Script Collection, WSHS.

24. *Guiding Light* script, 22 February 1965, Reel 57, Procter and Gamble Television Script Collection, WSHS.

25. *Guiding Light* script, 27 January 1965, Reel 57. Procter and Gamble Television Script Collection, WSHS.

26. Letter from Lessell C. Rucker to *Days of Our Lives*, 23 March 1971 and letter from William J. Bell to Reverend Rucker, 10 April 1971. Box 1, Correspondence 1967–77, 1971 Correspondence, William J. Bell Collection, AHC.

27. *Love Is a Many Splendored Thing* script, 9 February 1972. Box 11, Scripts and Related Materials, 1969–73, #1142–#1145, Ann Marcus Collection, AHC.

28. Ibid.

29. *Love Is a Many Splendored Thing* script, 29 December 1972. Box 1, Production Files 1971–73, General—*Love Is a Many Splendored Thing*, Ann Marcus Collection, AHC.

30. "Events Leading Up to the Rape of Lucretia." Box 1, Production Files 1969–73, *Love Is a Many Splendored Thing*, "Laura's Storyline / Catholic Church," Ann Marcus Collection, AHC.

31. Marcus believed that Spence could not find out the truth about baby Maggie's parentage for a variety of reasons, among them that revealing this secret would defeat "the purpose of this rape business," which was to give the writers story material to draw from over the years (perhaps as the *Days of Our Lives* Bill/Laura/Mickey story line did). "Love Is a Many Splendored Thing," Box 1, Production Files 1971–73, LIAMST General, Ann Marcus Collection, AHC.

32. Because *Love Is a Many Splendored Thing* was canceled about a year after the rape (the final episode aired 23 March 1973), not all of these ramifications could play out.

33. Allen, *Speaking of Soap Operas*, 171. Allen argues that the quick end to the inter-

racial story line is typical of the television soap opera's tendency to endorse normative values.

34. "CBS Discovers Soaps in Magazine Opener," *Broadcasting*, 22 April 1974, 55.

35. Some audiences clearly did pick up the intended meaning. See letter from Mrs. Walter Larkin, "Letters to the Editor," *Daytime TV*, September 1974, 52.

36. Gilbert, *All My Afternoons*, 165.

37. Ibid.

38. "The History of Y and R," *My Soaps Online*, http://www.mysoapsonline.com/yr/history/index.html.

39. I will not discuss all nineteen rapes and attempted rapes that I have identified as occurring on daytime soaps between 1978 and 1981, both in interest of space and because my information on some is quite limited. The following are rape stories I will not discuss: In 1978 or 1979, Nurse Carolee Simpson on *The Doctors* (NBC, 1963–82) was kidnapped and raped. During the same period, on *Another World*, Eileen Simpson was raped by Phil Higley, a sleazy figure who also sexually abused runaway teens. In January 1979, Hank Robinson raped Carol Stallings on *As the World Turns*. Hank was the employer of Carol's husband, Jay, as well as his sworn enemy (Hank believed Jay had stolen his girlfriend). Hank apparently raped Carol as an act of revenge against Jay (David R. Jackson, email to author, 20 August 2001). In November 1979, a former prostitute on *One Life to Live*, Karen Wolek, was raped by her brother-in-law, Brad. In 1980 on *All My Children*, Billy Clyde Tuggle escaped from prison and drugged and raped his wife, Estelle. Tuggle was caught and returned to prison, but Estelle was pregnant with his child. In 1981, there was a rape on *Texas* (NBC, Procter and Gamble, 1980–82), about which I have not been able to find any more information (letter from Pat Smith to *Daytime TV*, "You the Viewer," *Daytime TV*, July 1981, 40.) Also in 1981, Kellam Chandler raped Dr. Marlena Craig on *Days of Our Lives*. In 1980 or 1981, Duke Lafferty kidnapped and raped Morgan Richards on *Guiding Light*. Neither will I discuss the following attempted rape story lines: Greg Barnard attempted to rape Pat Randolph on *Another World* in 1978, but she killed him with a letter opener in self-defense, flashing back to an earlier encounter with Tom Baxter, the father of her illegitimate child. In 1979 on *All My Children*, a cosmetics company executive attempted to rape Erica Kane. She was saved by her husband, Tom Cudahy. Friends Michael and Margo scared off an attempted rapist who tried to attack Trish on *Days of Our Lives* in June 1979. Finally, there are two ambiguous rape story lines that I will not discuss: Late in 1979 on *The Doctors*, an angry Colin ripped Nola's clothes, slapped her, and "[took] her brutally, leaving Nola crying." Nola had been waiting for Colin in a sexy negligee and was presumably interested in having sex with him, but the

Soap Opera Digest summary of these events does not make entirely clear whether they were identified as rape in the story line. ("The Doctors," *Soap Opera Digest*, 8 January 1980.) And on *As the World Turns* in 1981, John Dixon was tried for raping his wife, Dee. However, Dee had consented to sex with him under the mistaken impression that he was the man she truly loved, Brad.

40. The information I have gathered on these stories suggests that they were not modeled after *The Young and the Restless*'s treatment of rape as a social issue but instead on the old-fashioned rape stories of the 1960s and early 1970s. On *Somerset* (NBC, 1970–76, a spin-off of *Another World*), Virgil Paris raped Ginger Kurtz in a mafia-murder mystery plot in late 1973 or early 1974. On *General Hospital* in late 1974 or early 1975, the scoundrel Phil Brewer raped his former lover, Diana Taylor, impregnating her (for the second time) and leading her to conceal the rape (and her child's parentage) from her husband, Peter. On *Another World* in 1976, a group of sailors attempted to rape Sharlene Frame as her evil brother Willis looked on, but she was rescued by Russ Matthews.

41. "Love of Life." Box 20, Production Files 1979–80, *Love of Life*, Ann Marcus Collection, AHC; and "Love of Life," *Soap Opera Digest*, 4 September 1979, 77.

42. "Love of Life." Box 20, Production Files 1979–80, *Love of Life*, Ann Marcus Collection, AHC.

43. Ibid.

44. Geri Jefferson, "Daytime Drama Explores the Crime of Rape," *Soap Opera Digest*, June 1978, 29.

45. Ibid., 75.

46. Episode #3099 outline. Box 18, Production Files 1977–78, *Days of Our Lives*, Ann Marcus Collection, AHC.

47. Julie's therapist is Laura Horton, the woman raped in the 1968 *Days* plot by the man she has since married, Bill Horton. The rape crisis center is run by Dr. Marlena Evans, who will herself become a rape victim in 1981. The past and future handlings of rape on this soap have an impact on the meaning of this story line, at least for the longtime viewer.

48. Episode #3157 script. Box 18, Production Files 1977–78, *Days of Our Lives*, Ann Marcus Collection, AHC.

49. Letter from D.R.P. to Ann Marcus, 10 March 1978. Box 18, Correspondence 1977–78, *Days of Our Lives* Fan Mail, Ann Marcus Collection, AHC.

50. Peggy was quite morally upstanding and Roger saw her as his chance at salvation. But he is forced to testify to his affair with Rita when she is tried for murder. Because the circumstances of their affair had been so disreputable (Rita was married to another man at the time), Peggy leaves Roger. Roger blames Rita for this.

51. *Guiding Light* script, 6 October 1978 and 9 October 1978. Reel 113, Procter and Gamble Television Script Collection, WSHS.

52. *Guiding Light* script, 9 October 1978 and 10 October 1978. Reel 113, Procter and Gamble Television Script Collection, WSHS.

53. *Guiding Light* script, 9 October 1978. Reel 113, Procter and Gamble Television Script Collection, WSHS. Though I have not been able to view these specific episodes to confirm that the revised dialogue was actually taped and aired, I have seen a similar style of revision (lines crossed out, with different lines written in by hand) in other *Guiding Light* scripts from this period and these revisions do match the actual scenes that I have been able to view. As soap episodes before the early 1980s (when fans were first able to videotape episodes at home) are nearly impossible to view, this kind of historiographic problem is unavoidable. Most pre-1980s soap episodes simply do not exist, as many were produced live and those that were videotaped were sometimes not kept for more than a few months by producers.

54. *Guiding Light* script, 12 October 1978 (flashback to October 11 episode). Reel 113, Procter and Gamble Television Script Collection, WSHS.

55. "You the Viewer," *Daytime TV*, February 1979, 37.

56. Schemering, "*Guiding Light*," 45–46.

57. *Guiding Light* script, 26 February 1979. Reel 115, Procter and Gamble Television Script Collection, WSHS.

58. *Guiding Light* script, 27 February 1979. Reel 115, Procter and Gamble Television Script Collection, WSHS.

59. *Guiding Light* script, 28 February 1979 and March 2, 1979. Reel 115, Procter and Gamble Television Script Collection, WSHS.

60. *Guiding Light* script, 2 March 1979. Reel 115, Procter and Gamble Television Script Collection, WSHS.

61. *Guiding Light* script, 7 March 1979. Reel 115, Procter and Gamble Television Script Collection, WSHS.

62. *Guiding Light* script, 9 March 1979. Reel 115, Procter and Gamble Television Script Collection, WSHS.

63. Ibid.

64. The instances of this stance being reiterated are almost too numerous to list. One other key moment took place on 13 March 1979, when Holly was questioned by the police. Here, Lieutenant Ruiz grills Holly, asking why this event was any different from other times she and her husband had fought and she hadn't reported it to the police. When Holly insists, "But this was different! He . . . he was violent!," Ruiz asks, "How about 'passionate,' Mrs. Thorpe?" In this way, the program set forth the typical objections to claims of marital rape and allowed Holly to reject

them forcefully. *Guiding Light* script, 13 March 1979. Reel 115, Procter and Gamble Television Script Collection, WSHS.

65. "You the Viewer," *Daytime TV*, March 1979, 55.

66. "You the Viewer," *Daytime TV*, July 1979, 43.

67. Letter from P. R., Morgantown, W.V., "Sound Board," *Soap Opera Digest*, 14 August 1979, 6.

68. It is relatively common for soap writers to "rewrite" their show's history to expedite a later narrative thread, allowing characters to go through significant changes but still be intelligible as the same character. Mimi White has referred to this process of "rewriting" as "retrofitting." Cited in Mumford, *Love and Ideology in the Afternoon*, 157 n. 11. Allen indirectly recognizes the typicality of soap characters experiencing changes in their identities and values. See Allen, *Speaking of Soap Operas*, 170–71.

69. Jay Cocks, "*General Hospital*: Critical Case," *Time*, 28 September 1981, 64.

70. Schemering, *The Soap Opera Encyclopedia*, 112.

71. Michael Logan, "Dad's Dirty Little Secret," *TV Guide*, 7 March 1998.

72. See, for example, Harry F. Waters et al., "Television's Hottest Show," *Newsweek*, 28 September 1981, 62; and Doris G. Worsham, "Luke and Laura: Soap Opera's Hottest Lovers to Wed at Last," *Tribune/Today*, 16 November 1981, http://mcamy .hispeed.com/geary/artint/art10.html.

73. Seli Groves, "A New Love for Laura?" *Soap Opera Digest*, 18 August 1981, 26.

74. Lardine, "Anthony Geary Is a Reformed J. R.," 98.

75. My access to these scenes is thanks to Stacey (CurlyQgrl), Joan R., and an unknown *General Hospital* fan who was videotaping and archiving these scenes in 1979 and 1980.

76. Laura yells, "Don't expect me to play Scarlett to your Rhett Butler! You rape me and I won't wake up the next morning with a smile on my face!" The suggestion that Scotty could rape her and that Laura could identify such a famous popular culture example of a rape fantasy as a myth is quite ironic, given that Luke has proven himself to be the much more likely threat and that, eventually, Laura's relationship with Luke will, in certain senses, conform to just the sort of rape fantasy put forth in *Gone with the Wind*.

77. Gelman and Huck, "A Perfect Couple," *Newsweek*, 28 September 1981, 63; Denis, *Inside the Soaps*, 84; Schemering, *The Soap Opera Encyclopedia*, 112.

78. Marilyn Henry, "Tony Geary — The Man Who Made Luke a Legend," *Afternoon TV*, November 1981, 19–20.

79. "You the Viewer," *Daytime TV*, June 1980, 40.

80. Clair, "Sweet Subversions," 69.

81. John Fiske identifies such pleasures as distinctly gendered and specific to gendered cultural forms such as the soap opera. Fiske, *Television Culture*. Fiske draws on the work of Modleski, *Loving with a Vengeance*. See Radway, *Reading the Romance* for further discussion of the gendered appeals of the romance novel.

82. Brownmiller and other feminists argued that women's rape fantasies were a product of patriarchal conditioning and could be eliminated through feminist consciousness-raising. For examples of discussions of rape fantasies in the popular press, see Martha Weinman Lear, "The Sexual Fantasies of Women," *McCall's*, March 1973, 64–65+; Molly Haskell, "The 2,000-Year-Old Misunderstanding: Rape Fantasy," *Ms.*, November 1976, 84–86+; Robin Morgan, "What Do Our Masochistic Fantasies Really Mean?" *Ms.*, June 1977, 66–68+; Louisa Rogers, "Four Years Ago I Was Raped," *Glamour*, September 1978, 192+.

83. Haskell, "The 2,000-Year-Old Misunderstanding," 85.

84. See, for example, "You the Viewer," *Daytime TV*, December 1980, 40; and the letter from Hemlock, Michigan in "Sounding Board," *Soap Opera Digest*, 19 February 1980, 4.

85. "You the Viewer," *Daytime TV*, July 1981, 40.

86. "You the Viewer," *Daytime TV*, March 1980, 28.

87. "Sounding Board," *Soap Opera Digest*, 10 November 1981, 6.

88. "You the Viewer," *Daytime TV*, December 1980, 40.

89. "Sounding Board," *Soap Opera Digest*, 26 May 1981, 6.

90. "A Year after Laura's Rape, the Viewer Uproar Continues," *Daytime TV*, March 1981, 49; and "You the Viewer," *Daytime TV*, January 1981, 41.

91. "A Year after Laura's Rape," 49.

92. "Sounding Board," *Soap Opera Digest*, 24 November 1981, 4.

Conclusion

1. Todd Gitlin essentially makes this argument about the social issue-driven programming of the early 1970s. Gitlin, "Prime Time Ideology."

2. The concept of television as a "cultural forum" draws from Newcomb and Hirsch, "Television as a Cultural Forum."

3. Battles and Hilton-Morrow, "Gay Characters in Conventional Spaces," 87–105. Becker, "Straight Panic!"

4. Becker, "Straight Panic!" 213–22.

5. Rufus Wainwright, "California," *Poses* (Dreamworks, 2001); Rufus Wainwright, "I Don't Know What It Is," *Want One* (Dreamworks, 2003).

6. Rufus Wainwright, "Oh What a World," *Want One* (Dreamworks, 2003).

7. Burroughs, *Running with Scissors*, 70, 43, 5, 29, 69.

8. Emily Wylie, "At an All-Girls School, Boys Are Still a Factor," *All Things Considered*, National Public Radio, 14 December 2004, available online, http://www.npr.org/templates/story/story.php?storyId=4227885, accessed 27 December 2004.

9. Steinecke, *The Bionic Woman*. Gretchen Stoeltje, *Bionic Beauty Salon*, 22 min. (Ho-Ho-Kus, N.J.: New Day Films, 1999).

10. Tillity, "Desperately Seeking Farrah," 292–95.

— BIBLIOGRAPHY —

Alcoff, Linda. "Cultural Feminism vs. Post-structuralism: The Identity Crisis in Feminist Theory." *Signs* 13, no. 3 (spring 1988): 405–36.

Allen, Robert C. *Horrible Prettiness: Burlesque and American Culture*. Chapel Hill: University of North Carolina Press, 1991.

———. *Speaking of Soap Operas*. Chapel Hill: University of North Carolina Press, 1985.

Allyn, David. *Make Love, Not War: The Sexual Revolution, an Unfettered History*. Boston: Little, Brown and Company, 2000.

Altman, Dennis. *The Homosexualization of America, the Americanization of the Homosexual*. New York: St. Martin's Press, 1981.

Aries, Philippe. *Centuries of Childhood: A Social History of Family Life*. Translated by Robert Baldick. New York: Vintage, 1962.

Atkinson, Ti-Grace. *Amazon Odyssey*. New York: Links Books, 1974.

Auster, Albert. "If You Can't Get 'Em into the Tent, You'll Never Have a Circus: An Interview with Len Hill." *Journal of Popular Film and Television* 8 (1981): 10–17.

Bailey, Beth L. *From Front Porch to Back Seat: Courtship in Twentieth-Century America*. Baltimore: Johns Hopkins University Press, 1988.

———. *Sex in the Heartland*. Cambridge, Mass.: Harvard University Press, 1999.

Baker, Robert K., and the Media Task Force Staff. "The Views, Standards, and Practices of the Television Industry," appendix III-K. In *Report to the National Commission on the Causes and Prevention of Violence*. Vol. 9, *Mass Media and Violence*, edited by Robert K. Baker and Sandra J. Ball, 593–613. Washington: U.S. Government Printing Office, 1969.

Battles, Kathleen, and Wendy Hilton-Morrow. "Gay Characters in Conventional Spaces: *Will and Grace* and the Situation Comedy Genre." *Critical Studies in Media Communication* 19, no. 1 (March 2002): 87–105.

Beauvoir, Simone de. *The Second Sex*. Translated and edited by H. M. Parshley. New York: Alfred A. Knopf, 1975.

Becker, Ron. "Straight Panic!: Gay-themed Television and American Culture in the 1990s." Ph.D. diss., University of Wisconsin, Madison, 2004.

Bedell, Sally. *Up the Tube: Prime-time TV and the Silverman Years*. New York: Viking Press, 1981.

Bevacqua, Maria. *Rape on the Public Agenda: Feminism and the Politics of Sexual Assault*. Boston: Northeastern University Press, 2000.

Boddy, William. "Senator Dodd Goes to Hollywood: Investigating Video Violence." In *The Revolution Wasn't Televised*, edited by Lynn Spigel and Michael Curtin, 161–84. New York: Routledge, 1997.

Bodroghkozy, Aniko. *Groove Tube: Sixties Television and the Youth Rebellion*. Durham, N.C.: Duke University Press, 2001.

Brownmiller, Susan. *Against Our Will: Men, Women and Rape*. New York: Simon and Schuster, 1975.

———. *In Our Time: Memoir of a Revolution*. New York: Delta, 1999.

Brunsdon, Charlotte. "*Crossroads*: Notes on a Soap Opera." In *Screen Tastes: Soap Opera to Satellite Dishes*, 13–18. London: Routledge, 1997.

Burroughs, Augusten. *Running with Scissors*. New York: Picador, 2002.

Capsuto, Steven. *Alternate Channels: The Uncensored Story of Gay and Lesbian Images on Radio and Television, 1930s to the Present*. New York: Ballantine Books, 2000.

Carroll, Peter N. *It Seemed Like Nothing Happened: The Tragedy and Promise of America in the 1970s*. New York: Holt, Rinehart and Winston, 1982.

Chauncey, George. *Gay New York: Gender, Urban Culture, and the Making of the Gay Male World, 1890–1940*. New York: Basic Books, 1994.

Clair, Daphne. "Sweet Subversions." In *Dangerous Men and Adventurous Women: Romance Writers on the Appeal of the Romance*, edited by Jayne Ann Krentz, 61–72. Philadelphia: University of Pennsylvania Press, 1992.

Coakley, Mary Lewis. *Rated X: The Moral Case Against TV*. New Rochelle, N.Y.: Arlington House Publishers, 1977.

Cole, Barry, and Mal Oettinger. *Reluctant Regulators: The FCC and the Broadcast Audience*. Reading, Mass.: Addison-Wesley, 1978.

Cowan, Geoffrey. *See No Evil: The Backstage Battle over Sex and Violence on Television*. New York: Simon and Schuster, 1979.

Cuklanz, Lisa M. *Rape on Prime Time: Television, Masculinity, and Sexual Violence*. Philadelphia: University of Pennsylvania Press, 2000.

D'Acci, Julie. *Defining Women: Television and the Case of "Cagney and Lacey."* Chapel Hill: University of North Carolina Press, 1994.

——. "Nobody's Woman? *Honey West* and the New Sexuality." In *The Revolution Wasn't Televised*, edited by Lynn Spigel and Michael Curtin, 73–94. New York: Routledge, 1997.

Daly, Mary. *Gyn/Ecology: The Metaethics of Radical Feminism.* Boston: Beacon Press, 1978.

Daniels, Les. *Wonder Woman: The Life and Times of the Amazon Princess.* San Francisco: Chronicle Books, 2000.

Davis, Angela Y. "Rape, Racism and the Myth of the Black Rapist." In *Women, Race and Class*, 172–201. New York: Vintage Books, 1983.

Davis, Elizabeth Gould. *The First Sex.* Baltimore: Penguin Books, 1973.

Deiter, Newton E. "The Last Minority: Television and Gay People." *Television Quarterly* 13 (fall 1976): 69–72.

Denis, Paul. *Inside the Soaps.* Secaucus, N.J.: Citadel Press, 1985.

D'Emilio, John, and Estelle B. Freedman. *Intimate Matters: A History of Sexuality in America.* 2nd ed. Chicago: University of Chicago Press, 1997.

Diner, Helen. *Mothers and Amazons.* Edited and translated by John Philip Landin. Garden City, N.J.: Doubleday, Anchor Books, 1973.

Doty, Alexander. *Making Things Perfectly Queer.* Minneapolis: University of Minnesota Press, 1993.

Douglas, Susan J. *Where the Girls Are: Growing Up Female with the Mass Media.* New York: Times Books, 1994.

Dow, Bonnie J. *Prime-time Feminism: Television, Media Culture, and the Women's Movement since 1970.* Philadelphia: University of Pennsylvania Press, 1996.

Echols, Alice. *Daring to Be Bad: Radical Feminism in America, 1967–1975.* Minneapolis: University of Minnesota Press, 1989.

——. "The New Feminisms of Yin and Yang." In *Powers of Desire: The Politics of Sexuality*, edited by Ann Snitow, Christine Stansell, and Sharon Thompson, 439–59. New York: Monthly Review Press, 1983.

——. "The Taming of the Id: Feminist Sexual Politics, 1968–83." In *Pleasure and Danger: Exploring Female Sexuality*, edited by Carole S. Vance, 50–72. Boston: Routledge and Kegan Paul, 1984.

Edgerton, Gary. "High Concept, Small Screen." *Journal of Popular Film and Television* (fall 1991): 114–27.

Ehrenreich, Barbara, Elizabeth Hess, and Gloria Jacobs. *Re-Making Love: The Feminization of Sex.* New York: Doubleday, Anchor Books, 1986.

Eliot, Marc. *Televisions: One Season in American Television.* New York: St. Martin's Press, 1983.

Felsenthal, Carol. *Phyllis Schlafly: The Sweetheart of the Silent Majority*. Chicago: Regnery Gateway, 1981.

Firestone, Shulamith. *The Dialectic of Sex: The Case for Feminist Revolution*. New York: William Morrow and Company, 1970.

Fiske, John. *Power Plays, Power Works*. London: Verso, 1993.

———. *Television Culture*. London: Routledge, 1987.

Foucault, Michel. *The History of Sexuality*. Vol. 1, *An Introduction*. New York: Vintage Books, 1990.

Geller, Henry, and Gregg Young. "Family Viewing: An FCC Tumble from the Tightrope?" *Journal of Communication* (spring 1977): 193–201.

Gerhard, Jane. *Desiring Revolution: Second-Wave Feminism and the Rewriting of American Sexual Thought 1920 to 1982*. New York: Columbia University Press, 2001.

Gilbert, Annie. *All My Afternoons: The Heart and Soul of the TV Soap Opera*. New York: A and W Visual Library, 1979.

Gilbert, James. *A Cycle of Outrage: America's Reaction to the Juvenile Delinquent in the 1950s*. New York: Oxford University Press, 1986.

Gitlin, Todd. *Inside Prime Time*. New York: Pantheon Books, 1985.

———. "Prime Time Ideology: The Hegemonic Process in Television Entertainment." In *Television: The Critical View*, 6th ed., edited by Horace Newcomb, 574–94. New York: Oxford University Press, 2000.

Goldenson, Leonard H., and Marvin J. Wolfe. *Beating the Odds: The Untold Story Behind the Rise of ABC*. New York: Charles Scribner's Sons, 1991.

Gordon, Linda. *Woman's Body, Woman's Right: Birth Control in America*. Revised and updated ed. New York: Penguin Books, 1990.

Gramsci, Antonio. *Selections from the Prison Notebooks*. New York: International Publishers, 1971.

Hall, Stuart. "Gramsci's Relevance for the Study of Race and Ethnicity." In *Stuart Hall: Critical Dialogues in Cultural Studies*, edited by David Morley and Kuan-Hsing Chen, 411–40. London: Routledge, 1996.

Heath, Stephen. *The Sexual Fix*. London: Macmillan Press, 1982.

Hendershot, Heather. *Saturday Morning Censors: Television Regulation before the V-Chip*. Durham, N.C.: Duke University Press, 1998.

Hofbauer, Diane L. " 'Cableporn' and the First Amendment: Perspectives on Content Regulation of Cable Television." *Federal Communications Law Journal* 35 (summer 1983): 139–207.

Hofstede, David, and Jack Condon. *Charlie's Angels Casebook*. Beverly Hills: Pomegranate Press Ltd., 2000.

Holmes, John P., and Ernest Wood. *The TV Game Show Almanac*. Radnor, Pa.: Chilton Book Company, 1995.

Irwin, Barbara. "*The Young and the Restless*": *Most Memorable Moments*. Los Angeles: General Publishing Group, 1996.

Jeffreys, Sheila. *Anticlimax: A Feminist Perspective on the Sexual Revolution*. London: Woman's Press, 1990.

Kaplan, Herb, and Rick Houlberg. "Broadcast Condom Advertising: A Case Study." *Journalism Quarterly* 67, no. 1 (spring 1990): 171–76.

Kimball, Gayle, ed. *Women's Culture: The Women's Renaissance of the Seventies*. Metuchen, N.J.: The Scarecrow Press, 1981.

Klatch, Rebecca E. *Women of the New Right*. Philadelphia: Temple University Press, 1987.

Koedt, Anne. "Lesbianism and Feminism." In *Radical Feminism*, edited by Anne Koedt, Ellen Levine, and Anita Rapone, 246–58. New York: Quadrangle Books, 1973.

———. "The Myth of the Vaginal Orgasm." In *Radical Feminism*, edited by Anne Koedt, Ellen Levine, and Anita Rapone, 198–207. New York: Quadrangle Books, 1973.

Lafferty, William. "Feature Films on Prime-time Television." In *Hollywood in the Age of Television*, edited by Tino Balio, 235–58. Boston: Unwin Hyman, 1990.

LaGuardia, Robert. *The Wonderful World of TV Soap Operas*. New York: Ballantine Books, 1974.

Levine, Elana. " 'Having a Female Body Doesn't Make You Feminine': Feminine Hygiene Advertising in 1970s TV." *The Velvet Light Trap* 50 (fall 2002): 39–58.

———. "Wallowing in Sex: American Television and Everyday Life in the 1970s." Ph.D. diss., University of Wisconsin, Madison, 2002.

Maltin, Leonard. *TV Movies and Video Guide*. New York: Signet, 1987.

Mansbridge, Jane J. *Why We Lost the ERA*. Chicago: University of Chicago Press, 1986.

Marc, David. *Comic Visions: Television Comedy and American Culture*. Boston: Unwin Hyman, 1989.

Marcus, Daniel. *Happy Days and Wonder Years: The Fifties and the Sixties in Contemporary Cultural Politics*. New Brunswick, N.J.: Rutgers University Press, 2004.

Marill, Alvin H. *Movies Made for Television: The Telefeature and the Mini-series, 1964–1979*. Westport, Conn.: Arlington House, 1980.

Marshall, Susan E. "Keep Us on the Pedestal: Women against Feminism in Twentieth-century America." In *Women: A Feminist Perspective*, 3rd ed., edited by Jo Freeman, 568–82. Palo Alto, Calif.: Mayfield Publishing, 1984.

Marston, William Moulton. *Wonder Woman*. New York: Holt, Rinehart, and Winston, 1972.

Mathews, Donald G., and Jane DeHart Mathews. "The Cultural Politics of ERA's Defeat." *The Organization of American Historians Newsletter* (November 1982): 13–15.

McGilligan, Patrick. "Movies Are Better Than Ever on Television." *American Film* 5 (1980): 50–54.

McNeil, Alex. *Total Television*. 4th ed. New York: Penguin Books, 1996.

Medea, Andra, and Kathleen Thompson. *Against Rape*. New York: Farrar, Straus and Giroux, 1974.

Mittell, Jason. *Genre and Television: From Cop Shows to Cartoons in American Culture*. New York: Routledge, 2004.

Modleski, Tania. *Loving with a Vengeance: Mass Produced Fantasies for Women*. London: Methuen, 1982.

Montgomery, Kathryn Christine. "Gay Activists and the Networks: A Case Study of Special Interest Pressure in Television." Ph.D. diss., University of California, Los Angeles, 1979.

———.*Target: Prime Time—Advocacy Groups and the Struggle over Entertainment Television*. Oxford: Oxford University Press, 1989.

Mumford, Laura Stempel. *Love and Ideology in the Afternoon*. Bloomington: Indiana University Press, 1995.

Murray, Matthew. "Broadcast Content Regulation and Cultural Limits, 1920–1962." Ph.D. diss., University of Wisconsin, Madison, 1997.

Newcomb, Horace, and Paul M. Hirsch. "Television as a Cultural Forum." In *Television: The Critical View*, 6th ed., edited by Horace Newcomb, 561–73. New York: Oxford University Press, 2000.

New York Radical Feminists. *Rape: The First Sourcebook for Women*, edited by Noreen Connell and Cassandra Wilson. New York: New American Library, 1974.

Nixon, Agnes Eckhardt. "Coming of Age in Sudsville." *Television Quarterly* 9, no. 4 (fall 1970): 61–70.

Ozersky, Josh. *Archie Bunker's America: TV in an Era of Change, 1968–1978*. Carbondale: Southern Illinois University Press, 2003.

Peiss, Kathy. *Cheap Amusements: Working Women and Leisure in Turn-of-the-Century New York*. Philadelphia: Temple University Press, 1986.

Pekurny, Robert George. "Broadcast Self-Regulation: A Participant-Observation Study of the National Broadcasting Company's Broadcast Standards Department." Ph.D. diss., University of Minnesota, 1977.

Poll, Julie. "*Another World*": *35th Anniversary Celebration*. New York: Harper Entertainment, 1999.

———. "*As the World Turns*": *The Complete Family Scrapbook*. Los Angeles: General Publishing Group, 1996.

———. "*Guiding Light*": *The Complete Family Album*. Los Angeles: General Publishing Group, 1997.

Projansky, Sarah. *Watching Rape: Film and Television in Postfeminist Culture.* New York: New York University Press, 2001.

Quinlan, Sterling. *Inside ABC: American Broadcasting Company's Rise to Power.* New York: Hastings House, 1979.

Radner, Hilary. "Introduction: Queering the Girl." In *Swinging Single: Representing Sexuality in the 1960s,* edited by Hilary Radner and Moya Luckett, 1–38. Minneapolis: University of Minnesota Press, 1999.

Radner, Hilary, and Moya Luckett, eds. *Swinging Single: Representing Sexuality in the 1960s.* Minneapolis: University of Minnesota Press, 1999.

Radway, Janice. *Reading the Romance: Feminism and the Representation of Women in Popular Culture.* Chapel Hill: University of North Carolina Press, 1984.

Rapping, Elayne. *The Movie of the Week: Private Stories, Public Events.* Minneapolis: University of Minnesota Press, 1992.

Robbins, Trina. *The Great Women Superheroes.* Northampton, Mass.: Kitchen Sink Press, 1996.

Rowland Jr., Willard D. *The Politics of TV Violence: Policy Uses of Communication Research.* Beverly Hills: Sage, 1983.

Russell, Diana. *The Politics of Rape: The Victim's Perspective.* New York: Stein and Day, 1975.

Ryan, Barbara. *Feminism and the Women's Movement: Dynamics of Change in Social Movement, Ideology and Activism.* New York: Routledge, 1992.

Schaefer, Eric *"Bold! Daring! Shocking! True!" A History of Exploitation Films, 1919–1959.* Durham, N.C.: Duke University Press, 1999.

———. "Gauging a Revolution: 16mm Film and the Rise of the Pornographic Feature." *Cinema Journal* 41, no. 3 (spring 2002): 3–26.

Schemering, Christopher. *"Guiding Light": A 50th Anniversary Celebration.* New York: Ballantine Books, 1986.

———. *The Soap Opera Encyclopedia.* New York: Ballantine Books, 1985.

Schlafly, Phyllis. *The Power of the Positive Woman.* New Rochelle, N.Y.: Arlington House Publishers, 1977.

Schulman, Bruce J. *The Seventies: The Great Shift in American Culture, Society, and Politics.* New York: Free Press, 2001.

Schulze, Laurie. "The Made-for-TV Movie: Industrial Practice, Cultural Form, Popular Reception." In *Hollywood in the Age of Television,* edited by Tino Balio, 351–76. Boston: Unwin Hyman, 1990.

Schwartz, Nancy. "TV Films." *Film Comment* 11 (March–April 1975): 36–38.

Silverman, Fred. "An Analysis of ABC Television Network Programming from February 1953 to October 1959." M.A. thesis, Ohio State University, 1959.

Spigel, Lynn. *Make Room for TV: Television and the Family Ideal in Postwar America.* Chicago: University of Chicago Press, 1992.

———. "Seducing the Innocent: Childhood and Television in Postwar America." In *Welcome to the Dreamhouse: Popular Media and Postwar Suburbs*, 185–218. Durham, N.C.: Duke University Press, 2001.

Spigel, Lynn, and Michael Curtin, eds. *The Revolution Wasn't Televised: Sixties Television and Social Conflict.* New York: Routledge, 1997.

Stamp, Shelley. *Movie-Struck Girls: Women and Motion Picture Culture after the Nickelodeon.* Princeton, N.J.: Princeton University Press, 2000.

Steinecke, Julia. *The Bionic Woman.* Toronto: Flying Camel Press, 1996.

Stone, Douglas. "TV Movies and How They Get That Way: Interviews with TV Movie Makers Frank von Zerneck and Robert Greenwald." *Journal of Popular Film and Television* 7 (1979): 146–57.

Streeter, Thomas. "Blue Skies and Strange Bedfellows: The Discourse of Cable Television." In *The Revolution Wasn't Televised: Sixties Television and Social Conflict*, edited by Lynn Spigel and Michael Curtin, 221–44. New York: Routledge, 1997.

Swanbrow, Diane. "Talking T-shirts: America's Raunchy New Ritual." *Human Behavior* (March 1979): 12–13.

Taylor, Ella. *Prime-time Families: Television Culture in Postwar America.* Berkeley: University of California Press, 1989.

Tillity, Jennifer. "Desperately Seeking Farrah." In *The BUST Guide to the New Girl Order*, edited by Marcelle Karp and Debbie Stoller, 292–95. New York: Penguin Books, 1999.

Tropiano, Stephen. *The Prime Time Closet.* New York: Applause Theatre and Cinema, 2002.

Tuchman, Gaye, Arlene Kaplan Daniels, and James Benet, eds. *Hearth and Home: Images of Women in the Mass Media.* New York: Oxford University Press, 1978.

United States Commission on Civil Rights. *Window Dressing on the Set: Women and Minorities in Television.* Washington: U.S. Government Printing Office, 1977.

Vidmar, Neil, and Milton Rokeach. "Archie Bunker's Bigotry: A Study in Selective Perception and Exposure." In *"All in the Family": A Critical Appraisal*, edited by Richard P. Adler, 123–38. New York: Praeger, 1979.

Waldrep, Shelton, ed. *The Seventies: The Age of Glitter in Popular Culture.* New York: Routledge, 2000.

Warner, Gary. *"All My Children": The Complete Family Scrapbook.* Los Angeles: General Publishing Group, 1996.

———. *"General Hospital": The Complete Scrapbook.* Los Angeles: General Publishing Group, 1995.

Weeks, Jeffrey. *Sexuality and Its Discontents*. London: Routledge and Kegan Paul, 1985.

Williams, Raymond. *Marxism and Literature*. London: Oxford University Press, 1977.

Wyatt, Justin. "Selling 'Atrocious Sexual Behavior': Revising Sexualities in the Marketplace for Adult Film of the 1960s." In *Swinging Single: Representing Sexuality in the 1960s*, edited by Hilary Radner and Moya Luckett, 105–32. Minneapolis: University of Minnesota Press, 1999.

Zenba, Lorraine. *"Days of Our Lives": The Complete Family Album, A 30th Anniversary Celebration*. New York: Regan Books, 1995.

—INDEX—

220–21, 227, 232; made-for-TV movies and, 29–30, 44, 119, 264 n. 19; promotion of, 36; reputation of, 19–20, 27; sex symbols and, 31, 36–40, 138; standards and practices of, 80, 98, 234; turn to relevance and, 21–23, 131, 174–77; X-rated films and, 52–53

Censorship, 12; advertiser pressure and, 196–98; regulation vs., 47, 266–67 n. 2

Charlie's Angels, 7, 11, 31, 45, 120, 210, 257, 259–60; criticism of, 147; femininity vs. feminism in, 147–48, 259; imitations of, 37–41, 138–39, 157–62, 283 nn. 83–84; sex symbols in, 124–25, 128, 135, 145–47, 282 n. 68; sexual difference and, 13, 133, 149–57, 168, 282 n. 67, 283 n. 69; stars of, 152–57

Charo, 124

Chico and the Man, 32

CHiPs, 18

Cigarette advertising ban, 23–24

Clark, Susan, 31

Coakley, Mary Lewis, 48–49

Coalition for Better Television, 197–98

Cohen, Mark, 115

Columbia Broadcasting Company. *See* CBS

Comedy: homosexuality and, 186–90, 190–93; protests against, 106, 196–98; race and, 185–86; radical potential of, 171, 198–207; sex symbols and, 162–68; of sexual suggestion, 33, 170–71, 179–85, 193–96, 205, 284 n. 3; social issues addressed in, 22–23, 172–77; variety shows, 172–73, 284 n. 2, 284 n. 5

Commission on Civil Rights (U.S.), 129

Commodification of sex, 1–2, 10, 68, 183, 253–54

Common sense: new sexual culture and, 6, 10, 15, 254–55; of sexual difference, 125–26

Communications Subcommittee (U.S.

Senate): challenges to TV content from, 173; porn and, 50; pressure on FCC from, 96–97; radio sex talk and, 54–55; study of TV violence and, 81–82

Comstock, Anthony, 79

Condoms: attitudes toward, 67–68, 70; as birth control, 69; marketed to women, 70–71; as matter of public health, 74; print advertising of, 70–71, 272 n. 83; regulation by TV Code Board, 68, 71–74, 253–54; television advertising of, 12, 47–48, 72–73

Congratulations, It's a Boy!, 25

Congress (U.S.), 75; the pill and, 69; TV sex and violence and, 96–97, 100; X-rated culture and, 46, 50, 52–53, 56. *See also* Communications Subcommittee (U.S. Senate)

Conrad, Robert, 18

Continental Airlines, 67, 129–30

Contraception. *See* Birth control

Corday, Barbara, 145, 282 n. 58

Cornell, Lydia, 41, 124, 162

Cosell, Howard, 17–18

Cover Girls, 39, 159–62

Cox, Kenneth A., 50–51

Cramer, Douglas S., 36, 115–17, 132–35, 137, 146, 182–85, 282 n. 54. See also *Love Boat, The; Wonder Woman*

Crosby, Cathy Lee, 18, 137

Cry Rape!, 29–30

Cultural feminism, 126–28, 279 n. 8

Cultural forum, television as, 255

Dallas, 44–45, 113

Dallas, Jodie. See *Soap*

Dallas Cowboys Cheerleaders, 38, 124, 283 n. 83

Damned, The, 52–53

Dark Shadows, 26

Dating Game, The, 26

Fox network, 4, 45
Foucault, Michel, 261–62 n. 11, 266–67
    n. 2
Francis, Genie. See *General Hospital*: Luke
    and Laura rape story
Funny Face, 131

Game shows, 14, 26, 169–71, 193–96,
    198–200
Gay content, 181; in characters, 23, 187–90,
    202, 253; in humor, 172–73, 174, 187–
    93, 198–99; in made-for-TV movies, 25,
    112; in 1970s TV nostalgia, 258; protests
    against, 90, 187–88, 190, 196–98, 256;
    in themes, 23, 196, 253
Gay culture: backlash against, 8, 172–73;
    co-optation of, 183, 207; mainstream
    visibility of, 2, 6, 186–90, 199, 255–57
Gay Media Task Force, 116, 275 n. 40, 277
    n. 82; *Soap* and, 187–88
Gay rights movement, 4, 9, 172–73, 177–
    78, 182, 186, 188, 257, 260
Geary, Anthony, 209, 221, 239–40. See also
    General Hospital
General Hospital: audience responses to
    rape story, 246–50; early rape stories
    and, 214, 217–18, 291 n. 24; 293 n. 42;
    history of, 21, 26, 34–35, 45; Luke and
    Laura rape story, 15, 208–9, 214, 221,
    224, 238–51, 260, 295 n. 78; sexual con-
    tent on, 28; youth audience for, 34–35,
    238
Georgia Peaches, The, 39
Get Christie Love!, 31, 124, 134–35, 137, 149,
    281 n. 39
Gitlin, Todd, 84, 296 n. 1
Goldberg, Leonard, 25–26, 146–47. See
    also *Charlie's Angels*
Gone with the Wind, 219, 276 n. 60, 295
    n. 78
Good Times, 178–79

Gramsci, Antonio, 261 n. 5. *See also*
    Common sense
Grant, Lee, 132
Graves, Teresa. See *Get Christie Love!*
Green Acres, 22
Guiding Light, 21, 292–93 n. 41; audience
    responses to rape stories, 234–35, 237–
    38; Mike and Julie rape story, 214–19,
    237–38; Roger and Holly rape story, 7,
    232, 235–38, 251, 294–95 n. 66; Roger
    and Rita rape story, 232–35, 293 n. 52,
    294 n. 55
*Guilty or Innocent: The Sam Sheppard
    Murder Case*, 102
Gunsmoke, 21

Happy Days, 14, 45, 170; promotion of,
    35–36; sex symbols and, 39–40, 159;
    sexual humor of, 178–81, 284 n. 3, 285
    n. 19
Harold Robbins' 79 Park Avenue, 42
Harris, Susan. See *Soap*
Hartke, Vance, 81
Harvey, James, 50
Haskell, Molly, 247–48
Hawaii Five-O, 210
*Hearth and Home: Images of Women in
    the Mass Media*, 130
Hee Haw, 22
Hegemony: in history of women's roles
    on television, 128–29; in television's
    handling of sexual change, 5–6, 43,
    171, 254–56. *See also* Common sense;
    Gramsci, Antonio
Helfrich, Stockton, 98
Helter Skelter, 102
Hendrickson, Robert C., 79
Heterosexuality: challenges posed to, 9,
    14, 98–99, 191, 197–200; dominant
    ideology of, 5–6, 14, 171, 183, 194–96,
    199, 253, 256; endorsed through sex

acterized as, 37, 41, 48–49; theatrical
exhibition of, 2, 50. *See also* X rating
Portrait of an Escort, 44, 106
Portrait of a Stripper, 44, 106
Post-feminism, 158, 161–62, 168
Post-network era, 15, 45
Prime Time Access Rule (PTAR), 23–24
Procter and Gamble, 197–98; CBS and, 21,
221, 232; sexual content in soaps and,
35, 233–35, 248–49; threats to daytime
dominance of, 26, 220
Project 120, 24
Promiscuity, 25, 181–82, 187, 193–200,
201–2, 205, 207, 287 n. 38
Public Broadcasting Service. *See* PBS

QBVII, 30
Quark, 39
Question of Love, A, 106
Queerness of television content, 14,
198–99, 256, 287–88 n. 45

Race relations: civil rights movement and,
9, 171; inequalities in, 9, 212; representations of, 94–96, 160–61, 173–74,
185–86. *See also* African Americans,
representations of
Radio, 54–55
Rape: acquaintance, 222–23, 239–40;
activism against, 7, 14, 211–13, 216,
220–24, 230–31, 235, 238, 243, 248, 251;
fantasies of, 209, 246–48, 250–51, 296
n. 84; legal system and, 210–12, 220,
222, 230–32, 289 n. 8; in made-for-
TV movies, 25, 29–30, 87–91, 104–5,
109; marriage and, 214, 219, 224, 232,
235–38, 291 n. 23; media attention to,
210, 289 nn. 5–7; myths regarding,
208, 212, 222, 226, 230–31, 237, 239,
242, 245, 251; as sexual passion, 210,
212–14, 217–20, 222, 227, 232, 238,

240–41, 249–51; as violence, 210–14,
222, 230–38, 242, 249–51, 253; women's
liberation movement and, 208, 210–11,
226, 231, 251
Rape storylines on soap operas, 14, 209–
10, 254–55, 292–93 n. 41; ambiguity
in, 213–14, 238–50; audience response
to, 209, 218, 222, 231, 234–35, 237–
38, 246–50; consequences for rapists
and, 215–16, 218, 232, 238–39, 242–45;
generic conventions and, 213–19, 223,
226, 228, 235–36, 238, 242, 246, 250,
291 n. 33; old-fashioned plot of, 213–
20, 223–24, 226–29, 233, 238, 291 n. 24;
pedagogical mission of, 213, 220–24,
229–38, 248–49; pregnancy and, 213–
20, 223, 227–28; sexual passion in,
217–20, 227–28, 233–34, 240, 242–45;
victims' experiences and, 216, 200,
223, 229–39, 241–44, 248; women's
movement and, 229, 231
Rapping, Elayne, 105, 106, 117–18
Rayburn, Gene. *See Match Game*
Red Skelton Hour, The, 21, 284 n. 5
Regulation, 47–48, 75, 207, 210; censorship
vs., 47, 266–67 n. 2
Reilly, Charles Nelson, 198–99, 258, 260.
See also *Match Game*
Religious groups, 14, 44, 73, 171, 190,
196–98, 206, 287 n. 40
Repression: during 1950s vs. 1970s, 175–81;
production vs., 47–49, 61, 66, 75, 254;
of sexual content, 12, 74
Reproduction, as purpose of sex, 10, 48,
254, 260
Rhoda, 131, 258
Rich Man, Poor Man, 105
Rigg, Diana, 132
Rollergirls, 39
Romance novels, 220, 247
Roots, 105

White, Betty, 170

White, Mimi, 295 n. 70

Wild and Wooly, 158, 266 n. 63, 283–84 n. 84

Wild Women of Chastity Gulch, The, 266 n. 63

Wiley, Richard, 89, 97. *See also* Federal Communications Commission

Willa, 39

Will and Grace, 255–56

WKRP in Cincinnati, 40, 162, 166–67

Women audience: radio sex talk and, 54–55; for soap operas, 214; as target for television industry, 29, 111, 129–30, 146, 279 n. 12; women's liberation's effect on, 129–30

Women's liberation movement, 4, 7, 182, 206, 257, 260; anti-rape activism and, 211–13, 220, 222, 226, 231, 251; bra banning and, 62–63; *Charlie's Angels* and, 147–49, 153–54; contraception and, 69–70; on media, 64, 129–30; opposition to, 127–28, 134; sex symbols and, 125, 135, 137, 162, 165–68; on sexual difference, 126–28, 279 n. 8; TV representations of, 25, 28, 132, 171, 173–74, 177–78, 203–5; *Wonder Woman* and, 135–40, 145

Women's sexuality, 3, 5–9, 48, 171, 254–57, 262 n. 15; bra advertising and, 59–67; condom advertising and, 68, 70–71, 74–75; in made-for-TV movies, 91, 104, 106; in radio content, 54–55; rape and, 212, 222–23, 229–31, 233–37, 240; as subject of comedy, 7, 172, 192–93, 199–207, 288 n. 53. *See also* Sex symbols

Wonder Woman, 4, 133, 260, 281 n. 49; ABC series, 31, 37, 138–42, 282 n. 53; CBS series, 39, 138–39, 143–44; comic book, 133, 135–36, 281 n. 40; as sex symbol, 128, 135, 138, 144–45; sexual difference and, 13, 140–45, 158–59, 168; TV movie, 133–34; women's liberation movement and, 125, 136–39, 145, 281 n. 47, 282 n. 54

Wood, Robert, 22

World Premiere (NBC), 25, 83–84. *See also* Made-for-TV movies

Writers Guild of American, 99–100

Wylie, Emily, 258–59

X rating, 110; applied to radio, 54–55, 268 n. 25; applied to television, 48, 89; barred from television, 74, 254; cable television and, 56–58, 269 n. 35; feature films and, 50, 267 n. 12; for films to air on television, 12, 46–48, 50–54

Young and the Restless, The: as new style of soap opera, 28, 221, 228, 264 n. 29; rape stories and, 221–24, 226, 229; sexual content and, 28, 48, 233

Youngs Drugs Products Corporation, 72–73, 272 n. 83

Your Show of Shows, 284 n. 5

Youth: attempts to appeal to, 22, 26, 32–33, 36, 107, 110, 112–13, 171, 220–21, 228, 238, 249–51; concerns about sex and, 12–13, 46, 48, 51, 55, 61–62, 77, 79, 253; counterculture and, 9, 172, 186; dangers of television for, 12–13, 78, 80–82, 89, 99, 120–21, 249–50; representations of sexual endangerment of, 13, 77–78, 91–96, 104–13, 119–22, 255; television's role in the lives of, 4, 121–22, 123, 250; representations of sexuality of, 99, 110, 171, 174, 183–85, 228, 253, 260; widened range of threats to, 121

Elana Levine is an assistant professor of journalism and mass communication at the University of Wisconsin, Milwaukee.

Library of Congress Cataloging-in-Publication Data
Levine, Elana, 1970–
Wallowing in sex : the new sexual culture of 1970s American television /
Elana Levine.
p. cm. — (Console-ing passions)
Includes bibliographical references and index.
ISBN-13: 978-0-8223-3902-1 (cloth : alk. paper)
ISBN-13: 978-0-8223-3919-9 (pbk. : alk. paper)
1. Sex on television. 2. Television broadcasting — Social aspects — United States.
3. United States — Social life and customs — 1971– I. Title.
PN1992.8.S44L49 2007
791.45′6538097309047 — dc22   2006020436